S0-EVI-435

Published by
Edward Elgar Publishing Limited
The Lypiatts
15 Lansdown Road
Cheltenham
Glos GL50 2JA
UK

Edward Elgar Publishing, Inc.
William Pratt House
9 Dewey Court
Northampton
Massachusetts 01060
USA

A catalogue record for this book
is available from the British Library

Library of Congress Control Number: 2009936754

ISBN 978 1 84844 194 1

Printed and bound by MPG Books Group, UK

Contents

Contributors

Manuel Brandão Alves, Associação Nacional de Direito ao Crédito (ANDC), Portugal.

Peter Arnaudov, Nachala Cooperative, Bulgaria.

Mohammad Naveed Awan, Business Advisor, EVU, Copenhagen, Denmark.

Diana Bialus, Consultant on Microfinance, ShoreBank International, Chicago, USA.

Georgi Breskovski, Microfond.

Allan Bussard, Managing Director, Integra Co-op, Bratislava, Slovakia.

Annika Cayrol, Researcher, Réseau Financement Alternatif, Brussels, Belgium.

Karl Dayson, Senior Lecturer in Sociology and Executive Director, Community Finance Solutions, University of Salford, UK.

Simone di Castri, Policy Analyst, CGAP/The World Bank, USA.

Beata Dobova, Executive Director, Integra Foundation, Bratislava, Slovakia.

Maria Doiciu, Senior Consultant on SMEs and Microfinance, Eurom Consultancy and Studies SRL, Bucharest, Romania.

Iveta Erlichova, Loan Officer, Integra Foundation, Lucenec, Slovakia.

Dr Jan Evers, Managing Partner, EVERS & JUNG GmbH, Hamburg, Germany.

Véronique Faber, Appui au développement autonome (ADA), Luxembourg.

Grzegorz Galusek, Executive Director, Microfinance Centre for Central and Eastern Europe and the New Independent States, Warsaw, Poland.

Michel Genet, Director of Crédal.

Niamh Goggin, Community Development Finance Association.

Trude Emaus Holm, Researcher, Nordland Research Insitute, Norway.

Bárbara Jayo Carboni, Director of Research, Fundación Nantik Lum, Madrid, Spain.

Per Jonsson, CFO, ALMI Företagspartner AB, Stockholm, Sweden.

Jill Kickul, Director, Stewart Satter Program in Social Entrepreneurship, Berkley Center for Entrepreneurial Studies, New York University – Stern School of Business, USA.

István Kovács, President, Hungarian Enterprise Development Network Consortium and Managing Director, PRIMOM Foundation for Enterprise Promotion, Nyíregyháza, Hungary.

Maricruz Lacalle Calderón, Senior Advisor, Fundación Nantik Lum, and Professor of Universidad Autónoma de Madrid, Spain.

Stefanie Lämmermann, Junior Programme Manager, European Microfinance Network, Paris.

Stefanie Lahn, Researcher, EVERS & JUNG GmbH, Hamburg, Germany.

Andrea Limone, CEO, PerMicro, Italy.

Elisabet Ljunggren, Research Manager, Nordland Research Institute, Norway.

Margot Lobbezoo, Director, 360° Responsibility, Netherlands and Project Leader Professorship, Microfinance and Small Enterprise Development, INHOLLAND University, Netherlands.

Jean Marchand, Intern, Réseau Financement Alternatif, Brussels, Belgium.

Horst Maunz, ÖSB Consulting GmbH, Austria.

Sarah McGeehan, Head of Social Finance, The Lab, National Endowment for Science, Technology and the Arts (NESTA), London.

Américo Mendes, Associate Professor, Portuguese Catholic University, Porto, Portugal.

Klaas Molenaar, General Director, TriodosFacet BV, Vice President, European Microfinance Network and Professor of Microfinance and Small Enterprise Development, INHolland University, The Hague.

Kostadin Munev, Financial Leasing Manager, UNDP–JOBS Project, Sofia, Bulgaria.

Michael Ploder, Research Fellow, Institute of Technology and Regional Policy, Graz, Austria.

Anka Rajska, Training Manager, Integra Foundation, Ruzomberok, Slovakia.

Silvia Rico Garrido, Director, Fundación Nantik Lum, Madrid, Spain.

Monika Smolova, Microcredit Program Manager, Pontis Foundation, Bratislava, Slovakia.

Lenka Surotchak, Executive Director, Pontis Foundation, Bratislava, Slovakia.

Ranjula Bali Swain, Assistant Professor, Department of Economics, Uppsala University, Sweden.

Tibor Szekfu, Managing Director, Fejer Enterprise Agency, Székesfehérvár, Hungary.

Agata Szostek, Micro-credit Consultant.

Tom Theves, Ministry of Work and Mayra Arvioti, ADA.

Jela Tvrdonova, Executive Director, VOKA, Banska Bystrica, Slovakia.

Mario Vircik, Director of International Relations, Slovak Ministry of Finance, Bratislava, Slovakia.

Tuija Wallgren, independent researcher, European Microfinance Network, Paris, France.

Susanne Zurl-Meyer, ÖSB Consulting GmbH, Austria.

Introduction

Karl Dayson, Bárbara Jayo Carboni, Jill Kickul, Maricruz Lacalle Calderón and Silvia Rico Garrido

While Grameen Bank has attracted public attention, with its founder Muhammad Yunus, being awarded the Nobel Peace Prize in 2006, most Europeans are probably unaware that the continent has a flourishing microfinance sector. Yet some of the world's most successful (and probably some of the smallest) microfinance providers are based in the continent. There are many reasons for this but the most straightforward is a desire to contribute to national economic growth, particularly by those considered economically and socially excluded.

In environments where information asymmetries, intense competition and changing market conditions are ever-present, the debate over which factors within and across countries facilitate the rate of growth of entrepreneurial and emerging firms continues to thrive in many forums and research arenas (Dickson and DeSanctis, 2001; Tapscott et al., 2000). Firms in countries with less support and structure for enabling entrepreneurship may be at a disadvantage when compared to their counterparts in countries that have public and private resources, personnel and funding – especially at the microcredit level. As such and with a supply-side perspective, the actions, policies and programmes taken by government and practitioners to ensure survival of their microcredit organization and to improve the service to their borrowers should not be overlooked. The onset of the credit crunch and subsequent recession has highlighted the precarious nature and availability of credit, particularly to entrepreneurs and micro-enterprises. Thus those nations that have the policy tools to ensure a stable flow of credit to all sectors of the economy, while balancing this against the need for prudent lending, are likely to be well placed to take the advantage that the future will present. For this reason, *Handbook of Microcredit in Europe: Social Inclusion through Microenterprise Development* offers a unique opportunity to consider national contexts and the performance of microcredit initiatives within the European Union.

Our work draws on authors from a multi-disciplinary background and provides complementary perspectives in this field. The themes developed in the 18 national reviews are drawn together in the conclusion to offer an interpretation of microfinance in Europe. It is intended that this *Handbook* will contribute to the evolving European discourses on microcredit, inclusion through microenterprise, and social exclusion. Additionally, by providing a robust examination of microcredit activity across numerous EU countries, it is possible to examine which strategies and policies may influence and affect how any given nation's initiatives can foster future entrepreneurial behaviour. In particular, evidence of successful programmes may be replicated by nations in similar economic positions. Such an improved understanding of these factors may further inform and assist government and policy makers in prioritizing a target set of improvements, initiatives and programmes that foster entrepreneurship and growth-oriented activity through microcredit.

This handbook is concerned with the idea that microcredit granted to financially excluded entrepreneurs can play an important role in creating small businesses, reducing unemployment, improving welfare and establishing financial and social inclusion (The SEEP Network, 2000; Lacalle, 2008). In turn, these collectively contribute to general economic well-being and growth. This is a significant change in many European nations and has not been without controversy. For most of the post-war years, the European economic models were either reliant on the state as an economic actor or the state in combination with large private sector organizations. Although small businesses have always been present, they received modest political support and were treated as marginal actors. However, from the 1980s onwards, one of the consequences of the expanding influence of neo-liberal economics was a greater emphasis on individual entrepreneurship as an indicator of economic success. Today, most European governments seek to encourage the development of small businesses and work to develop a supportive infrastructure.

One aspect of this was the need to provide financial support, particularly for entrepreneurs with minimal investment capital. A number of approaches were adopted to address this which can be broadly categorized as 'carrot and stick' for the banks and small grants for the entrepreneurs. Ironically, neo-liberals, while endorsing entrepreneurship, were critical of enabling grants, arguing that they undermined competition as the state offered support that the banks could provide in the form of a loan, and came at a high cost to taxpayers. The entrepreneurs also suffered because the practice encouraged a dependency culture and a reliance on the state to support their businesses.

Though these criticisms were aimed at certain Western European nations, they had a more immediate effect in Eastern Europe, where in the flush of post-Communism the neo-liberal arguments helped shaped policies, including business support. An impact of this was that loans for small businesses were more prevalent in Eastern rather than Western Europe.

Much of this was in the form of aid via international donors, especially those based in the USA. These aid agencies drew on their experiences of assisting the developing world and promoted notions of microfinance, whereby new financial institutions would be established to offer credit to entrepreneurs. The argument was that it was financial poverty, not entrepreneurship, that was withholding development. Consequently, new financial institutions would be required to serve this latent demand. Therefore, the evolution of microcredit in Europe has an unusual genealogy, beginning in the developing world before its implementation in Eastern Europe and gradual spread into Western Europe, though the process was not linear, with promoters of microcredit being found across the continent.

What is microfinance?

In its broadest sense, microfinance comprises a range of financial services aimed at individuals and micro (or very small) enterprises, both for-profit and those with social missions. Usually, the term excludes the 'mainstream' banking community and it is assumed it serves those not served by the mainstream. Furthermore, it is often used interchangeably with microcredit, which is a loan worth up to 25000 euros[1] made to those unable to access the mainstream financial market. Microcredit is the dominant service offered by microfinance institutions (MFIs) in Europe, hence the focus on loan products. However, and it's a big however, the situation is far more complex than the aforementioned definitions. Firstly, there are microcredit providers who don't see themselves as MFIs, and in the UK there are even microfinance providers who don't even see themselves as MFIs – instead they adopt the American nomenclature 'community development finance institution'. Then there are credit unions;[2] though nominally MFIs, they rarely present themselves as microfinance providers. This is because for many years microfinance was associated with enterprise lending, while credit unions specialized in personal credit.

These artificial divides have now begun to crumble as European governments have argued that their welfare state systems appeared to work against entrepreneurship, creating poverty-traps in which those engaging in marginal utility activity found their benefits cut, thereby reducing the incentive to work. It was thought that credit-based systems may help overcome some of these structural problems. Secondly, academics (Dayson et al., 1999) began to argue that the demarcation between business and household finances was deeply problematic, especially among sole traders and other micro-entrepreneurs, with allocation of resources depending on need at a specific moment in time. Encapsulating this were the popular 1980s British television comedies 'Only Fools and Horses' and 'Bread', in which families of micro-entrepreneurs negotiated the 'breadline' through processes of informal economic activity and financial reciprocity. The outcome of this is that a limited number of MFIs engage in both enterprise and personal credit, while the majority continue to serve one of these markets. However, this transition is still in its infancy, and can be seen as the next stage of financial inclusion policy and practice in Europe. Thus for the purpose of this book, and in common with the majority approach throughout Europe, we are focusing on microenterprise lending.

Beyond the arcane discussions about definitions, Europe's highly developed financial sector has a rich history of microfinance and of serving excluded communities that long preceded activity in the rest of the world. As noted earlier, credit unions were invented in Germany by Franz Hermann Schulze-Delitzsch before being exported across Western Europe and North America. As the forthcoming chapters will demonstrate, virtually every European country had incipient MFIs in the eighteenth and nineteenth centuries, whether they are savings banks in Sweden and Spain or building societies in the UK. However, in Italy financial services for those on low incomes have their origins in the fifteenth century, and were provided by religious orders (namely the Montes Pietatis). This connection with religion continues today, as with the Catholic Church's promotion of credit unions in Ireland. Thus the state has been a relatively late actor in the provision of financial services and it has only been in Sweden and to a lesser extent in France were there has been a desire for universal provision. Elsewhere, as the chapters will indicate, the role of local and regional agencies have been of primacy. But what of policy at a European level?

European Union policy

While the European Union supports microfinance in African, Caribbean and Pacific countries (ACP) through its Microfinance Framework Programme, there is no equivalent provision within Europe. As the European Microfinance Network (EMN)[3] argues, European microfinance policy straddles economic and social inclusion policy areas (http://www.european-microfinance.org/index2_en.php, accessed 13 June 2008). Much of this activity has been the responsibility of national governments, supported or supplemented by the EU. Adding to the complexity, microfinance has different roles in Eastern and Western Europe. In the former, it was an important policy tool during the transition from communist control and has contributed to the construction of private financial architecture. Consequently, as the chapters on Poland, Romania and Bulgaria will show, the sector has grown rapidly and in some cases is operationally self-sufficient. By contrast, microfinance in Western Europe has been an ancillary service aimed at those considered economically excluded. In particular, there has been a focus on encouraging self-employment, an issue

Table 1 The nature of microfinance in Europe

Part of Europe	Central and Eastern	Western
Policy motivation	Transition, building a market economy	Encourage self-employment, address unemployment particularly among disadvantaged groups
Policy location	Economic	Socio-economic – link to welfare state
Ownership	Self-sufficient independent financial institutions	Partially operationally sufficient. Some non-profits and some extension of private and state sector entities

Source: Dayson (forthcoming).

which concerns policy makers because of the lower level of entrepreneurship when comparing Western Europe to the United States of America. Thus microfinance policy, if such a thing can be said to exist in Western Europe, bridges the two sides of the mixed economy. Complicating the matter still further, the majority of microfinance organizations in Europe are non-governmental organizations (NGOs)[4] and see themselves as operating in the social economy. Given this sectoral matrix (see Table 1) it is perhaps unsurprising that a single European policy has not emerged. It should be noted that Table 1 is a generalized synthesis and simplification of microfinance provision in Europe, and there will be numerous exceptions.

However, the European Union has permitted microfinance providers to access general funding sources, such as the European Regional Development Fund (ERDF) and the European Social Fund (ESF). Since 2007, there has also been a commitment to the Microcredit Guarantee Window which can be accessed through the European Investment Fund (EIF). To date eight organizations across Europe[5] have successfully applied for this status which enables them to offer loans to micro-entrepreneurs (up to 10 staff and turnover below 2 million euros) worth up to 25000 euros, 75 per cent guaranteed. In addition, the JEREMIE initiative (Joint European Resources for Micro to Medium Enterprises Initiative) enables nation-states to convert regional strategic funding from the European Union into loan capital and other financial instruments. By December 2008, only Greece, Romania, Latvia and Lithuania have agreed to JEREMIE funding arrangements, with negotiations ongoing with five other nations and regional agreements made with Languedoc-Roussillon in France and Campania in Italy. Though as the need for JEREMIE is decided at a national level, it is likely that there will be further fragmentation in the provision of support for microfinance across the European Union. Beyond direct funding for microfinance, the EU has also supported the intellectual development of the sector by funding transnational learning projects including training events, supporting women entrepreneurs and a character-based lending approach.

Although policy development at a European level is often a protracted affair as the various nations seek a consensual approach, there are indications of how the sector will look in the future. The most ambitious to date came from the European Commission in November 2007[6] in which they recommended that nation-states ensure they remove barriers to the development of microcredit, and that a central support agency is created for microcredit providers. These infrastructural changes are supplemented by the proposal for a microcredit fund partially funded by the European Union. There was also a recognition that loan repayment was partially dependent on the quality of business support and it was recommended that this occurred in conjunction with the loan process. The same report also attempted to assess the potential scale of the microcredit market in Europe and estimated that it was worth 6145 million euros (an estimated 712 900 loans). To help achieve these objectives, the Commission suggested that the environment was made more supportive of entrepreneurship through promotion, welfare transitional schemes for those moving from unemployment to self-employment, and greater training and support for micro-entrepreneurs.

The European Commission proposed agenda reflects much of the discourse within the literature. Evers and Lahn (2006) discussed the concept of the 'moveable island' to describe the difficult transition of those from welfare to self-employment. They continued the analogy by suggesting the construction of a bridge to overcome the barriers. In particular, they highlighted Ireland's tapering of welfare benefits for those moving into self-employment. This obsession with 'serving the poorest' is questioned by Guichandut who wonders if this commitment results in financial viability being a 'distant viability' (Guichandut, 2006: 55) for Western European MFIs. This MFIs performance has been the focus of work by Underwood (2006), Evers and Lahn (2006), McGeehan (2008), Dayson (2005) and Copisarow (2005), all of whom have discussed the 'sustainability gap' that MFIs face across the continent. However, this debate represents an advance on the earlier literature which first had to explain why MFIs were needed (Mayo et al., 1998) and the case for a benign legal environment

(Reifner, 2002; Nowak, 2006; Copisarow, 2000). Unsurprisingly, given the relative youth of the sector in Europe, there are few debates about mission drift, exploitive credit rates, and whether they are targeting the poorest customers that are increasingly prevalent among development workers, MFIs and aid agencies in the developing world (Dichter and Harper, 2007). Perhaps with maturity these debates will be replicated in Europe, but for the present the focus remains helping those most excluded.

Our aim for the handbook

In writing this handbook, we have several intentions, including the following:

1. to bring together the experience of microcredit throughout Europe;
2. to analyse critically microcredit activity in specific nations in Europe;
3. to identify commonalities in practice and examples of innovative activity;
4. to reflect critically on the relationship between social welfare policy and the role of microcredit in Europe and possible links to policy globalization.

This handbook consists of 20 chapters, including the introduction and conclusion written by the editors. The bulk of the chapters are national case studies exploring the nature of microcredit in each country. It is intended that the majority will be examined in detail (Austria, Belgium, Bulgaria, France, Germany, Hungary, Italy, Poland, Portugal, Romania, Slovakia, Spain, United Kingdom) with a further chapter discussing those nations with less extensive microcredit markets (the Netherlands, Luxembourg, Norway, Sweden and Denmark). Each of the national case study chapters has a similar format, enabling the reader to compare key characteristics easily. Each begins with a contextual discussion that assesses the prevailing social welfare ideology and how this has informed policy. Linked to this is an exploration of the policy evolution that resulted in microcredit being introduced. The origin of microcredit in each nation is discussed and includes aspects of policy implementation and operationalization of microcredit. The third section focuses on the infrastructure of microcredit in the country, including the key microcredit providers, supporting institutions and the role of individual social actors who influenced the development of the sector. Following this, there is an analysis of the target audience and a description of the organizational form used to deliver microcredit. Finally, the role of the government and regulation is explained before an analysis of the financial and operational sustainability of the sector. Our concluding thoughts for each chapter/country attempt to chart the likely future of microcredit in the country and the key risks and opportunities that lie ahead.

Austria

The concept of microcredit has only recently begun to make inroads to the Austrian economy and is still treated with a degree of apprehension by the financial establishment. Initiatives are currently being overseen by the AWS (Austria Wirtschaftsservice – Austrian Business Service Agency), SFG (Steirische Wirtschaftsförderung – Austrian Business Promotion Agency), with the recent addition of the EQUAL programmes – coordinated by the European Social Fund (ESF) and the Federal Ministry of Economics and Labour. Microcredit operations did not begin here until 2004. Now, available products and services are limited to liability programmes, subsidies, low-interest loans, consultation and related services. All are solely aimed at the SME sector.

Belgium

Originating in the early seventeenth century, SME financing has a notable history in Belgium. Today, Belgium's microcredit market is serviced by three major lenders: Fonds de Participation, Crédal and Brusoc, where Fonds is the predominant provider (42 per cent of all approved credit provision). The three offer a range of credit products that target two general groups, those vulnerable to poverty (for example the unemployed and elderly) and micro-entrepreneurs who are otherwise excluded from credit access. Central to the current discourse on Belgium's microfinance market are the respective roles and responsibilities of the private sector and public authorities.

Bulgaria

Microfinance in Bulgaria emerged in the early 1990s primarily as a donor-driven tool to address some urgent aspects of transition. It offered vital assistance to support the reestablishment of entrepreneurship and the private sector, whose traditions and potential were largely interrupted during the previous centrally planned system. With micro, small and medium-size enterprises accounting for about 99 per cent of business activity in Bulgaria (data from the Ministry of Economy and Energy, see Chapter 4), the need for microcredit is bound to remain a key factor for enterprise development. It is important for all sectors of the Bulgarian economy, whose structure is dominated by service and trade companies (60 per cent) followed by industrial enterprises (31.4 per cent) and the agricultural sector (8.6 per cent) (Invest Bulgaria Agency: Economy, Investment, Business and Industry, see Chapter 4). The ability to meet that need will be decisive, not only for the good performance of microfinance actors and the banks, but also for Bulgaria's overall success in achieving the ambitious social and economic goals ensuing from EU membership.

Denmark

With a per capita GDP near US$57 000, Denmark is home to one of the world's wealthiest populations. The strong national economy is based in the SME sector where one enterprise exists for every 10 Danes, and 92 per cent of those enterprises have fewer than 10 employees. Recognizing that entrepreneurial activity is clearly the foundation of the Danish economy, the government has implemented a range of schemes to foster growth and success within the sector. The government's strategy has been diversified, and the holistic approach has proven very effective. Yet the immigrant population remains economically marginalized and the lack of any microcredit institution that specifically targets potential ethnic entrepreneurs has forced many to rely on informal financing with its inherently limiting and negative consequences.

France

In the last decade, France has undergone modest economic growth. With an average 2.3 per cent growth in its gross domestic product over the last 10 years, France has a slightly lower growth rate than the EU 25 (2.4 per cent). In France, different types of organizations provide microcredit directly or indirectly. They differ in the kind of products they offer, in their functioning, sources of funding and with regard to the target group they serve. They fall into three different categories: non-bank microcredit; organizations that facilitate access to micro-loans from banks; and para-bank actors. However, a huge yet unmet demand for microcredit still exists in France. Adie estimates the potential market for non-bank microcredit at business start-up at between 48 000 and 98 000 per year, resulting in a gap of between 40 000 and 90 000 microloans per year. For bank microcredit, a shortage of 100 000 loans per year has been observed.

Germany

In Germany, the past decade has seen a growing interest in and practice of microlending. In recent years, an increasing number of specialized microcredit programmes have been created for start-ups and microenterprises with low capital requirements. While the number of microcredit programmes has risen from 24 to 33, the clear sign of a dynamic process is not reflected in the number of loans disbursed, which is disappointingly low in practice. It makes sustained business development almost impossible: 14 of the programmes surveyed disburse only up to 10 loans and a further five programmes disburse up to 50. Microfinance in Germany will only become significant if more players accept responsibility and really look at the demands of microenterprises and entrepreneurs, develop and implement loan processes, and aggressively enter the current financing market in order to make microfinance a core business.

Hungary

Hungary has proved to be fertile ground for the evolution and proliferation of microcredit initiatives. The Hungarian microfinance industry is considered a success. Its dynamic 15-year history provides interesting insight into the methodology and science of implementing microfinance. Beginning as early as 1992, formal microcredit projects were run by Local Enterprise Agencies (LEAs) with the backing of the EU PHARE programme. Through the 1990s, the success of the SME financing industry in Hungary garnered international recognition. The success encouraged efforts to move the industry toward greater sustainability, thereby reducing PHARE fund dependence. Attempts at sustainability began with a restructuring of the industry, placing funds and greater oversight control in the National Microcredit Fund. Certain indications suggest the new structure helped increase the amount of funds loaned, specifically because the maximum loan was increased significantly. On the other hand, it appears centralization proved to be an impediment to *positive* growth in the sector due to politicization coupled with the increased cost structure of the bureaucracy. The short attempt at sustainability was abandoned and the industry returned to the decentralized model with responsibilities mostly left to the now semi-autonomous LEAs. While considered a success, Hungary's microfinance experience has still tended toward favouring SMEs, perhaps forgetting some of society's neediest.

Italy

If a wide definition of microlending activity is taken into consideration, as the provision of small loans to people who lack conventional collateral, up to 2007 almost seventy microcredit projects have been activated in Italy. The analysis of mission, institutional typology, governance, lending practices and model of granting of the Italian microcredit projects shows remarkable differences in the way projects deal with their microlending activity. Two main discriminating factors are: (1) the awareness of each entity as viewing microcredit as an activity that aims to spur economic development or to redistribute wealth; and (2) the purpose of achieving financial inclusion of the borrowers or their social inclusion through and with financial inclusion. The microcredit sector in Italy is a dynamic scenario populated by many small actors that are using different ways to provide marginalized groups with financial services, in a context where social finance has generally experienced difficulties in growing and has never received the adequate support from the policy makers and public opinion. This scenario is evolving quickly due to three main factors: the growing relevance of migrants in the Italian economy and the discovery by financial intermediaries of this new target; the creation of joint projects involving the third sector; and the growth of microcredit initiatives in the wake of the worldwide success of microfinance. The challenge for the sector is to become more professionalized and thereby to improve approach, strategy and practices.

Luxembourg

Microcredit does not officially exist in Luxembourg and its future prospects are decidedly limited. With a population of over 460 000, unemployment around 4.5 per cent and a GDP of 58 000 euros per capita – the highest in Europe – the potential microcredit market is small. The public sector employs 98.6 per cent of Luxembourg nationals. In the private sector SMEs predominate, and many of them are micro in nature. For financing, SMEs in Luxembourg rely on four main providers but the available microcredit products are limited and geared toward the entrepreneurial sector alone. There is no focus on social inclusion of the unemployed. In a national 2005 report, it was concluded that there is neither prospect nor significant need for a national microcredit institution in Luxembourg, due to the limited market, low self-employment rates, and the risk-aversion of Luxembourg nationals.

Netherlands

There has been little awareness of microfinance in the Netherlands itself. There is for instance no unanimous accepted definition for microfinance in the Netherlands. Ironically, although the Netherlands has been sending microfinance experts to developing countries for over 20 years and there have been many campaigns about microfinance in developing countries by the development NGOs, only recently has there been a growing awareness that something needs to happen to reach more people with microfinance in the Netherlands. There is no official model for microfinance and provision of microcredit in the Netherlands. Based on an analysis of the initiatives, three organizations play dominant roles: (1) regular banks that carry out the actual lending and administration of the loan to the microenterprise, (2) intermediaries such as enterprise development agencies, NGOs or schools that provide business development services like coaching and help with preparation of business plans; the costs of these are paid by external parties, and sponsors or volunteers are used; and (3) others (for example, government, European funds, projects) which support banks with a guarantee.

Norway

Norway's economy has benefited greatly from natural gas and oil reserves. Exports of these resources have facilitated impressive economic growth in recent history and an expansion of the public sector as well as a strong welfare state. Norway's labour market is considered relatively fair in terms of gender equality, but women are traditionally underrepresented in the entrepreneurial sector. Microcredit first appeared in Norway in 1992 and has tried to target female and immigrant entrepreneurs. Norway's public authorities and MFIs have made gender equality their chief priority. Network Credit Norway (NCN) and Innovation Norway (IN) dominate the microfinance market; both operate with funding assistance from the national government. Effectively, these two organizations, in conjunction with governmental programmes, provide a variety of products and services, including entrepreneurial grants, loans and training.

Poland

Current microcredit providers in Poland include commercial and cooperative banks, credit unions, specialized non-bank financial institutions, and microloan programmes. The banks' market share is 98 per cent (in terms of the value of loans). Although the banks seem to be the only significant players, they have interest in the market segment and have sufficient infrastructure to physically reach the consumers, there are several constraints, which make their role in market development questionable. Apart from the strategies to stimulate demand, the key issue for the microcredit market development in Poland is to scale up the supply schemes. The analysis conducted by the Microfinance Centre for Central and Eastern Europe and the New Independent States (MFC), clearly indicates the need for linking specialized non-bank financial institutions with commercial and cooperative banks and the network of guarantee schemes. This kind of partnership is a win–win solution that combines strengths of all key actors. It is unlikely that the Polish example is unique in Europe. In the opinion of MFC experts, the huge market gap does not show the failure of microcredit. It demonstrates a need to move from the experiment to the scaling-up phase. It can be done only if there are delivery models, which are viable for all the stakeholders, especially for commercial players.

Portugal

Social solidarity financing projects have existed in Portugal since the fifteenth century, although, in spite of this extensive experience, Portugal's current microfinance market is relatively limited in size, range and diversity. The industry currently revolves heavily around the Associação Nacional de Direito ao Crédito (ANDC), a non-profit organization founded in 1998. The ANDC, and more recently Santa Casa da Misericórdia de Lisboa (SCML), are the two major practitioners of microfinance and microenterprise promotion. As is common throughout Europe, Portugal prohibits these and similar MFIs from actually lending and collecting funds. This regulatory constraint, coupled with the current MFIs' inability to reach sustainability have resulted in a dependence structure that involves a number of traditional banks as well as the public sector through the Ministry of Labour. Despite the involvement of three distinct types of actors, product and service offerings have been limited. Ultimately, Portugal's microfinance industry and social solidarity efforts in general would benefit from an expansion of awareness and diversity about the potential of microfinance.

Romania

Microfinance has a rich 15-year history in Romania beginning in the 1990s when the economy underwent the transition from a centralized to a market-based model. Many of its largest, most established MFIs today were started by international NGOs and MFIs, but today the Romanian microfinance sector is very much independent, and in many cases, tending toward sustainability. The sector provides a wealth of services and financial products with both social and commercial ends. Overall diversification, coupled with supportive legal framework reforms has made the Romanian MF sector very successful in terms of overall growth and sustainability. A variety of services and products, lending methods and targeting criteria have made the industry's overall penetration wide, but depth is still the major challenge as some studies conclude that 30 per cent of demand for financial services is still unmet.

Slovakia

A sparsely populated country with double-digit unemployment and a legacy of communism, Slovakia (formerly part of Czechoslovakia) unexpectedly qualifies as one of Europe's fastest-growing economies. Home to no more than 5.5 million, Slovakia has frequently posted GDP growth figures at, or exceeding, 9 per cent (Slovak Statistical Office, 2007, http://portal.statistics.sk/showdoc.do?docid=4). Within this unique context, microfinance has struggled to succeed. Uneven geographical wealth distribution and strong overall economic performance obscure the demand for microfinance services and products. A late beginning and a cultural aversion to entrepreneurship have compounded the difficulties that the sector faces. But, in the face of all these obstacles, over a thousand microloans have been made, and many more clients have been provided with educational services that have proven invaluable to their economic security and overall social inclusion.

Spain

The Spanish microfinance sector grew at a considerable rate from the outset of the twenty-first century. Beginning with international NGO initiatives in the 1990s, the home-grown industry took its roots in the Spanish savings bank system; first with the Caixa Catalunya's programme, Fundació Un Sol Món, founded in 2001, and soon followed by the Caja Granada's own proprietary programme. Currently, nearly all 46 recognized savings banks in Spain have their own microcredit programmes. This impressive growth was facilitated by public subsidization from both the national level (ICO Microcredit line) and the European level (European Investment Fund and the European Social Fund). In addition to traditional financial institutions and public sector actors, Social Microcredit Support Organizations (SMSOs) play a vital role. These organizations serve the sector in a variety of ways, most importantly acting as informal guarantors and liaisons between potential micro-entrepreneurs and the institutional lenders. Impressive growth and ongoing governmental support promise that the industry will maintain stability but other concerns do exist. The sector can be criticized for a general avoidance of financing initiatives for the poorest strata of society as well as the lack of diversification in product and service offerings.

Sweden

Microfinance in Sweden experienced a late start in comparison to much of Europe, and is currently in a markedly developmental stage. There are no true MFIs so to speak, but the state-sponsored organization ALMI has recently (May, 2007) released new microcredit products. The lack of progress in the areas of social inclusion and poverty alleviation through entrepreneurship promotion are due in part to a cultural bias for wage employment as well as associated legislative obstacles. This is not to say that the demand is not there. Female and immigrant groups are the most excluded and the administrative burdens for start-up entrepreneurs are well known. Sweden is at a critical point in the development of the sector, but it remains to be seen whether or not the microfinance industry will be made a priority by either public or private sector actors.

United Kingdom

The community development finance sector in the UK encompasses a wide range of social finance organizations providing access to personal finance, microfinance, small business loans, social enterprise investment and community development venture capital. Despite the recent changes within the UK Community Development Finance Institution (CDFI) environment, the government, both at national and regional level, remains committed to CDFIs as a mechanism for the delivery of a range of policy priorities. There is no political appetite for a return to a grant or soft loan-based policy, though this could change if the UK were to undergo a period of extended recession. As microfinance grows and diversifies and particularly as products diversify and organizations increasingly raise investment, the right to raise capital will come with responsibilities. Ensuring that the regulatory burden and behaviour of CDFIs remain proportionate will be a challenge for practitioners and the regulatory authorities. Microfinance continues to flourish in the UK and although the funding environment has tightened, it is likely to remain supportive, providing it serves individuals and businesses that the mainstream sector lacks the ability to assist.

Conclusion

In Europe, microfinance policy has emerged from both the 'developing world' and the USA, combining with indigenous historical precedent. Moreover, the contested nature of economic policy and the rise of neo-liberalism have created the conditions and explanations for the interest in microfinance policy. The composition of this cocktail has differed across the continent, and each nation has produced its own unique microfinance sector. However, in terms of operationalization, similarities can be seen in the importance of charismatic leadership and the reliance on debt finance (predominantly underwritten or supplied by the state). Differences are stronger in the relationship with banks and other mainstream financial institutions, and views on sustainability. Overall, the sector in Europe is dependent on the support of the state and to a lesser extent the banks, while at the same time many practitioners seek greater autonomy. This creates a dynamic environment involving a continual redefinition of microfinance in Europe, a series of what we call Complex Interrelationship Microfinance Initiatives.

Notes

1. In many European nations microfinance loans can be issued up to 40 000 euros.
2. Mutual savings and loans organizations, which also offer other financial services. In Europe they have a significant presence in Poland and Ireland, and to a lesser extent elsewhere. Credit unions were actually invented in Germany by Franz Hermann Schulze-Delitzsch and popularized by Friedrich Wilhelm Raiffesein, before being exported to Austria, England, France, Italy and the Netherlands, and subsequently to Canada and the USA. Near the end of the twentieth century, having become major players in the USA and countries under the American sphere of influence, they were re-exported to

Europe, predominantly through the Catholic Church, Caribbean migrants to the UK, and lastly United States of America aid agencies.

3. EMN represents microfinance providers and national/regional trade associations on the European stage. It is supported by the European Commission and French Caisse des Dépôts et Consignations (CDC).
4. For our purposes an NGO is a body that is not a for-profit entity or a public sector agency.
5. Fonds de Participation/Participatiefonds in Belgium; Kreditanstalt für Wiederaufbau in Germany; Instituto de Crédito Oficial (ICO) in Spain; Association pour le Droit à l'Initiative Economique (ADIE) in France; The Prince's Trust and The Prince's Scottish Youth Business Trust in the UK; First Step Ltd in Ireland; and Cultura Sparebank in Norway (http://www.eif.org/guarantees/resources/ec_programme/micro_credit_guarantees/index.htm).
6. European Commission (2007).

References

Copisarow, R. (2000), 'The application of microcredit technology to the UK: key commercial and policy issues', *Journal of Microfinance*, **2** (1), 13–42.

Copisarow, R. (2005), *Street UK – A Micro-Finance Organisation: Lessons Learned from its First Three Years' Operations*, Birmingham: Street UK.

Dayson, K. (2005), 'Are community development finance institutions doing too much?' paper presented at the *ISBE Conference*, Blackpool, 1–3 November.

Dayson, K (forthcoming), 'Financing small business development in the UK', in A. Southern (ed.), *Understanding Enterprise Inclusion*.

Dayson, K., R. Paterson and J. Powell (1999), *Investing in People and Places*, Salford: University of Salford.

Dichter, T. and M. Harper (eds) (2007), *What's Wrong with Microfinance?*, Rugby: Practical Action Publishing.

Dickson, G.W. and G. DeSanctis (2001), *Information Technology and the Future Enterprise: New Models for Managers*, USA: Prentice Hall.

European Commission (2003), *Microcredit for Small Businesses and Business Creation: Bridging a Market Gap*, Brussels: European Commission Directorate for Enterprise and Industry.

European Commission (2007), *A European Initiative for the Development of Microcredit in Support of Growth and Employment*, COM (2007) 708 Final.

Evers, J. and S. Lahn (2006), 'Promoting microfinance: policy measures needed', *Finance for the Common Good/Bien Commun*, **25**, Autumn, 47–53.

Guichandut, P. (2006), 'Europe occidentale et reste du monde: parle-t-on des mêmes pratiques?', *Finance for the Common Good/Bien Commun*, **25**, Autumn, 54–60.

Lacalle, M. (2008), *Microcréditos y Pobreza*, Madrid: Ediciones Turpial.

Lacalle, M., S. Rico, J. Marquez and J. Duran (2006), *Glosario básico sobre microfinanzas*, Cuaderno Monográfico no. 5, Foro Nantik Lum de Microfinanzas, Madrid, available at http://www.nantiklum.org/CUADERNO_5.pdf.

McGeehan, S. (2008), *Inside Out 2007*, London: CDFA.

Mayo, E., T. Fisher, P. Conaty, J. Doling and A. Mullineaux (1998), *Small is Bankable: Community Reinvestment in the UK*, York: Joseph Rowntree Foundation.

Nowak, M. (2006), 'Croissance et cohésion sociale. Le microcrédit et l'Union Européenne', *Finance for the Common Good/Bien Comme*, **25**, Autumn, 37–43.

Reifner, U. (2002), *Micro-lending: A Case for Regulation in Europe*, Baden-Baden: Nomos.

SEEP Network (The) (2000), *Learning from Clients: Assessment Tools for Microfinance Practitioners*, Assessing the Impact of Microenterprise Services (AIMS), Washington, DC, SEEP Network.

Tapscott, D., A. Lowy and D. Ticoll (2000), *Harnessing the Power of Business Webs*, Boston, USA: Harvard Business School Press.

Underwood, T. (2006), *Overview of the Microcredit Sector in Europe*, Paris: EMN.

Yunus, M. (2003), *Banker to the Poor*, USA: PublicAffairs.

1 The microcredit sector in the United Kingdom: the role of CDFIs

Niamh Goggin, Karl Dayson and Sarah McGeehan

As with many aspects of British life the development of microfinance was strongly influenced by the experience of the USA, especially the nomenclature, in which the term 'Community Development Finance Institution' (CDFI) is used to describe the broad social finance sector, rather than 'microfinance' or 'microcredit institution'. The UK's CDFIs have enjoyed extensive support from American CDFI practitioners and the sector has drawn on the USA policy experience. However, the UK has also been shaped by practitioners from Europe, particularly Poland (Copisarow, 2000), the developing world and indigenous pre-CDFI provision. This synthesis of perspectives led to a sector that has emerged in an environment with expectations of self-sustainability, while engaged in what American CDFI activists described as the highest risk activity within their model; namely enterprise finance.[1] The reason for this apparent contradiction resides in the UK Government's ideological commitment to Third Way politics (Giddens, 1998): a desire to address unemployment (social democratic impulse), while ensuring any solution does not 'distort' the marketplace (neo-liberal impulse). Consequently, the UK Government did not replicate the USA model of imposing reporting obligations on the banks. An irony of this outcome is that the UK now has a more neo-liberal microfinance policy environment than a Republican-led USA Government.

This chapter will explore how UK CDFIs have been established and adapted in response to national and more recently, regional policy. Although these policies may sometimes offer divergent objectives, enterprise, creation and encouragement of an enterprise culture has been a constant feature of successive UK governments. However, the interest in microfinance has coincided with the arrival of the New Labour Government in 1997. An active strategic policy environment coupled with a variety of quasi-independent and independent delivery vehicles has created a vibrant and challenging microfinance environment.

National context

The community development finance sector in the UK encompasses a wide range of social finance organizations providing access to personal finance, microfinance, small business loans, social enterprise investment and community development venture capital. While the sector is certainly older than the current Labour Government, with the oldest CDFI within the CDFA[2] membership having formed in the mid-1970s, the superficially disparate group of organizations have formed into a discernible sector, and have been joined by a variety of new institutions as a result of a broadly supportive policy environment.

The public policy priorities have shifted and changed over the last decade – but they retain a firm focus on the connection between economic development and social change. This agenda was largely set in 1999 with the reports of the Government's social inclusion policy investigations, known as Policy Action Teams (PAT). PAT 3 and 14 focused particularly on access to financial services and the broader support environment for enterprises and individuals respectively. While the PAT 14 report recommendations saw little progress, the recommendations from PAT 3 were reflected immediately with the announcement of the creation of the Phoenix Fund in 1999. The fund was heavily modelled on the US CDFI fund and focused on supporting organizations to develop and extend financial services for businesses that were unable to access the finance they needed from the commercial banking sector. Between 2000 and 2006, the Phoenix Fund provided more than €60.77m of grant support to cover existing and emerging organizations.

The community development finance sector received another boost from the implementation of the recommendations of the Social Investment Task Force (SITF) which was also set up in the wake of the policy action teams. It reported in 2000, and its five recommendations aimed 'to obtain higher social and financial returns from social investment, to harness new talents and skills and to address economic regeneration and to unleash new sources of private and institutional investment' (SITF, 2000).

The SITF's first recommendation was the introduction of a community investment tax relief (CITR) that would create an incentive by enhancing return, to encourage private investment in underinvested communities. The CITR legislation was enacted in 2002 and gives investors in accredited CDFIs 5 per cent tax relief on the value of their investment for five years. The CITR scheme has already levered more than €57.2 million into the CDFI sector. While there remain some design issues with the scheme, its greatest potential lies in the future as CDFIs increasingly focus on accessing investment rather than grants to grow their portfolios. There has been some criticism of the effectiveness of the scheme – but this can largely be attributed to the timing of its introduction: three to five years before effective demand for external capital had grown within the CDFI sector.

The SITF's second recommendation focused on the introduction of the community development venture capital model (CDVC) in the UK. CDVC focuses on using an equity model (rather than debt-based models which dominate the CDFI sector in the UK) to support growth businesses in underinvested communities and areas. The first of these was Bridges Ventures, which was launched in 2002 with a €57.2 million fund invested by the Government and private investors. In June 2007, Bridges closed its second fund of €107 million raised entirely of private institutional and individual investors. The CDVC model has not seen significant growth in the UK, although smaller initiatives by local CDFIs to provide equity or equity-like investments have developed, and two larger, publicly backed organizations – Futurebuilders and Adventure Capital Fund – have been launched to provide packages of support including equity-like products to the increasingly enterprising voluntary and community sector.

The task force also recommended that charitable trusts and foundations should be given greater latitude to invest in, as well as to offer grants to community development finance institutions. Charity Commission[3] guidance on social investment followed in 2001 and since then a number of charities have developed investment strategies for CDFIs and other third sector lenders, such as credit unions. Currently, these strategies include provision of long-term, subordinated debt at low or no cost, purchase of share capital and mixed packages of risk-taking granted capital, grant support to cover the costs of operations and access to returnable capital.

The fourth recommendation from the task force focused on increasing disclosure from the formal banking sector on their lending activities in deprived areas. The task force recommended voluntary disclosure, and while some banks have disclosed some information about their activities, not all have done so. This is probably the recommendation that has seen the least activity or systemic change. However, as community development finance grows, banks and CDFIs are increasingly finding ways of working together in mutually beneficial ways including indirect investment, product development and delivery (such as delivery of basic bank accounts, savings and budgeting products) and through referrals programmes where retail bank declines are passed to non-bank partners.

The final recommendation from the task force was for further support for the sector with the launch of a trade association dedicated to building a thriving community development finance sector, which would bring economic and social benefit to every disadvantaged community in the UK. The CDFA was launched in 2002 and now has 76 members representing the majority of the UK's CDFIs – from an initial base of 23 CDFIs.

Since the task force reported and its recommendations have been acted upon, there have been further developments in the public policy arena. The Graham Review of the Small Firms Loan Guarantee Scheme (SFLG) reported in 2002 recommending the opening of the scheme to CDFIs. The SFLG is a government-backed guarantee scheme. It provides up to 70 per cent guarantees on individual loans made by registered lenders. Originally focused on extending lending policy of commercial providers, it has been formally extended to CDFIs although registration of CDFIs for the scheme is presently limited. However, one CDFI is acting as a regional pilot for CDFI use and a further three applications are in the pipeline. The SFLG is likely to be available to all CDFIs by the end of 2007. The SFLG (as a publicly backed guarantee) cannot be used in conjunction with CITR on the same loans, although both tools can be used within the same portfolio.

The origin of microfinance in the UK

Credit transactions played an important role in the development of modern Britain and the gradual shift from relational to codified approaches was evident from the fifteenth century onwards (Kermode, 1991; Muldrew, 1993). By the seventeenth century letters of credit and rudimentary bank notes were in circulation and by the 1740s Dean Jonathan Swift, the author of *Gulliver's Travels*, started a small loans fund for the tradesmen of Dublin (Hollis and Sweetman, 1997). Over the next couple of centuries numerous enterprise funding schemes, often in specific geographic locations, were established, though it was not until the post-war period that these became more extensive.

While the USA provided the impetus for independent CDFIs to arise in the UK, those that initially concentrated on peer lending schemes drew lessons from Poland and Grameen Bank (Copisarow, 2005; Esmée Fairbairn, 2005). However, the majority of CDFIs were engaged in direct lending to micro businesses and small and medium sized enterprises (SMEs) and many of these had their antecedents in local authority business loan schemes. These funds became known as 'soft loan schemes', as the lending and collection criteria were weaker than banking standards and in the main, there were lower expectations of fund performance and recovery of loans. For much of the 1970s and 1980s, soft loan funds were the conventional means to fund businesses, often in tandem with enterprise grants and allowances. However, the survival of these funds averaged less than three years (Klett, 1994) and this failure was an additional spur to a sustainable approach. Today most of the remaining 'soft loan funds' have been incorporated into CDFIs (such as the Warwickshire Fund into the Coventry and Warwickshire Reinvestment Trust), or have adopted more

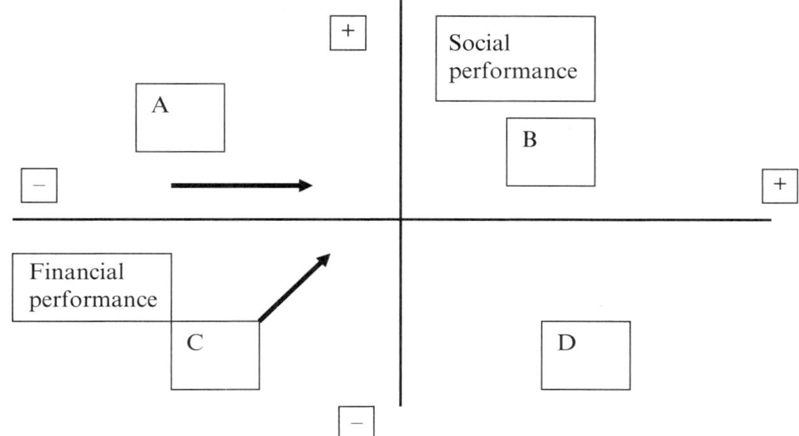

Source: Dayson (forthcoming).

Figure 1.1 Theoretical matrix of UK CDFIs

sustainable characteristics, such as morphing into CDFIs (North West Business Finance as part of Bolton Business Ventures). Often the latter are part of wider business support groups, known as Enterprise Agencies, and microfinance lending forms a subsidiary activity.

Completing the UK sector are CDFIs that serve social, cooperative and charitable enterprises, and others that offer personal financial credit (McGeehan, 2006).[4] These two sub-sectors have been particularly dynamic, with social enterprise lending being the largest financially and personal credit providers having the most customers. Although not the focus of this chapter it is worth noting that these two sub-sectors have received more government interest and/or financial support than conventional microenterprise lenders.

In summary, the UK has a blended approach framed within a context where microcredit seeks to serve those most at need, while working towards institutional sustainability, often through support of the Government and other interested agencies. These conflicting dichotomies can be represented by Figure 1.1. In general UK CDFIs have twin objectives of financial sustainability and delivering social benefit. Figure 1.1 seeks to show the alternative theoretical strategies that are available to a CDFI; it also represents the overall status of CDFIs in the UK.

- Box A-type CDFIs are driven by a social mission. These types of CDFIs engage in extensive partnership working to ensure they are

embedded in the local enterprise support environment. However, their financial management may be underdeveloped or inadequate. This tends to be the status of new CDFIs or those operating in hard-to-serve markets where outreach is prioritized.
- Box B could be described as the ideal type. These CDFIs have strong financial management and levels of self-sufficiency but also pursue a social agenda. They are socially innovative, providing this accords with fiscal stability, though they will not exploit clients financially. To date, with the possible exception of Charity Bank, no UK CDFI fulfils these criteria.
- Box C is the most problematic status with minimal financial management or too few loans accompanied by high central costs. In addition these CDFIs display no overt attempts to reach and measure social objectives. The majority of the former soft loan funds could fulfil these criteria.
- Box D CDFIs tend to be driven by sustainability. They believe in the need to be profitable in order to make a difference. They may accept the need for social objectives but this is never at the expense of the business. To date few, if any, CDFIs are Box D types, though if core funding is removed some may adopt this as a survival mechanism.

Figure 1.1 should enable a CDFI to develop a series of indicators to place itself within the grid. In lieu of any statistical frame it can be estimated that most CDFIs are attempting to improve their self-sustainability, while retaining a strong social ethic. These trends are represented by the two arrows in Figure 1.1.

Main actors within the microfinance sector in the UK

Public agencies

The strategy for funding CDFIs and in particular maintaining and extending the legacy of the Phoenix Fund has been transferred to England's Regional Development Agencies (RDAs) and the devolved administrations of Scotland, Wales and Northern Ireland. The nine English regions and the devolved administrations are now individually responsible for adopting and implementing plans and budgets to support CDFIs. Following the 2005 Comprehensive Spending Review, a total of €16 million was ring-fenced to be passed to the English regions for support for CDFIs from March 2006–2008. Since then, the RDAs have developed a variety of approaches, at varying speeds, to supporting CDFIs, although the majority have now committed or distributed support for CDFIs in their regions. A recent report from the New Economics Foundation has noted that CDFIs feel that the transfer of funding from government to RDAs has not been accompanied by a satisfactory level of strategic understanding about the sector (NEF, 2007).

Banks

While the government has set policy, created an effective environment for growth and provided grants to grow and build capacity, there are a number of other stakeholders that have played and continue to play an important role in the growth and development of the sector. Indeed, the largest amongst these stakeholders – charitable trusts and foundations and formal financial institutions (most commonly the retail banks) – are significant. Foundations are increasingly focusing on funding risk and revenue gaps while the banks' approaches move away from purely Corporate Social Responsibility (CSR) perspectives to providing capital on commercial and quasi-commercial terms.

The banking sector has been a key partner in the growth and development of community development finance. While some retail and investment banks have long-term relationships with individual CDFIs, a portfolio approach from the banking sector can only really be said to have emerged since the late 1990s. To date, banks have taken varying approaches. The most heavily engaged in the sector are those that have committed dedicated teams to build relationships through support and funding. As the majority of past support has focused on grants, most of these teams have been based within CSR departments or as special policy teams. More recently these banks have developed a more commercial approach to CDFIs – seeking to provide capital or develop projects that create financial and social returns for the bank and the CDFI, for example through referral programmes. For example, banks[5] provided 3 per cent of all revenue support for microfinance providers in the UK in 2006, but 15 per cent of new loan investment funds. This type of relationship is dominated by the two banks with which CDFIs[6] consistently have the strongest relationship – RBS NatWest and Barclays.

A number of large and small banks are increasingly focusing on the CDFI sector as a market niche requiring specific capital products. HBOS (indirectly through BIGInvest), Unity Bank and Co-op Bank have all provided capital through term debt or revolving lines of credit for CDFIs. Although deals of this kind have been slow to begin there are signs that this area of opportunity is expanding. When CDFIs reported in 2005, as a sector, for every £1 they raised in grants for onward lending they raised £0.74 in investment. Given the challenges of microfinance lending, that ratio is reduced significantly to £0.19 in investment for every £1 raised in grants for onward lending.

Experience of approaches to date suggests those banks that are closest to CDFIs are most successful at creating deals. The majority of CDFIs are still developing a track record and longitudinal information on portfolio performance, while standardized reporting processes and templates have only recently emerged. It has also taken time for some investors to understand the risk/return profile of CDFIs and the variety of ways in which CDFIs cover one of their biggest costs – write-offs – through other forms of earned income, grants and guarantee funds. As firmer assessments of risk emerge and with the introduction of Community Investment Tax Relief (CITR), such deals are changing, with banks requiring no or lower cash deposits against CDFI borrowing, more flexible use of capital with returns delivered – at least partly – through the CITR, enabling CDFIs to deliver a larger spread between the rates at which they borrow and lend (McGeehan, 2007).

Social investors

One sub-set of investors in the sector that currently have a smaller stake, but are likely to grow, are individual social investors. As individual CDFIs grow their portfolios and their profile and understanding of the philosophy behind their activities increases, social investment from individuals is likely to increase. Many CDFIs want to cultivate investors from the communities they serve and a number have succeeded in creating a particular niche amongst social investors in their communities.

Charitable trusts and foundations

Foundations have always been an important stakeholder for the sector and can be credited for providing a significant proportion of the support needed to start up and maintain lending activities for CDFIs. The data from across the sector from 2007 shows that charitable trusts and foundations contributed 9 per cent of all revenue grant incomes for CDFIs.

In the past, foundation support has focused on traditionally structured grants. However, as the sector has developed and demand for capital has grown, the environment is changing as foundations are increasingly either providing low or zero-cost capital. For instance, the Northern Rock Foundation committed €1.43 million in interest-free loans to five CDFIs in March 2007. Foundations are also funding the explicit cost of losses or contributing to guarantee pools from a variety of sources for the same purpose. Finally, the foundations that are most engaged with the sector have embraced the new CDFI performance framework – Change Matters. In the second quarter of 2007 two foundations have chosen to adopt some of the key indicators from the performance framework to understand individual CDFI performance and potential.

Table 1.1 Target markets served by microfinance CDFIs

Finance products	Percentage of microfinance CDFIs
Microfinance, small and medium enterprise lending, social enterprise lending	24%
Microfinance, small business lending, social enterprise lending	24%
Microfinance, social enterprise lending, personal lending	21%
Microfinance only	15%
Microfinance and social enterprise	6%
Microfinance and small business lending	6%
Microfinance, small and medium enterprise lending, social enterprise lending, personal lending	3%
Microfinance and personal lending	3%

Although community development finance does not yet represent a discernible asset class for different investors and risk/performance differs across the sector, it seems likely that the metrics will emerge to enable a variety of stakeholders more readily to assess propositions and make investment in the sector.

Model of microcredit granting in the UK: general description of the model

This section reports on the results of the annual Community Development Finance survey, 'Inside out', carried out by the Community Development Finance Association and covering the year to March 2007. Thirty-four of the responding Community Development Finance Institutions (CDFIs) provided microfinance loans, defined as an average loan size of less than €25 000.[7] This does not include the largest microfinance provider in the UK, The Prince's Trust, which does not report on its performance to the CDFA.

In 1042 microfinance loans in the UK last year, €9 840 233 was lent, bringing the total microfinance portfolio outstanding to €17 474 261 in 3088 loans. All are individual loans. Most CDFIs provide microfinance as part of a wider range of finance products, as Table 1.1 demonstrates.

Microfinance CDFIs are increasingly diversifying their services and are looking at other financial services. Other services currently provided or under consideration include back office services for other CDFIs (3.57 per cent, planned to rise to 17.5 per cent by 2008), wholesale capital and leasing purchase products (under consideration by 4 per cent of organizations).

Sixty-four per cent of loans were to new-starts and the remainder is to established businesses, more than six months old. Sixty-six per cent were to male clients and an estimated 25 per cent of loans are to members of black and ethnic minority communities. Thirteen per cent are to households headed by a lone parent and most clients (57 per cent) are between the ages of 30 and 49. Twenty-two per cent of them are rural-based, with 64 per cent in urban areas and the remainder in semi-urban areas.

CDFIs reported that their most important priorities in terms of target groups were to reach those who suffer exclusion from mainstream financial services and to create jobs (scoring 44 out of a possible 100). This is followed by improving the local economy (scoring 41 out of 100) and retaining jobs (scoring 38 out of 100). Lower priorities were increasing financial literacy and improving quality and availability of local services (scoring 20 out of 100).

Financial terms and conditions

Interest rate

There are no caps or limits on interest rates in the UK. Most UK microfinance CDFIs have used interest rates to ensure that they are targeting the financially excluded, rather than providing soft loans to those who can access mainstream bank services. The average interest rate charged was 12.40 per cent, with a large range from 0 per cent to 26 per cent. Some organizations reduced interest rates for repeat customers or larger loans.

Others: grace period, amount, repayment period, collaterals and so on

Loan size in 2006/07 ranged from €286 to in excess of those to microenterprises, but the average microfinance loan was €9447. Loan terms range from 18 to 60 months, with the average at 38 months. Fifty-three per cent of loans were for working capital and the remainder were for equipment purchase. Seventy-eight per cent of loans were totally unsecured; while 21 per cent of organizations sometimes take security in the form of charges over property, they only do so for 5 per cent of their loans. Debentures are taken by 20 per cent of organizations, but for 35 per cent of their loans. Personal guarantees were the most common form of security, taken by 48 per cent of organizations for 46 per cent of their loans. Only one organization takes peer group guarantees.

Main business services provided

Sixty-eight per cent of microfinance institutions provided formal business support services, in addition to finance, with the remainder providing finance only. All of the organizations provided referral or signposting to other service providers and informal advice by email, phone or in person.

All but one provide informal advice during loan processing and 84 per cent provide one-to-one mentoring advice. Fifty-six per cent provided brokerage or co-financing services, where they lend jointly with other finance providers such as banks. Fifty-two per cent provide training courses or seminars for their clients and 23 per cent provide peer mentoring.

Other financial products for inclusion

Twenty-six per cent of microfinance organizations also provided personal financial inclusion services including loans for consumption, training and education, debt consolidation, home purchase and home improvement. Organizations providing assistance in opening commercial bank accounts totalled 5.77 per cent, with 21.05 per cent planning to provide the service by 2008; 5.56 per cent provided savings accounts or facilities, with 11.36 per cent planning to provide the service by 2008.

Government support

The transfer of funding responsibility from central government to RDAs and the devolved administrations has caused funding difficulties for CDFIs and has led to an increase in the range of funding sources with which they have to negotiate. The average revenue support provided by government and other agencies is €137 000 per organization, ranging from €0 for three organizations to €390 000 for one. The contributions of the different types of organizations are summarized in Table 1.2.

Regulation: fiscal treatment, regulation of micro-enterprises and so on

Different regulatory requirements apply to CDFIs which are credit unions, Industrial and Provident Societies, Companies Limited by Guarantee, and Community Interest Companies, a new legal structure which permits investment through shares.

Only one of the microfinance providers in the UK is a credit union and therefore regulated[8] under the Industrial & Provident Societies Act 1965 and the Credit Unions Act 1979. Credit unions are regulated by the Financial Services Authority under the Financial Services and Markets Act 2000 and must be authorized by the FSA before they can do business. Registration as an Industrial and Provident Society gives credit unions corporate status and limited liability. Credit unions may only lend to 'natural persons', rather than corporate entities, but may lend to sole traders for business purposes.

CDFIs registered under the Industrial & Provident Societies Act only, may invite investment in withdrawable share capital once the invitation to invest is approved by 'a suitably qualified person'. No person may be appointed to the management committee of an IPS CDFI or shall be

Table 1.2 Funders of microfinance CDFIs in the UK

Funder	No. of organizations funded	% of total funding provided
RDAs	21	37%
Miscellaneous	8	19%
Charitable trusts and foundations	6	9%
European funding	5	9%
Local regeneration	8	8%
Local economic development / business support	6	6%
Banks / Building Societies	5	3%
Non-bank corporate and individual donations	3	2%
Financial inclusion growth fund	4	1%
Big lottery	1	1%
Housing associations	1	1%

appointed as chief executive or secretary who has been declared bankrupt, disqualified as a Company Director, been convicted of an offence which is not treated as spent, or is subject to a County Court Judgment relating to debt. IPS CDFIs must take reasonable steps to verify the identification of members and must establish a system to prevent money laundering. They must maintain fidelity insurance to provide cover against loss or liability caused by fraud or dishonesty. They must provide a copy of their audited accounts and an assessment of their performance and prospects to members. These CDFIs are also required to:

a. conduct their business with integrity;
b. conduct their business with due skill, care and diligence;
c. take reasonable care to organize and control their affairs responsibly and effectively with adequate risk management systems;
d. maintain adequate financial resources;
e. pay due regard to the interests of their customers and treat them fairly.

All non-credit-union CDFIs lending up to €37 000 are minimally regulated under the Consumer Credit Act, and CDFIs must apply for a licence in order to lend, and pay a fee of €400 – €700.

CDFIs which are structured as Companies Limited by Guarantee or as Community Interest Companies are not registered or regulated by the

FSA. The Community Development Finance Association is introducing a system of self-regulation which will be binding on all members and monitored by a third party. This includes a Code of Practice and the broader performance framework, Change Matters, including quantitative and qualitative indicators and covering finance, operations, organization, market awareness and impact.

Financial and operational sustainability

Loan officer productivity is low. It ranged from 3 to 100 loans per loan officer and averages 24. Annual write-off rates averaged 12 per cent, slightly lower than the cumulative rate of 13.24 per cent. Following a benchmarking exercise, the CDFA has set a draft good-practice benchmark for write-offs of 9 per cent. Portfolio yields averaged 8.71 per cent, with a wide range from 0 per cent to 16 per cent, against a good practice target of 16.5 per cent. Operational sustainability data is not yet available, but again, the CDFA benchmark for stand-alone microfinance organizations is 40 per cent, with a cost-per-loan target of €815 and an operating expense ratio of 64 per cent.

Challenges for the sector in the UK

CDFI business models and development needs

The figures above mask a cross-section of rather different organizations facing different challenges and opportunities as they build and consolidate their business. Within the sector, there are at least four different stages of development, which demand different strategies.

Well established CDFIs These CDFIs have established and developed organizational infrastructures, a clear route to market and a track record of lending. They are the most likely of all the groups to be investing in research and development, to have accessed and deployed external sources of capital, to be benefiting from increasing operating efficiencies and achieving greater scale. They are most likely to require additional capital as they grow. However, this group continues to struggle to ensure their customers have access to quality business support and financial advice to complement the finance they provide, and they require revenue funding to cover the costs of this support when they provide it themselves (Dayson, 2005).

CDFIs that are still maturing and developing their business model In the main these CDFIs have been financing for less than five years. They have invested in organizational development, product refinement and tested routes to market. They still have some way to go before their models are mature and they have effective routes to market. These organizations have used and will continue to require grant support for both revenue and capital to consolidate their business model and refine their products. These newer entrants offer a variety of business support and money advice services in their delivery (Dayson and Conaty, 2006). If this remains a significant part of their business model, payment for these kinds of services will continue to be a crucial part of their funding.

CDFIs who are 'front office' providers These are organizations that provide much of the client liaison and support for other CDFIs that provide back office and loan monitoring services. Front office providers are becoming more important as the provision of financial services becomes more and more segmented (see trends below). Although there are currently fewer front office providers operating in the UK, it is likely that operations like these will emerge in the next one to three years. These locally-based operations clearly have a role to play in penetrating and supporting the market place and offer one possible consolidation and scale development route. Clear funding and infrastructure support is still needed to assist replication of these models.

CDFIs offering new products at the national level This includes large-scale but newer entrants that are relatively well resourced and able to deliver their finance. They could benefit from increased market support and capital to enable customers to access their products, particularly where they have lower representation or in areas which are physically further away from their administrative centres.

The CDFA survey included a series of questions on the issues facing the sector. It showed that the top three issues facing UK CDFIs over the next three years were revenue funding, access to capital for on-lending and improving and increasing the quality of the portfolio.

Revenue funds are resources that are generally granted to CDFIs to cover the costs of the delivery of their services including accommodation, staff, infrastructure (such as management information systems), marketing and outreach, business support and money advice and product development. Capital contributions, by contrast, are funds (granted, lent or invested with varying returns) that are deployed in CDFI portfolios in investments and loans.

The survey returns suggest that for this new sector, a supportive funding environment remains the biggest identified need as it moves forward. For those who are starting out, securing their immediate financial future and ensuring their funds are reaching their chosen market is paramount. Unsurprisingly, as CDFIs mature, their concerns broaden as they face a variety of operational and reaching scale issues including improving and increasing their access to capital for on-lending. They are interested in finding a variety of different sources of capital which will enable them to grow, improving their portfolios and reaching more people while simultaneously increasing their levels of generated income to cover the costs of their operations.

Sector-wide perspectives

This broader environment, including the policies and actions of both statutory and non-statutory stakeholders, has created both opportunities and challenges for the sector going forward. In the main CDFIs are thought to be effective institutions, with 80 per cent of the respondents to a recent NEF[9] survey emphasizing the positive impact of CDFIs and their critical role in tackling access to finance and their importance in disadvantaged communities (NEF, 2007). With the right support CDFIs are likely to continue to innovate and develop. The biggest opportunity currently facing individual CDFIs is to continue to grow the size of portfolios and increase coverage while maintaining or improving portfolio quality. Some of the products in development in different markets include access to savings, insurance and budgeting products for individuals; home improvement and purchase products for householders; leasing, equity, accommodation and support packages for small and micro businesses; and long-term and quasi-equity products for social enterprise. For individual CDFIs, one of the key challenges will be to continue to secure the right mix of grants and investments to increase generated income (normally measured by the operational self-sustainability ratio) and to cover any shortfall with grants and contributed income.

Understanding performance – developing standards in the sector

One of the key ways in which CDFIs will succeed in securing the support they need to continue to grow and develop will be to provide greater transparency about their performance. One way to achieve this could be through Change Matters. In addition, an effective performance framework could enable the sector to develop its own self-regulatory regime on which future formal regulation can be based.

Change Matters is a financial, organizational and impact monitoring and assessment tool based on three key areas: finance, business operations and impact. Its objectives are to:

- drive up performance and support growth;
- provide a tool for stakeholders to assess CDFIs and understand differing performance;

- enable funders and stakeholder to develop capacity-building priorities;
- help funders and stakeholders make decisions about policy and strategic development;
- minimize/reduce funding and investment assessment, reporting and monitoring costs.

The tests – or indicators – within each domain are based on a series of both quantitative and qualitative ratios and principles. However, Change Matters does not seek only to reveal performance, but to drive up standards with the inclusion of key benchmarks for different markets. The benchmarks were published in draft at the 2007 CDFA conference and are currently under consultation with members and stakeholders.

Maturity and segmentation

At a sector level there are also increasing signs of maturity. There is a growing distinction amongst the newer entrants between those CDFIs that are developing a track record and those that are struggling to reach scale and streamline operations. This has already led to some consolidation and mergers and this trend is likely to continue, also driven by a tendency for CDFIs to coordinate more effectively at the regional level to provide coverage and liaise with individual RDAs. With the regional authority now involved in shaping the sector, a more locally strategic approach will be adopted. This will mean that some CDFIs will enjoy greater public funding, while others are excluded. Although this will lead to some takeovers, there is no guarantee that these will involve the strongest CDFIs. Instead it is possible that political status, as much as economic or social performance, will become predictors of survival, with the ability to promote the CDFIs to public officials becoming a priority. In addition, the creation of independent CDFIs means that some of these will survive even without state support, either by down-scaling, by drawing financial assistance from charitable foundations and other parties, or by pursuing pure financial sustainability. Even during funding under the Phoenix Fund, which had a deliberately 'light touch' reporting structure, most CDFIs sought additional and alternative funding sources, partly to ensure some independence from the state.

There are also signs of increasing segmentation of the functions of lending, creating opportunities to drive efficiency and improve services. As different parts of the outreach, underwriting, portfolio management process and capitalization of CDFIs are separated, specialists are emerging to provide particular services. A number of back office providers offering varying levels of management and underwriting have developed and continue to grow in effectiveness. A number of organizations that tested direct provision of lending have now transformed themselves into front office providers providing a pipeline of customers for the CDFIs they work with and crucial pre- and post-loan support. In the last three years a number of wholesalers have also emerged to provide capital for CDFIs and although demand has been slow to emerge, absorption of capital in the sector is likely to increase, fuelling demand for external capital and increasing interest in using wholesale intermediaries.

As the CDFIs strive for sustainability it is likely that the sector will fragment, with a small group of those 'almost sustainable' who will be the main innovators, followed by a rump reliant on public support and delivering similar services to those offered today. Perhaps the greatest challenge for this group will come when the first CDFI becomes totally self-sustainable, which is likely to cause all funders to re-evaluate their support for the sector. At this stage it is likely that any remaining resources are concentrated still further on the most sustainable, with funding for the others linked to specialized markets where they seek to achieve specific social outcomes.

Future policy perspectives

At present, there is little evidence that the ongoing regionalization of CDFI funding is going to be reversed. This is likely to result in policies which differ by location and according to whether the local priority is entrepreneurial culture through micro-enterprise or reducing unemployment through support for established SMEs. It is possible that both approaches will be adopted in some regions, although delivered by one or a number of institutions. Most RDAs are being more instrumental in selecting which CDFIs to support, leading to fewer supported CDFIs across the country. This does not necessarily mean that there will only be one CDFI per region, but it is unlikely the current proliferation of institutions will continue.

Conclusion

Despite the recent changes within the UK CDFI environment, the Government, both at national and regional level, remains committed to CDFIs as a mechanism for the delivery of a range of policy priorities. There is no political appetite for a return to a grant- or soft loan-based policy, though this could change if the UK were to undergo a period of extended recession.

The wide variety of CDFIs seems certain to continue, though some consolidation is likely in the next few years. However, CDFIs have come a long way since the inception of the Phoenix Fund, and the sector continues to have a strong pattern of growth. An outcome of the multifaceted sector is the continual improvement in business strategies and search for sustainable models. Stable funding streams which focus on performance and step changes in capacity and development will remain a central agenda for many organizations, together with the availability of affordable capital at the right price and on the right terms. It is also probable that the existing dichotomy of social and financial objectives will need to be continually balanced. Finally, there is no doubt that this new sector has been able to emerge within a light regulatory environment. As microfinance grows and diversifies and particularly as products diversify and organizations increasingly raise investment, the right to raise capital will come with responsibilities. Ensuring the regulatory burden and behaviour of CDFIs remain proportionate will be a challenge for practitioners and the regulatory authorities. Microfinance continues to flourish in the UK and although the funding environment has tightened, it is likely to remain supported providing it serves people and businesses which the mainstream sector is unable to help.

Notes

1. In the USA the majority of sustainable CDFIs are predominantly engaged in property and land-related lending (CDFI Data Project, 2004).
2. Community Development Finance Association, the trade association for social finance organizations in the UK: www.cdfa.org.uk.
3. The regulator of UK charities.
4. These are in addition to the UK's credit unions.
5. McGeehan (2007).
6. McGeehan (2007).
7. £17 482 at the exchange rate current in November 2007 (xe.com).
8. 'The regulation of microcredit in Europe', Expert Group Report, April 2007.
9. New Economics Foundation, a London-based 'think-and-do-tank'.

References

CDFI Data project (2004), *Providing Capital, Building Communities, Creating Impact: Community Development Financial Institutions*, 3rd edn, Fiscal Year 2003.

Copisarow, R. (2000), 'The application of microcredit technology to the UK: key commercial and policy issues', *Journal of Microfinance*, **2** (1), 13–42.

Copisarow, R. (2005), *Street UK – A Micro-finance Organisation: Lessons Learned from its First Three Years' Operations*, Birmingham: Street UK.

Dayson, K. (2005), 'Are community development finance institutions doing too much?', paper presented at the *ISBE Conference*, Blackpool, 1-3 November.

Dayson, K. (forthcoming), 'Financing small business development in the UK', in A. Southern (ed.), *Understanding Enterprise Inclusion.*

Dayson, K. and P. Conaty (2006), *Community Banking Partnerships*, Salford: University of Salford.

Esmée Fairbairn (2005), *Street (UK): Learning From Community Finance, a Briefing Paper*, London: Esmée Fairbairn.

Giddens, A. (1998), *The Third Way: The Renewal of Social Democracy*, Cambridge: Polity Press.

H.M. Treasury (1999a), *PAT 3: Enterprise and Social Exclusion*, London: H.M. Treasury.
H.M. Treasury (1999b), *Pat 14: Access to Financial Services*, London: H.M.Treasury.
Hollis, A. and A. Sweetman (1997), 'Complementarity, competition, and institutional development: the Irish loan funds through three centuries', March, unpublished paper.
Kermode, J. (1991), 'Money and credit in the fifteenth century: some lessons from Yorkshire', *The Business History Review*, **65** (3), 475–501.
Klett, M. (1994), *A Directory of Soft Loan Schemes 1993, 1994*, Kingston, UK: Small Business Research Centre, Kingston University.
McGeehan, S. (2006), 'Inside out', with N. Goggin, London: CDFA.
McGeehan, S. (2007), 'Inside out', with N. Goggin, London, CDFA.
Mosley, P. and L. Steel (2004), 'Microfinance, the labour market and social inclusion: a tale of three cities', *Social Policy and Administration*, **38** (7), 721–43.
Muldrew, C. (1993), 'Credit and courts: debt litigation in a seventeenth century urban community', *Economic History Review*, **XLVI** (1), 23–38.
New Economics Foundation (NEF) (2007), *Reconsidering UK Community Development Finance*, London: NEF.
Social Investment Task Force (SITF) (2000), 'Enterprising communities – wealth beyond welfare', report, UK Social Investment Forum, London, October.

2 Microcredit in France: financial support for social inclusion[1]

Stefanie Lämmermann

Introduction

Two different types of microcredit can be distinguished: microcredit referring to microloans for business start-up and self-employment, and 'social microcredit', that is small loans intended to assist excluded persons to borrow money for expenses facilitating their social and economic integration. This chapter deals mainly with business microcredit. 'Social microcredit' will be mentioned marginally, as it only began to develop very recently in France. In the same way, the notion of 'social venture capital', which more globally designates the funding of socially responsible economic projects and activities through credits, trust loans, guarantees, savings and equity, will be treated separately.

National context

In the last decade, France has undergone modest economic growth. With an average 2.3 per cent growth in its gross domestic product over the last ten years, France has a slightly lower growth rate than the EU 25 (2.4 per cent). Unemployment has steadily decreased from nearly 11 per cent in 1997 to 7.8 per cent in December 2007, but is still higher than the EU 27 average (6.8 per cent). It is twice as high in the French overseas territories (DOM-TOM) as in France itself. Unemployment is also higher for women than for men, and more than 18 per cent of young persons under the age of 25 are unemployed (EU 27 average: 15.4 per cent).[2] This holds especially true for young men and women in the most deprived French urban and suburban areas. Although risk of poverty in France is below the EU 27 average, an estimated seven million people in France live in poverty, and this rate is higher amongst women than amongst men.[3] There has been an increase in so-called 'precarious jobs', due to particular forms of contracts such as temporary, short-term, part-time and state-sponsored contracts (*contrats aidés*).

Setting up a business can be an active response to combating poverty and (re-)integrating into the labour market. In France, 40 per cent of new enterprises were launched or taken over by unemployed persons in 2006 – 6 per cent more than in 2002 (Insee, 2007c). However, France has a relatively low overall self-employment rate. While the EU 25 average self-employment to total employment rate is 16 per cent, this rate is only 10 per cent for France (Jouhette and Romans, 2006). For several years the French government has made significant efforts to encourage the setting up and taking over of micro, small and medium-sized enterprises by improving the regulatory and general environment for business. Thus it has become much easier to establish and register a business, especially microbusiness. However, the World Bank still ranks France toward the bottom of OECD countries with respect to the ease of doing business (World Bank, 2008).[4] Moreover, France has a strong culture of salaried work, with an educational system that does not sufficiently stimulate entrepreneurial spirit (Volery and Servais, 2000; Torrès and Eminet, 2004). Only 30 per cent of new entrepreneurs are women (Insee, 2007a).

More than 91 per cent of enterprises in France are microenterprises with fewer than five employees, employing one out of five people (Ministère de l'Economie, 2001/02) and microenterprises make up the biggest part of new enterprise start-ups. Indeed, in 2007, 87 per cent of all new enterprises in France were started without employees, an increase of 57 per cent since 2002, and 64 per cent of new entrepreneurs started their business in order to assure their own job, which is 10 per cent more than in 2002 (Insee, 2008). Most microenterprises are established in Southern France and in the Ile-de-France region, while the Northern and Eastern regions are more intensively marked by agriculture and large industrial sites that absorb a large part of the labour force (DCASP, 2007).

The financial resources used for setting up an enterprise tend to be relatively low. In 2002, 45 per cent of entrepreneurs in the Insee SINE panel claimed to have started without any form of external finance. In the Insee SINE 2006 panel surveying 48 000 businesses, 54 per cent of entrepreneurs started with less than 8000 euros. About 40 per cent of all new entrepreneurs took out a bank loan and one third started exclusively with their own resources (APCE, 2006). Levels of initial investment vary strongly depending on the business sector. In all sectors, women start their businesses with fewer financial resources than men (Insee, 2007a). It is not clear if this low initial investment is a consequence of low financial demand on the part of entrepreneurs (demand side) or of refusal by banks (supply side).

Origins and main actors

In France, different types of organizations provide microcredit directly or indirectly. They differ in the kind of products they offer, in their functioning, sources of funding and with regard to the target group they serve. They fall into three different categories: non-bank microcredit, organizations that facilitate access to (micro-)loans from banks, and para-bank actors.

Non-bank microcredit for business start-ups, as it is today, began to develop early in France compared to other European countries. This is principally due to the personal initiative of one person, Maria Nowak, founder of Adie, the Association au Droit à l'Initiative Economique (Association for the Right to Economic Initiative). In 1989, at a point in time when unemployment caused by the restructuring of the economy became a major problem in France and the minimum social allowance scheme RMI was set up,[5] Maria Nowak, at that time programme manager at the French Development Agency, together with two other volunteers, founded Adie with the financial support of several private foundations, the government, the Caisse des Dépôts et Consignations (CDC)[6] and a European anti-poverty programme. Their aim was to fight unemployment and social exclusion by providing finance and support to unemployed individuals who wished to start their own businesses, but who did not have the necessary guarantees to receive a standard bank loan.

The founding of Adie was inspired by the success of the Grameen Bank microfinance model in Bangladesh. At the beginning, Adie transferred the Grameen Bank's solidarity group model to the French environment. This approach, however, failed. The association therefore turned to individual loans. Since then, Adie has forged partnerships with several cooperative banks and private financial institutions, as well as with other public actors such as local government. It has also diversified its financial products following changes in the institutional framework to assist those in difficulty to set up an enterprise.[7]

Adie is the only organization that fits the definition of a non-bank microcredit provider. It has defined the provision of microcredit as its main mission and strategy. Socially and financially excluded people are its main target group. In fact, the organization has continually promoted the idea of self-employed work as means of inclusion for unemployed and minimum income beneficiaries. Adie's lobbying activities have played a huge role in ameliorating the administrative and regulatory environment for microlending and microenterprises in France.

As of December 2007, 369 staff members[8] worked in 18 regional Adie offices, 131 sub-offices and 400 'stand-by spots'[9] spread over the French territory and overseas[10] (Adie, 2008a). In addition, more than 1000 volunteers support Adie entrepreneurs. More than 50 000 people contact Adie every year.

In two locations, different associations benefit from Adie's back-office system, GAIA. In the Languedoc-Roussillon region AIRDIE has been supporting the unemployed in starting a business since 1994. In the Seine-et-Marne, in the region of Ile-de-France, Afile 77 was founded in 1991 with the same purpose. It uses a business incubator and has had a special focus on the Romany population for several years.

In addition to Adie, other organizations operate in the field. They provide quasi-equity or guarantee schemes in order to facilitate access to bank loans for new entrepreneurs who lack the necessary guarantees. However, only part of their activity reaches excluded individuals and enables them to access loans below 25 000 euros.

France Initiative was created as a public and para-public initiative[11] in 1985 as a federation of 20 local business support programmes, combining the provision of financial support with additional 'human' support, that is mentoring. Today, France Initiative brings together 242 such programmes, called 'France Initiative's platforms'. Spread all over France and the overseas territories, these platforms are often located in Chambers of Commerce and Industry buildings. Each local structure is supposed to develop its own priorities of intervention depending on local economic needs and its specific partnerships in the field. Moreover, each platform itself mobilizes and manages funds locally. In 2007, 509 employees worked within France Initiative with 14 staff in the Federation's head office. The average size of a local team is 2.9 people. These are on average assisted by 55 volunteers active in one platform. Overall 13 100 volunteers were actively engaged in the work of France Initiative in 2007 (France Initiative, 2008).

Another organization called France Active was founded in 1988 by the Fondation de France,[12] the Caisse des Dépôts et Consignations (CDC), the French National Agency for Enterprise Start-up (APCE) and Crédit Coopératif. France Active federates a network of 38 territorial funds (Fonds Territoriaux France Active). It is today the main provider of guarantee schemes to French microenterprises and SMEs. The association had 280 employees and worked with around 800 volunteers in 2007. A great part of its funds are provided by the CDC. Finally, OSEO was founded in 2005 as a public development bank under the supervision of the French Ministry of the Economy, Finance and Industry. OSEO provides guarantees and financial support to French micro, small and medium-sized enterprises with a focus on innovation.

Moreover, two para-bank actors exist. These are Nef (Nouvelle Economie Fraternelle) and Parcours Confiance. Nef is a solidarity finance cooperative founded in 1988 that supports responsible and innovative business projects with social, cultural or environmental value through collection of savings and credit provision with approval of the Banque de France. The Parcours Confiance associations were set up by the French Savings Banks, Caisses d'Epargne, in 2006 and provide microloans for business purposes as well as 'social microloans'.[13] In a part of the

Aquitaine region the association Caisse Sociale du Développement Local has been appointed to carry out the work of Parcours Confiance. Created in Bordeaux in 1998 by the local government and banks, the association receives funds from several public actors, banks and the EU. In the region of Provence-Alpes-Côtes d'Azur the association Créa-Sol acts on behalf of the Parcours Confiance.

Microcredit products

Non-bank, bank and para-bank actors in France provide different kinds of products. These either serve to finance a business directly or to facilitate access to bank loans. The different products are shown in Table 2.1.

Non-bank microcredit

Adie's mission is to finance and support (long-term) unemployed individuals and welfare recipients who would like to set up their own businesses but do not qualify for a standard bank loan. The association disburses several types of microloans and provides pre- and post-loan advice and support.

Before 2001 French banking law did not allow associations to on-lend to their clients. Adie therefore had special refinancing agreements with banks that provided loans to Adie clients. However, through intense lobbying, Adie obtained an amendment to the French banking law which now allows the association to borrow for on-lending. For the association, this facilitates its management of loan provision, enables it to reach a larger number of clients and accelerates the disbursement of the loans. Within Adie, on average 30 days pass between the first contact and the provision of the microcredit.

The main part of the association's credit activity (82 per cent) consists of so-called solidarity loans implying interest rates which, due to the high costs of additional business support, the relatively risky target group and the unprofitability of small loans, are higher than those charged by mainstream banks.[14] For its solidarity loans, Adie charged an interest rate of 7.98 per cent in 2007. Increasing the interest rate became possible through the abolition of the usury rate in 2005.[15] The association also applies a 5 per cent commission and requests one or several people from the entrepreneur's environment to guarantee 50 per cent of the loan amount. Beside risk management, this measure also aims at encouraging members of the entrepreneur's entourage to support him or her if necessary. By offering a product with an interest rate, Adie aims to assist not immediately-bankable would-be entrepreneurs to integrate progressively into mainstream financial services and to cover their own cost progressively. The association provides approximately 85 per cent of its loans to new businesses and 15 per cent to existing enterprises.

Table 2.1 The French microcredit market: organizations and products

Classification	Product	Organization	Loan amounts	Outreach (2007)
		Non-bank microcredit		
Microloans	Short/medium-term interest-bearing loans with alternative guarantee arrangements	Adie	Maximum €5500 (average: €2750)	9853 loans
	Local finance providers facilitating access to bank (micro-)credit			
Prêts d'honneur	Medium-term interest-free loans without guarantee to leverage bank loans	France Initiative	€3000 – 40 000 (average: €7400 + €59 400)	12 500 *prêts d'honneur* (~5000 below €25 000)
		Adie	Maximum €5000 (average: €2508)	2391 prêts d'honneur
		France Active	Maximum €10 000	749 *prêts d'honneur* (2006)
Guarantee Funds	Guarantees facilitating access to bank loans for underprivileged persons	OSEO Sofaris	Guarantee up to 70% and PCE loan: €2000–7000 (average: €5500 + €20 000)	23 261 PCE loans
	France Active Garantie (FAG)	France Active	Guarantee up to 65% with a limit of €30 500 (average loan: €11 835)	790 FAG guarantees
	FGIF	France Active	Guarantee up to 70% with a limit of €27 000 (average loan: €14 600)	745 FGIF guarantees

Table 2.1 (continued)

Classification	Product	Organization	Loan amounts	Outreach (2007)
		Para-bank microcredit providers		
Microloans	Medium-term loans with preferential interest rate and without guarantee	Parcours Confiance	Max. €30 000	1500 loans ('social' microloans included)
	Medium- and long-term loans	Nef	€10 000 – €125 000	~158 loans below €25 000

Adie's microloans have to be paid back within 24 months. The average loan amount is 2750 euros for a period of 18 months. It can take different forms: step loans from 1000 to 3500 euros for the transformation of an informal activity into an enterprise; regional start-up loans of up to 2000 euros from local authorities; the PCE; repayable advance EDEN loans;[16] as well as *prêts d'honneur* (subsidized quasi-equity loans). In addition, Adie provides different types of equity or quasi-equity: test loans up to 1500 euros for evaluating the feasibility of a project, loans for the development of an enterprise (renewal of material, stocks, diversification of products and so on) and loans for material. Total financing of a project does not exceed 10 000 euros.

In the overseas territories Adie provides microloans in a way that is adapted to the local context. It works with local staff and in collaboration with local political leaders. Since 2003 it has tested family loans. The loan amounts are smaller: 40 per cent of the loans are below €1500 (Adie, 2005).

Adie has several partnerships with banks which, overall, provide 80 per cent of loan funds. In 2007 the most important were: Crédit Coopératif/Banque Populaire (24 per cent), BNP Paribas (16 per cent), Crédit Mutuel (11 per cent) and Société Générale (6 per cent). The French Development Agency, AFD provides a credit line to Adie branches overseas.

Having provided 34 loans in 1990, Adie disbursed nearly 10 000 loans in 2007 representing a 30 per cent growth compared to the year before. The repayment rate of loans was 93.1 per cent in 2007. Adie financed 10 450 new jobs in 2007. From its inception in 1989 to the end of 2007, the association has disbursed 53 600 microloans and more than 11 100 *prêts d'honneur*, has financed more than 45 600 new enterprises and created more than 54 000 jobs. The survival rate for new enterprises after three years was 57 per cent in 2007, and 80 per cent of the people Adie supported in the last five years have quit welfare schemes and have become reintegrated into the labour market[17] (Adie, 2008a).

Facilitated access to bank (micro-)credit

France Initiative – prêts d'honneur ('quasi-equity') In contrast to Adie, France Initiative has the broader mission of stimulating enterprise set-up on the local level and does not explicitly focus on excluded individuals. The association disburses quasi-equity in the form of so-called *prêts d'honneur*. These are personal, reimbursable, interest-free loans without guarantee that target relatively experienced, 'almost-bankable' persons with projects aimed at creating three to ten jobs. The great majority of the projects financed by a France Initiative *prêt d'honneur* (89 per cent) are used to leverage a bank loan. The average amount of a *prêt d'honneur* was 7400 euros (between 3000 and 40 000 euros) in 2007, accompanied by more than seven times that amount in bank lending (France Initiative, 2008). Thirty per cent of the projects funded by France Initiative are business take-overs.

Each platform sets its own loan terms and conditions and decides itself on the maximum amount of a *prêt d'honneur*, the period of reimbursement (between two and five years) and grace periods. Loan reimbursement is made via the respective local platform or bank. The average reimbursement period is three years, with a grace period of four months. Like Adie, France Initiative may also provide entrepreneurs with other public loans or guarantee schemes. France Initiative does not ask for a guarantee but applies a strict selection process: once pre-selected, the entrepreneur has to present his or her business plan to an Expert Committee which accepts or rejects the decision to provide a loan and tutoring. In 2007 the repayment rate was 96.6 per cent.

In 2007, France Initiative provided 12 500 *prêts d'honneur*, out of which an estimated 5000 enabled the beneficiary to access a bank microcredit (Adie/EMN, 2008).[18] The network supported the start-up or take-over of 13 500 enterprises with a total of 30 500 jobs created. In 2007, the survival rate of enterprises supported by France Initiative after three years was 86 per cent (France Initiative, 2008).

France Active (guarantee schemes) France Active facilitates access to bank credit for would-be entrepreneurs via guarantee schemes and provides financial support through access to equity without requiring collateral. Its solidarity investment funds primarily target associations and social enterprises including those employing people from deprived areas and those with disabilities.

France Active has its own guarantee scheme called FAG (France Active Garantie) and has been awarded the management of four government guarantee schemes since 2002: the FGIF (Fonds de Garantie pour la création, la reprise ou le développement d'entreprises à l'initiative des femmes) for women entrepreneurs; the FGIE (Fonds de Garantie pour l'Insertion Economique); the FGAP (Fonds de Garantie pour le Développement des Ateliers Protégés) and the FGES (Fonds de Garantie pour la création, la reprise et le développement des Entreprises Solidaires). Whilst the last two guarantees target social enterprises, the FGIE is used to cover the risk of microloans, for instance by Adie.

Only the FAG and the FGIF can be used by micro-entrepreneurs directly. While the FAG targets unemployed people who would like to set up their own business, the FGIF is exclusively reserved for female entrepreneurs who have launched their business at most five years previously. The FGIF was barely used until 2002 due to its heavily-centralized structure and a lack of awareness. The government then undertook a number of programme reforms and notably selected France Active, with its nationwide business support network, as the guarantee fund manager. The France Active grassroots network has had a very positive impact on the provision of the FGIF. In addition, in 2006, accessing the guarantees was made easier. The number of FGIF guarantees granted therefore increased sevenfold from 2003 to 2006. In 2007, 745 FGIF guarantees were provided, guaranteeing on average 14 600 euros (CDC, 2007). Moreover, the association makes governmental unsecured interest-free loans and advances available to microenterprises. France Active helped to start up 3270 microenterprises in 2006.[19] A partnership was also established between the French Savings Banks Caisses d'Epargne in 2006 through the Parcours Confiance associations.

OSEO – the business start-up loan PCE In October 2000, the former SME Minister launched the enterprise start-up loan PCE (Prêt à la Création d'Entreprise) and entrusted its management to OSEO's Sofaris branch. The PCE consists of an unsecured loan between 2000 and 7000 euros with an interest rate based upon state bonds (approximately 5.6 per cent), a six-month deferment on principal payments and a maximum loan term of five years (54 monthly instalments). PCE loans are disbursed to registered new microenterprises not more than three years old as well as to take-overs, regardless of their sector of activity (except for agriculture and real estate). An accompanying bank loan two or three times the amount of the PCE is obligatory. In order to reassure banks, OSEO may in addition guarantee up to 70 per cent of the value of the bank loan. The average amount of a bank loan is 10 882 euros. The whole amount of money mobilized with the help of the PCE, including *prêts d'honneur*, equity, PCE, EDEN, bank loans and so on, must not exceed 45 000 euros. While the PCE covers costs such as computer software or start-up fees, the bank loan is intended for investment in material, machinery and so on. The PCE can be obtained directly from a bank[20] or from Adie. Its provision can be facilitated by social business support structures (see below).[21]

Access to the PCE was simplified and extended to a larger audience in November 2006 in order to double the number of loans provided per year. In 2007, 23 261 PCE loans were provided with an average amount of 5500 euros and an average associated bank credit of 20 000 euros. Approximately 80 per cent of the associated bank loans were less than 25 000 euros (Adie/EMN, 2008). OSEO's aim is to disburse 30 000 PCE loans per year.

Para-bank microcredit

With approval of the Banque de France, the solidarity finance cooperative Nef supports responsible and innovative projects with a social, cultural or environmental value through savings and credit. The cooperative provides medium- and long-term loans of between 10 000 and 125 000 euros with interest rates that are calculated on the basis of market rates, and takes into consideration the characteristics of each loan (amount, period, risk, and so on). In 2006, it provided 264 loans with an average loan of 53 000 euros.[22] Approximately 60 per cent of the association's loans are for less than 30 000 euros.

In addition, since 2006 the savings banks Caisses d'Epargne have created associations called Parcours Confiance, providing microcredit to combat financial exclusion. These not-for-profit associations are distinct from the bank but directly linked to it. One of their pillars is microcredit for business start-ups by people excluded from the banking sector – with preferential interest rates and without guarantee. Partnerships have been established with business support networks.[23] All in all, almost 1500 ('social' and business) microcredits were provided in 2007 (Adie/EMN, 2008). The loans provided are for less than 30 000 euros; however, the amounts differ from one region to another. The savings banks provide the credit lines and also cover part of the risk. France Active guarantees cover the rest of the risk (70 per cent).

Target groups

Adie mainly reaches socially and economically excluded people (welfare recipients, long-term unemployed and inactive people) who are not immediately bankable due to a lack of the collateral banks require as a pre-condition for lending. In fact, Adie's non-bank microcredit aims at progressively integrating persons with low incomes into the normal bank circuit. Equally, France Active targets excluded people. In contrast, France Initiative and OSEO serve a nearly-bankable clientele.

Eighty-three per cent of Adie clients are welfare recipients and unemployed persons with an average unemployment period of two years. Out of these, 42 per cent receive social minima paid to those who have exhausted employment-based income support. The remaining clients are self-employed or come from low-paid jobs. Adie entrepreneurs above all wish to create their own job. They have limited financial assets to invest in their businesses. Supported projects need on average a relatively low start-up capital of 10 000 euros and are mainly new sole proprietor businesses (Adie, 2008a). In 2007, 29 per cent of Adie clients had passed the baccalaureate. Thirty-seven per cent possessed a professional certificate (BEP/CAP) and 21 per cent had no or very little formal education. One third of Adie clients are foreign-born or children of immigrants and 36 per cent of clients are female (Adie, 2008a). Adie particularly tries to reach more young people, especially in deprived urban areas, as well as residents of rural areas.[24] The association's clients mainly start their business in the trade and service sectors.

In contrast, France Initiative entrepreneurs bring in 25 per cent of the global start-up capital themselves. Projects have average start-up capital needs of 71 000 euros (that is seven times as high as Adie's average start-up capital) and create on average two or three jobs. Twenty-eight per cent of France Initiative's support to enterprises concerns business take-overs. Fifty-five per cent of enterprises financed for take-over have budgets of more than 75 000 euros (France Initiative Réseau, 2007). Nevertheless, a relatively high percentage of France Initiative clients, 66 per cent in 2007, are unemployed. It is possible that a part of this client group gives up their job voluntarily in order to start a business. Client profiles also vary from platform to platform. As for Adie, France Initiative clients start their business in the trade and service sectors. Thirty-three per cent of France Initiative clients are women (France Initiative, 2008).

Adie and France Initiative reach a slightly higher percentage of women than the national average of female entrepreneurs.[25] However, this is not enough if one takes account of the fact that women's businesses are generally clustered in the very competitive service sector and that women have higher poverty levels, greater unemployment rates and fewer assets than men.

Business development services

The finance providers intervene at different points in time. Adie and France Initiative may already assist the would-be entrepreneur before

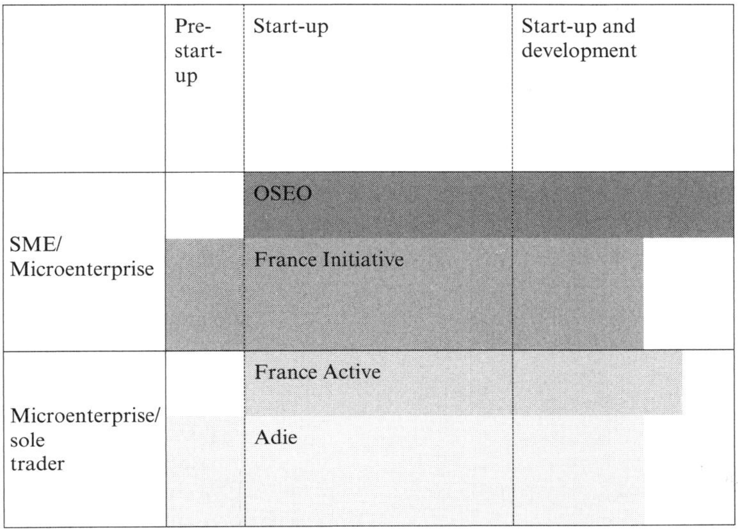

	Pre-start-up	Start-up	Start-up and development
SME/ Microenterprise		OSEO France Initiative	
Microenterprise/ sole trader		France Active Adie	

Figure 2.1 Map of financial tools

actually providing the business loan, that is by financing feasibility studies. In contrast, France Active and OSEO do not intervene until the business has actually been set up, but stay with the entrepreneur for a period of time, as they engage in financing the further development of businesses. This can be illustrated by Figure 2.1.

Besides the credit itself, BDS[26] services are of the highest importance in France, as in the whole of Europe. They enable new entrepreneurs to face administrative procedures, implement accountancy and management systems, establish a relationship with the bank and identify commercial opportunities. In fact, studies show that business survival five years after start-up is three times as high if the new entrepreneur has received business support when setting up his or her business (Agence des PME, 2003). In addition, it reduces the risk of non-repayment of the loan. The organizations therefore cooperate closely with business support networks such as the Chambers of Commerce and Industry/Chambers for Crafts[27] and the Boutiques de Gestion (see Table 2.2).

Adie provides pre- and post-loan business support during the whole period of reimbursement of the loan, which is on average two years. Until 2007, the association provided individual advice and training in four major fields: administrative procedures, management and accounting, marketing and banking. Since 2007, the association has revised its support strategy and has set up a strategic plan for the period 2007–2009 in order

Table 2.2 'Pure' BDS providers in France

Organization	Status	Services
Chambers of Commerce and Industry (CCI)/ Chambers for Crafts	Not state entities but with a duty to serve the public	Training and support; advice on financing possibilities; national and European-level information (websites database)
Boutiques de Gestion	Network of associations	Pre-start-up support, training and advice; business incubators (*couveuses*); post-business start-up support in the first two years of a newly-established business
APCE – Agence National Pour La Création d'Entreprises	60% state-financed and 40% financed by revenue (professional training, online data sales)	Website: information on programmes and formalities; technical assistance and training to support organizations

to provide high quality services and disseminate them in a homogeneous way. In June 2007, a hotline (Adie Conseil) was set up as a pilot project in five of its offices.[28] It is run by volunteers and is thought to reduce Adie loan officers' workload. In addition, volunteers train the entrepreneurs in so-called '*cercles de créateurs*' (business clubs) which at the same time provide space for the exchange of experiences. Technical partnerships with companies such as Microsoft, Leroy Merlin and Linklaters have also been developed. Since 2005 the project 'L'informatique en 3 clics' ('Computing in 3 clicks') in cooperation with Microsoft provides a three-day free computer training course as well as the opportunity to buy a used computer at preferential prices. Seventy training sessions of this kind were provided in 2007 with very positive feedback (Adie, 2007).

France Initiative network members assist the entrepreneurs in the development of their business plans and access to finance, and help link them to an appropriate bank. In addition, each entrepreneur may be individually mentored by a 'godfather/godmother' (*parrain*), a (former) business director who monitors and supports the would-be entrepreneur and introduces him or her into local business networks. In 2007, 6600 entrepreneurs, or about 30 per cent of entrepreneurs supported by France Initiative, had a mentor of this type (France Initiative, 2008). France Active also provides technical training to entrepreneurs and develops tools and methods for the network.

The organizations rely heavily on volunteers. For instance, Adie works with an extensive network of 1000 volunteers, and overall 4700 mentors were engaged in the work of France Initiative in 2007. Most volunteers are recent retirees and active professionals in the business and banking environment, who help the associations as advisors, mentors and trainers.

Other financial products

'Social microcredit'

Beside microcredit for business start-up, other types of financial product exist or are being developed in France. In 2005 the government set up the Social Cohesion Fund (Fonds de Cohésion Sociale FCS) under the Social Cohesion Programme.[29] Endowed with €73 million for a period of five years it is governed by the Caisse des dépôts et consignations (CDC) on behalf of the State. The Social Cohesion Fund provides its guarantee to microcredit organizations through the FGIE guarantee fund and can guarantee up to 50 per cent for 'social microcredits' offered by microfinance organizations or banks.

Social microcredit is still in the testing period. These loans are intended to enable financially and socially excluded people to borrow money for expenses that promote their social and economic inclusion such as a driver's licence, a means of transport, further education or the acquisition of new equipment. The social microloan amounts vary between 300 and 4000 euros, to be paid back over a maximum period of 48 months. An exception exists for severe accidents leading to work incapacity, with loan amounts of up to 12 000 euros to be paid back within 60 months. The interest rate applied should not exceed 8 per cent. Actual applied interest rates lie between 1 per cent and 6 per cent. The loans are granted by certain credit institutions that have agreed a contract with the CDC, while additional support to lenders is provided by national and regional social associations such as Secours Catholique, community centres or public bodies. The Social Cohesion Fund guarantees up to 50 per cent of the social microcredit loan portfolio.

Up to 31 December 2007, the FCS had established partnerships with 14 banks and financial organizations, including the Parcours Confiance (Caisses d'Epargne), and 12 national support networks. All in all, 132 pilot projects were counted at the local level (ANSA, 2008). Adie has tested social microcredit in three regions (Ile-de-France, Pays de la Loire and Aquitaine) since November 2006, but has not yet decided whether to continue the activity.[30]

Up to 31 December 2007, approximately 2500 'social microloans' had been provided through the FCS with an average amount of €1800. The relatively small outreach of the programme is the result of various factors. First of all, up until now, there has been no legal definition of social microcredit. Therefore it tends to be put on a level with consumer credit. Moreover, while the actual aim of the programme is to facilitate labour market integration, in reality 50 per cent of the loans cover needs that are not directly linked to employment. Finally, another important reason for the low take-up is the fact that people who are registered as a bad credit risk in the national credit databases are not eligible for social microcredit. However, these people represent approximately 40 per cent of all applicants (ANSA, 2008; CDC, 2008).

Microinsurance

In addition to loan products, microinsurance aimed at excluded persons is being tested. A study conducted by a student at ESSEC[31] and Adie in September 2006 revealed that 20 per cent of entrepreneurs, formerly unemployed or those receiving the minimum revenue RMI, are financially unable to access insurance coverage. Without insurance, microentrepreneurs may fail to sustain their enterprise in the case of a simple unforeseeable professional, family or health incident. In fact, 14 per cent of entrepreneurs cease their activity during the first five years due to noneconomic problems (notably accidents), of which 5 per cent are due to health problems (MACIF/AXA/Adie, 2007).

In Lyon, in the Rhône-Alpes region, a microinsurance association called Entrepreneurs de la Cité was established in December 2004. It offers microinsurance to excluded people who start their enterprise with assistance from a microcredit and/or a business support structure. Funded with an initial budget of 5.7 million euros by several 'traditional' insurance companies as well as the CDC and the Banque Postale, the association covers its operating costs through funds from individuals and enterprises. The collaborating insurance companies do not request commission; guarantee terms, accessibility, payment and price delays are adapted to those with a low income. Insurance covers liability, multi-risk at work and health expenses as well as rental of a car and office/computer insurance. Besides the insurance itself, the association provides training to the entrepreneur, especially with respect to risk prevention. While insurance was initially tested exclusively in the Rhônes-Alpes region from December 2006 to May 2007, availability was extended to the entire French territory in September 2007. Up to the end of 2007, 260 insurance packages had been provided to microentrepreneurs.[32]

Another microinsurance initiative has been set up by Adie in partnership with the insurance companies Macif and AXA who merged in May

2007. The offer comprises several pillars that can be chosen depending on the entrepreneur's specific needs. After a maximum period of three years the micro-entrepreneur is integrated into the usual insurance contracts. So far, this offer has been launched in four pilot regions and a national extension is planned for the year 2008. Up until the end of 2007, 68 microinsurance contracts had been subscribed (Adie, 2008a).

Social venture capital

Several organizations also enable entrepreneurs to increase their own funds by providing venture capital, often with the aim of accessing a bank loan. As such, since spring 2006, the NGO PlanetFinance, which primarily works in developing countries, has been providing equity and quasi-equity of between 5000 and 70 000 euros to businesses in deprived urban areas in France (Zones Urbaines Sensibles, ZUS) through the share capital fund FinanCités. The first funding decisions were taken in July 2007 and 11 projects were funded in 2007 with between 30–40 000 euros (Adie/EMN, 2008). Smaller amounts are provided by the CIGALES Federation ('Club d'Investisseurs pour une Gestion Alternative et Locale de l'Epargne Solidaire' – Club of Investors for an Alternative and Local Management of Solidarity Savings), which unites five territorial associations mobilizing their members' savings for the start-up or development of small local and social enterprises. In 2006, the CIGALES Federation had 82 active clubs with an average monthly saving of 24 euros per participant and an average investment of 2204 euros per club (Fédération des CIGALES, 2007). The clubs work in collaboration with the venture capital cooperative Garrigue which, since 1985, has invested in enterprises with a social focus as well as cooperatives. Finally since 1991, the Racines association has been running the so-called CLEFE structure ('Clubs d'épargne pour les femmes qui entreprennent'). These clubs operate under the legal status of voluntary co-ownership ('indivision volontaire'). Within each CLEFE a group of between five and 15 members (men and women) build savings by regular transfers to a bank or postal account. The average amount of these transfers is 46 euros. After twelve months on average, the accumulated capital is lent to one or several women who have decided to start up or further develop their business. The savings make it easier for the women to receive a loan from a traditional financial institution and can be a complement to other financial assistance programmes. At the end of 2006, 35 CLEFEs were spread over the different regions of France. From the start, the clubs have supported 85 new enterprises, out of which 70 were still active at the end of 2006. All in all, 118 jobs have been created with the help of CLEFE. The reimbursement rate of these clubs in 2006 was 97.2 per cent, proving that women pay back well.[33]

Laws and regulations governing microenterprises and microcredit

While the business environment in France has for a long time been disadvantageous for microenterprises, several measures have been taken to improve the legal and administrative environment for small businesses. These improvements are in part a result of Adie's strong lobbying activities in favour of self-employment. Through several recently adopted laws in the field of business regulation, the government explicitly acknowledges self-employment as a tool for inclusion and social cohesion.

Administrative procedures for microenterprises have been eased through the introduction of a highly simplified tax system for microenterprises called *'régime micro'* in 1999. The main objective of this regime is to reduce fiscal obligations for solo entrepreneurs (not companies), so they can focus more intensely on their activity. It applies to individual enterprises with an annual business volume limited to 73 000 or 27 000 euros, depending on the type of activity (Adie/EMN, 2008).

Administrative measures for small enterprises were also eased through two laws, Law for Economic Initiative (Loi pour l'Initiative Economique) and SME Law (Loi en faveur des petites et moyennes enterprises) adopted in August 2003 and August 2005 respectively. They introduced online business registration through Business Formality Centres (Centres de Formalités des Entreprises, CFE) which act as one-stop business registration windows and ease the transition from a salaried to a self-employed activity. New entrepreneurs were also given the right to create their own activity whilst continuing to work on a part-time basis in their old job over a period of 12 months. Moreover, the ACCRE programme (Aide au Chômeurs Créateurs ou Repreneurs d'une Entreprise – Assistance for unemployed persons) was progressively extended. It allows the unemployed, beneficiaries of social minima, those over 50 and young people up to 26 years of age, and people between 26 and 30 who have not worked long enough to have the right to receive unemployment allowances and who wish to set up their business, to maintain their welfare benefit. People benefiting from ACCRE are also exonerated from social charges (illness, pregnancy, old age) during the first year of operation, may receive training and support, and can apply for an interest-free government loan entitled EDEN (Encouragement au Développement d'Entreprises Nouvelles – Promotion of New Enterprise Development) to start their business. These loans have a five-year term and a deferment period of 12 months. The maximum loan amount is €6098 for a sole trader and €9000 for a limited liability company. This has to be complemented with an additional loan from another institution (bank or non-bank) totalling at least half of the advance.

Moreover, since March 2007 self-employed people registered under the 'micro-regime' (agricultural workers excluded) can benefit from a system of capped contributions (*bouclier social*). This measure intends to make sure that social payments do not represent too large a part of the revenues earned from the activity. It corresponds to an exemption of social contributions proportional to the turnover:

- 14 per cent of the turnover for businesses in the trade sector;
- 24.6 per cent of the turnover for enterprise in the handicraft and service sectors.

Those enterprises created under the 'micro-regime' after 1 January 2008 can also opt for a simplified calculation of their social contributions in the first year after the establishment in the two following years, proportionally to the turnover of the preceding trimester (Adie/EMN, 2008). Finally, at the end of May 2008 the first chapter of the 'Draft of the Law for the Modernization of the Economy' (Projet de Loi de la modernisation de l'économie) was adopted by the National Assembly. It introduces a flat rate for fiscal and social charges of 13 per cent for small entrepreneurs in the trade sector and 23 per cent in the service sector.

Adie has also carried out significant lobbying to create better opportunities for microcredit providers. In 2001 Adie obtained an amendment to the French banking law allowing certain microcredit providers to borrow for on-lending to unemployed persons and minimum income recipients during the first five years of a newly established enterprise. The Law for the Modernization of the Economy extends this permission to all kinds of micro-entrepreneurs without excluding beneficiaries of social minima.

In addition, under the SME Law in 2005 the usury rate for loans provided to individual entrepreneurs was abolished. The Law included the drafting of a report from Banque de France evaluating the impact of an abolished usury rate.[34] This document points out that the abolition of the usury rate has improved the funding mechanisms for MSMEs globally and has not produced the perverse effect feared by many. Moreover, in 2005, the government also introduced the Law for Social Cohesion (Loi de programmation pour la Cohésion Sociale) which set up the Social Cohesion Fund, providing its guarantee to financial institutions that disburse microcredit for business purposes and promote access to 'social microcredit' (Adie/EMN, 2008).

Finally, the Law for the Modernization of the Economy authorizes MFIs to access the national database recording borrowers' history. It also provides the authorization to MFIs to provide 'social microcredit' to foster labour market integration. These measures significantly improve the environment for microcredit providers and encourage growth.

Financial sustainability

One of the main challenges for microfinance providers is reaching financial sustainability. It is a measure of the microlender's ability to sustain itself over the long term, that is to cover all operational expenses through operating revenue such as interest and fees, the cost of borrowing and loan loss provision (adapted from Underwood, 2006). Being self-sustainable reduces dependency from public donors as government and EU subsidies are decreasing. Adie aims to reach partial financial self-sustainability in the next three years, that is to cover the operating costs *regarding its credit activities.* In contrast, organizations such as France Initiative do not intend to reach sustainability. This organization and its product, the *prêts d'honneur*, are wholly financed through subsidies from local districts and EU funds, the CDC, banks and donations from enterprises[35] (France Initiative, 2008). It is very hard for Adie to compete with a fully subsidized organization, even if the target group is not necessarily the same.

In order to reach its objective of partial sustainability, Adie has established a strategic plan for 2008–2010. The association is also establishing six pilot branches during 2007 and 2008 in districts with high population densities. The aim is to test the possibility of covering the lending costs of these pilot branches until approximately 2012.[36] The association has adopted or strengthened a range of mechanisms to reach this aim. Some of these are:

1. Strict separation of credit and support: since the beginning of 2007 Adie has been in the process of restructuring. In order to track its microlending costs separately from the costs of training and technical assistance and to manage funds as effectively as possible, the association has separated the management of its credit poles from its accompanying service poles. The regional Adie offices are from now on made up of three poles: credit, client monitoring/training and support, with this last pole building a link between the first two.
2. Outreach and productivity: Adie aims to extend its outreach through providing more credits to self-employed people in a precarious situation, that is those working in the informal economy, those who live in deprived urban areas and in rural areas. Adie carries out studies in order to improve communications with these target groups and has developed a marketing strategy. In addition, it trains its staff with regard to the target population.

   Another aim is to double the loan officers' productivity and to halve the period between the first demand for credit and its actual provision. The goal is the provision of 11 322 microloans in 2008, 15 000 in 2009, 18 000 in 2010 and 22 000 in 2011 (Adie, 2008b).
3. Demand: the association aims to diversify its financial services, for

instance through stronger development of microinsurance. In addition it tries to reach more people who are not yet bankable after having received a first loan and who need a second microloan (Adie, 2008b).

4. Risk management: in 2007 Adie's repayment rate was 93.1 per cent, and write-offs constituted 2.97 per cent. Different strategies are applied to hold this rate as low as possible. At Adie the underwriting and due diligence process combine the features of character lending with 'credit scoring'. More important than the project itself is the nature of the match between the entrepreneur and his or her business. A strict assessment process is applied and the presentation of the project by the entrepreneur before a selection committee plays a huge role. The loan itself is managed based on relations of proximity and confidence, and specific kinds of guarantee and security methods (solidarity guarantees, co-signatories) are used to reduce the risk of non-repayment (Guérin and Vallat, 2005).

   In order to obtain a lower portfolio at risk rate and to have a more cost-effective decision-making process, Adie has also simplified procedures and, in April 2006, began using a tool designed in collaboration with CERISE,[37] to help decision-making based on data collected about clients' credit history (profiles and reimbursement over a period of 15 years) (Adie, 2007). With the help of this tool, Adie aims to reach more self-employed people in a precarious situation, that is, those working in the informal economy. Besides, through the adoption of the first chapter of the Law for the Modernization of the Economy, for which Adie has carried out intensive lobbying, the association is now authorized to access the national borrowers' database of Banque de France. The purpose is not to increase the selection of entrepreneurs, but to take prevention measures regarding the credit amount and support in order to ensure reimbursement and increase the chances of the business succeeding.

   Private and public institutions also share part of the risk. Adie is counter-guaranteed to 48 per cent by the FGIE guarantee fund (itself funded by the Social Cohesion Fund), to 20 per cent by bank partners and to 9 per cent by the European Investment Fund EIF. The rest is secured by local guarantee funds and the Adie entrepreneurs themselves (Adie, 2008a).

5. Funding possibilities: Adie aims to diversify its sources of funding through balanced agreements with different banks. It also tries to arrange more medium-term refinancing agreements with banks instead of short-term agreements to ensure liquidity.

6. Business support: pre- and post-loan training and support costs for the start-up of one microenterprise were estimated by Adie to average

1600 euros in 2007. This cost was 2000 euros in 2003. It has been reduced as a result of increased efficiency. Adie has established a distinct monitoring pole with specialized staff and additional human and financial resources with the aim of strengthening efficiency and developing the diversity of support offered to entrepreneurs. The support pole is therefore recruiting specialized staff. In addition, an information system will be developed specifically for the support services.

Support also relies heavily on the involvement of volunteers. In fact, in 2007, 1034 volunteers dedicated three days a month to Adie. This represents the work of 176 full-time jobs. The aim is to double the support from volunteers. The volunteers are also offered the opportunity to attend training organized in regional offices, allowing volunteers from different regions to exchange experiences. However, despite strengthened efficiency, Adie's support pole will continue to rely on public funding due to high cost. Today, the main part is funded by the European Union, the French government, local authorities, the CDC and socially responsible companies (Adie, 2008a).

Future challenges

Since its introduction at the end of the 1980s the French microcredit sector has grown steadily. Microcredit as a tool for social inclusion has become more and more accepted by political decision-makers and a range of laws have been adopted to improve the administrative and fiscal environment for self-employment, microenterprises and microcredit. Adie's lobbying activities have played a huge role in this regard. Due to the abolition of the usury rate and the ability for Adie to borrow for on-lending, combined with simplified administrative procedures for microenterprises and business starting out of unemployment, growth has become possible. Adie's lending activity has grown from 34 loans in 1990 to 9853 loans in 2007 and the association today has 131 sub-offices spread over the French territory and overseas. Equally, the France Initiative association, which only partly acts in the microcredit field, started as a federation of 20 local business support initiatives in 1986 and regroups 242 such programmes today.

However, a huge, yet unmet demand for microcredit still exists in France. Adie estimates the potential market for non-bank microcredit at business start-up at between 48 000 and 98 000 per year, resulting in an existing gap of between 40 000 and 90 000 microloans per year. For bank microcredit, a shortage of 100 000 loans per year has been observed (Adie/EMN, 2008). However, this demand can only be met if certain conditions are fulfilled. The French microcredit market will face three main challenges in the years to come.

First of all, social charges and administrative burdens still remain high.

The measures implemented in 2007 to simplify social contributions only apply to enterprises registered under the micro-regime. They still remain too complex for many to encourage them to register. In addition, access to self-employment remains limited due to a number of barriers related to the different types of businesses (restricted access and right to carry out a business). In particular, this bars self-employed people who work in the informal sector from legalizing their business. The Law for the Modernisation of the Economy, which had been partly adopted at the time of the drafting of this chapter, provides crucial improvements in this regard.

Moreover, better knowledge of the informal sector should be fostered. There are no statistics available on the informal sector, which is described revealingly by the OECD as 'unobserved work'. Most of the time informal activities are self-employed activities whose productivity and profitability are not high enough to be worth registering with the standard social protection system, as this represents too high charges for too low profits. Therefore, the potential of these activities is not sufficiently exploited (Raabe, 2007).

Finally, non-bank microcredit providers face the challenge of reducing to a minimum the relatively high risk the target group implies and of covering the costs of the lending activities. Moreover, they need to be extremely efficient in their business support activities and ensure sufficient funding. They have to engage strongly in seeking grant monies from more private players such as banks and enterprises (CSR). Regular evaluation of activities and impact studies are important means to optimize practices and convince possible donors. Sharing of experiences based on good practices may be another way to optimize products while keeping expenses low.

The overall aim of microcredit is to give citizens who are today the objects of welfare policy the opportunity to become people who may determine their own destiny. Adie is an impressive example of the impact microcredit can have in an environment that promotes entrepreneurship and access to microfinance. Adie envisages a 15–30 per cent growth of lending each year. This trend will certainly continue, taking into account the huge untapped demand for microcredit in France.

Notes

1. This chapter relied heavily on the opinion of experts in the field. In particular the assistance of Maria Nowak, founder and president of Adie, Audrey Raabe, research manager of Adie, Marc Olagnon, Representative of the General Deputy of France Initiative, Benoît Granger of MicFin as well as Philippe Guichandut and Tamara Underwood of EMN, were invaluable in a number of areas.
2. Insee, Eurostat.
3. Observatoire des Inégalités, Insee. Eurostat's definition of poverty risk refers to individuals living in households where the equivalized income is below the threshold of 60 per cent of the national equivalized median income.

4. France is ranked 19th out of 24 by the World Bank Doing Business Survey 2008 (http://www.doingbusiness.org/economyrankings/?regionid=5).
5. Revenu Minimum d'Insertion (RMI) is a social allowance that applies to persons over 25 years of age who have exhausted their unemployment benefits or whose resources are below a fixed ceiling.
6. The Caisse des Dépôts et Consignations (CDC) is a French public institution founded in 1816. It executes missions of general interest upon request of the French government through its 25 regional offices. It is mainly involved in local economic development initiatives in cooperation with the municipalities.
7. For instance, the ACCRE support scheme, a support programme for start-ups and business takeovers out of unemployment that has existed since 1979, was restricted to a more limited group of people at the end of 1996.
8. Out of these, 170 are loan officers.
9. In these cases Adie staff are present for a certain period of time (several hours or days) in partners' offices or Chambers of Commerce and receive would-be entrepreneurs.
10. Réunion, Mayotte, Guyana, New Caledonia, Martinique.
11. Para-public means the involvement of the Chambers of Commerce and Chambers for Crafts, for instance.
12. Fondation de France is the biggest independent private charity foundation created in 1969 by Michel Pomey, advisor to André Malraux, a French writer and politician.
13. 'Social microcredit' will be presented in more detail later in the section about 'Other financial products'.
14. Interest rates of mainstream banks lie between 4 per cent and 5 per cent.
15. In August 2005, the SME Law abolished the ceiling on interest rates for loans to individual entrepreneurs. This allowed Adie to continually increase its interest rate. In 2005, the interest rate had been 5.2 per cent. For more information on the abolition of the usury rate and the positive effect for the users, please see the section on 'Laws and regulations governing microenterprises and microcredit'.
16. These programmes are described in the section about 'Law and regulations governing microenterprises and microcredit'.
17. This rate is called 'rate of integration' ('taux d'insertion') by Adie.
18. This number is very approximate. It is based on the approach used in the Microfinance Market Study (Adie/EMN, 2008) used to calculate the number of microcredits provided by France Initiative in 2006: 41 per cent of clients presented a budget of less than 30 000 euros corresponding to bank loans of 25 000 euros.
19. Information taken from webpage: http://www.franceactive.org/fiches/chiffres.php.
20. OSEO has signed an agreement with 180 banks and branches of banks such as Crédit Coopératif and Crédit Mutuel.
21. http://www.pce.oseo.fr/pce_beneficier.php.
22. Microfinance Market Study, Adie/EMN, 2008.
23. See section on 'Business development services'.
24. Since 2006 Adie has run a project called 'Projet Banlieues' in collaboration with the BNP Paribas bank aimed at supporting the start-up of 700 new enterprises in deprived French suburbs from 2006 to 2009. Adie therefore created eight new branches and developed new adapted communication strategies. In addition, in 2007, the association launched the 'Créajeunes' programme, which is intended to boost enterprise start-up amongst young unemployed persons in deprived urban areas. It provides pre- and post-start-up training and a start-up grant of 500 euros plus a microcredit. In 2007, 12 per cent of Adie clients were young people under the age of 26 living in deprived urban areas. Finally, Adie also tries to improve information to people in rural areas about the possibilities of microcredit, and to estimate the demand for this service. It has therefore launched a rural development project based on the idea of mobile branches.
25. According to Insee SINE data for 2002 and 2006, the rate of female business start-ups and take-overs is 30 per cent.
26. Business Development Services.

27. Les Chambres de Commerce et d'Industrie et les Chambres des Métiers.
28. 'Adie Conseil' is based on a telephone consultancy tool called 'Firmenhilfe', developed by the German business consultancy service EVERS & JUNG.
29. The Social Cohesion Programme (Plan de Cohésion Sociale) has been implemented by the Ministry of Employment, Social Cohesion and Housing since January 2005. The programme aims to combat unemployment and discrimination and to confront the housing and education crisis with a special focus on deprived (sub-)urban areas.
30. Information based on an interview with an Adie representative in autumn 2007.
31. École Supérieure des Sciences Economiques et Commerciales.
32. Data from www.entrepreneursdelacite.org and based on a telephone interview with the association in March 2008.
33. This information is based on a telephone interview with the association in March 2008.
34. 'Rapport au Parlement. Les incidences de la réforme de l'usure sur les modalités de financement des petites et moyennes entreprises' (Report to Parliament. The effects of the reform of the usury on the funding modalities for small and medium enterprises).
35. 21.5% 'conseils régionaux'; 16.2% 'conseils généraux'; 12.3% 'communes'; 6.3% EU funds (FEDER/LEADER); 17.3% CDC; 9.7% from banks; and 8.2% from the private sector.
36. This information is based on an interview with an Adie representative in autumn 2007.
37. CERISE is a group of French NGOs that are specialized in microfinance.

Bibliography

Annual reports

Adie (2008a), 'Rapport d'Activité 2007', Paris.
Adie (2008b), 'Plan Stratégique 2008–2010', Paris.
Adie (2007), 'Rapport d'Activité 2006', Paris.
Adie (2005), 'Rapport d'Activité 2004', Paris.
Caisse des Dépôts et Consignations (CDC) (2007), 'Rapport d'Activité 2006', Paris.
Fédération des CIGALES (2007), 'Rapport d'Activité 2006', Pantin.
France Initiative Réseau (2007), 'Rapport Annuel 2006', Paris.
France Initiative (2008), 'Rapport Annuel 2007', Paris.

Studies

Adie/EMN (2008), 'Microfinance Market Study in France', Report 3, Paris.
ANSA (Agence Nouvelle des Solidarités Actives) (2008), 'Microcrédit Social: diagnostic et perspectives de développement', summary of report submitted to the Caisse des Dépôts et Consignations (CDC), 25 February, Paris.
Caisse des Depôts et des Consignations (CDC) (2008), 'Le microcrédit personnel garanti – un nouvel outil au service de l'insertion sociale, Paris.
European Commission (2007), 'The Regulation of Microcredit in Europe', Brussels: EC DG Enterprise and Industry.
Jouhette, S. and F. Romans (2006), 'EU Labour Force Survey, Principal Results 2005', Luxemburg: European Communities.
KFW Bankengruppe (2007), 'Microfinance in Germany and Europe, Market Overview and Best Practice Examples', Frankfurt-am-Main.
MFC/EMN/CDFA (2007), 'From Inclusion to Exclusion through Microfinance', London: MFC/EMN/CDFA.
Torrès, O. and A. Eminet (2004), 'Global Entrepreneurship Monitor, Rapport 2003–2004 sur l'Entrepreneuriat en France et dans le Monde', Lyon: EM Lyon Business School.
Volery, T. and I. Servais (2000), 'Global Entrepreneurship Monitor, Rapport 2000 sur l'Entrepreneuriat en France', Lyon: EM Lyon Business School.
World Bank (2008), 'Doing Business France', Washington.

World Bank Doing Business (2008), available at http://www.doingbusiness.org/economyrankings/?regionid=5.

Books

Allemand, S. (2007), *La Microfinance n'est plus une Utopie*, Paris: Editions Autrement.

Nowak, M. (2005), *On ne Prête (pas) qu'aux Riches, La Révolution du Microcrédit*, Jean-Claude Lattès.

Articles

Agence des PME (2003), 'PME: l'appui à la création', Regards sur les PME no. 2.

APCE (2005), 'Les hommes et les femmes, créations pures et reprises', Paris.

APCE (2006), 'La création d'entreprises en France 2006: profil des entreprises et de leur dirigeant', Paris: APCE.

DCASP (Direction du commerce, de l'artisanat, des services et des professions) (2007), 'PME/TPE en bref', no. 28 December.

European Commission (2007), 'Communication from the Commission to the Council, the European Parliament, the European Economic and Social Council and the Committee of Regions: A European initiative for the development of micro-credit in support of growth and employment' (COM 2007, 708 final), Brussels.

Guérin, I. and D. Vallat (2005), 'La micro-finance en France', Centre Walras, Université Lumière Lyon II, CNRS, Lyon.

Insee (2007a), 'Créer son entreprise: assurer d'abord son propre emploi', Insee Première no. 1167, Paris.

Insee (2007b), 'Les créations d'entreprises poursuivent leur hausse en 2006', Virginie Fabre, Insee Première No. 1120, Paris.

Insee (2007c), 'Créations et créateurs d'entreprises: première interrogation 2006, Profil du créateur', Paris.

Insee (2008), 'Un rythme des créations d'entreprises très élevé en 2007', Insee Première no. 1172, Paris.

MACIF/AXA/Adie (2007), Press release: 'La MACIF et AXA France lancent une offre de micro-assurance en partenariat avec l'Adie', Paris.

MINEFI (Ministère de l'Economie, des Finances et de l'Emploi) (2001/2002), 'Microentreprises: un tremplin pour l'emploi', Cahier Industries No. 73, Paris.

Raabe, A. (2007), 'Improving the institutional framework for self-employed workers: a necessity for microcredit operators in France', Microfinance Europe, European Microfinance Network, no. 1, April, Paris.

Underwood, T. (2006), 'Overview of the microcredit sector in Europe 2004–2005', Paris: European Microfinance Network.

Websites

Adie: http://www.adie.org.

AIRDIE: http://www.airdie.org/.

Afile 77: http://www.afile77.org/.

CIGALES: http://www.cigales.asso.fr/.

France Active: http://www.franceactive.org/fiches/chiffres.php.

France Initiative: http://www.fir.asso.fr/.

PlaNetFinance France: http://france.planetfinance.org/.

La Nef: http://www.lanef.com/.

Profession Créer: www.micfin.org.

Racines Clefe: http://www.racines-clefe.com/.

3 The microcredit sector in Italy: small initiatives in a dynamic scenario

*Simone di Castri**

1 National context

Financial inclusion has been the subject of many initiatives in Italy since the fifteenth century, when several projects took place in order to provide poor people with access to financial services. From the end of the nineteenth century, these projects became structured financial institutions, progressively integrated into the formal sector. Most of them have been absorbed into the range of mainstream commercial providers, subjected to strict regulation and supervision and engaged in competition with the rest of the suppliers. They adapted their practices, mission and strategy; they lost outreach and eventually they became incapable of adapting to the emerging needs of the new poor. Basically, they lost their characterization as actors for financial inclusion. The origin of the inclusive financial sector will be examined in the next section.

Financial exclusion, meaning the lack of access to basic financial services, such as a bank or postal account, has been addressed in different ways for more than a century, but an inclusive financial sector has never been achieved. During the 1970s, this led to the creation of Mutue di Auto Gestione (self-management mutual associations – MAGs), and more recently to the emergence of microfinance initiatives and the development of services for migrant banking. These new financial services and providers are emerging to serve the needs of the uncollateralized, the unbanked, the marginalized and the poor.

If a wide definition of microlending activity is taken into consideration, as the provision of small loans to people who lack conventional collateral, up to 2007 almost seventy microcredit projects have been activated in Italy.[1] Many initiatives began recently: in 2004 there were almost forty programmes,[2] while in 2005 almost twenty new initiatives started and several new initiatives came up in 2007.[3] The approximate total amount of loans given within these projects is €75 million, to almost 8000 clients, and the average amount of the loan was €10 000.[4]

Italian microfinance projects, which will be analysed more in depth in the following sections, appear to be of a small size and scale. Almost all have lent to less than a hundred borrowers and focus on local markets.

It seems that few projects are pursuing financial sustainability and many projects lack proficiency and transparency, for instance in the disclosure of financial and operative results. The growth of the sector is strongly subsidized by public and private entities. Significantly, 78.2 per cent of the projects work thanks to guarantee funds.[5] Microfinance seems to have been taken as a welfare policy by public providers (and in some cases it sounds more like a populist initiative than a long-term policy). Looking at the private sector, the provision of microfinance services looks to be linked more to philanthropy or social oriented marketing than to the idea of a profitable business to invest in, challenging (and investing in) the development of new methodologies, technologies and philosophy to serve the financial 'outcasts'. That said, it does not mean there is a dearth of promising projects in the Italian sector.

It is difficult to get a comprehensive picture of the active experiences, due to their number, their small and local scale, the continual setting up of new programmes, the lack of coordination of the various experiences and finally the absence of a shared definition of microcredit and microfinance. With the available data, it is impossible to get a global assessment of outreach and impact at present.

The analysis of mission, institutional typology, governance, lending practices and model of granting of the Italian microcredit projects shows remarkable differences in the way projects deal with their microlending activity. Two main discriminating factors are:

- the awareness of each entity as viewing microcredit as an activity that aims to spur economic development or to redistribute wealth;
- the purpose of achieving financial inclusion of the borrowers or their social inclusion through and with financial inclusion.

The first affects (and is reflected in) several aspects of each project, like the intent to be sustainable, the control of operational costs, the attentiveness in defining adequate interest rates and the containment of unmet repayments. The second enables those projects to be distinguished from one another and to be included in two general categories. It also has an effect on the selection of clients coming from different social and economic backgrounds and in the provision of professional and financial education to support clients and their households, in order to allow them to attain long-term social inclusion. The number of initiatives in progress clearly signals a dynamic scenario, where many different entities are working for financial and social inclusion. Those projects provide loans to initiate or develop a business, for housing purposes, for emergencies faced by households, to prevent or get out of usury, and to facilitate basic consumption. From a different point of view, it could be argued that if microcredit is considered as the provision of loans by institutions which pursue sustainability to people who lack conventional collateral in order to allow them to attain long-term social inclusion; enhancing the role of the community where the borrower lives and her/his social relationship; and establishing a rapport based on acquaintance and confidence with her/him – thus stressing the multidimensional nature of microlending, the number of microcredit projects in Italy would be limited to less than twenty.

With the rise of a microcredit sector, steps toward financial inclusion have been taken by both public and private entities, which aim to serve those who lack access. In fact, many groups of people and categories of entrepreneurs experience credit rationing and inadequate savings and payment services. The rise of immigration from developing countries and the unsettling excess of temporariness and flexibility in the job market have increased the number of people who are socially and financially marginalized, which traditionally includes mainly females, young people, farmers and factory workers, and the chronically or periodically unemployed. Furthermore, even though the unemployment rate is decreasing, the size of the underground and informal job market is still significant, the inequitable distribution of wealth is amplifying and, in southern regions, the gap of development, opportunities and financial inclusion is notable, as detailed below. However, private financial intermediaries have been very reluctant to reach new segments of the market. Commercial banks have only recently recognized the profitability of migrant banking, low-cost banking and microfinance.

In Italy[6] there are approximately 789 banks and more than 30 000 counters. The total amount of savings and deposits is €729 billion, whereas the banks' portfolio is €1000 billion (almost 50 per cent are mortgages).[7] In 2004, 5917 out of 8101 municipalities in the country had a bank. However, 14 per cent of Italian households do not have access to any kind of financial service in the formal market, including the *BancoPosta* network.[8] A European survey conducted in 2003 shows that 22.4 per cent of Italian citizens do not hold a bank account, compared to of 8.6 per cent of adults in the European Union.[9] These data are close to those collected in a study conducted by Eurisko, which says that 23.4 per cent of the adult population does not hold a bank account. Furthermore, 45 per cent of those between 20 and 30 years old have never saved, and in 2005 the total number of Italians who were not able to save rose to 51.4 per cent.[10] Furthermore, lack of confidence in financial institutions among Italians is widespread and consumer associations often warn the authorities and the media on the fairness of the sector. Recent financial scandals, which hurt many retail clients, have increased mistrust.[11]

The relationship between Italians and the banking sectors is weak. A study on the public opinion of financial services conducted by the European Commission makes it clear that lack of trust affects banks' customers in Italy more than it does on average in the European Union. In particular, people deplore a lack of information and transparency. Also, Italians think their country's legislation does not guarantee protection of consumers' rights and security. Finally, 62 per cent of Italians regard the cost of a bank account as too high (against the average of 42 per cent of European citizens), and 65 per cent believe that it is very difficult to win a judicial dispute against a bank.[12] During his latest speech at the annual meeting of the Associazione Bancaria Italiana (ABI – Italian Banking Association), the chief of Banca d'Italia pointed out some shortcomings of the national banking sector. For example, the cost of mortgages and consumer credit in Italy are above the European average.[13]

When examining the internal market for credit, one will notice that in some areas these issues become even more problematic. In the south of Italy, six regions are included in the list of the poorest regions in Europe,[14] 25 per cent of the population live in conditions of relative poverty (almost double the national average) and 13.2 per cent of households live in absolute poverty[15] (meaning almost 3 million people, 75.1 per cent of the country's poorest). In this part of the country, usury is still extensively practised[16] and working in the informal and underground sectors is widespread.[17] The rationing of financial services is a pressing requirement for local development. Several studies have suggested that there is a lack of credit in the south, compared with the centre and the north of the country, with a relevant trade-off between the collection of savings and deposits and the disbursement of loans in this area; this trend is denied by the Central Bank.[18] A recent survey has emphasized that in 2006 the outstanding portfolio of banks in southern Italy increased 17.3 per cent, more than in the rest of the country.[19] Also, higher interest rates are charged to southern borrowers.[20] This could be due to a higher risk in lending (because of the small size and major risk of the business sectors where southern enterprises are more involved; but unmet repayments are decreasing constantly[21]), as well as to a high rate of unmet repayments. However, considering that different interest rates are imposed to fully worthy enterprises in different areas,[22] doubt persists about the efficiency of the allocation of capital. Several public programmes have tried to address the matter of credit rationing: incentives for the start-up of microenterprises in depressed areas; female and young entrepreneurs have been targeted with projects like *prestito d'onore* ('loan upon the honour'), and further measures to facilitate the access to risk capital have been carried out. However, the responses of governments and policy makers are still inadequate, discontinuous and, frequently unsuccessful. Public programmes have failed to reach a large number of people and have had a modest impact on their target, despite their costs.

2 Toward an inclusive financial sector

The provision of financial services to marginalized groups has long been considered in Italy. Many initiatives have taken place since the nineteenth century, providing savings and credit services to individuals, micro and small business activities. Casse di Risparmio, Banche Popolari and Banche di Credito Cooperativo come from this tradition of financial institutions that have paid particular attention to the poor. Since 1462, *Monti di Pietà* have been strongly involved in giving the poor the opportunity to borrow on pledge at a lower interest rate than the pawnshop. Alongside these institutions, informal systems were used to secure savings and grant loans, like *Casse Peote* in Veneto.

The first part of this section considers the development of these entities to their current status and summarizes the legislative initiatives that have led to their evolution. The second part addresses the emergence of two new pre-eminent subjects, MAGs (Mutua Auto Gestione, Mutual Self Management) and *Banca Popolare Etica*. Finally, the third part gives an overview of some microcredit projects and providers.

2.1 The origin of inclusive finance

Savings banks (*casse di risparmio*) were created, as in other European countries, with the aim of encouraging and protecting retail savings of the poorest class. They tended to mitigate some of the most evident social injustices, by removing as many sources of instability as possible and, at the same time, they allow a flow of new funds 'to mitigate on behalf of the State and other public entities whose securities in which that money invested'.[23] Very soon, savings banks began lending, and legislators became aware of the risks connected to the mobilization of savings. On 15 July 1888, law number 5546 regulated their activities by isolating company assets from those of their founders, forbade the distribution of dividends, and established minimum capital requirements and capital adequacy. *Monti di pietà* originated to give poor people access to loans on security, then some of them started collecting savings. These were progressively regulated following the model of savings banks.[24] Savings banks and *monti di pietà* are the first banking institutions with a special status and regulation, because of the public relevance of their activities and the inherent risks.

Other types of highly specialized banking institutions for marginalized borrowers grew during the same time. Rural banks (*casse rurali*, now called credit cooperatives) and *banche popolari* were both organized as cooperatives.[25] The former were characterized by unlimited liability, founded by catholic entities and were committed to serving the agricultural sector. The latter had limited liability and mainly provided financial services to small businesses and manufacturers in urban contexts. Different institutions provided specific financial services to specific segments of clients, and many of them were allowed to operate only at the local level.[26] These intermediaries have been the main providers of 'bottom targeted' financial services for a century. Of course, both market and regulatory evolutions have modified their practices and mission, but some of them are still active with regards to financial inclusion.

The specialization of banking intermediaries, including those cited above, was a characteristic of the Italian banking sector until the 1980s, along with the absence of competition, due to legal disincentives for mergers and acquisitions and the state dirigisme which set up barriers to new competitors. Then, the conservatism of the sector was challenged by the integration of European markets[27] and the diffusion of new financial products provided by non-banks. In particular, the Legislative Decree (D.Lgs.) 356/1990[28] removed the geographic specialization of the various intermediaries and allowed them to provide a wide range of services to a larger clientele involved in different economic sectors. The complete 'despecialization' of banks was achieved with D.Lgs. 481/1992 and the D.Lgs. 385/1993 (Consolidated Banking Law).[29]

Legge 218/1990 radically transformed savings banks and *monti di pietà*. In fact, they had to transform their institutional types into credit corporations, owned by bank foundations, which are currently relevant entities of the microcredit sector. A major reason for this legislative choice was the inefficiency of savings banks, particularly on governance, due to the difficult coexistence of the demands of social mission and profitability.

2.2 MAGs and Banca Popolare Etica

At the end of the 1970s MAG promoters challenged the mainstream use and conception of finance, to support the creation of a financial network as an alternative to the mainstream bank industry, beginning a project that has greatly contributed to social finance in Italy and remains as a benchmark for later experiences. MAGs arose out of the social scenario of that period, with the aim of achieving (together with several other players in civil society) democratization of governance, and to challenge the dominance of corporations and financial institutions, which were based on top-down decision making and on the supremacy of capital over work.[30] Starting in Verona[31] and developed soon after in northern Italy, better advocating for a new financial culture and promoting socially responsible employment of money, MAGs also satisfied the needs of those who were not served by the mainstream financial providers.

In 1991, due to the new anti-money-laundering law,[32] MAGs were gradually transformed into financial cooperatives, with a minimum capital of €600 000, regulated under article 106 of the Consolidated Banking Act and placed on the register of the *Ufficio Italiano Cambi* (Italian Foreign Exchange Office: UIC). MAGs are not allowed to collect capital through savings and deposits, but only through members' ownership of equity. MAGs4 Piemonte has a slightly different legal status and can collect savings from legal entities such as cooperatives. There are currently six MAGs, most of them operating in the north of Italy.[33] They provide various services to the third sector, mainly credit, savings, consulting and training. They operate with different methodologies to serve local needs. Only three of them[34] provide loans for business activities to single entrepreneurs, cooperatives and associations, without requiring any financial collateral.

In 2005, MAG Servizi launched a specific microcredit project, Economia di Condivisione e Microcredito (Ec.co.mi.) in collaboration with the Minister of Labour, Regione Veneto, and a local network of entities (Banca di Credito Cooperativo della Valpolicella and Banca Popolare di Verona). The project helped people wanting to apply for a loan to develop a business plan and become trustworthy for the lenders. Rates are from 5.9 to 7.9 per cent, for loans up to €2500 for emergencies related to outstanding bills, rent and debts, and €20 000 for business purposes. Repayment is due within five years and a grace period of six months can be granted on capital repayment.

In 1994 some MAGs and 21 not-for-profit organizations (ARCI, ACLI and other protagonists of the third sector) set up an association to create an alternative to the traditional financial system, specializing in serving the third sector and those enterprises active in socially responsible markets, Banca Popolare Etica. Then in 1999 they merged in a cooperative in order to attain the amount required by Italian banking law to incorporate a popular bank (12 500 000 000 lire: €6.5 million).[35] The group Banca Popolare Etica finances socio-economic initiatives that aim to implement sustainable social and human development in Italy as well as in developing countries. In order to achieve its goal, the bank adopted a system of three different entities. One of them, Consorzio Etimos, collects savings in Italy to support microbusinesses and microfinance programmes in developing countries and areas affected by economic crisis.[36] Etica sgr provides socially responsible investment solutions for its customers, who surrender 1 per cent of their investments (as a fee) to a guarantee fund for microfinance projects in Italy. Finally, Banca Popolare Etica established several microcredit initiatives in collaboration with local partners. The bank has provided 204 microloans to a total value of €1 722 751. By October 2006, 48 loans (€883 570) had been provided to finance microenterprises, while the rest were granted under '*socio-assistenziale*' programmes.[37]

3 Overview of the microcredit sector

Commercial banks and other financial intermediaries, banking and non-banking foundations, not-for-profit organizations and public entities play an important role in the promotion of microcredit projects, mainly in collaboration with local entities (associations of workers, migrants and women, business incubators, and so on) which allow proximity with clients and often give them those non-financial services that are necessary for effective financial and social inclusion. Projects have different approaches, missions and methodologies. Most of them have been set up in the last five years and are not yet large enough to be sustainable. Local activity is a common attribute, while institutional typology and models of granting of loans differ. Who is involved in the sector-promoting projects?

Banks

Banks have recently increased the supply of financial services to serve new customers who belong to financially marginalized groups. Mainly, those programmes address the needs of migrants, workers with flexible working contracts and young people. Several banks are entering the microcredit market to check its potential, as part of their social responsibility or for marketing purposes, but their investments are still very limited compared to their portfolio. Furthermore, in many cases banks participate in micro-credit projects as a lending partner, without taking the risk of unmet repayments. In fact, this risk is greatly mitigated by the other partners or by a guarantee fund provided by a third party, public or private. In the words of Zadra, the Director General of ABI:

> For those banks interested, [microfinance] could represent an opportunity of business growth and development, enlarging operativeness and developing a new role with the aim of taking action for and promoting financial inclusion. [. . .] The purpose is to develop new methodology to get profit and to allow the banks which are interested to carry out strategies of corporate social responsibility, meaning a modality of strategic corporate management oriented to a multistakeholders approach.[38]

Operation in this market was analysed in a 2006 survey on 39 Italian banks:[39] 82.1 per cent state they are active in the microfinance sector and 10.3 per cent would be considering the supply of microfinance services in the next five years. They offer savings, credit and payment services, mostly to migrants, households, students and microenterprises. The activity is greatly concentrated in northern Italy, where 67.7 per cent of those services are provided (16.3 per cent in the centre, 16.0 per cent in the south). The authors of the survey pointed out that these Italian banks were not yet developing 'specific models for microcredit and microfinance that do not imply simply transposing and adapting those services and know-how which already exist in the bank'.[40]

Pre-scoring of new borrowers, evaluation of proposed projects and collaterals, drawing up of the business plan and generation of fiduciary relation are often done by the partners in the project. Only 15 per cent of the financial institutions surveyed were educating staff and dedicating specific methodologies of analysis and monitoring, forms and software to meet the specificity of microfinance clients. 'Thus it is possible to say that the majority of the surveyed banks consider microcredit as an ordinary credit that is developed in collaboration with third entities. Methodology and internal organization do not change, a necessary filter is added instead.'[41] The survey does not show clear evidence of the involvement of banks in the microcredit sector besides their role as lenders. Banks almost never take any financial risk for unmet payments, but sometimes support part of the operational costs of the project they are involved in through grants disbursed to the entity that manages the project.

Some institutions have entered the microcredit sector participating in projects as lender or promoting their own initiatives. Earlier in the section the programme of Banca Popolare Etica was described. The bank is not the only *banca popolare* involved in microcredit. Banca Popolare Pugliese three years ago launched a pilot project called Everywhere targeting Senegalese migrants in Lecce, in collaboration with a local cooperative that guarantees the loans. Banca Popolare di Ancona collaborates in a project with the local Caritas, lending and sharing the risk through participation in the guarantee fund. Banca Popolare di Milano, Banca Popolare di Bergamo and Banca Popolare dell'Emilia Romagna also participate in microcredit initiatives, mainly as lender.

Banche di credito cooperativo (BCCs) play a major role in banking for local communities. As illustrated in section 2, they have changed significantly since their inception, but they are still consistent with their original mission and they could play a major role in microfinance in the coming years, due to their structure and governance scheme based on mutuality, their implementation in local contexts and their impressive size. All together, they represent the largest Italian banking group in terms of number of counters and the second largest in terms of geographic spread. There are 445 BCCs with 3478 counters in 98 provinces and 2375 municipalities (in 526 municipalities the local BCC is the only bank available).

BCCs have 729 000 members and 27 000 employees serving more than 4 million clients, who save more than €94.4 billion. The consolidated portfolio of BCCs amounts to €76.4 billion, 21.6 per cent of which is disbursed to artisan enterprises that employ up to 20 workers; 16.5 per cent given to other enterprises that employ up 20 workers; and 10 per cent is given to non-profit entities.

Major national banks are looking at microcredit as a possible way to expand their business or to promote their social responsibility. In the next section the experience of Microcredito di Solidarietà spa, a company established by Banca Monte dei Paschi di Siena, will be analysed. Intesa San Paolo, the second major Italian bank group, has joined the microcredit sector with four initiatives that are described in the next section and has recently launched a new bank, Banca Prossima, which aims to serve the third sector and would probably shake the entire national industry of social finance. Furthermore, some local banks have established or joined microcredit projects. For example, Banca di Bologna lends to those entrepreneurs presented by micro.Bo and supports the institution with a three-year grant (see next section). Banca del Piemonte, which operates on a regional scale, started in 2003 with provision of microcredit with the aim of meeting new clients, most of all migrants. Loans are mainly given for consumption. The effective interest rate (*Tasso di interesse effettivo globale* – TAEG) is 4.61 per cent.[42] The parish of Sant'Agostino and the Ufficio Pastorale Migranti dell'Arcidiocesi di Torino refer potential borrowers to the bank and are in charge of gathering information from the prospective client.

Furthermore, 167 Italian banks, equivalent to 84 per cent of the industry, have recently been involved in the consortium PattiChiari, an initiative promoted by ABI with the aim of simplifying and clarifying the offer of basic financial services,[43] in order to implement transparency, lower prices and to contribute to financial education.[44]

Foundations

Foundations are a relevant actor in several microcredit projects, according to the social mission that leads their activities. Fondazione San Carlo is a non-banking foundation established by Caritas Ambrosiana (a Catholic organization) and Arcidiocesi di Milano, which is active in microcredit, providing loans of up to €7500 at 2.25 per cent interest rate to the unbanked for their businesses. From 1999 to date, 75 people have borrowed from it, the majority being migrant men with an average age of 35. The average loan amount is €5800. The unmet repayments rate is around 15 per cent. Fondazione di Venezia and Terre in Valigia joined in a microcredit project dedicated to migrant women who live in Venezia and who are willing to get professional training and to start or expand a business. Loan size is between €1000 and 20000, reimbursed in a period ranging between 18 and 60 months. For those women who belong to cooperatives or partnerships (*società di persone*), borrowing is up to €35000. The association Terre in Valigia is responsible for evaluating credit applications, monitoring borrowers, and educating women on financial and business items in collaboration with further local entities. Cassa di Risparmio di Venezia, a savings bank, deals with lending. Fondazione di Venezia has a peculiar mission in the microcredit sector as it intends to support the start-up of several microcredit projects in Italy.

Fondazione Field, created by Regione Calabria, aims to promote economic development and the emergence of underground and informal businesses through a wide range of tools, including a guarantee fund for microcredit. In 2006, the foundation provided 143 loans through a bank partner, for an average of €54576, almost never requiring any collateral. At the moment, overdue payments are less than 1 per cent. Eight microcredit projects established by non-banking foundations address the problem of usury through small lending.[45] These allow people to borrow to pay unsustainable loans, as prescribed under Law 108/1996, which has established a public fund for this purpose. Fondazione Antiusura Interesse Uomo, in collaboration with Banca Popolare Etica, also has a microcredit project to help workers who are made redundant or who are subject to difficulties due to temporary unemployment, or who experience social and financial instability due to atypical contracts.

Fondazione La Casa, among its activities connected with social housing, gives its clients credit through Banca Popolare Etica, in order to rent or buy a house. Loans to rent are up to €2500, to be reimbursed in 36 months: loans to buy go up to €20000, payable in 60 months. Borrowers are migrants from developing countries and southern Italy. Since 2004, 77 loans have been provided.

Not-for-profit entities

The majority of microcredit projects have been established by not-for-profit organizations that act on a local scale and connect potential borrowers with available banks. Usually the organizations are responsible for the selection of the borrowers and guarantee their loans through donors' grants, ad hoc guarantee funds given by third parties or members' capital. Organizations help draw up business plans, offer professional training and financial education and often support borrowers for months to help them to address their business affairs. Micro.bo is a great example of a non-profit entity that has promoted a microcredit project (see next section). Furthermore, Catholic entities in the network of Caritas Italiana are engaged in many microcredit initiatives. Caritas Italiana is the charitable entity of the Conferenza Episcopale Italiana (The Italian Episcopal Conference: CEI), established in 1971, whose activity is based on a network of 220 Caritas diocesane spread around Italy. Caritas Italiana has a frame agreement with Banca Popolare Etica within which several Caritas diocesane act as local partners for microcredit projects in collaboration with the bank. Some other Caritas have launched further microcredit programmes.

Public agencies

Various public agencies are involved in microcredit as it is seen as an effective active workfare policy tool. Microcredit is more and more preferred to credito a fondo perduto – money disbursed without the aim of recovering it, the main instrument of credit given within public programmes in the past – because it allows part of the amount disbursed to be recovered. Even though many public initiatives are defined as microcredit projects, this definition is probably mistaken. In fact, following the analysis of principles and rules that regulate lending, those initiatives seem to suit favourable credit given at low interest rates better than microcredit. Public agencies represent almost 30 per cent of the entities that promote microcredit projects. Their role can be crucial in the launching of new initiatives in partnership with local networks of social entities and banks, but the efficiency of public projects could be limited because in public agencies the attention given to financial sustainability of microcredit projects, to reducing costs and to the selection of clients could be inadequate. Furthermore, Messina emphasizes the worry of technical incompetence and of the negative influence of political priorities and electorally oriented decisions and suggests that the matters that have affected Prestito d'Onore programmes, with an insolvency rate of 20 per cent, could be replicated in microcredit projects.[46]

BIC Lazio is the largest public project in Italy providing small loans. BIC Lazio is an agency that manages a guarantee fund of €3.5 million established by Regione Lazio to support lending from €5000 to 20 000 to those people who lack access to financial services, targeting microenterprises, cooperatives, ex-prisoners and those who urgently need credit to face emergencies related to housing and other primary needs (from €1000 to €10 000). The interest rate is 1 per cent and the repayment period varies from 36 to 84 months. Similarly, in Toscana Dipartimento delle Pari Opportunità della Regione Toscana established a network of entities to process the demand for credit by individuals facing economic difficulties.

Also present in the microcredit sector are the Municipality and the Province of Turin. The first has been operating a project since 2004 constituting a guarantee fund of €500 000 (Fondazione Cassa di Risparmio di Torino has added €250 000) and has lent to almost 80 new entrepreneurs through seven banks an amount totalling €670 000. The latter, within the Mettersi in Proprio (MIP) project, assists migrants who are seeking entry into the job market. They are provided with vocational guidance, professional training, administrative and legal support and assistance with accommodation.

Social funds

Finally, in Tuscany, Fondo Etico e Sociale Le Piagge and Fondo Essere raise money in the neighbourhood of Le Piagge and Quartiere4 of Florence, and lend to local borrowers. Since 2000, the members of the social cooperative Il Cerro have deposited €25 to €5000 at MAG6, creating a fund, Fondo Etico e Sociale Le Piagge, of more than €100 000 to lend to those neighbours who need money for bills, health care, car insurance or for their enterprises. Loans for business constitute 20 per cent of the lending activity and can be up to €7000, while for the other loans the maximum amount is €2000. The loan request is evaluated by a commission of 12 members and is subsequently approved by the assembly of the members of the fund who meet almost every month, and finally by MAG6, which gives the loans (70 to date) with an interest rate of around 4 per cent to cover the expenses of the project, almost €700 per year. Since 2002 Fondo Essere has allowed residents of Quartiere4 to access 155 'loans for solidarity', with no interest rate, for a total amount of €209 818, for housing, health and education (up to €2500) and business start-up (up to €5000). Then, in 2007, Fondo Essere launched a microcredit project where it carries out the preliminary investigation and the cooperative bank *Banca del Chianti Fiorentino* lends €5000 and €10 000 for business, at an interest rate of 0.50 over Euribor, to be paid back in 60 months. The bank participates in the guarantee fund and takes up to 50 per cent of the financial risk. This element is unusual within Italian microcredit initiatives. Furthermore, in 2007 the guarantee fund was increased through a local issue of bonds provided by the bank, giving subscribers the opportunity to give 0.50 per cent of their return to the fund.

4 Main actors within the microfinance sector

As pointed out in the first section, in a country that experiences such problems of financial service rationing and with immigration constantly increasing, there is room for initiatives pursuing social and financial inclusion. A microcredit sector seems to be growing to serve this demand. In this section some microcredit initiatives are analysed to illustrate the activity of the main actors of the sector. The projects described meet the following characteristics:

- Target: borrowers are people excluded from the financial sector, the so-called unbanked; non-bankability is evaluated through the analysis of the financial and economic situation of the client, looking at their wages, balance sheet, rent, etc.
- Type of activities financed: within the range of activities and needs financed by the sampled microcredit projects, entrepreneurship prevails. The borrower is financed to start up her/his enterprise or to support an already active business, for self-employment purposes or to finance non-individual entities, such as cooperatives.
- Guarantees: social and moral guarantees prevail on collateral security. The relationship with the borrower and the selection are based on credibility of the business plan and trust, based on a social network that supports the client.
- Interest rate: an interest rate is applied, thus part of the cost of lending is charged to the borrower.

Furthermore, the projects described here have been selected because they offer a likely outline of the plurality of microcredit initiatives in Italy, considering the institutional typology of the promoters, the type of guarantee fund (if present) and several other characteristics that are summarized in Table 3.1. The projects are:

- Microcredito di solidarietà SpA
- MAG2 Finance coop
- Microcredito sociale della Compagnia di San Paolo
- Micro.Bo Onlus

Microcredito di Solidarietà SpA

Banca Monte dei Paschi di Siena (MPS), a major Italian bank, entered the microfinance sector in 2006 through the incorporation of a dedicated entity, Microcredito di Solidarietà SpA. This is a limited liability corporation whose shareholders are MPS (at 40 per cent), Comune di Siena and Provincia di Siena at 15 per cent each, 33 local municipalities at 10 per cent and associations and ecclesiastical entities for the remaining 20 per cent. MPS provides part of the salaries, the information technology and logistics. Loans are disbursed for various purposes, to face a wide range of needs or related to setting up an enterprise, adapting the processes for evaluating creditworthiness to clients lacking suitable collateral. Microcredito di Solidarietà does not require collateral and grants loans on the basis of a judgement of morality and responsibility on the part of the borrower. Loans are up to €7500, at a fixed interest rate of 4.5 per cent, with no extra charges except taxes. Repayments are tailored to customer needs and the

Table 3.1 Main actors within the microfinance sector in Italy

	Compagnia di San Paolo – Microcredito Sociale	MAG2 Finance coop	Micro.Bo Onlus	Microcredito di Solidarietà SpA
Institutional typology	Banking foundation	Limited liability cooperative	Onlus (organizzazione non lucrativa di utilità sociale)	Limited liability corporation
Social capital	–	€2.5 million	Not required by the law	€1.4 million
Main funding sources	–	Capital subscribed by 1167 members	Grants	Shareholders' capital
Largest funder or shareholder	–	Individual members	Banca di Bologna	Monte dei Paschi di Siena Bank
Lender	Intesa Sanpaolo banks Sanpaolo Banco di Napoli banks	MAG2 Finance	Banca di Bologna	Monte dei Paschi di Siena Bank
Other partners	Fondazione Don Mario Operti Fondazione antiusura Santa Maria del Soccorso Onlus Fondazione San Giuseppe Moscati Onlus Fondazione Risorsa Donna Local groups of volunteers	Local social networks, public administrations, big social cooperatives, female associations, religious associations	Provincia di Bologna Associazione Intercomunale Terre d'Acqua (6 local municipalities) Fondazione del Monte di Bologna CRIF Assindustria Bologna	Provincia di Siena Comune di Siena 33 municipalities in the province of Siena Arcidiocesi di Siena Diocesi di Montepulciano ARCI Ass. Volontariato Senesi

Table 3.1 (continued)

	Compagnia di San Paolo – Microcredito Sociale	MAG2 Finance coop	Micro.Bo Onlus	Microcredito di Solidarietà SpA
Established in (year)	2003	1980	2005	2006
Geographical context	Provinces of Genova, Naples and Turin, Region of Lazio	Lombardia Region	Province of Bologna	Local
Contacts with potential clients	957	About 500 enterprises	550	70
Disbursed loans	200	About 300 enterprises About 100 individuals	64	46
Methodology	Individual loans	Mutual credit support	49 with group lending 15 with individual loans	Individual loans
Total amount disbursed	€2 291 050	€4 568 000	€541 000	€390 000
Maximum value of loans disbursed	€20 000 per person €35 000 per institution	€5000 to individuals €30000 to social cooperatives	€9000 per person with group lending €7000 per individual loan The same client can receive further loans for a maximum total amount of €15 000 €450 in the programme Sei Più	€7500

Average value of loans disbursed	€11 445	For individual: €2500 For enterprise: €25 000	€8580	€3800
Loans renewed to a same borrower	–	142 loans have been renewed to 52 members	30	–
Loans outstanding	–	€1 936 000	–	€27 500
Loans written off	–	219	14.3% (as from 2005)	–
Value of loans written off	–	€2 602 600	–	–
Grace period	6 months	3 months for business loan	6 months	–
Repayment period	18–60 months	2–3 years	36 months	12–60 months
Interest rate	EURIRS + 0.50% (e.g. EURIRS 2y updated to 13 November, 2007: 4.39%)	For enterprise: 10% annual For individual: 6–8% annual	6% with group lending 8% with individual lending	4.5%
Guarantee fund	€1 600 000 (€400 000 per project) with credit multiplier	Relation contract (personal *fideiussione*)	€450 000 (bank *fideiussioni* given by 20 local entrepreneurs) with credit multiplier	0
Types of activities/ needs financed	Start-up enterprises	Social responsible businesses Health and family emergencies	Start-up enterprises Businesses Professional training Basic consumptions (Sei Più programme)	Start-up enterprises Professional training Health emergency Liquidity needs Education

Table 3.1 (continued)

	Compagnia di San Paolo – Microcredito Sociale	MAG2 Finance coop	Micro.Bo Onlus	Microcredito di Solidarietà SpA
Start-up microenterprises financed	–	About 100	46.8%	2
Business sector of financed enterprises	Trade 38% Handicraft 15% Services 32%	Bio food producers Social editor Fair trade Cooperative services Environmental business	Trade 71% Handicraft 22% Services 7%	Trade – Handicraft – Services –
Other services provided	Professional training	Consultancy Start-up support Follow-up	Business support	None
Gender of borrowers	Female 46% Male 54%	For individual Female: 50% Male: 50%	Female 25% Male 75%	Female 26% Male 74%
Average age of borrowers	–	30–40	–	42
Origin of borrowers	Italy 59% Others 41%	For individual: Italy: 30% Others: 70% For enterprise: 100% Italian enterprise	Italy 20.3% Others 79.7%	Italy 48% Others 52%

Preliminary investigation and conditions to access	–	For enterprise: economic and ethical evaluation For individual loan: membership in a local network, MAG2 membership	Borrowers 1) are not creditworthy, meaning have already asked for a loan for their business to a bank which refused it because of insufficient collateral; 2) are in a disadvantaged economic situation; 3) live stably in the area of Bologna, for example have their family or other personal relationships in the local area and/or have their business in Bologna; 4) if migrant, have residence permit and have been in Italy for at least 4 years	Residence permit Wage packet Ethical agreement
Time to disburse the loan (average)	–	1 month for enterprise 3 weeks for individual loans	3 weeks	1 month
Network	European Microfinance Network (EMN)	None	European Microfinance Network (EMN)	None
Data updated to	30 September, 2007	30 November, 2007	17 October, 2007	4 November, 2007

institution identifies the sustainable length of the loan through an analysis carried out by its credit committee and the board of directors.

A pillar of Microcredito di Solidarietà's scheme of governance is the role of volunteer associations that investigate borrowers' morality, honesty and degree of need.

MAG 2 Finance coop

MAG2 Finance was created in Milan in November 1980 as a self-managing mutual association. It began to market nominative savings-books and used the collected sums to support cooperatives and associative projects that could not be backed by traditional financial loans. In 1982 MAG2 incorporated a cooperative society named Cooperative Mag2 Servizi, and included in the range of services was a consultancy for not-for-profit organizations. Like the other MAGs, MAG2 promotes democratization of the financial system and supports ethical finance through socially responsible employment of money (see section 2). MAG2 has been active in microcredit since 1996. Loans are provided to single people, cooperatives and associations for business purposes and, in particular cases, to face health and family emergencies (within a joint project with Caritas Ambrosiana). The financial cooperative has 1164 local entities and individuals as members who subscribe to its capital of €2.5 million. MAG2 provides loans to individuals (up to €5000), cooperatives and associations (up to €25 000) for those businesses considered socially responsible. Borrowers are assisted in the development of their activities until the debt is paid off. A free pre-enquiry checks whether a project is feasible or not, then a technical enquiry is carried out to check the economic and financial perspectives, and finally an ethical enquiry is conducted to verify if the project meets MAG2's principles and criteria.

Compagnia di San Paolo

Compagnia di San Paolo, founded in January 1563 as a charitable brotherhood, today is one of the largest private-law foundations in Europe. Since 2003, the Foundation has progressively developed the microcredit project Microcredito Sociale, which aims to assist those who need access to credit and professional training by providing loans and non-financial services. The project works thanks to a wide network of not-for-profit local entities (Fondazione Don Mario Operti, Fondazione antiusura Santa Maria del Soccorso Onlus, Fondazione San Giuseppe Moscati Onlus, Fondazione Risorsa Donna and local groups of volunteers) allowing proximity to the different targets, such as migrants in Turin, women in Rome, unemployed people in Campania. The local partners offer the clients several non-financial services that are necessary for the success of the project, like the financial education given by Fondazione Risorsa Donna to Italian and migrant women. Borrowers are not asked to have collateral, but to open a banking account to facilitate the loan conditions, and they are closely assisted after borrowing. Individuals and social cooperatives that wish to develop a business or to undergo training to access the job market can borrow up to €20 000 per person and €35 000 per institution. The interest rate (EURIRS + 0.50 per cent) depends on the repayment terms (18 to 60 months), with monthly instalments and six months pre-amortization. A guarantee fund of €400 000 per project has been created by the foundation to secure the lending of the banks Intesa Sanpaolo and Sanpaolo Banco di Napoli that lend at the end of the selection process. In February 2005 the banks decided to apply a ratio '1 to 2' between the guarantee fund and the overall loans, which doubles the amount of possible loans covered by the same guarantee fund. Consequently, the banks take on part of the risk. Furthermore, a credit multiplier allows the projects to increase their outstanding portfolio.

Micro.Bo Onlus

Since February 2005, micro.Bo, Association for the Development of Microfinance in Bologna Onlus, has been working in collaboration with Banca di Bologna, a local cooperative bank that is the lending partner, to allow people without traditional collateral to borrow to finance business start-ups; consolidate or renovate enterprises; and attend professional training. Local entrepreneurs have provided a guarantee fund that ensures the solvency of the borrowers, and the bank has agreed to apply a credit multiplier. Many partnerships with local public and private entities have been established. The mission of the project is to make people economically self-sustainable and to introduce them into the banking system. Borrowers are given free consulting and support for their business activity.

The association was established in 2004 within a project at the University of Bologna. The first loan was issued in June 2005. At the beginning micro. Bo used the Grameen methodology, based on sequential loans provided to self established groups of three to five entrepreneurs, each one borrowing for its own business activity. The model entails relying on peer selection and peer monitoring, meaning the monitoring of each member of the group by the others. In October 2006, the association began with the offer of individual lending, involving moral guarantors instead of the reciprocal monitoring in groups. Soon, new borrowers preferred individual lending to group lending. The maximum loan amount for an individual loan is €7000 and the interest rate is 8 per cent. For a group loan, the maximum amount disbursed is €9000, with an interest rate of 6 per cent. In both cases no further expenses are charged. The same client can receive further loans for a maximum total amount of €15 000. The approval or rejection of the project by the credit committee will depend on the economic feasibility of the business idea, the reliability and seriousness as demonstrated in the meetings, the desire to create a regular business or to formalize an existing business. In order to access microloans potential borrowers are required:

- not to be creditworthy, meaning they have already applied for a loan to a bank that has refused to lend because the client has insufficient collateral; the loan officer takes into consideration several elements such as wages, balance sheet, rent, etc. to verify bankability;
- to be in a disadvantaged economic situation;
- to be resident in the area of Bologna, for example to have their family or other personal relationships in the local area and/or to have their business in Bologna;
- and, if migrants, to have a regular permit of stay and to have been in Italy for at least four years.

Recently Micro.Bo has benefited from Microfinance Actions for Growth through Integrated Consultancy (MAGIC), a programme of training and technical support created by the European Microfinance Network (EMN) to help its members grow and to improve the quality, value and extent of services.[47] Under this programme, micro.Bo has taken some relevant steps to implement a lending procedure and governance to enhance its performance.

Finally, micro.Bo has recently launched two new initiatives. First, the project Sei più, in collaboration with a banking foundation, Fondazione del Monte di Bologna, intends to give credit to second generation migrants who are attending vocational school and need to have credit (available up to €450) in order to buy books, magazines, DVDs, a scooter, a helmet, bus and metro card, to pay fees to attend school outings, driving test, summer school, sport and cultural activities. Interest rates are fully subsidized by the foundation and repayments are flexible. Second, the project micro.Credem is an activity in six municipalities near Bologna allowing households and individuals who are experiencing a temporary lack of money or an unexpected expenditure to borrow. For example, loans can be used to pay for rent, home bills, health or legal assistance.

5 Models of microcredit granting

As shown in the previous sections, the microcredit sector in Italy involves hundreds of different entities engaged in around 70 projects. At present, it is very difficult to summarize their approaches and activities and to draw a few models of microcredit granting. The majority of the projects are characterized by three elements (see Figure 3.1):

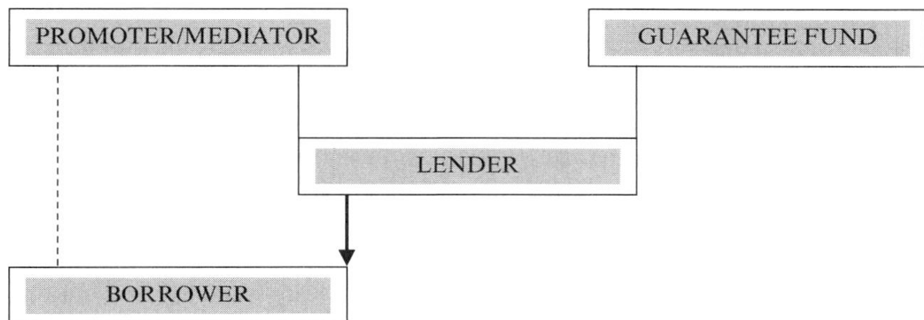

Figure 3.1 Common lending scheme in Italian microcredit projects

- Promoter/mediator: a public or private entity that is rooted in the local context and often close to target groups, which collects information and documents from the potential client, conducts preliminary investigations, selects borrowers to be presented to the lender, provides them with guarantees directly or through a third party, helps borrowers with business plans, offers professional training and financial education, gives other support such as business consulting;
- Lender: a bank or, sometimes, a public agency;
- Guarantee fund: created with the capital of the mediator or a third subject to secure the loan.

The main distinction is between public and private initiatives. The latter offer loans at lower interest rates, or sometimes at zero rate.

Most of all, projects address requests for loans for business purposes, even though many projects also lend to borrowers who are facing impelling needs and in particular to avoid or get out of usury. A few projects specialize in housing.

The main problem with having recourse to a guarantee fund is the risk of moral hazard by the lender, which may not care enough about the selection of worthy borrowers. In addition, for borrowers themselves, there is a disincentive to repay because unmet repayment will not be enforced or will be enforced less in the case of a guarantee fund participated in by members of its community; also, because unpaid loans are not formally written off when refunded by the guarantee fund, the credit bureau will not register the negative behaviour of the borrower. This means that a bad borrower will not have their credit reference updated. Guarantee funds can be public or private, and often are given by Confidi. In section 9, a critical approach about the activity of microfinance mediators in terms of compliance with the banking regulation is addressed.

6 Target groups

There is no specific data available to single out the targets of microfinance projects in Italy. A qualitative estimation of effective borrowers is not yet available and it seems to be quite difficult to collect a reliable database, because of the high number of projects and the absence of records within some lenders. Looking forward, it is very important to understand how many people below the poverty line are provided with loans thanks to microcredit projects. An analysis of the potential demand of the micro-credit sector has not been carried out; nevertheless, there are indications of probable capacity of the market, as indicated in the first section, while a quantitative assessment of the capacity of microcredit targets is as yet unavailable.

Although there is no qualitative and quantitative assessment of potential customers, some considerations and data can help understanding, in addition to what has already been highlighted. Many categories and groups of people are excluded from the mainstream financial sector and could take advantage of financial inclusion services. These include: migrants; young people with temporary work and flexible working contracts; students who do not attend schools in the town where they live; women who live in the south; third sector and not-for-profit entities; the self-employed; and microenterprises. Banca d'Italia has calculated that 14.1 per cent of Italian households do not have access to any financial services, including a bank or postal account. Financial services are less widespread among young people, people without education, people with low income, the working-class, retired people and southerners.[48] But this statistic does not clarify what triggers this exclusion. Most of all, there is no indication of the number of potential entrepreneurs who are denied access to loans. Osservatorio Bankimprese does not have records of the number of loans under €25 000 provided by banks or the characteristics of those who borrow at that level. Finally, income data is affected by a distortion produced by informal work and tax evasion. The extent of informal employment is approximately 7 per cent of the population.[49]

In general, credit rationing and the cost of borrowing in southern Italy are substantial and seem to have increased since the consolidation of the banking sector, which occurred following the 1990s.[50] It is predictable that, as Basel II rules come into force, this trend will worsen, because microenterprises could fail to meet the strict standards required to borrow, small banks could find it difficult to make their systems conform to the new rules and small bank agencies could risk closure, decreasing the availability of financial services in rural or depressed areas.

Migrants

Officially migrants in Italy number approximately 2.6 million, comprising 4.5 per cent of the population. The number has doubled from 2000 to 2004. The role of migrants in economic growth relates not only to subordinate work, as almost 2000 enterprises owned by migrants were active in 2004, which means 2 per cent of registered enterprises. According to a study conducted by ABI and CESPI, 1 200 000 migrants from developing countries are banked, meaning 55 per cent of legal migrants.[51] By June 2006, there were 141 393 (71 843 in 2004) foreign entrepreneurs, almost 4 per cent of the total number of owners of companies.[52] Almost all new foreign entrepreneurs were previously employees. Every year, migrants remit almost €5 billion to their families in their countries of origin. Half of that amount is transferred through informal channels. This informal market matters in terms of security of the transactions, money laundering and terrorist financing.

Among migrants, women are a sub-target which is very important for microcredit projects that aim to increase their social impact. Credit could be one of the instruments allowing women to become more integrated and for their progressive empowerment, leading them to participate actively in society. Among migrants, women represent 40 per cent of employees and 16.2 per cent of entrepreneurs. In general, in Italy, 44 per cent of women are in paid work. In the last decade, female employment has increased by 1.296 million, 4.5 times more than male employment. But disadvantages remain in terms of salaries and career opportunities. In 1992, female entrepreneurs were the target of a significant move to facilitate access to initial capital through law no. 215/1992.

Precari

The last category that could be particularly targeted by microcredit projects is that of employees with temporary work and workers with flexible working contracts. The result of Law no. 30, 14 February 2003, has been an increase in unsecured work and a decrease of open-ended contracts, resulting in less social protection for workers. This has led many young people and workers up to 40 years old to enter the so-called *precariato* category. Even though unemployment has decreased, people are often obliged to accept short-term contracts, to change jobs periodically and to accept low wages. Among the many problems arising from this situation, these people are excluded from the credit system because they do not have a regular wage.

Microenterprises

Finally, taking into account microcredit as the provision of loans for self-employment, it is interesting to note that the economic structure of the Italian market for micro and small enterprises is particularly favourable: 95 per cent of 4.2 million Italian enterprises employ fewer than ten employees, and 2.8 million of them do not have employees.[53] On average, each enterprise has 3.8 employees: 48 per cent of workers are employed in microenterprises, while 18 per cent work in large enterprises (more than 200 workers).

An example of the difficulties that small enterprises face in accessing credit and the quality of given loans comes from the annual report on credit to artisan enterprises:[54] those enterprises, which account for a third of Italian enterprises, receive only 4.8 per cent of the credit. Furthermore, only half of that credit concerns medium/long-term loans, which are necessary to finance fixed investments.

7 Financial terms and conditions

Looking at interest rates, microcredit projects can be classified in two categories: first, those that apply facilitated interest rates, frequently subsidized by public entities within welfare policies; second, a small number of projects that require the borrower to pay a market-oriented interest rate that typically ranges from 6 to 8 per cent of the amount of the loan. As already pointed out, in private initiatives the majority of microcredit projects involve two distinctive entities in the role of promoter/manager of the project and lender. The lender fixes the interest rate depending on the evaluation of its costs and its policy. The promoter/manager follows the borrower during the whole process, but cannot directly charge interest rates. In general, the promoted/manager is not mentioned in the contract signed between borrower and lender.

Interest rates are limited by the law. The UIC (Ufficio Italiano Cambi: Italian Exchange Office), in conjunction with the Bank of Italy, records the actual interest rates applied in the market so as to determine which level of rates represents usury. Quarterly, the agency identifies the average market interest rates for several financial services. Under Law no. 108, 7 March 1996, the defined value is the benchmark for fixing legal interest caps, which must not exceed double that value, otherwise they are classified as usurers and sanctioned. Concerning the grace period, amount, repayment period and collaterals, the operative and financial practices vary depending on the project and also on the single loan, as mediators and lenders often attempt to meet the need of the borrower and to get the terms and conditions of the loan as flexible as they can. The grace period, where it is foreseen, could be up to three months, to help those entrepreneurs who require an immediate high investment that is later repaid, after a period of low or zero activity. The average amount of the loan disbursed is around €7000. Loans are usually up to €10 000 or 25 000, depending on the client, which may be an individual or a legal entity, mainly a social cooperative. Typically loans are no lower than €2000. The repayment period is extended in many cases up to a year or more, and repayments are due weekly or monthly. Flexibility in scheduling repayments is particularly important in microcredit projects, even more so in Italy, where banks often face late repayments by enterprises.[55]

8 Other financial products for inclusion

As has been previously pointed out, financial inclusion in Italy is actually limited to the provision of loans for self-employment, for business purposes, for emergencies and for consumption. Some entities can collect and mobilize deposits, which banks do. A few of them are also offering payment and transfer services, but this is rare. There are no projects entirely dedicated to the provision of microfinance services, unlike microcredit. Recently banks began looking to that part of the population that does not use financial services, migrants in particular. Some banks have developed their commercial products, introducing new services and products tailored to this clientele, promoted through a targeted communication strategy. Banks are pursuing financial inclusion and reaching new clients through migrant banking, offering a range of products that includes credit, savings, and credit and debit cards.

Banca Popolare di Milano has published a study that indicates that 86 per cent of migrants demand remittance services. On average, each migrant makes three remittances a year for an average amount per transaction of around €258, which equates to €775 per year. Remittances move principally through informal channels and money transfer operators, from Lazio and Lombardia (77 per cent of the flows) towards Albania, Morocco, the Philippines, China, Senegal, Romania, Ecuador, Egypt and Peru. Caritas estimates the total amount in remittances from Italy is around €5 billion per year,[56] but in 2003 only €1.17 billion was sent through financial institutions[57] and €1.18 billion through money transfer operators.[58] It means almost 60 per cent of remittance flows are in cash or goods and take place through informal channels. Recently the central bank issued data on remittances, saying that in 2006 migrants remitted €4.5 billion, twice the amount in 2005. In 1995 remittances barely exceeded €100 million. More than a third of remittances go to China and Romania.[59] To increase the role of banks in the profitable remittances market, ABI promoted within PattiChiari a service to display and allow comparison of the features and the prices of national and cross-border credit transfers. Three experimental initiatives on remittances have been adopted by Microfinanza Srl, a consulting firm specializing in microfinance and rural finance, mainly in developing and transition economies, to direct remittances of Albanians,

Tunisians and Moroccans respectively resident in Puglia, Sicily and Livorno to savings in their countries of origin.

9 Government support

At national level, the involvement of government and policy makers in the microcredit sector is still limited. In July 2007 microcredit was first considered by parliament and government during the approval of several amendments to the regulation of consumer credit in order to increase consumer protection and decrease the number of financial intermediaries involved in this activity. The government approved the doubling from €600 000 to €1.2 million as the minimum capital required for financial mediators to be authorized to provide their services in the field of consumer credit, making an exception for the providers of microloans and those intermediaries engaged in solidarity finance. Several other initiatives must be taken into consideration when evaluating government support to microcredit strengthening and microenterprise set-up. First, the Italian government has promoted the creation of Sviluppo Italia SpA (SI), now Agenzia nazionale per l'attrazione d'investimenti e lo sviluppo d'impresa SpA (National Agency for the Inward Investments and Business Development), to help enterprises to develop and attract investments, most of all in the south. Its mission is to promote, accelerate and disseminate the production and entrepreneurial development in order to strengthen the country's competitiveness. Among other things, SI promotes initiatives of self-employment, microbusinesses and franchising activities in the goods manufacturing, service provision and trade sectors. The concessions are financial incentives and free technical and managerial assistance services and are granted only to those who are not yet on the labour market. Thus SI supports those who aim to set up a microenterprise that employs a maximum of 10 people. According to D.Lgs. 185/2000, the agency finances up to €129 114, without requiring repayment and financing the entire amount of the business project. Between 2001 and 2005, the programme financed the creation of 4893 enterprises. The government has recently taken the initiative to boost the activity of the agency as it has been subject to criticism concerning inefficiency. Second, in 2006, the Law no. 81, 11 March 2006, established the Comitato nazionale italiano permanente per il microcredito (Italian National Permanent Committee for Microcredit), with the aim of cementing the experience of the national committee created in 2005 to coordinate the activities for the International Year of Microfinance. In 2005, the Committee organized several conferences on microfinance and carried out several pieces of research that are now published in the book *Microcredito e Obiettivi del Millennio*.[60] From its consolidation to date, the Committee has been characterized by inadequate initiative and in particular it has failed to implement an adequate mechanism to promote dialogue among its members and to guarantee their effective participation. In fact, recently some members have claimed there is hardly any transparency and involvement in the decision making process regarding policy and activity of the Committee. Finally, in 2005 the Senate discussed a document that requires the government to provide incentives for ethical and social finance as a tool for inclusive social policies and poverty reduction, which the government welcomed.[61] To fulfil this, the report recommended that the Italian government should consider the adoption of a microfinance policy.

What could be the role of national and local governments in microfinance?

Facilitate the creation of new enterprises

The government should facilitate the creation of new enterprises by people who lack start-up capital and should provide incentives for the emergence of enterprises from the informal sector. In 2007, the government approved the *Decreto Bersani* (D.Lgs. 7/2007), article 9 of which provides for a simplified administrative procedure to create a new enterprise. The so-called *Impresa in un giorno* (enterprise in one day) decree seeks to reduce the bureaucracy for the entrepreneurs, merging the communications requested and preventing them from wasting time at least four different public offices.[62]

Promote and support guarantee funds

National government and local public agencies should promote the creation and partially support the costs of guarantee funds, which could also be supported by foundations and other philanthropists to underwrite microcredit provision. The members of the local community must also be involved in creating, financing and managing the guarantee funds, in tailoring the structure and the use of the funds to local needs and in enhancing the social enforcement on the borrower. Guarantee funds should be accessible only to microcredit projects promoted by those institutions that meet defined standards of governance, proficiency, transparency and accountability. Economic and social performance of each microcredit project should be measured to determine the quota of the guarantee fund available to the institution. Guarantee funds should progressively decrease their support to microfinance providers. Guarantee funds should never secure the entire amount of the loan, as those institutions that provide the loan and the lender take part of the risk of the microlending, in order to become accountable for their activity (the same ratio led the UK government to promote the Small Firms Loan Guarantee Scheme – SFLGS). In addition, the agreement on welfare, labour and competitiveness signed in July 2007 by the government and the national representatives of entrepreneurs and workers laid the way for the creation of two guarantee funds to support access to microcredit for women and young people. In April 2007 several deputies presented a proposal for a guarantee fund of €100 million to be established at the Ministry of Economic Development to collateralize loans of up to €30 000 at 2 per cent interest rate with a one-year grace period, accessible to unemployed people between 18 and 40 years old coming from low-income families. The same amount could also be borrowed by non-profit entities and associations that intend to start a microcredit project. Law 662/1996 already instituted a guarantee fund for those entrepreneurs who need loans of up to €75 000; thus the regulation of the fund could be amended to allow those microfinance projects to access part of the fund to guarantee borrowers within their programmes through a specific and simplified procedure.

Promote business incubators and professional support

National government and local public agencies should promote the revitalization of the role of the network of business incubators managed by Sviluppo Italia SpA (SI) and address these structures to help people to define a business plan to access microcredit projects and provide professional training to those people who seek to increase their skills. According to SI,

> the business incubator is a tool aimed at helping SMEs get off the ground. The offer includes locations and logistic facilities, as well as consulting, training and financial services exclusively addressed to the companies in the incubator. The Sviluppo Italia incubator network is the biggest network in Europe linked to one single agency: 24 already operating facilities, 10 under implementation and 7 in the programming stage.[63]

Finally, national government and local public agencies should promote the creation and partially support the costs of professionalized structures where potential clients of microcredit projects can get assistance for legal, administrative, bureaucratic and accounting matters that often discourage marginalized people from engaging in new entrepreneurship.

10 Legislation

Microcredit activity is not subject to any specific regulation under Italian law. The professional and stable provision of loans is regulated under the mainstream bank regulation. The engagement of so many different entities in the microcredit sector means that it is not possible to describe the whole of the norm regulating their activities. However, it is useful and necessary to mention some rules regarding the activity of lending and the practice of the profession of mediator.

The D.Lgs. 385/1993, Testo unico in materia bancaria e creditizia (TUB: Italian Consolidated Banking Law), contains the main rules that regulate the banking sector. Under the law, collection of savings and deposits and lending is mainly reserved for those financial institutions that have the status of banks (article 10). Financial intermediaries registered under article 106 can grant loans and provide payment services, but entry in the market is costly, as the minimum capital required is €600 000.

The activity of mediation in microcredit projects

At the moment, a critical issue from a legal point of view is the role of several entities which are involved in microcredit in collecting information and documents from the potential client, selecting borrowers to be presented to the lender, providing them with guarantees directly or through a third party, helping them with business plans, offering professional training and financial education and providing other support such as business consulting, which meet the definition of *mediatore creditizio* under Italian law. Article 16 of Law no. 108, 7 March 1996, reserves 'the activity of mediating and consulting in the provision of financing from banks and financial intermediaries [. . .] to the subjects registered in a specific register established at the Ministry of Economy, which makes use of the UIC'.[64] This means that the provision of mediation and consulting about the supply of 'monetary resources' by banks or financial intermediaries is reserved to those subjects registered at the UIC. Consistent with the definition of *mediatore creditizio* provided by article 1754 of the Italian Civil Code, the decree DPR 28 July 2000, n. 287, identifies the *mediatore creditizio* as one: 'who professionally, even if not exclusively, or regularly, brings into contact even through consulting, banks or financial intermediaries with potential clients for the provision of any type of financing'.[65]

Simplifying the content of the norm, but preserving its ratio, the credit mediator is the subject that:

- selects a borrower for a bank or financial intermediary and a bank or a financial intermediary for someone who is seeking a loan;
- helps the meeting of supply and demand of loans provided by a bank or a financial intermediary;
- preserves her/his neutrality and independence from both parties, because she/he is not a representative or an agent who acts in force of a contract by which she/he is entrusted to perform this service by the bank or the financial intermediary (otherwise the activity is placement of financial services/products);

- provides mediation or consulting, as described,
  - professionally, even though non-exclusively;
  - regularly;
  - not as an ancillary service to support its main activity.

Thus, it is likely that several people are illegally providing mediation and/or consulting in microcredit projects, and – unless the regulation is amended – must register at the UIC, or they will be sanctioned. Another regulated subject is the *agente in attività finanziarie* (agent in financial activities), which is regulated under article 3 of D.Lgs. 374/99 and article 2 of the Decreto del Ministero dell'Economia e Finanze no. 485/2001. Under article 106 of the TUB, the agent in financial services can promote and sign a financial contract on behalf of an intermediary registered under articles 106 and 107 of the TUB. Agents are registered in a specific register of the UIC. PerMicro acts in microfinance according to this status.

The proposal of the Italian microcredit committee

The Italian National Permanent Committee for Microcredit has published a study to propose a special law on microcredit.[66] First, the proposal asks for a definition of microcredit activity to subordinate all initiatives to regulation. The definition should focus on the objectives of microcredit: 'which aims to promote inclusive financial systems to support those activities of human, social and economic promotion that play a part in overcoming poverty and unemployment, through the creation and growth of micro and small enterprises'.[67]

The target of those initiatives should be financially and socially marginalized people, and most of all those who wish to start up a small business. Those entities active in microcredit, as defined, should be required to be financially sustainable, using a wide range of microfinance products (among the examples, deposits and savings collection are not mentioned). Thus microfinance activity must be oriented to profitability in the view of the authors of this study, who justify their strict approach by stressing the need to achieve efficiency, effectiveness and long-term self-sustainability. Moreover, the necessity of a special law, separated from banking and financial regulation, is explained as a requisite to preserve the 'mutual and humanitarian' scope of microfinance, which diverges from mainstream finance in the nature and technology of its products and economic conditions of their provision.

This special law and the regulation should determine capital requirements (minimum capital, capital adequacy, reserves and liquidity) of providers, forbidden activities, qualifications of people involved, transparency rules on interest rates and fees and duty of information, without interest caps. Some characteristics of clients should be fixed (significantly, maximum income and legal capacity) and it should be prohibited to ask borrowers for collateral securities more then personal collaterals. According to the proposal, the adoption of ethic codes, transparent fundraising and internal monitoring should also be undertaken. This is the core of the proposal, which includes a list of those amendments necessary to harmonize the special law on microfinance with the existent rules that regulate different kinds of banking and non-banking providers, in particular organizzazioni non lucrative di utilità sociale (Onlus), banche popolari and credit cooperatives.[68]

11 Challenges for the sector in Italy

In this chapter on the microcredit sector in Italy, the term microfinance institution (MFI) has not been mentioned yet because it is very difficult to identify an entity for which this definition is suitable. As has been illustrated, many different subjects are active in microlending, but none is completely responsible for the entire lending process, from the selection of the project to be financed, the act of lending money, the follow-up of the borrower, the taking on of the risk, the making of profits by repayments or the loss due to written-off loans. It has been considered fairer to refer to microcredit initiatives or projects, which involve different entities in various tasks of the process.

The sector is undergoing a growth phase and it is likely that in the next couple of years microcredit initiatives will become more professionalized and will improve their approach and strategy. The activity of the National Italian Permanent Committee for Microcredit will probably increase in order to create a channel of communication among the entities active in the sector and to establish transparent mechanisms to involve the practitioners in its activities. The setting up of a network of the institutions involved in the microcredit sector in Italy would be really important to support the activity of the Committee and to develop further activities. Some steps in this direction have been taken during recent meetings of microcredit practitioners in Bologna and Rome. First, the establishment of the Italian microcredit network would allow the promotion of a stable and transparent dialogue on ideas and practices, and the identification of common problems and sharing experiences and solutions. Second, the network could work to promote the role of the sector and to clarify the philosophy, mission and tools of microfinance institutions, their needs and opportunities arising from their growth, thereby contributing to the creation of a critical mass aware of the meaning and practice of microcredit in Italy. For example, the public perception of interest rates still remains related to anti-usury actions, while in the perspective of self-sustainability of microcredit projects it should be evaluated technically and without prejudice. Third, the network could require its members to increase their transparency and measure their social and financial performance,[69] collecting reliable and comparable data on the projects and their clients, which would allow a better understanding of the problems of the sector and address policy and regulatory initiatives. Fourth, the network is necessary to strengthen the identification of efficient policies by local and national governments and by the monetary and the financial authority and to improve their implementation. Finally, thanks to the proximity between institutions and borrowers, the network would help to give voice, and sometimes answers, to the needs of the clients, which of course are not limited to access to credit, and involve access to other financial and non-financial services, to welfare and to the legal system.

Moreover, microcredit needs a context that is favourable to entrepreneurship. To encourage people to take business initiatives it is necessary to lower costs and simplify procedures for start-ups, as law no. 40/2007 has done in part. 'Downscaling' of banks can obviously help the professionalization and the growth of the microcredit sector. In section 2, the phenomenon has been summarized, but the subject needs deeper investigation. Some banks are entering the market of migrant banking because it is highly profitable, and are opening dedicated branches, while microcredit is still seen as a marketing tool and not provided directly. But the earlier experience of credit cooperatives and the activity of MAGs has shown that social banking can be profitable. Probably banks are waiting for a microcredit project to demonstrate the capacity for making profits. In fact, considering that a forced downscaling – like the obligation to provide financial services in difficult neighbourhoods required by the Community Reinvestment Act in the United States – will never be envisaged in Italy, the development of projects must be carried out by those institutions that believe in the effectiveness of this tool, such as associations and financial cooperatives. The consolidation of some projects that act in the same context, for example in Turin and Florence, would help those initiatives to scale and to standardize their work in order to increase their efficiency. The problem mainly lies in the fact that it is impossible for non-banking institutions to access exogenous sources of capital, as they are not allowed to collect savings. An opportunity would consist of mobilizing savings and provident funds through ethical and socially responsible investment funds, but this would require transparent and accountable microcredit institutions enabled to lend to clients at tailored interest rates.

The microcredit sector in Italy is a dynamic scenario populated by many small actors that are using different ways to provide marginalized groups with financial services, in a context where social finance has generally experienced difficulties in growing and has never received adequate support from policy makers or public opinion. This scenario is evolving quickly due to three main factors: the growing relevance of migrants in the Italian economy and the discovery by financial intermediaries of this new target; the creation of joint projects involving the third sector; and the growth of microcredit initiatives in the wake of the worldwide success of microfinance. As noted earlier, the challenge for the sector is to become more professionalized and to improve its approach, strategy and practices. For all the stakeholders, the challenge is to create favourable economic, social and legal frameworks to support financial inclusion and to promote responsible behaviour by microfinance practitioners, and to strengthen best practice.

Notes

* Expert: Andrea Limone. The author is grateful to Andrea Limone for the supervision of the work and his valuable suggestions. I also thank my colleagues at IDLO for time spent with me collecting data and reviewing the chapter. Mistakes are my own fault only. The author has collected the data on different microcredit initiatives presented in this chapter in autumn 2007. I am grateful to those people who have answered my questions and provided me with updated information about their work.

1. This projection comes from a map-making of microcredit projects that I conducted for the Research group on microfinance of the University of Bologna (http://www2.cirig.unibo.micro) in March 2007, whose results have not yet been published and have been revised for this publication. Sixty-nine microcredit projects already launched have been identified, plus two recently closed. The selective criteria were: maximum amount of the loan below €25 000 (according to the definition given by European institutions in the Multi-Annual Programme, MAP); objective exclusion from the mainstream financial services (status of non-bankability) of those people served by the considered initiatives. The complete results of the map-making will be published in 2008 in the journal *Banca Impresa Società.*

   A survey on microcredit in Italy, edited in 2006, reports on 85 initiatives launched, of which 69 are actually active (see C. Borgomeo & Co, *2° Rapporto sul Microcredito in Italia*, Rubbettino Editore, 2006. The selection of the projects to be considered as microcredit initiatives for inclusion in the survey is open to differences in interpretation and some initiatives have been included even thought they are not microcredit projects. I refer particularly to those projects of *prestito d'onore* ('loan upon the honor') that target students only, which require the status of student and, often, good marks, but do not require the status of non-bankability of applicants, nor do they preview any kind of 'alternative' collateral.

   Associazione Finanza Etica issued the research *Il microcredito in Italia* in 2004 and analysed 19 microcredit projects.
2. C. Borgomeo & Co, *1° Rapporto sul Microcredito in Italia*, Rubbettino Editore, 2005. Data is cleaned to exclude *prestito d'onore*, as in note 1.
3. In Turin, PerMicro Srl, a limited liability company specializing in microloans, was incorporated in June and began lending in September. In the province of Modena, Fondazione Casa di Risparmio di Carpi has launched a microcredit programme, Avere Credito, targeting unbankable people with ISEE (Indicator of Equivalent Financial Status) income lower than €20 000, lending up to €4000, with an interest rate at 4 per cent, repayable in 48 months. A network of 18 local entities support the project and is available to potential clients for information and application, and Banca dell'Emilia Romagna is the lending partner.

4. Alessandro Messina, 'Una finanza etica per l'innovazione sociale', introduction to MAG Roma, *Finanza Creatrice, Indagine sul Microcredito nella Provincia di Roma*, 2007.
5. C. Borgomeo & Co, *2° Rapporto sul Microcredito in Italia*, op. cit., p. 93.
6. According to the World Bank, the total population in Italy was 57.6 million in 2004, 67 per cent of whom were between the ages of 15 and 64. The World Bank reports that in 2004 GDP per capita PPP adjusted was $30 116 (current international dollars) and the informal sector accounted for 27.0 per cent of GNI in 2003. Italy's GINI coefficient was 0.36 in 2000. The International Labor Organization (ILO) reports that the unemployment rate in Italy was 8.7 per cent in 2003.

   In 2005, 2.585 million households lived under the relative poverty line, that is 7.577 million people, 13.1 per cent of the country's population. The relative poverty line is fixed at €936.58 per month for a family of two. As from 2003, Istituto Nazionale di Statistica (Istat) has been reviewing the methodology for estimating absolute poverty. (Sources: www.yearofmicrocredit.org/docs/countryprofiles/Italy.doc and Istat, 'La povertà relativa in Italia nel 2005', 2006).
7. Banca d'Italia, 'I bilanci delle famiglie italiane nell'anno 2004', in *Supplementi al Bolletino Statistico, Indagini Campionarie*, year XVI, no. 7, 17 January 2006.
8. 77 per cent of Italian households have a bank account and 19 per cent have a postal account (Banca d'Italia, 'I bilanci delle famiglie italiane nell'anno 2002', in *Supplementi al Bolletino Statistico, Indagini Campionarie*, year XIV, no. 12, March 2004).
9. European Commission, Health and Consumer Protection Directorate General, 'Eurobarometer 56: Europeans and Financial Services', 11 September 2002. The survey considers the EU 15.
10. BNL and Centro Einaudi, *XXIII Rapporto sul Risparmio e sui Risparmiatori in Italia*, 2007.
11. Financial fraud's impact on the bank–client relationship has been recently overviewed in the yearly report of BNL and Centro Einaudi, *XXIII Rapporto sul Risparmio e sui Risparmiatori in Italia*, 2007: 75 per cent of those interviewed have less trust in banks. Financial frauds and market failures have shown an astonishing level of corruption and misconduct among Italian bankers, capitalists and gatekeepers and highlighted the incapability of public policies and regulations to address financial matters and to strengthen trust between financial intermediaries and consumers. See Marco Onado, 'I risparmiatori e la Cirio: ovvero, pelati alla meta. Storie di ordinaria spoliazione di azionisti e obbligazionisti', *Mercato Concorrenza Regole*, January 2002; Francesco Benedetto and Simone di Castri, 'There is something about Parmalat (on Directors and Gatekeepers)', November 2005, available at http://ssrn.com/abstract=896940; Francesco Benedetto and Simone di Castri, 'Il caso Parmalat e l'indipendenza dei controllori', *Banca, Impresa Società*, 2005, no. 2, pp. 211–45; Francesco Vella, 'Scandali finanziari e governo delle banche', 19 November 2005, available at http://www.lavoce.info.
12. European Commission, 2002, op. cit. Last February, Autorita' Garante della Concorrenza e del Mercato (AGCM – Antitrust Authority) presented a report on the retail price of banking services. The study addresses the cost of banking services for Italian households, which exceeds the rest of the EU countries significantly. Italian households spend almost €182 per year on their bank accounts, while in the Netherlands the same service costs €35, in Belgium and the United Kingdom less than €65, in France less than €99 and in Spain almost €108. The study considers different compositions of the retail clientele (10 typologies of households) and the less expensive bank accounts available for every category of them. The costs include both maintenance and operative costs for a bank account. For those people who have access to Internet banking, the cost decreases to €60 per year. See Autorità Garante della Concorrenza e del Mercato (AGCM), 'Indagine conoscitiva riguardardante i prezzi alla clientela dei servizi bancari', 1 February 2007, available at http://www.agcm.it.

   Furthermore, in 2006 the AGCM opened an investigation into the cost of withdrawal of cash using Automated Teller Machines (ATMs) and bank transfers known as RID (Rapporti Interbancari Diretti, Direct Interbank Transfers) and RIBA (Ricevuta Bancaria Elettronica, Electronic Banking Receipt), in order to evaluate whether costs are fixed at their maximum because of interbank anticompetitive agreements. See *Provvedimento* no. 15303, 4 April 2006. See AGCM, Press release, 'Banks: Antitrust authority opens inquiry into possible anti-competitive arrangement', available at http://www.agcm.it. On 24 November, ABI and CO.GE.BAN offered a reduction in interbank commissions ranging from 10.67 per cent on ATM withdrawals of other banks, to 57 per cent on fast RID, and proposed to eliminate the commission on the RIBA.

13. Mario Draghi, 'Politica monetaria e sistema bancario', speech at the Annual Meeting of the Associazione Bancaria Italiana, Roma, 11 July 2007, available at http://www.bancaditalia.it.
14. Before the enlargement of the European Union, in those six regions the GDP per capita was 75 per cent less than the EU average. Those regions are: Basilicata, Campania, Calabria, Puglia, Sardegna and Sicilia. See Law no. 104, 7 April 1995; Council Regulation (EC) of 21 June 1999, no. 1260.
15. Istituto Nazionale di Statistica (Istat), 'Indagine 2002 sulla povertà', Rome, 2004. The absolute poverty line was €574 per month for a family of two people.
16. See Lucia Dalla Pellegrina, Giuseppe Macis, Matteo Manera and Donato Masciandaro, 'Il rischio usura nelle provincie italiane', study commissioned by the Ministry of Economy and Finance, 2004, available at http://www.dt.tesoro.it.
17. See Censis, 'Tendenze generali e recenti dinamiche dell'economia sommersa in Italia fra il 1999 e il 2002', 2003, www.censis.it.
18. See Fabrizio Saccomanni, Testimony before the Commission on Finance at the Chamber of Deputies, 'Indagine conoscitiva sulla situazione e le prospettive del sistema creditizio con particolare riferimento alle aree meridionali. Sistema creditizio e attività economica nel Mezzogiorno', p. 13, 26 July 2007, www.bancaditalia.it/media/notizie/saccomanni_260707.
19. Osservatorio Bankimprese, 'Rapporto annuale', June 2007, www.bankimprese.it.
20. Fabrizio Saccomanni, op. cit., p. 15.
21. Osservatorio Bankimprese, op. cit.
22. See Vittorio Daniele, 'Il costo dello sviluppo. Note su sistema creditizio e sviluppo economico nel Mezzogiorno', *Rivista Economica del Mezzogiorno*, **17**(1–2), 2003; Adriano Giannola, 'Il credito nel mezzogiorno. Questione risolta?', *Rivista Economica del Mezzogiorno*, **17**(3), 2003. While considering the economy of southern Italy, it is important to recognize that the scenario is not homogeneous, with some areas and initiative that are fully engaged in the national economy.
23. Renzo Costi, *L'ordinamento bancario*, Bologna: Il Mulino, 2001. Original text in Italian.
24. Law no. 169, 4 May 1898, and Royal Decree (R.D.) 14 June 1923, no. 1936. Then, R.D. 25 April 1929, no. 697; *Testo unico* (a law issued to consolidate a number of rules for savings banks that would otherwise disperse in several regulations) and *monti di pietà*.
25. The chief of Italian Central Bank has recently called for a reform of governance of *banche popolari*, with the aim of maximizing their potential, guaranteeing full representation by the board and the other bodies and preserving their mutual mission (see Mario Draghi, op. cit.). For critics on governance, see Stefano Costa, 'Per le banche popolari una riforma complessa', 5 November 2007 available at http://www.lavoce.info; Francesco Vella, 'Popolari, un fronte ancora aperto', 14 December 2006, available at http://www.lavoce.info.
26. Regio Decreto Legge (R.D.L.) 12 March 1936, number 375, which regulated the whole banking sector for decades, did not provide a deep specialization, unless it distinguished between '*aziende di credito*' and '*istituti di credito*'. Specialization was mainly a consequence of special laws and different practices. See R.D.L. 6 November 1926, n. 1830 and R.D. 967/1929 for savings banks and *monti di pietà*; law no. 426, 23 January 1887, law no. 1760, 5 July 1928, D.M. 23 January 1928, law no. 657, 6 June 1932, and law no.

186, 25 January 1934, for rural banks. On the specialization of Italian banks, see Sabino Cassese, 'La "divisione del lavoro bancario". Distribuzione funzionale e territoriale del credito dal 1936 a oggi', *Economia Italiana*, no. 3, 1983, p. 375.

27. The mutual recognition of banking licences among European countries is effective as from the 1 January 1993, due to the previsions of the Directive 89/646/ECC (EC Official Journal N. 386 of 30/12/1989).
28. D.Lgs. 20 November 1990, no. 356.
29. D.Lgs. 14 December 1992, no. 481 and D.Lgs. 1 September 1993, no. 385.
30. Giambattista Rossi, 'La storia della MAG', 1990, available at http://www.magverona.it.
31. The project 'MAG Verona' dates back to 1975, to assist the workers of Salgraf, a graphic firm in Verona. The enterprise was going to restructure its production and lay off many of its workers, but instead, they obtained an insolvency declaration from the court enabling the possibility to continue production and self-manage the enterprise, creating a cooperative with a new chart aimed at promoting equally shared governance and profit among the workers. A group of citizens from the civil society assisted and advised this experience, which was replicated in several other enterprises. That group and the members of the eight self-managed cooperatives formally incorporated on 22 December 1978 as MAG Verona, a *società di mutuo soccorso* regulated under the law no. 3818, 15 April 1886. First, MAG Verona gave administrative and accounting advice, and then it soon provided its first financial service, collecting savings of members to lend to an associated cooperative in order to buy the enterprise.
32. D.Lgs. 197/91 which limited lending only to those intermediaries who have a minimum of 1 000 000 000 lire capital.
33. MAG Servizi in Verona; MAG Venezia in cooperation with Consorzio Finanza Solidale; MAG2 Finance in Milano; MAG4 Piemonte in Torino; MAG6 in Reggio Emilia; and MAG Roma.
34. MAG2 Milano, MAG4 Torino and MAG6 Reggio Emilia.
35. The bank has a share capital of €19 517 000, collects savings of €453 965 000, has an outstanding portfolio of €352 576 000 (2294 loans) and has 27 843 members (23 865 individuals and 3978 organizations) (data from http://www.bancaetica.com: accessed on 30 July, 2007).
36. Consorzio Etimos' portfolio amounts to more than €10 million. In Italy, Etimos supports Progetto Barnaba, a microcredit project of Caritas di Andria and Banca Popolare Etica.
37. Loans to microenterprises are provided within four partnerships: 1) Impresa al femminile with Provincia di Foggia, 2) Progetto Co.Me-Equal, Tutti i colori del mercato, parità di accesso al lavoro with Provincia di Torino and Confederazione Nazionale Artigiani di Torino, 3) microcredit with Gal Molise, 4) Capitalizzazione Cooperative Sociali with Etica sgr. 'Socio-assistenziale' programmes where Banca Popolare Etica lend are promoted, for example, by Caritas Italiana, Caritas Andria, Fondazione La Casa, Fondazione Anti-Usura Interesse Uomo, Comune di Venezia, Provincia di Potenza, Comune di Argenta and Caritas Pisa.
38. ABI and Fondazione Giordano Dell'Amore, *Banche e Microfinanza*, Bancaria Editrice, 2006, preface. Original text in Italian.
39. Ibid. The statistical sample represents 60 per cent of total counters of banks.
40. ABI and Fondazione Giordano Dell'Amore, *Banche e Microfinanza*, op. cit., p. 103. Original text in Italian.
41. Ibid., p. 105. Original text in Italian.
42. The average interest rate on loans for consumption in Italy is between 6.5 and 7.5 per cent.
43. See http://www.pattichiari.it. Within the services provided under PattiChiari, significantly Servizio Bancario di Base is a tool promoted to allow inexpensive access to savings and payment services. Under the programme, 78 banks offer products including cash deposits and cheques, cash withdrawals, crediting of salary or pension, payment of

utility bills, sending and receiving of credit transfers, account statements and information on movements, a withdrawal card and pre-paid card.

44. Unfortunately, the cost of complying with the procedures is sometimes an obstacle for the bank wishing to serve those clients who typically apply for microloans. For example, bankers require any borrower to supply copies of the latest three balance sheets, which must be kept in both paper and digital versions.
45. Fondazione Adventum, Fondazione Antiusura Interesse Uomo, Fondazione Antiusura Padre Pino Puglisi, Fondazione Antiusura S. Giuseppe Moscati di Napoli, Fondazione Jubilaeum, Fondazione Lombarda per la prevenzione del fenomeno dell'usura, Fondazione Lucana Antiusura, Fondazione S. Maria del Soccorso Catanzaro, Fondazione S. Zaccheo di Crotone, Fondazione Antiusura San Matteo Apostolo, Fondazione San Matteo – Insieme contro l'usura, Fondazione Santa Maria del Soccorso di Genova, Fondazione SS. Simplicio e Antonio, Fondazione Toscana per la prevenzione dell'usura.
46. Alessandro Messina, 2007, op. cit.
47. http://www.european-microfinance.org/magic.php.
48. Banca d'Italia, 2004, op. cit.
49. Eurobarometer, 'Special Eurobarometer 284. Undeclared work in the European Union', https://www.ec.europa.eu/public_opinion/archives/ebs/ebs_284_en.pdf, October 2007.
50. During the 1990s, a huge number of mergers and acquisitions took place in the Italian banking industries, due to the progressive commercialization of the sector, the new competition at European level and the new regulation of the industry, issued in 1993 with the D.Lgs. 385/1993, which strongly encouraged banks to increase their dimensions. In the same decade, interest rates decreased everywhere in the country.
51. ABI-CeSPI, *La Bancarizzazione dei 'Nuovi Italiani'. Strategie e Prodotti delle Banche per l'inclusione Finanziaria*, editors Gianna Zappi and José Luis Rhi-Sausi, Bancaria Editrice, 2006.
52. Caritas, *Immigrazione, Dossier Statistico 2007, XVII Rapporto sull'immigrazione*, Edizioni Idos, Rome, October 2007.
53. Istituto Nazionale di Statistica (Istat), 'Struttura e dimensioni delle imprese', in *Archivio statistico delle imprese attive. Anno 2003*, Rome, 2005.
54. Artigiancassa, 'Rapporto sul credito e sulla ricchezza finanziaria delle imprese artigiane', 2006, http://www.artigiancassa.it/Pagine/Rapporto%20sulla%20ricchezza.aspx.
55. Dun & Bradstreet, 'Studio pagamenti 2006', 2007.
56. Caritas, *Dossier Statistico Immigrazione 2005*, Rome: IDOS, 2006.
57. Caritas, *Dossier Statistico Immigrazione 2004*, Rome: IDOS, 2005.
58. Fondazione Rosselli, *Ottavo Rapporto sul Sistema Finanziario Italiano. Oltre la crisi. Le banche tra le imprese e le famiglie*, Donato Masciandaro and Giampio Bracchi (eds), Italy: Fondazione Rosselli, 2003.
59. Mario Draghi, 'L'azione di prevenzione e contrasto del riciclaggio', Testimony of the Governor of Banca d'Italia before the Commissione parlamentare di inchiesta sul fenomeno della criminalità organizzata mafiosa o similare, Rome, 14 June 2007.
60. Comitato Nazionale Italiano Permanente per il Microcredito, *Microcredito e Obiettivi del Millennio. L'impegno del Comitato Italiano per l'Anno Internazionale del Microcredito*, Venice: Marsilio Editori, 2006.
61. Proposal G15.1 discussed by the Senate on 5 October 2005.
62. In Germany, the success of the Hartz Law has shown the efficacy of such intervention: the Ich-AG is a type of company that has been introduced to allow individual workers to step out of the informal sector. New Ich-AG entrepreneurs receive favourable tax treatment and public subsidies for three years (€600 monthly the first year, 360 the second, and 240 the third) or until their businesses earn €25 000 per year. More than 300 000 new enterprises were created in three years thanks to this opportunity. In France, the government has adopted fiscal incentives and cut administrative expenditures for new enterprises. Such an approach has been taken through the Plan Dutreil,

which allows microenterprises in certain sectors to pay lower, or to be exempt from value added tax (VAT).

63. http://www.sviluppoitalia.it/.
64. Original text in Italian.
65. Original text in Italian.
66. Comitato Nazionale Italiano Permanente per il Microcredito, *Microcredito e obiettivi del Millennio*, op. cit.
67. Ibid. Original text in Italian.
68. The study also consists of a proposal for amending law no. 49/87 on Italian international cooperation, in order to implement microfinance initiatives in developing countries.
69. See also Daniele Ciravegna and Andrea Limone, *Otto Modi di Dire Microcredito*, Bologna: Il Mulino, 2006, p. 113.

4 The microcredit sector in Bulgaria

*Kostadin Munev**

1 National context

After a long and challenging period of reform and transition, Bulgaria opened a new chapter on 1 January 2007 when the country became, together with Romania, the most recent new members of the European Union (EU). The efforts of national governments, the citizens and the business world, supported by generous international assistance and guidance during the most difficult phases of transition, have led Bulgaria to achieve fiscal stability, sound economic performance and consistent policies for growth and alignment with common EU goals and standards. In 2006, Bulgaria continued a steady upward trend and reported a real GDP growth of 6.3 per cent, with a total GDP of 25.1 billion euros for the country's population of 7.7 million.

The financial sector and banking system have recovered from several dramatic crises in the beginning of transition which caused the introduction of a currency board in 1997, pegging the Bulgarian Lev (BGN) to the euro at 1.95583:1. Currently most of the commercial banks in Bulgaria are strong, internationally-owned entities and operate according to international banking practice. Recent years have seen intense competition between the banks and a powerful expansion of commercial bank lending in response to increasing demand from corporate clients and households, ultimately forcing the Bulgarian National Bank (BNB) to intervene with some moderate measures to offset debt concerns. In the fourth quarter of 2006, bank claims on the non-government sector rose by BGN 1981.7 million (1013.2 million euros), whereas their annual growth rate reached 24.6 per cent by end-December. By end-December the claims on the non-government sector to GDP ratio comprised 48.6 per cent, posting a 3.9 percentage point rise in 2006.[1]

Unemployment has been steadily falling, particularly over the past five years. It has come down from 18 per cent in 2000 to 7 per cent in August 2007 (259 300 unemployed people according to official unemployment figures of the National Statistical Institute). The main concern is that two-thirds of unemployed people have been out of work long term (longer than one year) as a result of their poor educational background (Guene and Kneiding, 2007), lack of professional skills and loss of working habits and motivation. Youth unemployment is also a major issue in Bulgaria, accounting for a quarter of the compound unemployment rate. Ethnic minorities were the hardest hit by the economic upheavals of transition and continue to struggle with very high unemployment, lack of opportunities, and poverty. The two largest minorities in Bulgaria are ethnic Turks and Roma, who accounted for 9.4 per cent and 4.6 per cent of the population respectively, according to the last national census (2001). More recent estimates place the Roma population in Bulgaria somewhere between 400 000 and 800 000 people (Tanner, 2005). Roma communities face the greatest hurdles in improving their livelihoods due to widespread poverty, exposure to an informal economy and social and financial exclusion. In a survey of the United Nations Development Programme (UNDP) and the International Labour Organization (ILO), Bulgarian Roma identified unemployment, economic hardship and discrimination in access to employment as major problems (Ivanov, 2002). In 2003, 64 per cent of Bulgarian Roma lived under the poverty line, defined at less than USD 2 per day, compared with 9 per cent of ethnic Bulgarians (National Deliberative Poll, 2007).

Current national research (Ivanov, 2000; Tomev et al., 2005) has identified two main groups exhibiting a significant potential as future target clients for microcredit products. There is a considerable share of highly qualified professionals who were laid off during the structural reforms of the past decade (Ivanov, 2000). These people tend to be difficult to place in the labour market due to their advanced age, but possess the skills and qualifications to set up their own enterprise. The second most important target group is young people, who can be stimulated to consider entrepreneurial activities through various incentives and support programmes. A research project that was carried out under the supervision of the International Labour Organization (ILO) focused on the attitudes and willingness of unemployed people to start their own business (Tomev et al., 2005). According to the survey, 5.3 per cent of respondents formed a 'core group' of people who 'do not hesitate and will start a business of their own despite difficulties' (p. 6). Typically, the members of this group are non-minority men of working age with secondary vocational education, who have good initial experience and are driven by the desire for higher living standards and financial autonomy. Increasing efforts are being made nationwide to promote inclusion of ethnic minorities and other vulnerable groups in the social and economic life of society, particularly by better access to jobs and economic opportunities. The growing microcredit industry in Bulgaria has a prominent role to play in this respect.

With micro, small and medium-size enterprises accounting for about 99 per cent of business activity in Bulgaria (data from the Ministry of Economy and Energy), the need for microcredit is bound to remain a key factor for enterprise development. It is important for all sectors of the Bulgarian economy, whose structure is dominated by service and trade companies (61.5 per cent) followed by industrial enterprises (32.3 per cent) and the agricultural sector (6.2 per cent) (Invest Bulgaria Agency, 2009). The ability to meet that need will be decisive, not only for the good performance of microfinance actors and the banks, but also for Bulgaria's overall success in achieving the ambitious social and economic goals ensuing from EU membership.

2 The origin of microfinance in Bulgaria

Microfinance in Bulgaria emerged in the early 1990s primarily as a donor-driven tool to address some urgent aspects of transition. It offered vital assistance to support the reestablishment of entrepreneurship and the private sector, whose traditions and potential were largely interrupted during the previous centrally-planned system. Massive unemployment, triggered by often inefficient restructuring, forced many people to engage in micro-scale business to provide for their families. As a rule, they were not supported by the newly created banks which were also changing gear and were about to cause, and suffer from, a major financial crisis which annihilated a substantial portion of personal savings that could be used for household and business needs. The growing ranks of small business owners and start-ups needed money and advice to strengthen their rudimentary or non-existent business and financial management skills in the new market-based economy. For almost a decade, commercial banks were unable and unwilling to provide tailored financial products and services to these clients, or requested terms that were too difficult or impossible for borrowers to meet (The Peoples Group, Ltd, 2002). The answer to that crucial combination of needs and potential was microfinance.

Most microfinance operations started as pilot projects or programmes initiated and funded by international donors, which included the United States Agency for International Development (USAID), the EU PHARE Programme, bilateral cooperation mechanisms (with Germany and Switzerland), the Soros Open Society Institute, and the Catholic Relief Services (CRS). These organizations provided loans to entrepreneurs and disadvantaged groups not only in the big cities but also in depressed areas and rural regions, where borrowers could not provide guarantees for bank loans and had no access to other legitimate sources of finance. Other important actors for microfinance were cooperatives and mutual aid funds, which were traditionally popular in Bulgaria but had very little leverage and experience in the new context and would not have adapted without targeted international assistance. Employee Mutual Kasas (literally, mutual cash funds) arose in the 1950s. The kasas existed in most companies and industries during the communist era and served as a means for employees to take small and relatively inexpensive loans. The only law acknowledging their existence is a reference to a 1989 trade union regulation. Most of the kasas are registered in the courts and have a bank account, but they do not pay any taxes on their income, though they do withhold taxes from the salaries of any full-time employees and pay employee social fund costs. Most of the kasas have only volunteer staff or part-time staff receiving very modest compensation. The Cooperative Mutual Kasas (or Popular Kasas) developed as a result of some changes in the cooperative legislation in 1997. Special efforts were made to revitalize the mutual kasas and to set up and support credit cooperatives under the EU PHARE programme (The Peoples Group, Ltd, 2002).

Among the pioneers in the industry were the foundation Nachala (established with USAID funds in 1993) and the EU PHARE credit cooperatives (1995). It took several years, however, before the Bulgarian government allowed the administration of microfinance programmes by non-banking financial institutions (NBFIs) despite the fact that lending was generally restricted to commercial banks. In 1997, as an exception to the banking law reforms, the EU PHARE programme gained the right to lend as credit cooperatives and they started effective operations in 1998. Other programmes also chose that model to take advantage of the credit cooperatives exemption, usually under a memorandum of understanding between the government and donors (The Peoples Group, Ltd, 2002). The World Council of Credit Unions launched its technical assistance programme for the kasas, and CRS began a microfinance group-lending programme through Ustoi. The United Nations Development Programme piloted alternative microfinance options through several small projects in 1998–2000, notably loan guarantees and financial leasing for business equipment. A service company model for delivering microfinance was launched by the Open Society Foundation in 1999 in an effort to comply with Bulgarian National Bank (BNB) restrictions on lending by non-banks.

Slowly but surely, all these efforts created a sufficient base for microfinance and brought access to MFI services to large groups of people, spreading business growth, community benefits and employment. Demand grew and the MFIs grew with it, becoming on the way more and more professional in terms of well developed management structure, service and portfolio quality, strategic planning and impact (based on data provided by Main Non-Banking Microfinance Institutions in Bulgaria). They offered a solution to the pressing need for access to capital in the most challenging years of the transition; they proved the feasibility of microfinance in Bulgaria and made it a winning proposition for the banks, transitioning microfinance clients to greater funding opportunities; and they continue to develop now with a strong potential to expand their outreach and to bring their activities to the next level.

The past five years have been a turning point with respect to microcredit in Bulgaria as the success of various microfinance operations outside the bank industry, even if on a very small scale initially, gradually turned the eye of commercial banks to the market potential of smaller, typically higher-risk borrowers. The banks started offering special products penetrating down to increasingly lower segments of the market, and today the microcredit sector in Bulgaria has unquestionably carved its place within the lending industry. It involves a growing range of commercial banks and a well established group of microfinancing institutions (MFIs) who pioneered a variety of microcredit products and built credibility for their target clientele, notably microenterprises, small entrepreneurs, business starters and disadvantaged borrowers. According to expert estimates, microcredit disbursed in Bulgaria in 2005 was around 61 million euros (Ministry of Economy and Energy, 2007). The figure includes loans provided by traditional MFIs and by the chief dedicated microfinance bank in Bulgaria, ProCredit Bank. The actual figure would be much higher if microloans from other banks and the substantial volume of consumer loans used as microcredit were taken into account.

3 Main actors within the microfinance sector in Bulgaria

The microfinance sector in Bulgaria includes a group of experienced MFIs who piloted various programmes over the past decade and currently have grown into the main providers of diverse microcredit products covering collectively around 130 000 borrowers in Bulgaria (based on data provided by main non-banking microfinance institutions in Bulgaria). Their profile and characteristics are presented in Table 4.1 and 4.2. The other major player in the industry is Bulgaria's first microfinance bank, called ProCredit Bank (Box 4.1).

The strategic focus of NACHALA Foundation is to expand opportunities for high-quality financial services for the poor and for small entrepreneurs in Bulgaria to improve their livelihoods. The foundation provides small business training and manages a micro and small business lending programme for the Bulgarian American Enterprise Fund (BAEF). During its ten years of existence, NACHALA Cooperative, with the essential financial support of the United States Agency for International Development (USAID) which provided almost 93 per cent of the equity, succeeded in establishing a stable and well functioning institution to support small businesses in Bulgaria. Through its 11 branch offices, 28 reception desks and two mobile offices, NACHALA Cooperative lends

Table 4.1 The main non-banking microfinance institutions in Bulgaria: the facts

Name of MFI	Launched in	Type of organization	Sponsored/ created by:	Target clients	Average loan balance (euros) 2006	Depth of outreach* 2006
Microfinance companies						
Nachala	1993	Foundation, first transformed into a credit cooperative in 1997 and then into a joint stock company (2007) owned by the Nachala Cooperative	Created by Opportunity International (OI), sponsored by USAID. USAID donations are the main source of equity (almost 93%)	Loans for support of small family business in all sectors (production, construction, tourism, agriculture, transport, trade, services, etc.); 49% of loans disbursed to women.	1597	49%
Ustoi	1998	Microfinance programme, transformed into a joint stock company in 2005	Catholic Relief Services (CRS)	Lowest income microentrepreneurs in Bulgaria, predominantly women operating their business activities both in urban and rural areas.	946	29%

Mikrofond EAD Microcredit Program of the Resource Center Foundation	1999	Transformed in 2003 into a joint stock company owned by the Mikrofond Foundation	Soros Open Society Institute, New York	Start-up, small and middle-sized companies.	1877	58%
Credit cooperatives and associations						
Cooperative Union of Popular Funds	1994	Brings together 22 credit coops with a total membership of 31 000 across the country	Credit cooperative members	Only members of the participating cooperatives are eligible for access to credit.	2838	87%
Cooperative Union 'Association of Popular Saving Societies on the Internet'	1994	Union formed by 12 credit cooperatives	Successor to the National Union of Popular Saving and Agricultural Societies	Clients should belong to a credit cooperative which is a member of the association and have shares of 10 to 30% of the amount of the loan.	4228	130%
The Federation of Private Mutual Rural Credit Associations (PMRCAs)	1996	Body for networking and cooperation between Private Mutual Rural Credit Associations	Agricultural Capital Fund Project of the Bulgarian Ministry of Agriculture and the European Commission	Support to members through organizational, technical and financial services.	960	29%

Table 4.1 (continued)

Name of MFI	Launched in	Type of organization	Sponsored/ created by:	Target clients	Average loan balance (euros) 2006	Depth of outreach* 2006
National Cooperative Union Evrostart	1996	Body for networking and cooperation between Private Mutual Rural Credit Associations	Agricultural Capital Fund Project of the Bulgarian Ministry of Agriculture and the European Commission	Support to members through organizational, technical and financial services.	2274	70%
Guarantee funds and projects						
Swiss Guarantee Fund	1999	International cooperation structure to the Federal Department of Foreign Affairs of the Swiss Confederation	Swiss Agency for Development and Cooperation (SDC)	Small and micro enterprises, farmers shifting from traditional to organic production	8911	273%
JOBS Project Financial Leasing Scheme	2000	Job Opportunities through Business Support – JOBS Project	Bulgarian Ministry of Labour and Social Policy and UNDP	Starting entrepreneurs, micro and small business, unemployed people willing to start a business, farmers and disadvantaged people.	3604	111%

Microcredit Guarantee Fund (MCGF)	2001	Microcredit Guarantee Fund Project	Bulgarian Ministry of Labour and Social Policy	Micro enterprises according to the Bulgarian SME law, cooperatives with up to 10 employees, farmers, craftsmen, unemployed people; loan interest subsidies for borrowers with disabilities	5925	182%

Note: * Depth of outreach is calculated as average loan balance per borrower divided by GDP per capita. Worldwide, many MFIs use depth of outreach as a proxy indicator to measure the poverty status of loan clients. It assumes that the smaller the loan size in relation to income, the poorer the client and the smaller his or her business. The facts in the table show that Ustoi served lowest-income microentrepreneurs in Bulgaria.

Source: Based on data provided by the respective MFIs.

Table 4.2 The main non-banking microfinance institutions in Bulgaria: the figures

Organization	Number of loans disbursed since start of activities until end-December 2006	Total amount disbursed since start of activities until end-2006 (in euros)	Number of active loans as of end-December 2006	Size of loan portfolio outstanding as of end-December 2006 (in euros)	Number of jobs created and sustained	Portfolio at risk (%) over 30 days	Summary results % of loans disbursed to women
1 Nachala Cooperative	15 813	33 372 860	2407	3 843 400	68 894	1.97%	49.00%
2 Ustoi	39 570	24 681 338	1566	1 480 784	NA	12.48%	70.03%
3 Mikrofond EAD	5500	16 361 340	1280	2 403 072	6000	3.6%	40.00%
4 Cooperative Union of Popular Funds	19 763	24 899 058	2683	7 616 504	22 952	4.30%	41.00%
5 Association of Popular Credit Societies on the Internet	13 586	19 173 446	156	659 567	110	1.60%	12.30%
6 Federation of Private Mutual Rural Credit Associations	9093	16 733 561	3590	3 447 130	4276	12.00%	32.00%
7 National Cooperative Union Evrostart	23 238	42 764 453	3873	8 810 070	15 724	8.00%	34.00%
8 Swiss Guarantee Fund	356	2 922 851	38	338 628	NA	3.10%	28.00%
9 JOBS Project	1245	6 084 645	772	2 782 395	6800	2.73%	31.00%
10 Microcredit Guarantee Fund Project	6396	37 652 999	3801	22 521 421	11 119	6.00%	34.00%
TOTAL:	134 560	224 646 551	20 166	53 902 971	132 127		

Source: Based on data provided by the respective MFIs.

BOX 4.1 THE MAIN MICROFINANCE BANK IN BULGARIA

ProCredit Bank Bulgaria is the first microfinance bank in Bulgaria with a corporate mission to offer credit to Bulgarian micro, small and medium-size entrepreneurs as well as a full package of financial services to give these businesses the means and economic opportunity to expand and develop. The bank started its operations in Bulgaria in October 2001 with the support of the International Finance Corporation (IFC), the European Bank for Reconstruction and Development (EBRD), Commerzbank, the German Development Bank and IMI Bank. It is a development-oriented, full-service bank with 60 branches and a capital of BGN 24 million (12.3 million euros). The bank provides a broad range of financial services, comprising various loan products tailored to meet the needs of micro, small and medium enterprises and private customers, as well as savings and deposit programmes and other banking services. The strong emphasis on lending to small and especially very small businesses reflects the bank's view that small enterprises and family-run businesses are the most effective means of ensuring human dignity, while combating marginalization and poverty in a difficult economic environment. The number of business customers of ProCredit Bank Bulgaria at the end of 2006 was 44000, up 28 per cent on the previous year. The ProCredit Group is committed to both social and commercial objectives. Its highly personalized approach is better suited to serve the needs of low-income clients. ProCredit Bank Bulgaria provides agricultural loans to a sector much neglected by the other banks, and thus it supports employment and social cohesion outside the main urban areas. Housing loan products are also available to help low-income families renovate their homes and improve energy efficiency.

Average loan balance at end-2006: 6234 euros.
Depth of outreach at end-2006: 191 per cent.

small loans to its members in 92 per cent of the territory of the country (based on data provided by Nachala).

The mission of Ustoi is to increase income and sustain employment of micro-entrepreneurs in Bulgaria. At present Ustoi has 19 offices throughout Bulgaria and provides quality financial support to small entrepreneurs from urban and rural areas. Ustoi clients are lowest income micro-entrepreneurs in Bulgaria, predominantly women, living and operating their business activities both in urban and rural places. Ustoi provides group or individual loans with interest rates depending on the loan size and term of repayment. Ustoi supports microbusiness development by providing entrepreneurs with sustainable access to financial and non-financial services while promoting partnership and mutual assistance (based on data provided by Ustoi).

Mikrofond EAD helps enterprising people in Bulgaria through alternative financial and non-financial services for micro and small start-ups that experience difficulties in funding their business projects. The fund operates in 215 municipalities and has 10 branches and one office. The company manages commercial funding and received a loan of USD 3 million from Raiffeisenbank Bulgaria for microlending, as well as funds from Dexia Microcredit Fund, Oikocredit, Etimos, Deutsche Bank, Alphabank Bulgaria and Soros Economic Development Fund. The Mikrofond vision is to grow into a Social Finance Institution which will accumulate capital from socially active community representatives – business, authorities, people and non-governmental organizations, and will invest it in microfinance and ethical businesses (based on data provided by Mikrofond).

The Cooperative Union of Popular Funds was formed in 1994. It brings together 22 credit cooperatives with a total membership of 31 000 across the country. In decision-making each member has a single vote, irrespective of the amount they have invested in the organization. This arrangement ensures that decisions are aimed at improving the services that the Union provides and not at bringing in more profit. Eligible for easy access to credit are only members of those cooperatives who have invested in the Union.

The Association of Popular Saving Societies on the Internet is the successor to the National Union of Popular Saving and Agricultural Societies established in 1994. The Union was formed by 12 credit cooperatives and primarily covers the Central South Region of Bulgaria. Union members include cooperatives that run their own mutual-help funds.

The Federation of Private Mutual Rural Credit Associations (PMRCAs) provides comprehensive support to its members through organizational, technical and financial services, promotes their development and ensures consistency of operational standards, including through participation in Bulgarian and international systems of financial institutions.

The National Cooperative Union Evrostart brings together 23 PMRCAs representing 8100 members. The total assets are BGN 21 million (10.5 million euros) and the share capital is a little over BGN 3.4 million (1.7

million euros). The lack of access to financial services for people who live and work in rural areas was the main reason for the Bulgarian Ministry of Agriculture and Forestry to support the setting up of the Project Agricultural Capital Fund Scheme (ACFS) in 1995. The irredeemable resources made available through the ACFS project enable the PMRCAs to finance mainly production and processing of agricultural products. Members operating outside agriculture access credit by attracted additional redeemable credit resources. The Union draws on the advice of the German Cooperative and Raiffeisen Union (based on data provided by National Cooperative Union Evrostart).

At the end of 1999 the Swiss Agency for Development and Cooperation (SDC) signed two agreements with the United Bulgarian Bank for the management of a Revolving Fund provided by the Swiss Confederation, in favour of i) private organic farmers and ii) independent SMEs in the Central Balkan region. A Credit Commission was established to enable 'marginally bankable' but economically sustainable organic farmers and entrepreneurs to have access to bank credit through the constitution of collateral warrants financed by the Swiss Confederation. The purpose is to privilege SME credits, which are conducive to job creation in rural areas; to encourage farmers to move from 'traditional' to 'organic' production methods; and to develop the skills of bank credit staff towards promoting and enabling a banking environment for micro and small credits. The total amount of the Collateral Facility Fund is CHF 1 500 000 (1 million euros) (based on data provided by the Swiss Agency for Development and Cooperation).

The Job Opportunities through Business Support – JOBS Project is a joint initiative of the Bulgarian Ministry of Labour and Social Policy and the United Nations Development Programme (UNDP). The project operates in rural communities with high unemployment rates, underdeveloped economies and a high percentage of vulnerable groups, including Turkish and Roma minorities. The JOBS network of 42 business centres (local NGOs) across Bulgaria provides an integrated package of business support services, including microfinancing. The JOBS Project Financial Leasing Scheme provides non-bankable business owners with microfinance for the purchase of enterprise equipment and machinery, combined with business support. The scheme is set up and operated with the close involvement of key community actors, ensuring local ownership, accountability and transparency. The JOBS leasing mechanism solves the main problem faced by the target group: lack of collateral, as the leased asset serves as the only collateral required. Ownership of the asset is retained until the final lease payment (based on data provided by Jobs Project).

The Microcredit Guarantee Fund (MCGF) Project was launched by the Bulgarian government with the aim of helping to create new jobs. The MCGF operates throughout Bulgaria and has a dedicated fund of BGN 36461400 (18642418 euros) from Bulgaria's national budget. The key project partners are the Ministry of Labour and Social Policy, the partner banks and the Labour Office Directorates acting as regional intermediaries. The commercial banks work with the Ministry on the basis of signed frame agreements that regulate the conditions of loan disbursement, target groups, loan types, size, maturity, collateral and interest rates. The Guarantee Fund provides monetary deposits based on a fixed percentage from the principal in the bank: 100 per cent for start-up businesses and 70 per cent for existing companies (based on data provided by Microcredit Guarantee Fund).

4 Model of microcredit granting in Bulgaria: general description of the model

The MFIs in Bulgaria have adopted various legal forms and strategies such as credit unions, not-for-profit NGOs, guarantee funds or for-profit operations enabling them to function effectively in the current legal environment which holds no explicit regulatory mechanisms for microfinance. Their capital for microfinance activities comes from a variety of sources, from international cooperation programmes and development banks or funds to, increasingly, commercial banks. Bilateral programmes and microfinance activities funded by the Bulgarian government would typically make framework agreements with partner commercial banks or MFIs, who are entrusted with the administration of the funds to the end beneficiaries. Specific arrangements are agreed upon for the funding institution's involvement in the selection of clients and programme supervision, and standard rules and procedures of operation are designed and put in place for each programme. The local staff of the implementing partners receive training in the proper performance of the microfinance programme and are responsible for its promotion to potential clients. Identification of clients and support for their participation as well as monitoring functions are also covered at the local level. In some programmes these functions can be divided between different partners.

Each MFI defines its own microcredit policy, principles and format of operation. The various programmes communicate their terms and rules for access to microcredit to the public and to potential clients by using different marketing and promotional tools. Standard client assessment protocols are used, which are again defined internally by the respective organization. As part of the application process the candidates can be asked to fill in customized client information forms of varying complexity and to present specific documents which are used for financial analysis.

Processing may take from 24 hours to several weeks. Approval can be made on the spot by the MFI's loan officer or involves several stages, sometimes including face-to-face interviews with a panel or some other body of the microfinance organization. The MFI staff inform clients about the available products, help them to choose the most appropriate option and generally support them during the application process and later on as needed. Depending on each programme's approach and requirements, the microfinance beneficiaries are required to formalize their engagement, usually by signing a loan agreement with the MFI defining the rights and obligations of the parties, terms of access, the full loan details and payment schedule, special conditions, if any, and so on. In some partnership operations the client may need to enter into separate agreements with an MFI (providing for instance guarantees or advisory assistance) and with a commercial bank providing the actual credit. Less formal arrangements are also used, particularly under group lending programmes and membership-based lending. MFIs report on their financial results and activities according to the provisions of the relevant law under which they have been incorporated. They also apply their own performance targets and indicators (based on data provided by Main Non-Banking Microfinance Institutions in Bulgaria).

In general, the applied microfinance model combines quick access to funds, often progressively increasing the funding limit based on the client's performance and strict payments, with a thorough risk analysis of the business, close and ongoing monitoring, adequate loan recovery provisions and hands-on assistance to build the client's business management skills.

Closer and broader coordination within the industry was initiated in late 2004 for the launch of the International Year of Microcredit (2005), designated by the United Nations. Supported by UNDP, Bulgaria and nine partnering organizations formed a National Committee and worked jointly to promote and strengthen microfinancing in the country. The group was set up as a platform open to all microfinance actors in Bulgaria, and by the end of 2005 had reached all major microfinancing organizations active in the country. This inspired dialogue and joint thinking on important aspects of the industry with the participation of NGOs, credit cooperatives, bilateral donors, international organizations, academia and trade unions. Commercial banks and business associations also attended the initiatives, and the EBRD office in Bulgaria emphasized the increasingly important role of the commercial banks in the microcrediting market. The EBRD is consistently providing additional credit capital and support to the development of microcrediting in Bulgaria through commercial banks. The United Nations Development Programme, the International Labour Organization, the United States Agency for International Development and the Swiss Agency for Development and Cooperation, who all have years experience of microfinance support initiatives in Bulgaria, played a prominent role in advocacy initiatives to reach key public/government institutions.

The National Committee convened two round table discussions on issues related to the effective functioning of the microfinance industry in Bulgaria and authored a joint appeal on the future of the microfinancing sector. A special round table on a conducive legal environment for microfinancing brought together high-level governmental officials (deputy ministers and heads of governmental agencies) who made commitments to further support the efforts of the MFI community. Members of Parliament declared that the respective parliamentary committees will bring to the agenda pending draft legislation on non-banking microfinancing institutions. The Speaker of the National Assembly recognized in an official letter the importance of the microfinancing sector in Bulgaria for sustainable human development and for reaching the Millennium Development Goals (International Year of Microcredit, 2005).

In the beginning of 2007, most of the active Non-Banking Microfinance Institutions created the Bulgarian Microfinance Alliance – a non-formal coalition aiming to facilitate the regular exchange of information amongst members, awareness campaigns and joint action for the future functioning of the microfinancing sector in Bulgaria. The Bulgarian Microfinance Alliance co-hosted the 10th International Conference of the Microfinance Center for Central and Eastern Europe and the Commonwealth of Independent States, which took place in Bulgaria's capital, Sofia, at the end of May and early June 2007.

5 Target groups in Bulgaria

Microfinance institutions in Bulgaria identify a range of client groups: micro and small businesses, start-up businesses, unemployed people, poor people, agricultural producers, self-employed, women, ethnic minorities, young people, disabled people, the rural population and the financially excluded. Some of the institutions target ethnic minorities and have special products for them. More than 35 per cent of clients in the microcredit sector in Bulgaria are women (based on data provided by main non-banking microfinance institutions in Bulgaria).

The target group of NACHALA Cooperative are its members – owners of small family businesses, and small entrepreneurs. The credit procedure includes submission of documents, evaluation of the existing business by a loan officer, and a subsequent decision by the Credit Committee of the Mutual Aid Fund. The entire procedure can take less than 24 hours (based on data provided by Nachala).

Loans from Ustoi are available for entrepreneurs with a functioning business in the field of trade, services and small production activities (with the exception of agricultural production). The tangible assets of the enterprise have to be below BGN 10 000 (5000 euros) and the companies should not employ more than three people, members of the family included. Ustoi provides loans with priority given to female entrepreneurs. To receive a loan, entrepreneurs should become members of a cooperative registered in the respective region. The members of the cooperative set up groups among themselves numbering 5 to 15 members. The purpose of the group is to secure a mutual guarantee for the loans received. At present, Ustoi also makes business loans on an individual basis (based on data provided by Ustoi).

Companies with a staff of 20, agricultural producers and the self-employed may apply for Mikrofond loan products. In the town of Sliven there is a project for lending to Roma people. The standard procedure is followed – a loan application is filed with information about the legal status of the applicant, the purpose of the loan, the business idea, and so on. Then the business idea is analysed, calculations and schedules are prepared and a credit file is opened. Depending on the loan level, the decision for the disbursement of the loan is made either by the manager of the branch or the Credit Committee at the respective branch. The loan disbursement procedure usually takes one to three days (based on data provided by Mikrofond).

Loan applicants with the Cooperative Union of Popular Funds need to be members of the cooperative. They have to submit an application and a set of all required documents. Loan inspectors review and analyse applications, focusing on their economic feasibility, expected efficiency of the business project, analysis of the solvency and creditworthiness of the applicant, and their liabilities to other lenders and so on. Other checks are also made depending on the specific case. Within a period of 10 days from submission of all necessary documents, loan officers are required to notify borrowers about the decision of the cooperative (based on data provided by Cooperative Union of Popular Funds).

Credit applicants with the Association of Popular Saving Societies on the Internet should belong to a credit cooperative that is a member of the association, and have shares of 10 to 30 per cent of the amount of the loan. The procedure includes the submission of a brief plan on how exactly the credit will be used and how it will be repaid. Depending on the amount of the credit, two to four guarantors are required who are members of the cooperative and who have a solid investment. For credits above BGN 10 000, there is a requirement for a mortgage (based on data provided by Association of Popular Saving Societies on the Internet).

The Federation of Private Mutual Rural Credit Associations grants loans to private agricultural farmers covered by the Federation.

The target groups of National Cooperative Union Evrostart are its members. The members are mostly farmers engaged in the food processing industry, craftsmen, turners, fitters and mechanics engaged in services, small shop owners or people who have workshops, studios and small processing units, most of them connected with the rural area's everyday life and local economy, as well as in small towns and partly in bigger cities. Members whose business does not relate to agriculture access credits by attracting additional redeemable credit resources (based on data provided by National Cooperative Union Evrostart).

The Swiss Development and Cooperation Agency sets the following requirements: applicants have to be below 50 years of age; they have to be registered with the respective regional agricultural service; at least 50 per cent of their output has to be intended for the market; they should have a minimum two years experience as managers of agricultural farms; they should own or lease arable land which is in the scope of the project; they should cooperate with Foundation Bioselena and participate in training courses for updating their knowledge with respect to organic produce; they should apply the rules of organic agriculture in their farms and use an accounting system for revenue and expenditure. With respect to eligibility for the programme for the support of micro and small enterprises, borrowers can be enterprises specializing in the processing of agricultural and forestry products, services, auxiliary production, marketing, traditional crafts and tourism. Priority is given to enterprises with two years of experience in the area for which the loan is wanted, that generates new jobs, stimulate and are contributing to the growth of the major source of economic development in the region and use local resources and materials. A major principle is to provide lending to companies that have had positive financial performance in the previous year. Special attention is also devoted to women involved in organic agriculture and small businesses (based on data provided by Swiss Development and Cooperation Agency).

To qualify for financial leasing under the JOBS Project, applicants should be among the following target groups: starting entrepreneurs, micro and small businesses, the unemployed, people willing to start up their own business, agricultural producers, and disadvantaged people in the labour market. Applicants for the lease schemes should meet only two conditions – to have a viable business idea and to generate new jobs (based on data provided by JOBS Project).

Enterprises eligible for the Microcredit Guarantee Fund should have a staff of up to 10 people and include: newly established and already existing cooperatives; agricultural producers; craftsmen and enterprises of craftsmen; and physical people. A business plan is prepared and has to be approved by the partnering banks and the Ministry of Labour and Social Policy. With regard to the financial feasibility of offered products (a collateral of 100 per cent in the case of new businesses, and 130 per cent in the case of those already in existence), the partnering banks have the say, and as to social aspects and meeting minimum social requirements, approval is given by the Ministry of Labour and Social Policy (based on data provided by Microcredit Guarantee Fund).

The target groups of ProCredit Bank are micro, small and medium-sized businesses. Lending terms are very easy – for loans below BGN 20 000, the company is required to have a market experience of only one month. Agricultural loans are also provided to agricultural entrepreneurs, and overdrafts are available to freelancers. The procedure is easy – filing a loan application, on-site check of the business and specification of loan repayment terms. The response to the loan application is as quick as possible, and in the case of microloans, the decision is made within 24 hours (based on data published on ProCredit Bank's website).

6 Financial terms and conditions

Microfinance institutions (MFIs) in Bulgaria use different models of microcredit granting: group and individual lending, business and consumer loans, microcredit guarantees, leasing for machinery and equipment, revolving loans and other products. A variety of products are made available that address in different ways the main barriers preventing clients from access to bank financing – lack of assets and property to cover guarantee/collateral requirements; poor financial skills and no credit history; lack of formal books, accounts and financial statements among micro and rural entrepreneurs; and reluctance to disclose business and income information to the institutions, and so on. Microfinance institutions in Bulgaria provide financial products with terms and conditions adapted for their target groups (see Table 4.3).

Provision of non-financial services

Nearly all microlending institutions perform non-financial services in the field of training: helping applicants draft microfinance business projects, and conducting training courses in entrepreneurial skills and attitudes and easier business conditions.

The Job Opportunities through Business Support (JOBS) Project has the best facilities at its disposal to provide non-financial services in support of small start-ups and operating businesses. Its business centres provide a complete package of information and office services, marketing surveys,

Table 4.3 MFIs products: terms and conditions

MFIs/ Products	Target clients	Loan size (euros) & purpose	Repayment period	Grace period	Annual interest rate (%)	Collateral required
Nachala Cooperative						
1. Investment loan		2500–30 000 investment	12–60 months	up to 3 months	8–12	Guarantors, pledge of machines and equipment, mortgage
2. Turnover funds loan		200–3000 working capital	3–12 months	up to 3 months	8–12	
Ustoi						
1. Loans for purchase of long-term tangible assets		Up to 3000 – investment	4–12 months	n.a.	1.5–2 per month	Mutual guarantee of the borrower's group
2. Turnover capital loan		Up to 3000 – working capital	4–12 months	n.a.	1.5–2 per month	
Microfond						
1. Start microcredit		Up to 5000 – small investment or working capital	18 months – turnover funds; 24 months – investment credits	Up to 6 months	15–17	Guarantors or clients' assets

2. Success microcredit		Up to 12 500 – investment or working capital	18 months – turnover funds; 24 months – investment credits	Up to 6 months	12–17	Guarantors or clients' assets
3. Micro microcredit		Up to 2500 – working capital	Up to 24 months		24	None
4. Quality microcredit		Below 12 500 – to introduce management systems	Up to 12 months		12–17	Real estate mortgage, equipment or vehicles
Cooperative Union of Popular Funds						
Business loans	Small companies in the service sector, manufacturing and agriculture	Up to 12 500	Up to 60 months	Looks at borrower revenues over the loan period	Depends on the shares of the borrower	Guarantors, pledges of movable assets and mortgages
Association of Popular Saving Societies on the Internet						
		4300 average	18 months on average		8.7	Promissory notes, pledge and mortgage contracts

Table 4.3 (continued)

MFIs/ Products	Target clients	Loan size (euros) & purpose	Repayment period	Grace period	Annual interest rate (%)	Collateral required
Federation of Private Mutual Rural Credit Associations (PMRCAs)						
1. Investment loan	Agricultural activity	Up to 15 000 – investment	Up to 36 months		10–15	Promissory note, pledge of property, mortgage, guarantors (cooperative members only)
2. Turnover funds loan	Agricultural activity	Up to 15 000 – working capital	Up to 12 months		10–15	
National Cooperative Union Evrostart						
Standard loans	Cooperative members	Between 500 and 20 000 euros – for investment and working capital	Up to 12 months – seasonal loans up to 36 months – short-term loans	Up to 12 months	10–16	Real estate mortgage, movable property, personal guarantees
Swiss Development and Cooperation Agency						
1. Bio-farmers loan	Bio-farmers	Up to 2500 – for working capital Up to 12 500 – for investments	Up to 12 months – for working capital Up to 60 months – for investments	Up to 12 months – for investment only	10–12	Mortgaged real estate, pledge on movable property, pledged

2. Small and medium enterprises loan	Small and medium enterprises	Up to 7500 – for working capital Up to 40 000 – for investments	Up to 12 months – for working capital Up to 60 months – for investments	Up to 6 months – for investment only	10–12	accounts, securities, bank guarantees, guarantors
JOBS Project						
1. Start with JOBS Leasing	Start-up entrepreneurs, registered unemployed people	7500 – investment	12–48 months	9 months	Base interest rate* (BIR)+10	No collateral required – leased equipment serves as collateral
2. JOBS Leasing for micro and small business	Active and start-up micro and small companies	15 000 – investment	12–48 months	6 months	BIR+10	
3. JOBS Agroleasing	Farmers and agricultural service providers	17 500 – investment	12–48 months	9 months	BIR+10	

Table 4.3 (continued)

MFIs/ Products	Target clients	Loan size (euros) & purpose	Repayment period	Grace period	Annual interest rate (%)	Collateral required
Microcredit Guarantee Fund						
1. Investment loan	Start-ups and operating businesses	25 000 – investment	Up to 84 months	Up to 12 months	7–9	Real estate mortgage, movable property, personal guarantees
2. Working capital loan	Start-ups and operating businesses	25 000 – working capital	Up to 36 months	Up to 6 months	7–9	
3. Mixed loan	Start-ups and operating businesses	25 000 – investment and working capital	Up to 84 months	Up to 12 months	7–9	
ProCredit Bank (Bulgaria)						
1. Agro loans	Agricultural producers and companies performing agricultural activities or services	No limit for working capital and investments	Up to 120 months – investment credits Up to 24 months – working capital		12–14	No collateral for loans up to 12 500 euros; guarantors, movable property, mortgages on real estate

2. Sprint loan	Companies in the trade, service and manufacturc areas	Working capital Investment up to 25 000	Up to 84 months for investment loans Up to 36 months for working capital loans	Up to 6 months	12–14	No collateral required
3. Dynamo loan	Entrepreneurs in the trade, service and manufacture areas	Working capital Investment 25 000–50 000	Up to 120 months for investment loans Up to 36 months for working capital loans	Up to 9 months	12–14	Guarantees special pledge on movable property and goods, mortgages on real estate

Note: * The BIR is set by the Bulgarian National Bank and is adjustable on a monthly basis and was 4.09 per cent in September 2007.

training, financial advice and access to the Internet. The business incubators now in place are also playing an important part in support of business start-ups as they lease space at beneficial rates and provide different kinds of information services. Every three months, the development of the leaseholder business is monitored, and sustainable development is ensured through timely advice in the event of problems (based on data provided by JOBS Project).

The Cooperative Union of Popular Saving Societies and Ustoi AD provide methodologies and expert support in the preparation of projects, accounting and audit services, as well as consultants and experts in different sectors of the country's economy (based on data provided by Ustoi and Cooperative Union of Popular Saving Societies).

NACHALA Cooperative does not offer any training courses; instead, it provides free on-site consultations that are very useful (based on data provided by Nachala), especially for start-up entrepreneurs who have no experience in cost and revenue accounting for their operations.

The Swiss Development and Cooperation Agency is working jointly with the foundations Faul and Bioselena (specializing in biological farming) to provide project consulting and training in business management. In 2004, they signed contracts with the Business Centres under the JOBS Project for consulting in relation to business plans and the preparation of loan dossiers (based on data provided by Swiss Development and Cooperation Agency).

Mikrofond EAD is focusing on poverty alleviation projects in areas with Roma ethnic minorities. Project activities, however, are channelled through Mikrofond Foundation in order to clearly separate financial from non-financial services.

7 Other financial products for inclusion

Some more targeted inclusion products are aimed at members of the Roma ethnic minority who have exceptionally limited access to financial resources. The JOBS Project financial leasing mechanism provided in two large urban Roma communities (with an estimated minority population of 20 000 each) was adapted especially to serve start-up entrepreneurs by offering a combined financial product – financial leasing for purchase of equipment packaged with a microgrant of up to 1000 euros for covering some of the start-up costs for the new business. Mikrofond EAD has a special approach to credit for Roma people – individual loans through a 'trust agent' in the urban ghetto. Ustoi runs a Roma group lending programme in rural and peri-urban areas (based on data provided by JOBS Project, Mikrofond and Ustoi).

8 Government support

The main goal of the National Strategy for Encouragement of SME Development for the Period 2002–2006 was creation of a favourable environment and conditions for the development of a competitive SME sector, including better and more varied opportunities for access to finance. In line with this declared policy, since 2000–2001 the Bulgarian government has been providing resources for two direct microfinance mechanisms implemented through specific projects of the Ministry of Labour and Social Policy: the Microcredit Guarantee Fund Project and the JOBS Project Financial Leasing Scheme. Both mechanisms have contributed to financial and social inclusion, disbursing collectively by end-December 2006 funds in excess of 43.7 million euros to over 7600 clients (based on data provided by JOBS Project and Microcredit Guarantee Fund).

9 Regulation: fiscal treatment, regulation of microentreprises, etc.

There is no special law concerning microcredit. Currently, the legal framework for micro-scale lending carried out by smaller institutions in Bulgaria is defined by five main laws: the Credit Institutions Act (CIA), the Commerce Act, the Cooperatives Act, the SME Act and the Non-Profit Legal Persons Act.

The CIA regulates credit institutions, banks and other financial actors that can provide loans as well as other matters related to banks and lending (in this sense also microcredit). A special section of the Commerce Act deals with bank credit, providing a definition and settling bank credit forms and requirements. Many of the local microfinance actors are registered under the Cooperatives Act (CA). Pursuant to Art. 36, par. 3 of the CA, cooperatives may perform deposit and lending activities, pursuant to a decision of its General Meeting and a decision of the Bulgarian National Bank under conditions and procedures stipulated in a special law. So far such a law has not been adopted. The SME Act envisages the provision of guarantees to SMEs to cover their credit risk and the provision of credits to SMEs by the state-owned Encouragement Bank, whose lending functions specifically for SMEs are established under the Act. Foundations and NGOs are registered under the Non-Profit Legal Persons Act. These organizations can provide loans with funds other than accepted deposits or other repayable funds and do not distribute profit. Non-Bank Financial Institutions (NBFIs) can provide loans with funds other than accepted deposits or other repayable funds, and through mutual aid funds extending loans only to their members on the account of contributions made by them and at their risk according to the CIA.

Regulation policies have ensured efficient regulation and supervision of commercial banks by the Bulgarian National Bank (BNB). At the same time, no blanket regulations are in place in Bulgaria with respect to microfinance and the BNB is as yet reluctant to cover non-banking financial institutions within its bank supervisory system. Under the current legal framework, there is no government authority to regulate and supervise NBFI activities. There is only some internal control on the part of the Management Board and the Cooperative Union of Cooperatives, the donors, private investors and lending banks. They analyse their operations and decide whether or not to give them a vote of confidence. It is generally believed that no regulation is necessary at this stage because, due to their limited scope, these activities pose no threat to the stability of the financial system in the country. NBFIs, however, are increasingly open to the view that the legal environment now effective does not facilitate the development of microcrediting and microfinance in Bulgaria. The renewal and amendment of the legal framework would result in greater transparency of loans granted to businesses and easier access to funding from these institutions (Tomev and Naidenova, 2005).

Regarding carrying out activities in the Bulgarian financial sector, at the moment there are a number of requirements for executing bank activities, following Directive 2000/12/EC for undertaking and carrying out the activities of credit institutions. According to Directive 2000/12/EC and its amendments, collection of deposits is defined exclusively as a bank activity, and the Member States ban the collection of deposits by people that are not credit institutions. According to the definition of the Directive (Art. 1, § 1), credit institutions are only banks and institutions running electronic banking operations. Bulgaria did not benefit from the legally valid opportunity to request an exception during the negotiation process for joining the European Union, whereby if an exception has been approved and negotiated, it is included in the list of institutions under Art. 2, towards which the Directive is not applied on the territory of the European Union.

NBFIs justify the need for special regulations with the following arguments:

- A unified system of loan assessment and loan risk assessment by independent external audit organizations and institutions would be applied for these institutions.
- NBFI management positions should be held only by people with suitable education, as in the banking system.
- Mechanisms would be put in place to seek personal responsibility in the event of losses caused by officials' faults (covered losses).

- A uniform procedure would be established for protection of borrowers against the moneylender's interest. Also, accurate, transparent and comparable information will be provided on all lending costs, including by making it necessary to specify the effective interest rate in loan contracts through the application of a uniform cost calculation formula.
- Non-bank institutions should also be allowed to have access to the existing debt register, and a general debt register should be introduced so that all actors in the industry can manage risks and raise funds more easily (Tomev and Naidenova, 2005).

10 Financial and operational sustainability

All MFIs in Bulgaria are carefully planning and monitoring their sustainability, striving for sustained growth that will enable them to broaden their outreach and serve their clients in the best possible manner. Since as of yet there are no commonly accepted indicators for all actors, various degrees of detail are available about the standing of individual organizations regarding sustainability (based on data provided by Main Non-Banking Microfinance Institutions in Bulgaria). Three organizations have provided summary data.

As of December 2005, Nachala reported low levels of profitability. The ROE[2] was 2 per cent and the ROA[3] was 1.8 per cent, while the adjusted values (AROA[4], AROE[5]) were negative respectively at –4.7 per cent and –3.9 per cent. After a strong positive trend in 2004, when profitability grew significantly, a negative pattern emerged in 2005, mainly due to a hike in inflation, increases in operating costs, depreciation and loan loss provisioning. A similar pattern was seen with respect to sustainability: Operational Self Sufficiency (OSS) decreased from 2004 levels but remained positive at 106.2 per cent, and Financial Self Sufficiency (FSS) was well below 100 per cent, at 86.7 per cent, dropping from 90.5 per cent in 2004. The increase of interest rates was reflected in the portfolio yield, which grew from 23.4 per cent to 26.5 per cent, but was not enough to balance higher costs and the growing effect of inflation (Nachala Final Rating Report, January 2006).

Ustoi is fully financially and operationally sustainable (based on data provided by Ustoi).

The analysis of the financial performance of Mikrofond is based on the audited financial statement of 2006. After reporting poor financial results for the years 2004 and 2005, Mikrofond managed to turn around the negative trend in 2006. The ROA reached 0.6 per cent and the ROE reached 3.7 per cent. The operational self-sufficiency is 109.3 per cent and the financial self-sufficiency is 107.1 per cent.

11 Challenges for the sector in Bulgaria

The key challenges for the sector in Bulgaria concern regulation, establishment of common standards of operation and strengthening of professional expertise, access to capital for microfinance activities and product diversification and closer and more efficient cooperation between actors.

The prime issue for the industry is to create a legal framework that will enable the functioning of a diverse range of microfinancing non-banking institutions and to establish a regulatory and monitoring mechanism for the work of non-banking MFIs. Legal requirements for non-bank microcredit providers should be addressed as a priority, although not necessarily through new legislation and include: registration and legal charters of entities, disclosure of ownership and control, reporting or publication of financial statements, professional qualification of NBFI management, transparent disclosure of interest rates to clients, and the status of their loans to credit bureaux. MFIs in Bulgaria need to find a legal existence and full recognition, and continued efforts are necessary on behalf of all actors to translate the growing public and government support for the role of this sector into practical, well focused mechanisms that will facilitate its development and will maximize benefits for society.

Now that microfinance institutions in Bulgaria are entering a phase of maturity, backed by a decade of experience in the difficult context of transition, they need to focus on their ability to tap new opportunities for growth to serve their unique market. They have gained momentum and must be even more innovative and proactive, diversifying and improving their approaches, products, services and operating practices. The biggest issue is to further broaden and deepen the outreach of microfinance to particular at-risk groups which may be more difficult to reach. Common, country-specific definitions need to be agreed upon and applied with respect to various target groups, such as ethnic minorities, young people, and other disadvantaged clients, and disaggregated data need to be collected and analysed to better monitor outreach, impact and improved participation.

Another challenge for the sector, which is particularly relevant for those NBFIs that are committed to serving the needs of socially excluded people and communities, is that most of the MFIs lack financial resources to expand their services. Development of long-term funding strategies is essential for increasing outreach and sustainability, and if such strategies are to work and be successful, they will require consistent strengthening of MFI capacities. The current clientele of the microfinance industry in Bulgaria – typically micro and small business owners and self-employed people, is becoming ready to graduate to formal financial services as a result of economic development, financial sector growth and the critical support they have received through microfinance. Therefore, the MFIs need to be prepared to adapt and fine-tune their products and delivery methods to the needs of the next generation of microcredit users, with an ever-growing shift to disadvantaged populations and inclusion.

Microfinance institutions in Bulgaria should seek to achieve improved cooperation and partnerships within the industry and with other actors such as non-governmental organizations, public institutions, the banks and the private sector. European Union programmes are already opening up valuable opportunities for microfinance growth and targeting. The JEREMIE[6] initiative presents a significant opportunity for additional funds for microfinance practitioners, and efforts should be made to ensure that these opportunities effectively reach out to support MFI target clients.

The need for better cooperation is also about: coordinating efforts to avoid overlap, sharing of information, feasible solutions and lessons learned to continuously improve impact, and understanding, agreement and work towards common performance benchmarks and standards for all NBFIs. The creation of the Bulgarian Microfinance Alliance in 2007 was a positive step toward future interaction between the leading microfinance organizations along these lines and it offers a high-profile platform for participation in policy efforts and international networking. The microfinance sector in Bulgaria has proved its viability, and its future is in its own hands if it wants to claim a lasting presence in the market, a tangible contribution to the growth of its clients, and real advancement in Bulgaria's development.

Notes

* Experts: Peter Arnaudov and Georgi Breskovski.

1. Economic review, Bulgarian National Bank (2007).
2. Return on equity is calculated as net operating income, minus taxes, divided by average equity.
3. Return on assets is calculated as net operating income, minus taxes, divided by average assets.
4. Adjusted return on equity is calculated as adjusted net operating income, minus taxes, divided by average equity.
5. Adjusted return on assets is calculated as adjusted net operating income, minus taxes, divided by average assets.
6. JEREMIE (Joint European Resources for Micro to Medium Enterprises) is a programme implemented in the framework of the new EU programming round 2007–2013. Its aim is to promote entrepreneurship and innovation through improving SMEs' access to finance. The programme enables the EU member states to use part of their Structural Funds dedicated to the development of micro to medium-sized enterprises in the form of loans, guarantees, venture capital and other similar non-grant instruments. JEREMIE programming is started by assessing the level of market failure in the various financial services segments within each Member State planning to implement the programme.

References

Bulgarian National Bank (2007), *Economic Review*, 1/2007.

Guene, Christophe and Christoph Kneiding (2007), 'Microfinance gap: assessment in Bulgaria', Update in Contribution to the JEREMIE Programme Bulgaria.

International Year of Microcredit (2005), progress report, Bulgarian National Committee, October.

Invest Bulgaria Agency (2007), 'Economy, investment, business and industry', report, March.

Ivanov, A. (2000), 'Microlending in Bulgaria: who will fill the gap and how?', MOCT-MOST: *Economic Policy in Transitional Economies*, **10**(2), 229–43.

Ivanov, A. (2002), *Avoiding the Dependency Trap: The Roma in Central and Eastern Europe*, Bratislava: Regional Bureau for Europe and the CIS, United Nations Development Programme.

Ministry of Economy and Energy (2007), 'Organisational and financial model for SME financial instruments in Bulgaria', Discussion paper, February.

National Deliberative Poll (2007), 'Policies toward the Roma in Bulgaria – Ghettos, Crime, Education', briefing material, Center for Liberal Strategies, Sofia.

The Peoples Group, Ltd. (2002), Bulgaria Microfinance Assessment.

Tanner, Arno (2005), 'The Roma in Eastern Europe: still searching for inclusion', available at http://www.migrationinformation.org/Feature/display.cfm?id=308.

Tomev, L. and Z. Naidenova (2005), 'Social finance for support to self-employment', in ILO *Main Actors and Institutions in the Area of Microfinance in Bulgaria*, Phase Three, Sofia: ILO/SRO Budapest.

Tomev, L., Z. Naidenova, D. Trakieva and K. Hristov (2005), 'Unemployed people's needs and attitudes to self-employment', in ILO, *Social Finance for Support to Self-Employment*, Phase Two, February, Sofia: ILO/SRO Budapest.

5 Microcredit in Denmark

Tuija Wallgren and Mohammad Naveed Awan

Denmark has a strong economy, with a GDP per capita among the ten highest in the world (Eurostat, 2007). Moreover, the Danish economy has experienced an economic upturn, with growth rates above 3 per cent during the previous years. The National Bank is predicting slower growth for the next few years, estimating growth rates between 1.3 and 2.3 per cent per year. The main reason for these lower predictions is the overall decline in private consumption. Unemployment is at its lowest in 30 years, below 4 per cent of the labour force, and is expected to remain low, as demographic development will increase the demand.[1] Inflation has been under 2 per cent, but is expected to increase to 2.25 per cent by the end of 2009, mainly due to increasing energy and consumer prices (Danmarks Nationalbank, 2007).

The Danish economy is characterized by small and medium-sized businesses. There are 283 000 active enterprises in Denmark, averaging one company for every ten Danes in the labour market; 92 per cent of the enterprises have fewer than ten employees (Statistics Denmark, 2007).

Every year, there are between 14 000 and 18 000 start-ups in Denmark, which is on a level with the best performing entrepreneurial countries. Start-ups account for approximately 10 per cent of the total number of enterprises in the Danish economy (Regeringen, 2006). Measured by the number of people considering a start-up or already managing an early-stage business, approximately 5 per cent of the Danish population is engaged in entrepreneurial activity (Schott, 2006).

Denmark ranks seventh in ease of doing business among the OECD countries.[2] According to the government's competitiveness report, if one has a good business plan access to bank loans is easier in Denmark than in many other European countries. Several private investment companies and so-called 'business angels' also provide financing for small businesses (for example Connect Denmark[3]). The Danish venture investments are estimated to reach DKK 475 million (€63.7 million) during the first quarter of 2008. This is 30 per cent less than in 2007, which is in line with the global economic trend of lower investment rates.[4] Denmark is among the top five OECD countries when business friendliness is measured by the time and cost needed to establish a business. The overall development has been positive, although the share of so-called high-growth entrepreneurs among the new start-ups is still lower than in some other countries (Økonomi- og Erhvervsministeriet, 2007). Also, while it is relatively easy to start an enterprise, there are strict governmental regulations especially for small businesses, which make the new business survival rate rather low (Schott, 2006).

The Danish government has adapted strong strategic policies supporting small and medium sized enterprises and start-ups by focusing on 1) education and culture; 2) general guidance, networking and sparring; 3) capital and taxation; and 4) administrative burdens. The government aims to develop entrepreneurial educational programmes, and is creating accessible and competent advice centres. It is also promoting access to capital by supporting private venture capital structures and new financial instruments, among them microfinance. Measures aiming to reduce the administrative burdens through easier registration and electronic governance, as well as tax reductions, are also being planned and implemented. The government's measures are mainly targeted towards high-growth start-ups (Regeringen, 2006).

The Danish state-backed investment company, Vaekstfonden, provides financing to Danish companies and venture funds with its €300 million capital base. It also administers Vaekstkaution, which is a national loan guarantee scheme.[5] The scheme provides loans to businesses, which fulfil certain criteria including collateral requirements. However, the success of the scheme has been limited, partly due to relatively high loan expenses, lack of information and a tedious administration process. In 2005, the Danish government set up a new loan structure targeting the vast group of entrepreneurs who might not be able to gather enough collateral for normal loans. These start-up loans ('Kom-i-gang-lån') are distributed through regular banks. The loans carry a public guarantee, covering 75 per cent of the possible loss of the banks. In addition to the loan, the entrepreneur is given access to business support and counselling provided by the banks in collaboration with local partners. Twenty-nine entrepreneurs received these types of loans amounting to DKK7 million (about €940 000) during the first quarter of 2007. However, this is DKK15 million less than during the first quarter of 2006, which might indicate that financing through regular loans and venture funds has become easier to achieve.[6] On the other hand, the decline might also be due to the banks' failure to reach all of the target groups. Further, it was observed that banks use this scheme as a marketing tool to sell other products.

Financing and business counselling is available from various venture funds and government-supported loan programmes. The business administration has been facilitated by the creation of a business portal 'Virk.dk', which is a website combined with telephone support. For already existing companies, personal expert visits may also be arranged upon request. The website provides the entrepreneurs a one point access to the public sector, and the government aims to reduce the administrative burdens by up to 25 per cent by 2010.[7]

Immigrants comprise 8.5 per cent of the Danish population of 5.4 million, with a higher rate of unemployment than the native Danes. The activity rate[8] of immigrants from non-western countries is only 56.4 per cent, while the activity rate of the population as a whole is 78 per cent[9] (Statistics Denmark, 2007). The immigrants tend to attend fewer higher education programmes than the population as a whole. The difference, however, has been diminishing during the past decade, partly due to an increasing proportion of second generation immigrants taking short and medium-cycle higher education[10] (Statistics Denmark, 2007). As in many other European countries, the higher education received especially in third world countries is often not recognized in Denmark, which makes it difficult for immigrants to find employment. Thus, many immigrants find starting their own business as the only way to earn a living. However, the new entrepreneurs lose all welfare rights, making starting their own business a very risky venture.

Currently, there are five regional business counselling centres in Denmark, providing support and free business counselling for small and medium-sized businesses. The centres also create business networks, run specific 'greenhouses' for new entrepreneurs and organize workshops and courses in business-related topics. The centres function in two major areas; the regional level concentrates on counselling and developing existing companies with higher investment and income levels and more than 50 employees, while the municipality level is focused on encouraging the establishment of new businesses by providing shared facilities and expertise to the start-ups. The centres receive funding from the regional municipalities, the Danish Ministry of Economic and Business Affairs and the European Social Fund (EVU, 2005).

For people with a lower standard of education, and especially for immigrant entrepreneurs, the administration procedures remain difficult, and the existing counselling services do not always reach them. In 2005, Denmark's biggest business counselling centre, EVU (Erhvervscenter for Etablering, Vækst og Udvikling) gave individual consulting services to 1578 entrepreneurs: 60 per cent of them possessed a higher education diploma,[11] 32 per cent were professionals and only 8 per cent were non-professionals. The ethnic entrepreneurs do not actively seek business counselling, either because they do not know about the existing opportunities, or because they find it difficult to understand the information given. To improve the situation, the EVU established a Knowledge Centre for Ethnic Entrepreneurship

(Videnscenter for Etnisk Erhvervsfremme) aimed at collecting and distributing information concerning the various possibilities and challenges facing ethnic entrepreneurs. The centre received funding from the City of Copenhagen and the EU's social funding projects (EVU, 2005). The EVU, together with the three largest municipality areas of Denmark, also started an outreach advice programme targeting the ethnic minority business entrepreneurs in the Odense, Århus and Bornholm areas.

The EVU reports that the ethnic entrepreneurs generally find it difficult to obtain financing through regular bank credit, due to the lack of banking history in Denmark, an inadequate business plan or a lack of savings and collateral. Some entrepreneurs choose the alternative, often private, borrowing market, as they are convinced that it will be too difficult to obtain a standard bank loan. Various forms of private borrowing exist in Denmark, and the minorities often find it easier to borrow from their family, friends or people they know in their business circle. Some minority entrepreneurs turn to loan sharks, or obtain financing from rotating cash pools (haqba). However, the interest rates are higher than in the regular bank loans, and the irregularity of these arrangements creates problems of accountability, additional risk and unhealthy dependency for the entrepreneurs. Thus, outreach advice, including information on how to find regular start-up financing through formal channels, is needed (Degn, 2006).

The EVU outreach advice projects proved successful. The advisers reached 18 per cent of the 2500 ethnic entrepreneurs in the Copenhagen area alone in the first two years (Degn, 2006). The method improved the access of ethnic entrepreneurs, as the advisers approached them directly, often in their own language. As word of mouth spread, and the ethnic communities learned about the possibilities of obtaining free business counselling, they became more active in seeking support. This resulted in healthier businesses and easier start-ups (Stoumann, 2007).

While the level of the Danish government's support for SME start-ups is rather high, the main target of the government is to create more high-growth businesses. These entrepreneurs can also find support from private business angels and organizations. The Knowledge Centre for Ethnic Entrepreneurship and the outreach advice programme of the EVU aimed specifically at reaching ethnic entrepreneurs. As the EVU did not provide microcredit itself, it focused on business counselling and helping the entrepreneurs to find the traditional sources of financing. There is a lot to be done in the microfinance area in Denmark. The organizational structure of Danish business counselling companies is largely dependent on public funding and thus is related to political decision making, which makes the long-term strategic planning, such as providing microcredit, somewhat challenging.

Meanwhile, the experiences from the EVU concept have been very promising, and similar projects have been launched throughout the country. From 1 January 2008, the EVU project in Copenhagen was replaced by a Business Contact Center (Erhvervskontaktcenter), an independent organization administered entirely by the Copenhagen Municipality. The centre is continuing the successful outreach business advice practice created by the EVU. Currently, few private banks in Denmark offer microloans, and these have higher interest rates and administration costs and have certain terms which are difficult to fulfil. Hopefully Copenhagen Business Contact Center (Erhvervskontaktcenter) as a part of Copenhagen Municipality will combine its advisory services with the microloans for both the socially excluded and small businesses in Denmark. As the government of Denmark has stated that it wants to develop entrepreneurship in Denmark, it might want to further improve microfinance opportunities in the country.

Although there are no registered microcredit institutions specifically targeting excluded people and immigrants in Denmark, the European microfinance sector can learn a lot from the success of the Danish practice of outreach business counselling.

Notes

1. The number of people in the 20–59 years age group is declining by approximately 18 000 annually (Statistics Denmark, 2007).
2. http://www.doingbusiness.org/ExploreEconomies.
3. http://www.connectdenmark.com.
4. Danish Venture Capital & Private Equity Association.
5. http://www.vaekstfonden.dk.
6. http://www.vaekstfonden.dk.
7. http://www.eogs.dk.
8. Self-employed and employees.
9. Foreigners with high levels of education and good jobs often obtain Danish nationality, and are thus considered as Danes in the statistics.
10. Short cycle = two years, long cycle = seven years of education after high school
11. Bachelor's Degree or above.

References

Danmarks Nationalbank (2007), *Kvartalsoversigt – 3. kvartal 2007*, Denmark: Nationalbanken.

The Danish Government (2006), *Progress, Innovation and Cohesion: A summary of the Government's Globalisation Strategy*, Denmark: Datagraf.

Degn, D.M. (2006), *Outreach Advice for Ethnic Minority Entrepreneurs, Method Catalogue, Knowledge Centre for Ethnic Entrepreneurship*, Copenhagen: EVU Business Center.

EVU (2005), 'Ehrvervscenter for etablering, vækst og udvikling', Årsberetning 2005, Copenhagen.

Økonomi- og Erhvervsministeriet (2007), *Danmark i den globale økonomi – Konkurrenceevneredegørelse 2007*, Denmark: Schultz grafisk.

Regeringen (2006), *Globaliseringsstrategien: Fremgang, fornyelse og tryghed*, Denmark: Datagraf.

Schott, T. (2006), *Entrepreneurship in the Regions in Denmark 2006 – Studied via Global Entrepreneurship Monitor*, Kolding: University of Southern Denmark.
Statistics Denmark (2007), *Denmark in Figures 2007*, Copenhagen: Statistics Denmark.
Stoumann, J. (2007), *Dokumentation og analyse af effekterne af opsøgende rådgivning til etniske virksomheder og iværksættere i Københavns Kommune*, Copenhagen: Videnscenter for Etnisk Erhvervsfremme.

Websites

http://www.doingbusiness.org/ExploreEconomies.
http://www.dvca.dk (Danish Venture Capital & Private Equity Association).
http://www.eogs.dk (The Danish Commerce and Companies Agency).
http://epp.eurostat.ec.europa.eu (Eurostat).
http://www.globalisation.dk.
http://www.vaekstfonden.dk.

6 Microcredit in Portugal

*Manuel Brandão Alves**

1 National context

Portugal is today considered a developed country, albeit with levels of well-being still somewhat removed from the average of other Western European countries. There has been remarkable progress in the past decades, but it has been accompanied by an increase in economic and social instability hardly permissible in a modern and competitive society capable of generating progress. This is not only the result of internal dynamics but is also due to structural changes in the way economies work globally. One of the major effects of these recent structural changes has been the increase in the unemployment rate. In a relatively short time, Portugal changed from being one of the countries in the EU with the lowest unemployment rate to one whose rate is above average.

This accelerated change has caught most of the international community by surprise. Capital, goods and people move at a speed and complexity which makes it very difficult to carry out medium and long-term projections. Political maps are drawn and re-drawn as countless ethnical and political groups emerge to make new claims and demand new territories. These changes cause social tension that development policies are incapable of controlling. Simultaneously, it has been assumed that by applying the same economic principles that work for market economies, social questions will solve themselves; dynamic and functional markets would not only generate wealth but would solve people's problems with levels of well-being. Every analysis that has been carried out leads us to conclude that this is a profound mistake and to the realization of its catastrophic consequences.

Both the silent impoverishment of millions of people pushed to the fringes of economy, and the shocking scenes of open war that is destroying whole countries are a clear demonstration of the high price the whole world is paying for having placed social issues on hold. On the other hand, we are witnessing an unbridled growth of the black economy: the 'informal' sector has been the only option for families wanting to avoid greater poverty. It is a spontaneous survival response for all those who have no other way out and who still have the will to react and the imagination to find a solution.

In Portugal, a European Commission study (2006) revealed that around 20 per cent of the population (2 000 000 people) are at risk of poverty and clearly seek a better life. Part of the solution could involve a little support by providing them with access to a small loan and allowing them to create a small business or company and consequently their own employment. The traditional banking system has always marginalized the poor, only granting credit to people with property or collateral, thus perpetuating a vicious circle; we cannot solve the poverty problem by applying the same theory that originated the problem in the first place. The poor are considered to be bad payers, with no entrepreneurial spirit and lazy. The experience of the institutions recently created in Portugal, who specialize in microcredit for those excluded from the traditional banking system, confirmed what has also been happening in other countries, that on average, beneficiaries of microcredit default much less on their loans than other economic agents, the survival rate of these microenterprises is high and their productivity is also high.

2 The origin of microfinance in Portugal

Microfinancing experiments, driven by social solidarity usually at a local level, have a long history in Portugal, dating back to the fifteenth century with the Misericórdias (Portuguese charity organization). In the second half of the sixteenth century there was the 'Common Granary' experience in which seeds were lent to farmers in years of poorer yields. Reimbursement, namely of interest, was also made in commodities. In the second half of the nineteenth century, the work carried out by the Misericórdias stimulated the creation of agricultural and industrial credit institutions, leading to the birth of the Caixas de Crédito Agrícola Mútuo in the beginning of the twentieth century. As small local banks, the Caixas de Crédito Agrícola played, and still play, a very important role in supporting small farmers, granting them small loans to face the challenges inherent in their activity. Finally, at the end of the 1970s, Caritas, a humanitarian organization of the Catholic Church, provided small loans to Portuguese people returning from the former colonies to help with their social and economic integration.

Unfortunately, most of the dynamics of these and other components of the so-called 'Third Sector' that existed in the first quarter of the twentieth century were suppressed by the long-lasting authoritarian regime that governed the country from 1926 until 1974. So, it was after democracy was restored in the country and the initial period when most of the focus in the fight against poverty was placed in the public sector, that the time came for the 'Third Sector' to take the lead in promoting microfinance and other forms of support to the excluded population. More recently, and following the strong boost given to microcredit by Muhammad Yunus, in Bangladesh in the late 1970s, new forms of microcredit emerged in Portugal, the most relevant of which being undertaken by Associação Nacional de Direito ao

Crédito (ANDC), in 1998, with others following later. Thus these are the foundations for the construction of a microfinance system in Portugal.

3 Main actors within the microfinance sector in Portugal

In Portugal, it is still hard to speak of a consistently structured microfinance activity. The microfinance activity that it has been possible to implement has focused on microcredit, leaving aside all other microfinance products and services. As previously mentioned, the organization which first promoted and most consistently developed microcredit in Portugal was ANDC. ANDC is a microcredit non-profit association created in 1998, which began its field activity in May 1999. It aimed to allow those who have been excluded from the traditional banking sector, and who have an idea and a project to create their own job or their own microenterprise, to have access to credit (microcredit). ANDC does not grant loans directly, since this is not allowed by Portuguese law.

Since 1999, the architecture of the microcredit system in Portugal has been based on the following key organizations and partnerships:

a. ANDC, playing the following roles:
   - raising awareness in the Portuguese society at large about the relevance of microfinance as an effective means to fight against poverty;
   - providing advice and technical assistance to those who want to apply for microcredit;
   - presenting those applicants to the banks which provide the loans and remaining as last resort guarantor of those loans, in the event of default;

b. Some banks (Millennium BCP, Banco Espírito Santo and Caixa Geral de Depósitos) are willing to provide microcredit to the applicants recommended by ANDC at preferential interest rates;

c. A public institute from the Ministry of Labour (Instituto do Emprego e Formação Profissional) whose main role has been to finance most of the operating costs of ANDC, based on the assumption that ANDC promotes the creation of employment.

As a non-profit association, ANDC today has around 320 members who contribute to a guarantee fund on top of their obligatory contributions. Members participate voluntarily in the activities of the Association in areas such as corporate bodies, credit committees, legal support, monitoring and mobilization of micro-entrepreneurs promotion, administrative support, and so on. ANDC's qualified staff is divided into two groups: the management/back office group and the operations group. The back office is composed of a Secretary General, one Secretary in Lisbon and another in Porto. There is also a group of volunteer workers who give support to this area. The operations team comprises one coordinator and 11 microcredit agents: two in Porto, five in Lisbon, one in the Algarve and the remaining covering the other parts of the country. ANDC has five volunteers on its Board of Directors, three volunteers on the General Assembly Board and three volunteers on the Auditors Board. There are also four Credit Committees (three in Lisbon and one in Porto) which are composed of five volunteer members each.

ANDC provides a number of services which involve the setting up and monitoring of business projects. The project setting-up stage consists of several interviews with the potential micro-entrepreneur with the purpose of helping him/her to build the business project and evaluate the feasibility of his/her idea. This stage ends with the preparation of the business plan and subsequent presentation to a credit committee which decides whether or not the application should be submitted to the bank. Once the application is submitted to the bank and the loan is approved, ANDC carries out follow-up work, in particular helping applicants overcome any problems that may arise along the way. A team of volunteer workers offer assistance in certain specific areas.

Following the partnership experience already established with ANDC, Millennium BCP, one of the largest commercial banks, decided, at the end of 2005, to create its own credit line. This is mainly aimed at an audience that, due to the more restrictive criteria, may not be considered excluded, but who still need support in spite of above-average academic qualifications and training. For this purpose Millennium BCP has opened branches in Braga, Lisbon and Porto. Besides this new type of microcredit the bank is maintaining its partnership with ANDC to provide microcredit to the applicants recommended by this organization, as has been happening since 1999.

Santa Casa da Misericórdia de Lisboa also created a microcredit bureau at the beginning of 2006, by means of a protocol signed with the financial institution Montepio Geral, to work with issues that arise in the communities within Lisbon, which they assist with social support services and subsidies. There is also word that microcredit activity is being implemented by some Caixas de Crédito Agrícola Mútuas in partnership with Superação SPA Consultoria, a project consultancy company.

4 Model of microcredit granting in Portugal: general description of the model

ANDC targets people who are socially and economically excluded and who do not have access to traditional bank credit. ANDC has only one type of loan, with a maximum amount of €10 000 and the minimum of €1000. However, the first block of the loan cannot exceed €7000, and only after a year of activity can a second one, to a maximum of €3000, be made available after an evaluation of the business. At the moment, ANDC has provided more than 800 loans for a total of nearly €3 400 000. These projects led to the creation of more than 930 new jobs. During 2006, ANDC granted 122 loans for a total of €524 000. A recent study (Mendes et al., 2007) concluded that these loans have been effective in the fight against poverty because on average, they increased the annual income of the applicants by €3740 in a country where the 'at-risk-of-poverty' income threshold for a household with two adults and two dependent children is €9864 (European Commission, 2006).

ANDC also aims to raise awareness and promote the concept of microcredit in Portugal. This is being achieved through the media, by meetings and conferences and also by publishing a regular newsletter, *Noticias do Micro Credito* (Microcredit News). In addition ANDC undertakes:

- intermediary work between promoters and financial institutions;
- monitoring and support to the micro-entrepreneurs after financing has been granted and during consolidation of the project.

Both Millennium BCP and Santa Casa da Misericórdia have set their credit line limits at €15 000 while Superação SPA Consultoria has a much higher limit of €25 000.

In every situation there is a microcredit model which, with the exception of Millennium BCP, has on one side the institutions that promote and monitor the development of projects (ANDC, Santa Casa da Misericórdia de Lisboa) and on the other side the financial institutions whose main role, by means of protocols signed with the former institutions, is to supply credit to promoters. The third partner in the system is the public sector, whose main role is to finance the operating costs of those organizations such as ANDC and whose main role is to reduce the transaction costs preventing the poor population from accessing the existing banking system.

5 Target groups in Portugal

The target groups are approximately the same for all the microcredit projects mentioned. In ANDC's case a solution is sought to the difficulty of accessing regular credit on the part of people who normally live on the fringes of society, provided they are in possession of a sustainable investment project. Potential clients would include those who are unemployed, who have never held a job but who have skills, or even with people who have a job but who are at risk of losing it. Other characteristics identified in a recent study (Mendes et al., 2007) covering the period from 1999 to the end of 2006, found that 52.8 per cent were women and 76.1 per cent were 45 years old or younger.

Millennium BCP's microcredit operation is designed to support entrepreneurship and fight social exclusion, having as its main beneficiaries unemployed people, family-run microenterprises, young graduates, immigrants and pensioners. Through microcredit, Millennium BCP finances and promotes people and microenterprises with viable entrepreneurial initiatives who otherwise, would have no access to the financial instruments traditionally made available by banks.

In the case of Santa Casa da Misericórdia de Lisboa (SCML), the objective is to provide financing through microcredit operations for small business projects identified by SCML, for the purpose of integrating the respective promoters into a work culture and to improve social cohesion. The conception and preparation of these business projects, the promotion and development of the entrepreneurial initiative, the setting up of the credit process, its concession and the support and monitoring of the people as they develop their enterprises, are all tasks promoted by SCML. Microcredit applicants must be between 18 and 65 years old, must reside in the city of Lisbon and have a limited family income.

The microcredit system promoted by SPA and the Caixas de Crédito Agrícola Mútuo aims to finance local entrepreneurial initiatives, self-employment and the creation of companies by people who are unemployed, who hold precarious jobs or who are looking for a first job.

6 Financial terms and conditions

Interest rate

The interest rate used for microcredit contracts promoted by ANDC is Euribor (6 to 9 months) plus a spread of 2 per cent, in the cases of Caixa Geral de Depósitos and Millennium BCP, and a spread of 3 per cent in the case of Banco Espírito Santo. The microcredit product as developed exclusively by Millennium BCP uses a variable interest rate depending on the risk presented by the promoter. The other two microcredit initiatives use preferential rates equivalent to those practised by the ANDC protocols.

Grace period, amount and others

The grace period varies among the various initiatives but is usually kept within the 0 to 6 months range. In the case of ANDC the grace period is usually 3 months and the tendency is to limit it to this period. In general, collateral is not needed but personal guarantees are required to cover part of the capital involved. In the case of ANDC, a guarantor responsible for

20 per cent of the capital is required, which together with the capital collateral has the purpose of providing the promoter with someone who may act as counsellor during the ups and downs of their project development. Repayment periods vary between a maximum of 36 to 48 months and are carried out in monthly instalments.

Main business services provided

It has previously been pointed out that in Portugal, microcredit institutions are not permitted to carry out credit operations or to accept deposits. This is the reason why they do not handle the credit contract side of the microcredit process. For the same reason, they are not authorized to supply other microfinance products. There is no information as to the relevance they may have in the everyday operations of financial institutions, although that is not to say that they do not exist in certain cases, namely under Millennium BCP's specific project. Utilizing Mendes et al. (2007), there are some indicators of what has been achieved:

- 780 loans;
- €3 530 000 of loans;
- average loan of €4548;
- 970 jobs created;
- 91.8 per cent of the total amount of loans outstanding on 1 January 2007, reimbursed;
- increase of €3740 in annual household income;
- survival rate of microfirms funded by microcredit: 69 per cent, well above the national average which is 47.6 per cent for firms with 3 years' trading or more;
- average cost (for ANDC) per loan, in 2005: €2734.

7 Other financial products for inclusion

It is not easy to say that there are, in Portugal, other financial products designed to promote inclusion. Indirectly, there are subsidy-type schemes that may be considered as such, sponsored by the Ministry of Labour and Social Welfare. There is a first category designed to promote inclusion directly: the 'Social Inclusion Income', a subsidy granted monthly to families in a serious economic and social situation, created to provide sustenance and simultaneously to produce incentives so that family members may find paths for inclusion (school attendance for children in care and job-seeking). In a second category, we may include a set of policy measures designed to protect employment operating under the supervision of IEFP (Employment and Vocational Training Institute). These include unemployment benefit (in various forms), granted to workers who are unemployed and who have contributed in the past to the National Welfare System. We can then find a wide range of options to promote self-employment or the creation of businesses (employment projects promoted by the beneficiaries of unemployment benefits, Local Employment Initiatives and Company Incubators), to support immigrants, people with disabilities and other specific groups.

8 Government support

Support has been granted to ANDC to help finance part of its operational activity in proportion to the number of microcredit projects developed. This financial assistance is justified because ANDC does not charge promoters for any transaction costs and because, since the government grants companies, in certain circumstances, with subsidies in proportion to the number of jobs created, it was accepted that ANDC's activity could similarly be regarded as a job-promoting activity.

9 Regulation: fiscal treatment, regulation of microenterprises, and so on

In Portugal, there is no specific legal framework designed for micro-entrepreneurs. There are only financial and fiscal regulations aimed at small and medium enterprises (SMEs).

ANDC has, for many years, been stressing the importance of creating a specific statute for the micro-entrepreneur, arguing that this should incorporate in a single document the existing regulations that may be applied to micro-entrepreneurs and provide a better understanding of the present omissions, while identifying policy measures that are lacking and need implementation. ANDC has pointed out that the type of micro-entrepreneur they work with has specific characteristics which should be taken into account within the legal framework. The first months of the enterprise's life, in particular, should be regarded as a process of vocational training at no cost to the government. Consequently, those who, justifiably, have no success with their enterprise should be considered as unemployed and thus be entitled to unemployment benefit. For the same reason, microenterprises should benefit from more favourable fiscal measures than companies that do not promote inclusion or that do not have inherent inclusion programmes.

10 Financial and operational sustainability

When analysed from a strictly financial perspective, the microcredit activity in Portugal has not been conducted in a sustainable way. The Millennium BCP project is, perhaps, the only exception since it is the only one to apply non-preferential interest rates. Lack of financial sustainability does not mean the absence of economic and financial sustainability. In the case of ANDC, in particular, this sustainability is obtained through the support of volunteers, member contributions and transfers from the government. It is not fair to assume that this results in hidden deficiencies. A recent study promoted by the Ministry of Labour and Social Welfare revealed that the work carried out by microcredit institutions is as efficient, if not more so, than that carried out by other similar institutions or with similar objectives, in Portugal and abroad (Mendes et al., 2007).

As in many other countries for similar organizations, a very high percentage of the ANDC's costs is supported by donors. The difference lies in the fact that for ANDC, public funding donations represent a very high share: the funds received from the Ministry of Labour total 91 per cent of the total expenditures of ANDC in 2004 and 2005. So the share of voluntary private contributions is still very small. This is not the case if we take into account what has been and continues to be the major resource on which ANDC has lived since its creation: the voluntary work of all those who have supported ANDC in different roles.

11 Challenges for the sector in Portugal

As previously pointed out, there is great market potential for the development of microcredit in Portugal. Any financial, administrative and institutional support that can be channelled to microcredit activities should not be regarded solely as an expense, but rather as a highly profitable investment in the near future. Consequently, there are three main challenges ahead:

1. The creation of a greater number of microcredit institutions; it is important that they are adequately sized with a strong participation from the civil society while assuming their citizenship responsibilities.
2. The mobilization and the raising of awareness on the part of social solidarity institutions working with the excluded, regarding the microcredit option for those living in precarious conditions who nevertheless, have the will and ability to be independent, autonomous and create their own business.
3. The raising of awareness of public authorities about the importance of work carried out on ethical finance. To create the necessary conditions for the introduction of alterations to the Financial Institutions Regulation that may, in the future and under specific conditions, allow the development of ethical finance institutions, a development that will bring financial, economic and social advantages to public administration.

Note

* Expert: Américo Mendes.

References

European Commission – Directorate-General for Employment, Social Affairs and Equal Opportunities (2006), 'Joint report on social protection and social inclusion, 2006', Luxembourg: Office for the Official Publications of the European Communities.

Mendes, Américo M.S.C. (coord.) (2007), 'Estudo de avaliação do sistema do microcrédito em Portugal', final report, Porto: Universidade Católica Portuguesa – Centro de Estudos de Gestão e de Economia Aplicada & Quaternaire Portugal.

7 Microcredit in Austria

*Susanne Zurl-Meyer and Horst Maunz**

National context

Austria, with its geographic situation in central Europe and its political and economical development, is widely respected for its achievements. With a population of 8.3 million people it has a GDP of 197.14 billion euros. As far as the economic situation and wealth of the population is concerned, it cannot be denied that the income gap is growing constantly. Around 12 per cent of the population is endangered by poverty. The groups especially affected are elderly people, women and migrants. The number of 'working poor' is also rising, especially among women, mainly caused by the increasing number of part-time jobs. Female participation in the labour force reached 64 per cent by the end of 2006 (Statistik Austria). In June 2006, 44 per cent of women in Austria were working part-time, whereas only 6 per cent of men held part-time jobs.

Another recent topic is the integration of migrants. In general, it must be stated that the period of unemployment is relatively short among migrants; the ratio of long-term unemployment among this group is also below average (AMS, 2006). In short, it could be said that migrants find jobs easily, but also get dismissed more often (ibid.). Another problem for migrants is recognition of their qualifications. According to a study done by the OECD, 21.1 per cent of migrants living in Austria are overqualified – their potential is not properly used (Der Standard, 2007).

From the year 2000 up to 2006 the unemployment rate was growing. Since the beginning of 2007 the economic situation has turned around, which also has a positive influence on the labour market. Flexibility and geographical mobility are still the big challenges for the Austrian workforce – and people are starting to adjust slowly (WKÖ, 2007). This problem is widely regarded as a result of an economic system deeply influenced by nationalized industry for over more than three decades. Jobs were secure, trade unions were strong, wages rose gradually, and most people planned to stay in the same job until they retired, and entrepreneurship was something reserved to a small group. The motto of the social democrat government then was, 'better to accept higher budget deficit than losing only a single job' (one of the most popular slogans of Chancellor Bruno Kreisky (1970–83)). From the beginning of the 1990s, the Austrian state started to

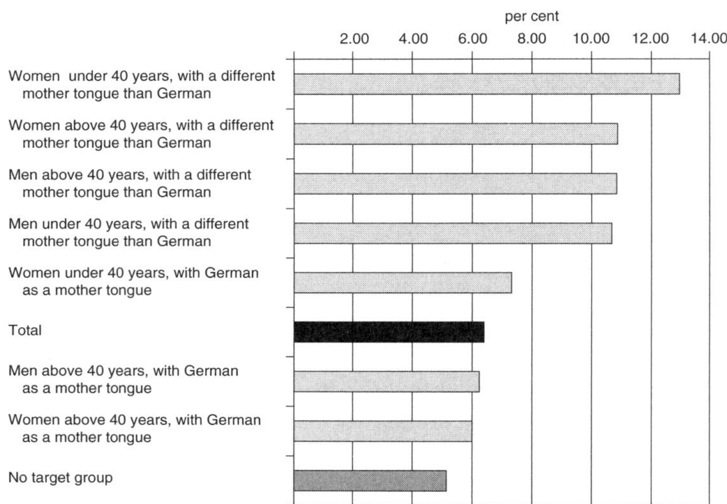

Source: Statistics Austria, *Handbook of Population Census* 2001, in TeReg-Evaluation report of the EQUAL project 'ESCAPE' 2006, p. 20.

Figure 7.1 Average rate of unemployment among target groups of the project ESCAPE (%)

sell its companies – which naturally had a strong effect on working conditions all over the country (ibid.).

Obviously, in a more competitive environment it is getting more difficult to succeed. Typically the groups which are excluded more easily from the labour market are: migrant women under 40 years old, followed by migrant women over 40 years old. Figure 7.1 shows the groups mainly affected by unemployment in more detail.

As an answer to the growing flexibility and job reductions, Austrians have gradually started to see self-employment as a possible alternative. The Austrian chambers of commerce are therefore confronted with a totally new situation – more than 70 per cent of its members belong to the group of micro and small enterprises (http://www2.wkstmk.at/wko.at/wup/statistik/ms2006.pdf). At the same time, the general conditions for future entrepreneurs are improving: there is a variety of support mechanisms to promote self-employment, as well as an improvement in the viability and growth of business start-ups. Support programmes are being initiated by the federal government and its institutions, as well as by the chamber of commerce. Besides various awareness measures, entrepreneurship is being enhanced particularly by training and coaching programmes and public loans. These instruments are open for potential entrepreneurs regardless of whether they are employed or unemployed.

Within the last couple of years, public support programmes have been adapted and further developed for the needs of different target groups, especially for academic entrepreneurs (individuals with high skills but possibly a lack of access to entrepreneurship).

In Austria, the number of sustainable start-ups that lasted more than six months in 2005 was 31 635. That means that 5.3 per cent of the adult population have been involved in start-up activities. 99 per cent of all existing enterprises are SMEs (firms with fewer than 250 employees). Micro-enterprises (firms with fewer than 5 employees) employed 19 per cent and small enterprises (6 to 50 employees) 23 per cent of the Austrian employed population (WKÖ, 2006b; BMWA, 2005; Sammer and Schneider, 2005).

The origins of microfinancing in Austria

Until 2005, small loans were not discussed very extensively as a possible instrument to support business start-ups. One of the first examples has been the 'success-based loan guarantee fund' which has been initiated by the Austrian Business Promotion Agency (AWS). Since then, the AWS has further developed its subsidy programme for micro-entrepreneurs.

Being aware of successful international examples, the idea of developing and piloting a microcredit model began in the region of Styria in 2004. In 2005 the Styrian Business Promotion Agency, SFG, and the EQUAL Partnership project ESCAPE developed two microcredit programmes. The SFG programme was dedicated to encourage and support existing one-person enterprises to employ their first employee. However, the microcredit programme ESCAPE focused on three target groups that were excluded from the labour market and had limited access to conventional financing alternatives offered by the banking sector. These groups were:

1. female entrepreneurs;
2. migrant entrepreneurs; and
3. male entrepreneurs over 40 years old.

Main actors and models within micro-finance in Austria

AWS: Austria Wirtschaftsservice (Austrian Business Promotion Agency). Austria Wirtschaftsservice, as sponsorship and financing bank of the Republic of Austria, provides subsidies, liabilities, low interest loans as well as consultation and services. The mission of the bank is to support the sustainable development of the Austrian economy. The AWS provides two microcredit programmes – one aimed at making businesses more sustainable, the other to enhance business start-ups. The two models developed by the AWS are called 'Jungunternehmerförderung' (Young Entrepreneur Fund) and 'Mikrokredite für kleine Unternehmen' (micro-credits for SMEs).

SFG: Steirische Wirtschaftsförderung (Austrian Business Promotion Agency). The SFG is the main actor for liability programmes and economic promotion projects in the province of Styria. The organization is owned by the regional government. Target groups for the SFG are in all sectors, except companies acting in the fields of tourism and agriculture. In 2006 the SFG was testing a microcredit model designed for existing businesses, especially sole traders. The SFG model was called 'Mikrofinanzierung 2006'.

In 2005 three EQUAL Projects were started in Austria – one in Tirol, one in the eastern part of Austria and one in Styria. Each was focusing on different microcredit models. The pilot project in Styria ESCAPE was based on the existing national framework concerning the legal system and banking, and concentrated on women and migrants, reaching around 450 people interested in the project. The microcredit concept in ESCAPE was developed and realized by the ÖSB Consulting GmbH.

General description of the models

'Jungunternehmerförderung'[1] *by the Austrian Wirtschafts service (AWS)*

The AWS 'Jungunternehmerförderung' is aimed at the promotion of start-ups and firm successions. One prerequisite is that the applicant has not been an entrepreneur before. This programme is a subsidy-programme for start-ups and therefore is not bound to the legal structure of a company.

Target group – premises for participation

1. People who are self-employed for the first time (or who have not been self-employed in the last 5 years).
2. People who started their business in the last 3 years.
3. Funding is only possible with a trade licence.
4. People with no salaried income.

Validity

1. Funding has been available since January 2007.
2. The programme comprises guarantees for investment loans as well

as overdraft credits. The investments could be up to a maximum of 600 000 euros; for the overdraft the limit was 300 000 euros.

Duration

1. Investment: 10 years (maximum 20 years).
2. Current account: 5 years maximum.

Interest rate per annum
Guarantee:

1. Investment: 0.6% per annum.
2. Current account: 2% per annum.

Loan:

1. Fixed interest rate must be given at the bank.[2]
2. Depends on dimension of guarantee.

Handling fees/taxes

- Guarantee: 0.5% and less than 25 000 euros: no single handling fee.
- Loan: depends on the bank.
- Tax: 0.8% for the loan.
- Handling fee per quarter: depends on the bank.

Special characteristics

- It is a guarantee for the bank.
- Extent of guarantee: maximum 80%.
- The request must be made by the bank.
- No counselling, no support before, during and after the loan is given.
- Cooperation between retailer banks and subsidy bank is complicated and difficult.

'Mikrokredite für kleine Unternehmen'[3] *– Austrian Wirtschaftsservice 2007*
This programme is meant to facilitate the access to microcredit for the self-employed and SMEs, excluding businesses in the field of tourism. The overall goal is to raise the competitiveness of SMEs by providing subsidized financing.

Target group

1. All foundations with a trade licence.
2. Businesses with fewer than 50 employees.
3. Businesses with maximum turnover: 10 million euros.

Validity Application possible from 1 January 2007 until 30 June 2007.

Loan

- Guarantee for loan for investment or loan for current account.

Amount Maximum amount of credit 25 000 euros.

Duration

- Investment: 10 years (maximum 20 years).
- Current account: maximum 5 years.

Interest rate per annum

- Extent of guarantee: from 0.6% to 2% maximum, per annum, depending on the risk of the project.
- No handling fee.
- Interest rate is 5% per annum (based on the 3 months EURIBOR).
- Decision of allocation of the loan is made by the bank.

Tax 0.8% for the loan.

Handling fee per quarter Depends on the bank.

Special characteristics problems

- It is a guarantee for the bank.
- Extent of guarantee: maximum 80%.
- The request must be made by the bank.
- No counselling, no support before, during and after the loan is given.
- Cooperation between retailer banks and subsidy bank is complicated and difficult.

SFG: Mikrofinanzierung 2006[4] In 2006 the 'Steirische Wirtschaftsförderung' (SFG) was testing a microcredit programme in cooperation with the Raiffeisen banks. The aim was to offer around 30 microcredit programmes for sole traders employing their first employee and for small grocery stores. The credit was combined with a supplementary offer: if the client took part in special coaching and training sessions, the interest rates for the credit could be reduced. The success of the project showed that there was a need for microcredit even among existing businesses. Within a period of 18 months a total sum of 300 000 euros of microcredits could be allocated.

Target group

- SMEs hiring the first employee, all sectors, except tourism.
- SMEs in the branch of food trading, e.g. groceries (complete food assortment), bakeries, butchers, pastry shops.

Validity From April until December 2006.

Loan 2 categories of loans were offered: for investments and for current account/giro.

Amount The maximum amount offered is 25 000 euros.

Duration

- Investments: 4 years.
- Current account/giro: 2 years. Prolongation for 2 years possible.

Interest rate per annum

- 3 months Euribor + 1.5%.
- 3 months Euribor + 0.5% after coaching.

Single handling fee 0.5%, at least 50 euros.

Tax 0.8%.

Handling fee per quarter 10 euros.

Special characteristics/problems Development of an alternative and innovative financing programme.

Alternative decision-making methods using:

- Check of personality/soft facts.
- Check of economy/hard facts.
- Coaching package.
- Free for the borrowers.
- 15 hours of individual coaching.
- Topics: economic, marketing and/or personnel.
- Reduces interest rate by 1%.
- Closer communication with the borrower.
- 4 business reports per year by the clients.

Results

- More than 90 inquiries.
- Loan most requested = giro of 25 000 euros.
- 30 loans allocated to entrepreneurs.
- Average credit granted = 17 700 euros.
- Most borrowers are in difficult economic situations (high liabilities, negative capital etc.).

Goals of the programme   Additional service for the two target groups.

EQUAL project 'ESCAPE – start credit accounting'[5] The EQUAL project ESCAPE was tested between 2005 and 2007. The pilot project was restricted to male entrepreneurs over 40 years old, female entrepreneurs, and entrepreneurs with an immigrant background in Styria, Austria. The project was initiated and financed by the European Social Fund (ESF) and the Federal Ministry of Economics and Labour.

The idea of the project was to implement microfinance as a new instrument against the background of the existing legislative framework and structure of the bank sector in Austria. Therefore, cooperation with the Raiffeisen Bank and AWS, Austria Wirtschaftsservice, was initiated.

The programme provided pre- and post-start-up business support and counselling through intensive individual and group sessions. Raiffeisenbanken of Styria provided the loan capital and disbursed the loans. The Austrian business promotion agency (AWS) guaranteed 80 per cent of the loans and the remaining risk was taken by the lending bank.[6] The maximum loan size was 25 000 euros and the base interest rate was 5 per cent.

The project ESCAPE made use of existing structures and was aimed to help improve and adapt services to the target market. Similarly, through the guarantee scheme, banks were encouraged to lend to clients traditionally excluded from mainstream finance. Operational costs were funded by EQUAL with the Austrian government co-financing. Project partners

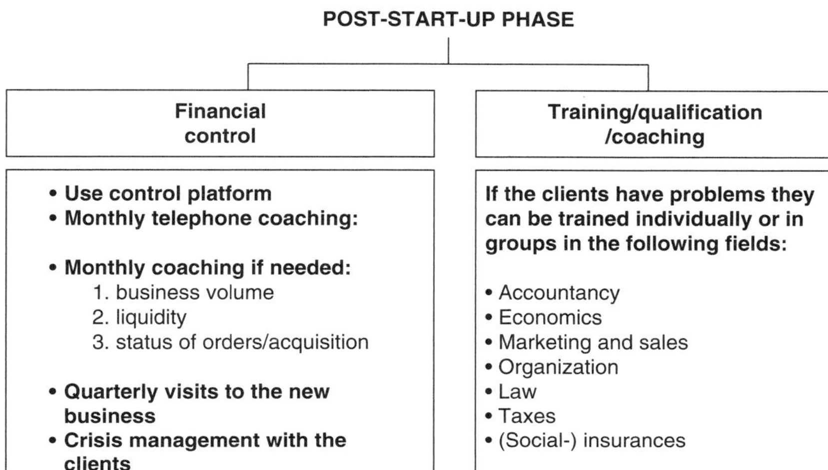

Source: Presentation EQUAL, project ESCAPE, ÖSB Consulting GmbH (2006).[7]

Figure 7.2 Support and counselling offers in the post start-up phase

were NGOs and start-up experts, and ÖSB Consulting GmbH developed the microcredit model.

The programme adopted several innovations to reach its target market which was considered one of the core tasks from the very beginning. This was characterized by an intensive outreach to existing immigrant and women networks. In addition, all programme partners, regional development staff, training organisations and bank staff, received gender-awareness and inter-cultural sensitivity training.

The counselling process in this concept was twofold – the 'pre-start-up phase' and the 'post-start-up phase'. In the phase before the funding, tailor-made counselling methods individually adjusted for each target group were applied. In the post-funding phase the funders were accompanied and supported with training programmes and offered personal coaching. One part of the post-funding counselling process was offered to all participants – the financial monitoring. ÖSB Consulting GmbH realized that in order to make a business sustainable, financial monitoring should be mandatory – preferably implemented in the loan contract.

Designed over a two-year period (including concept development), the first loans were disbursed in March 2006. Finally more than 450 people received initial advice, nearly 100 future entrepreneurs have attended training and support sessions, more than 50 people received microfinance counselling, and every third applicant received a microcredit loan, the

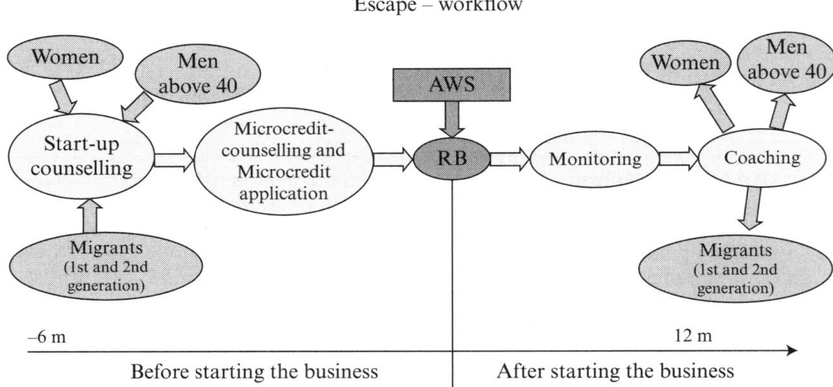

Source: Presentation EQUAL, project ESCAPE, ÖSB Consulting GmbH (2006).

Figure 7.3 Microcredit model of ESCAPE

average being 14 000 euros. Overall, 40 applicants were supported by the project (in some cases alternative financial means such as private funding and leasing were found).

Target Group

- Women.
- Men over 40 years old.
- Migrants (1st and 2nd generation).

The target groups were selected within the EQUAL framework, and were based on studies reporting that women, migrants and men over 40 were the most disadvantaged.[8]

Premises for participation

- Concrete start-up idea.
- Location in Styria.
- Professional qualification and/or experience.
- Need for financial support (less than 25 000 euros).
- Fulfilling the legal premises.
- Unemployment or in danger of becoming unemployed.
- Basic knowledge of German.

Valid From July 2005 until June 2007.

Loan For business start-up (loan for investment and loan for current account).

Amount Maximum 25 000 euros.

Experiences and recommendations for future microcredit programmes in Austria

Although the legal and economic background in European countries is quite heterogeneous, the main challenges and basic problems in connection with start-up financing are universal.

Similar structures could especially be detected with the situation in Germany. Thus, it was clear that many key points to a successful microcredit programme described by Jan Evers and Martin Jung were equally applicable for ESCAPE (Jung, 2006).

Experiences in accompanying and consulting the target groups within the project ESCAPE

Because of the nature of the target groups chosen by the project, it was clear that the need for consultancy would be quite high. In general, people with a migrant background have a greater need for coaching and training support in the area of microloan and business administration. Highly intensive counselling was needed especially in the area of general legal regulations, tax regulations and social security. The language barriers, limited, and in some cases even a complete lack of German, often demanded guidance in multiple languages. Through intensive preparation and personal support beforehand, but also directly at the bank and at other institutions, the insecurities of the applicant could be reduced significantly.

Recommendations

1. *Well prepared microloan applicants with professionally prepared bank- and microloan applications make it easier for the bank, allow an initial trusting relationship with the loan institution and lead to considerably faster decision making.*

   Experiences with the project ESCAPE and statements of bank officers who took part in the project show that without clear and transparent preparation, often five to eight contacts with the bank were necessary in order to come to a final loan decision. Surveys carried out by different experts showed that Austrian service users are rarely prepared for the loan application. Considering the countless start-up initiatives, this fact is especially amazing, since the support services are numerous and good. According to the banks it has to be said that in many cases the business concepts don't seem realistic. As far as the bank is concerned the main problem is selecting the right clients with a minimum of screening effort. A well prepared client coming with the right forms and reliable information could save the bank a lot of time – and more importantly increases the approval ratio.

Together with the project ESCAPE the applicants prepared a complete file containing all forms and information necessary for a loan decision. Thus, the time taken for the decision-making process in the bank was kept to a minimum (on average there were 1.5 visits to the bank, and the bank's decision was usually within a week).

2. *The function of the microcredit counsellor as a 'translator' between the applicant and the bank.*

   For the loan application the clients were accompanied by a microloan consultant. This was also highly appreciated by the banks. On the one hand the bank officers had a competent discussion partner who could be contacted in case of further questions. On the other hand a client seeking professional help and advice in the pre-start-up phase seemed more reliable to the banks.

3. *'Adverse selection' and the 'Pre-selection' of microloan applicants raise the number of lasting successes in granting microloans.*

   This argument is closely linked to the points mentioned above. During the project it became obvious that the counsellors also had an important selective function. The counsellors argued that socially and financially excluded people should not be led into self-employment, whether personal, commercial or other. Shortcomings could be detected. In many cases, the microcredit counsellor had to function as a case manager – showing the client realistic professional alternatives.

4. *Choose the right communication partner: 'Focus on a limited number of bank partners'.*

   Experience showed that the selection of the bank officers was crucial to the outcome of the loan application. For microcredit, a selection of only a few bank officers who can be contacted regularly is recommended. A good relationship between bank officers and the consultant has a positive effect on the microloan application (interviews carried out with bank officers involved in the programme). Nevertheless, the individual personality of the founder and his/her business concept stay at the heart of the decision-making process.

5. *Development of cooperation models between consultants, start-up centres and banks for the implementation of a future microloan sector in Austria.*

> In the Austrian banking sector, cooperative banks and savings banks have a high amount of client potential that can be described as 'bankable or nearly bankable'. Loan institutions and banks might look more closely at the international, successful microfinance organizations in order to have a better understanding in the area of active client acquisition, adverse selection and the use of alternative proof of loan eligibility, and the area of proof of securities.

Thus far, the existing start-up projects in Austria have concentrated on the economic effect, and not so much on the overall macroeconomic effects in terms of reducing social benefit costs, creating jobs for underprivileged groups, and so on. During ESCAPE local policy makers and stakeholders became more acquainted with the idea that self-employment and the necessary bankability even for such target groups sets up a positive impulse to raise employment among socially excluded groups.

The experiences mentioned above showed that the two-part structure applied in ESCAPE – counselling and financing – must be seen with different perspectives. Thus, evaluation criteria must be different. Efficiency is actually achieved through dividing tasks among highly specialized partners.[9]

In order to make microfinance in Austria more efficient, the liability programme of the Austrian Wirtschaftsservice GmbH (AWS), the loan procedures of the banks and the needs of the entrepreneurs have to be matched. Decision-making processes involving various partners slow down the process and make it impersonal. The development of offers specific to a target group has to be in the forefront.

The individual microcredit model should be adapted to the following factors:

1. Target group.
2. The actual microloan product.
3. The support service.
4. The policy of the bank.

Clear segmentation of target group, microfinance product, service system and the goal and motivation of the bank is absolutely necessary.

Follow-up programmes in Austria

Following the EQUAL project, the partner responsible for the microcredit counselling module, ÖSB Consulting, implemented microcredit into the most successful public start-up programme initiated and financed by the Austrian public employment service (AMS): the programme is called

'Unternehmensgründungsprogramm' (UGP). Microcredit counselling is now offered in five provinces in Austria. This programme reaches 9500 potential clients each year – and accompanies 4100 actual start-ups, which means that every seventh start-up in Austria goes through this programme.

Moreover, in Styria, ÖSB Consulting is also working on major start-up initiatives in cooperation with the Styrian Chamber of Commerce and the SFG, where the implementation of microcredit counselling is included. In the course of this initiative, innovative and young entrepreneurship is fostered in order to back up local economic structures.

Austria is definitely no longer a blind spot in the field of microcredit, though there is still a long way to convince the banking sector that this field is interesting in social as well as economic terms.

Notes

* External Expert: Michael Ploder. Research fellow at the Graz Office of the Institute of Technology
1. 'Young Entrepreneur Funding' (www.awsg.at), available since 2007.
2. In their newsletter of October 2007 the Austrian Business Promotion Agency published an interest rate of 6.54%.
3. Microcredits for SMEs (www.awsg.at).
4. 'Microfinancing 2006', (http://www.sfg.at/cms/1765/3969/).
5. The author of this chapter was a sub-project leader; concepts and results of the project are available on http://www.equal-esf.at/EqualDB/proceedBO.php?Entity=EP&EP_ID=128.
6. The Raiffeisenbanken of Styria and the AWS participated in the project as strategic partners.
7. Data drawn from internal reports (ÖSB Consulting GmbH).
8. Studies were taken from the Styrian Public Employment Service, http://www.ams.at/neu/stmk/start.html.
9. In the case of ESCAPE the counselling process started with a social worker, followed by start-up counselling, and finally microcredit counselling – which also represented the bridge to the bank.

Bibliography

AMS (2006), 'Jahresprofil', available at http://ams.at/ueber_ams/14172.html.

Arbeitsmarktservice Steiermark (2006), 'Arbeitsmarktinformation', available at http://www.ams.at/neu/stmk/600_inf_am_2006.pdf.

BMWA (2005), *Evaluierung der Novelle de Österreichischen Gewerbeordnung*, Vienna: BMWA.

Brickwell, D. (2006), 'The Tratoki toolkit: support and finance for small enterprises', Berlin: Tratoki Partnership.

Der Standard (2007), http://derstandard.at, 26–28 May.

ESCAPE (2007), 'Kleiner Kredit – grosse Wirkung: Mikrofinanzierung und zielgruppenorientierte Gründungsbetreuung', final report, Graz, Austria.

Evers, J. (2002), 'Kredite für Kleinunternehmen: Effiziente Betreuungssysteme von Banken', Frankfurt: Bankakademie Verlag.

Evers, J. and M. Habschick (2000), *Was können Anreize zur Weiterentwicklung der Mikrofinanzierung in Deutschland sein?*, Hamburg: Institute for Financial Services, International Labour Organization.

Förster, O., B. Maas and F. Zientz (2006), 'Handbuch', Berlin: Deutsches Mikrofinanz Institut.
Garrido, S. and M. Calderon (2006), 'Microcredit in Spain', Madrid: Foro Nantik Lum de MicroFinanzas.
Initiative.Frauen.Gründen et al. (2006), 'Kleinstkreditvergabe an Unernehmensgründerinnen', conference proceedings, Innsbruck.
Jung, M. (2006), 'Entwicklungen und Herausforderungen in der Mikrofinanzierung: Bewertung der Situation in Deutschland im Lichte der europäischen Entwicklung', presentation at the KfW sybosium Mikrofinanzierung, Berlin, December.
Ploder, M. and E. Veres (2007), 'Interne Evaluierung der Entwicklungspartnerschaft ESCAPE', Graz, Austria: Joanneum Research Forschungsgesellschaft.
Reifner, Udo (2002), *Micro-Lending: A Case for Regulation in Europe*, Baden-Baden: Nomos Verlagsgesellschaft.
Roider, J. and K. Hilkinger (2005), 'Ihr Leitfaden für den Bankenbesuch', Munich: LfA Förderbank Bayern.
Sammer, M. and U. Schneider (2005), 'Global Entrepreneurship Monitor: Bericht 2005 zur Lage des Unternehmertums in Österreiche', Graz.
Schwarz, C. (2006), 'Gründungsalltag, Gender und Gründungsfinanzierung: eine genderdifferenzierende Studie zum Gründungsprozess österreichischer UnernehmerInnen mit dem Schwerpunkt auf der Unternehmensfinanzierung', Vienna: ibw-Institut für Bildungsforschung der Wirtschaft.
Statistik Austria, http://www.statistik.at/web_de/services/wirtschaftsatlas_oesterreich/oesterreich_und_seine_bundeslaender/index.html.
Vondrak, Th., C. Schallauer and J. Zdrahal-Urbanek (2006), 'Funktionsweise von Mikrokrediten sowie erfolgreichen europäischen Mikrofinanz-Initiativen', Innsbruck: VondiConsulting.
WKÖ (2006), 'Mitgliederstatistik', available at http://www2.wkstmk.at/wko.at/wup/statistik/ms2006.pdf.
WKÖ (2006b), *Unternehmensneugründungen in Österreich 1993–2005*, Vienna: Österreichische Wirtschaftskammern.
WKÖ (2007), 'Österreich Diagnose: Einschätzung und Empfehlung zur Wirtschafts politik', Wirkschafts politik aktuell, available at http://portal.wko.at/wk/dok_detail_file.wk?AngID=1&DocID=649093&StID=310776.
Zdrahal-Urbanek, J. (2007), 'Internationale Literatur-Recherche zu Mikrokreditfinanzierungsmodellen: Erstellt im Rahmen der EQUAL-Partnerschaft Alternative: Selbständigkeit', Vienna: ibw-Institut für Bildungsforschung der Wirtschaft.

Recommended websites

www.ams.or.at: Arbeitsmarktservice Landesgeschäftsstelle Steiermark.
www.awsg.at: Austria Wirtschaftsservice Gesellschaft mbH.
www.oegb.at: Österreichischer Gewerkschaftsbund – Landesorganisation Steiermark.
www.oesb.at: ÖSB Consulting GmbH.
www.raiffeisen.at/rlb-steiermark: Raiffeisenlandesbank Steiermark.
www.sfg.at: Steirische Wirtschaftsförderungsgesellschaft mbH.
www.wko.at/stmk: Wirtschaftskammer Steiermark.

8 Status of microlending in Germany: an empirical survey of programmes in 2006

Jan Evers and Stefanie Lahn

General national context for entrepreneurship

Although GDP growth has been below the OECD average during recent years, the GDP per capita and the net real income per capita in Germany are still well above the OECD average.[1] The public support structure for enterprise development in Germany is comparatively well developed. The physical infrastructure is among the best around the world.[2] The level of entrepreneurial culture in Germany is low compared to the other countries in the study. In particular, the impact of risk avoidance behaviour on entrepreneurial activity is stronger than in other European countries.[3] Administrative burdens for conducting business activity are traditionally high in Germany, although recent reform efforts have improved the situation.[4] Income support programmes for self-employment out of (registered) unemployment are in place and have led to high numbers of start-ups out of unemployment in recent years. The access to external finance for start-ups in Germany has worsened rapidly during recent years. In particular, micro and small enterprises face greater difficulties compared to medium-sized enterprises.[5] A national microfinance sector is not well developed yet.

1 Introduction

Microfinancing is a success model of development cooperation. It refers to small financial transactions which are implemented very close to the clients, quickly and reliably through simplified procedures, and which support the clients in their economic independence.[6] The social objective is increasingly being backed by a business model and developed financial methodologies. Following Asia, Central and South America, now Central and Eastern Europe has become a region with high growth potentials and high returns on equity for microfinancing institutions. In Western Europe, microfinancing has been developing over the past ten to fifteen years and it is used primarily as an instrument for tackling unemployment and social marginalization. As a consequence, microlending in Western Europe concentrates more on start-ups than on growth financing. The focus is less on general financial services and more on small loans to be used for setting up or expanding businesses. The term microlending is used here to describe a loan of up to 25 000 euros. Despite the rising number of loan programmes and loans disbursed in Western Europe, the dynamic fails to match that of South-East Europe. An empirical survey by the European Microfinance Network (EMN) revealed that, of the 110 participating institutions in 2005, a total of 27 000 loans were disbursed and a growth rate of 15 per cent was reported. Only a few individual institutions can match international standards with several thousand loans per year and even these, at best, break even without so far generating any return on equity.[7]

In Germany, the past decade has seen a growing interest in and practice of microlending. In recent years, a growing number of specialized microcredit programmes have been created for start-ups and microenterprises with low capital requirements. Early in 2007, EVERS & JUNG carried out its third survey of German microcredit programme providers for KfW Bankengruppe. In 2007, 29 of the 33 programmes participated in the survey. A detailed analysis (including individual profiles of each programme) has been drawn up as an expert opinion and it will be summarized briefly here.

The objective of the survey was to provide an up-to-date overview of developments in the sector, including new providers, advances and trends. Following on the surveys of 2001/2002 and 2003, workshops were held aimed at positioning the sector and exchanging methods. Figures 8.1 and 8.2 set out the respective stages of development at the time.

How microlending in Germany has evolved in practice over the years since this analysis will have to be assessed. The following points highlight important changes in overall conditions during this period.

- The increased participation of regional promotional banks (*Landesförderinstitute*) in microlending: the Landesförderinstitute are regional development banks and, as such, are peculiar to Germany. Some offer microcredits directly (Investitionsbank Schleswig Holstein, Saarländische Investitionskreditbank); most, however, lend through principal bankers (L-Bank Baden-Württemberg, NRW-Bank and Investitionsbank Berlin).
- The establishment and expansion of the German Microfinance Institute (DMI), which now has 47 members and eight accredited microfinance institutions: in 2004, a funding tool was set up in the form of Microfinance Fund Germany to which the GLS Bank, the Federal Ministry of Economics and Technology and KfW Bankengruppe, among others, contributed.
- Improved empirical insights into the demand for microloans in Germany: according to the KfW-Gründungsmonitor, which monitors start-ups, almost half of all start-ups require funding of between

Source: Own considerations.

Figure 8.1 Summary of the first survey from 2001/02, discussed at the DtA-Workshop on 24 October 2002 in Berlin

1000 and 25 000 euros. Even if nearly half of these in turn meet their needs from their own resources, the remaining half form the ideal target group for microlenders.[8] In the KfW Mittelstandsmonitor, which monitors SMEs, particular attention is drawn to the rise in the number of businesses with low financing requirements, part-time enterprises and start-ups from unemployment.[9] Kritikos et al. (2006) conclude on the basis of a survey of 213 enterprises that a substantial, albeit small (15 per cent), number of those surveyed

What has been achieved?

1 Target groups reached

As a rule the programmes do reach the target groups which receive no loans from credit institutions.

2 Default rates

Default rates are partly below those of financial institutions in this market segment.

3 Financing and advisory support

Many programmes link financing and advisory support in an innovative manner.

4 Support effectiveness

Support through loans is more efficient, in economic and employment market terms, than through grants and subsidies (e.g. bridging money).

Institutional challenges

1 German Banking Act stipulations

Non-banks must cooperate with banks in granting loans. Regional and local authorities solve this by disbursing funds as repayable grants.

2 Low number of loans per organization

- Low-level standardization of procedures
- Unfavourable relationship between total lendings and overhead costs
- Poor economies of scale

3 Need for professionalization

- Products, support concepts and organizational structures and procedures
- International standards only partly implemented

4 High level of subsidization / Sustainability

Many programmes are heavily subsidized under time-limited project promotions. Customary operational and financial sustainability parameters rarely recorded and disclosed.

Source: Own considerations.

Figure 8.2 Summary of the second survey from 2003, discussed at a meeting of experts on 25 March 2004 in Frankfurt

would be prepared to pay interest rates of up to 20 per cent for quick, customer-friendly procedures. This group, with its demand for small working-capital loans following the start-up stage is not reached by the banking system partly due to its bad experience and/or low expectations.[10]

- The sharp rise in new business enterprises founded by unemployed people and promoted by funding from the German Federal Employment Agency (almost 1 million subsidized start-ups in the years 2003–05), which, at least in theory, ought to be requiring follow-up funding after the start-up grant.

2 Number of programmes and business policy orientation

Compared with the 2003 (2001) investigation, the number of identified microlending programmes has risen from 24 (21) to 33, of which 29 participated in the survey in 2007. Certainly, on the basis of the definition criteria in the international microfinancing literature, not all of these programmes would be covered by the term 'microlending' in the narrow sense. Their profiles were therefore already described as 'microcredit-type' programmes back in 2003.[11] However, the expectations vested in the procedures, products and results by microlenders have changed over recent years. It has become clear that microlending in a closely regulated environment of highly industrialized welfare states has a different function to fulfil.[12] While the dominant target group in international microlending is represented by existing microenterprises already integrated into economic life, microlending in Europe strongly supports not only start-ups and very young enterprises, but also disadvantaged target groups excluded thereby from economic life.

This strategy is clearly expressed in the term first coined at European level in 2006,[13] namely *inclusion lending*. Inclusion lending targets the reinclusion of financially and socially marginalized groups such as migrants and long-term unemployed persons, the *non-bankables*. Inclusion lending is distinguished from *microenterprise lending*, which looks to *bankables* and *nearly bankables* as target groups, namely traditional start-ups and small businesses already established on the market. Inclusion lending calls for distinctly more intensive advisory and support services in order to attain a high repayment ratio and economic survival rate among the borrowing enterprises.

With such target groups it becomes clear that there cannot be *one single* ideal lending model for the microfinancing sector in Germany. A range of different models must be available.

Given this setting, Table 8.1 differentiates the various initiatives according to *microenterprise* or *inclusion lending* schemes.

The programmes of the regional promotional banks (Landesförder-

Table 8.1 Exemplary division of German microcredit programmes according to type of target group

Inclusion lending	Micro-enterprise lending
• Enterbusiness GmbH, Berlin and Brandenburg • Förderung der Gründung von Kleinstunternehmen durch Erwerbslose, Hamburg State Ministry of Economic and Labour Affairs, Hamburg • GÖBI-Fonds, city and region of Göttingen • Gründerinnen-Consult Hannover, Hannover • GUM-Mikrofinanzierung, Bavaria and Saxony • KIZ Mikrofinanz, Offenbach • Microfinance for migrants, Mozaik Consulting, Bielefeld • Microloan of Mecklenburg-Western Pomerania's state ministry of economy, labour and tourism, Mecklenburg-Western Pomerania • Mikrofinanzfonds MaGNet, Rheinhessisches Gründernetzwerk (run), Mainz and Rhine Hesse • ProGES, Arbeitsförderung Kassel-Stadt GmbH, Kassel • Projekt Enterprise, iq consult e.V., Brandenburg • Starthilfefonds, Bremen's state ministry for employment, women, health, youth and social affairs, Bremen	• Berlin Start and KMU-Fonds, Investitionsbank Berlin, Berlin • Kooperationsvereinbarungen mit lokalen Akteuren der Wirtschaftsförderung, Savings Bank Düsseldorf, Düsseldorf • MikroDarlehen / Mikro 10, KfW, Germany • Mikrofinanzzentrum NRW, North Rhine-Westphalia and Lower Saxony • München Fonds, city and savings bank of Munich, Munich • StartGeld, KfW, Germany • Starthilfe, Investitionsbank Schleswig-Holstein, Schleswig-Holstein • Starthilfe, L-Bank, Baden-Württemberg • Startkapital, Saarländische Investitionskreditbank AG, Saarland • Startkredit and Ziel 2 – Hochschulgründerfonds, NRW.Bank, North Rhine-Westphalia

Note: The table only includes programmes where classification according to target group seemed possible and relevant. The classification merely indicates the target group to which the programmes tend in their loan disbursement.

Source: EVERS & JUNG (2007).

institute) and KfW Bankengruppe concentrate on microenterprise lending. The target group for inclusion lending, on the other hand, is not served by the regional and federal promotional banks. Here, the main participants are start-up centres together with the authorities and ARGEs (joint ventures between social services and municipal authorities). The underlying rationale reflects the closeness to the respective target groups and the capacity to provide subsidies. This differentiation in the market makes sense. Specifically tailored programmes, where appropriate with specialized actors and with higher subsidy rates, ought to be available for target groups with weaker creditworthiness but whose successful independence is nonetheless socially desirable. The regional promotional banks (Landesförderinstitute) are probably not suitable bodies for handling inclusion lending efficiently. That is the conclusion reached by the Investitionsbank Berlin, which since the last survey has stopped its labour-market-policy programme of interest-free lending for start-ups from unemployment. Now, it is offering BerlinStart, a new microcredit programme for start-ups with markedly higher creditworthiness, in cooperation with the Bürgschaftsbank Berlin-Brandenburg. In contrast, the Sächsische Aufbaubank – Förderbank –, which did not participate in this survey, has recently launched a programme financed by European funds under which interest-free loans are granted with low credit standing requirements of borrowers. No results are available as yet. Figure 8.3 sets out a more detailed breakdown of the target groups.

Compared with the earlier surveys, the focus has shifted. In 2003 seven programmes concentrated on start-ups *and* existing enterprises and 13, almost twice as many, concentrated *only* on start-ups, the present ratio is 18 to 11. However, there is so far no programme devoted exclusively to existing enterprises.

3 Geographical coverage and institutional framework

Table 8.2 sets out all of the 29 loan programmes surveyed and shows that the great majority of microloan programmes are offered at the local and regional level. The only nationwide player is KfW Mittelstandsbank with its two programmes, StartGeld and MikroDarlehen.

In Table 8.3, the programmes are listed according to their institutional background. There are three groups each with comparable size in terms of group members in Germany: promotional institutions (the Landesförderinstitute and KfW Bankengruppe), public sponsoring institutions, and initiatives accredited by the DMI with a private background Then, there are other institutions, which basically cannot be grouped into one of the above, such as the Feuerwehrfonds (fire brigade fund) self-help initiative in Westerwald and Goldrausch in Berlin.

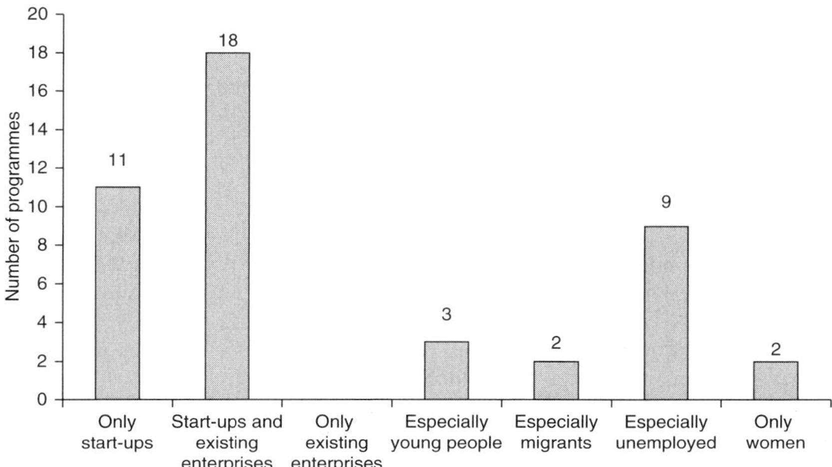

Source: Own data collection.

Figure 8.3 Target groups

4 Age of the programmes

According to the survey, the number of institutions disbursing microcredits rose by 12 between 2003 and 2006. As shown in Figure 8.4, most of the programmes were not started until after 2002. Four new microlending programmes each went to the market in 2002 and 2004, with a further eight in 2006.

Half of the new programmes created since the 2003 survey have been set up by the regional promotional banks (Landesförderinstitute). Five programmes appearing in the 2003 survey, on the other hand, are now no longer in the market: Enigma Siebte Säule Microlending GmbH and Emscher-Lippe Kleingründerfonds have ceased granting microloans. Three of these five programmes, however, are being continued in a radically modified form: the Investitionsbank Berlin's labour market policy programme has been transformed into Berlin Start; ProfiMannheim is a member of MONEX e.V. and handles loan disbursements through the latter; while Dresdner Exis Europa e.V. profits from the microcredit programme of the Sächsische Aufbaubank – Förderbank –. The microcredit programme of the promotional bank N-Bank was launched after 2003 but was already pulled from the market in January 2007 and is therefore not included here.

The discontinuation of the Enigma Siebte Säule credit programme

Table 8.2 Geographical coverage of German microcredit programmes, 2006

Local/regional programmes	*Länder*-level programmes	National programmes
• ELGO! Emscher-Lippe Gründungsnetzwerk, Region Emscher-Lippe • Feuerwehrfonds, Westerwälder Initiativen u. Betriebe Netz e.V. – WIBeN e.V., Altenkirchen and Westerwald • GÖBI-Fonds, city and region of Göttingen • Goldrausch – Frauennetzwerk Berlin e.V., Berlin • Gründerfonds, city of Paderborn • Gründerinnen-Consult Hannover, Hannover • KIZ Mikrofinanz, Offenbach • Kooperations-vereinbarungen mit lokalen Akteuren der Wirtschaftsförderung, Savings Bank Düsseldorf, Düsseldorf • Microfinance for migrants, Mozaik Consulting, Bielefeld • Microloan programme of the Dahme-Spreewald region • Mikrofinanzfonds MaGNet, Rheinhessisches Gründernetzwerk (run), Mainz and Rhine Hesse	• Berlin Start and KMU-Fonds, Investitionsbank Berlin, Berlin • Enterbusiness GmbH, Berlin and Brandenburg • Förderung der Gründung von Kleinstunternehmen durch Erwerbslose, Hamburg State Ministry of Economic and Labour Affairs, Hamburg • GUM-Mikrofinan-zierung, Bavaria and Saxony • Mikrofinanzagentur Thüringen, Thuringia • Mikrofinanzzentrum NRW, North Rhine-Westphalia and Lower Saxony • Microloan of Mecklenburg-Western Pomerania's state ministry of economy, labour and tourism, Mecklenburg-Western Pomerania • MONEX Mikrofinanzierung Baden-Württemberg e.V., Baden-Württemberg • Projekt Enterprise, iq consult e.V., Brandenburg • Starthilfe, L-Bank, Baden-Württemberg • Starthilfe, Investitionsbank Schleswig-Holstein, Schleswig-Holstein	• MikroDarlehen / Mikro 10, KfW, Germany • StartGeld, KfW, Germany

Table 8.2 (continued)

Local/regional programmes	*Länder*-level programmes	National programmes
• München Fonds, city and savings bank of Munich, Munich • ProGES, Arbeitsförderung Kassel-Stadt GmbH, Kassel	• Starthilfefonds, Bremen's state ministry for employment, women, health, youth and social affairs, Bremen • Startkapital, Saarländische Investitionskreditbank AG, Saarland • Startkredit and Ziel 2 – Hochschulgründerfonds, NRW. Bank, North Rhine-Westphalia	

Source: EVERS & JUNG (2007).

illustrates a phenomenon: the feasibility of a credit programme linked with the start-up centre Enigma was examined as part of a publicly financed project, and its establishment was funded. After all the documentation procedures, marketing work and so on had been completed, the first loans were disbursed – then the funding stopped and with it, the loan disbursements. The main problem was that the allocated resources for refinancing the loans had to be used solely for founders of new businesses, which had not yet formally licensed their businesses and which explicitly had to be unemployed. However, the willingness is especially low in this target group to take out a loan to finance a start-up. In this respect, Enigma Siebte Säule was confronted with a double problem: it had to reject a high number of loan applicants which did not fit the above-mentioned criteria, where at the same time there was a lack in demand of enterprise founders which at the time of credit application were still unemployed. A further problem was that the resources to cover the administration and advisory service costs, on the one hand, and the funding for the loans, on the other, had to be acquired from different sources, they did not become available at the same time, and they were geared towards different target groups. This further hindered the establishment of the scheme.

One source of financing for many programmes in Germany and the rest of Europe is promotional funding through grants. Those grants are

Table 8.3 Institutional types of German microcredit programmes (2006/07)

Publicly funded programmes	Programmes accredited by the German Microfinance Institute (DMI)	Development banks	Other microcredit programmes
• Microloan of Mecklenburg-Western Pomerania's state ministry of economy, labour and tourism, Mecklenburg-Western Pomerania Gründerfonds, city of Paderborn • Microloan programme of the Dahme-Spreewald region • Förderung der Gründung von Kleinstunternehmen durch Erwerbslose, Hamburg State Ministry of Economic and Labour Affairs, Hamburg • München Fonds, city and savings bank of Munich, Munich	• KIZ Mikrofinanz, Offenbach • Enterbusiness GmbH, Berlin and Brandenburg • Gründerinnen-Consult Hannover, Hannover • GUM-Mikrofinanzierung, Bavaria and Saxony • Mikrofinanzzentrum NRW, North Rhine-Westphalia and Lower Saxony • Mikrofinanzagentur Thüringen, Thuringia	• MikroDarlehen / Mikro 10, KfW, Germany • StartGeld, KfW, Germany • Startkredit and Ziel 2 – Hochschulgründerfonds, NRW.Bank, North Rhine-Westphalia • Starthilfe, L-Bank, Baden-Württemberg • Starthilfe, Investitionsbank Schleswig-Holstein, Schleswig-Holstein • Startkapital, Saarländische Investitionskreditbank AG, Saarland	• Feuerwehrfonds, Westerwälder Initiativen u. Betriebe Netz e.V. – WIBeN e.V., Altenkirchen and Westerwald • GÖBI-Fonds, city and region of Göttingen • Goldrausch – Frauennetzwerk Berlin e.V., Berlin • Projekt Enterprise, iq consult e.V., Brandenburg • ELGO! Emscher-Lippe Gründungsnetzwerk, Region Emscher-Lippe

• ProGES, Arbeitsförderung Kassel-Stadt GmbH, Kassel • Mikrofinanzfonds MaGNet, Rheinhessisches Gründernetzwerk (run), Mainz and Rhine Hesse • Starthilfefonds, Bremen's state ministry for employment, women, health, youth and social affairs, Bremen	• MONEX Mikrofinanzierung Baden-Württemberg e.V., Baden-Württemberg • Microfinance for migrants, Mozaik Consulting, Bielefeld	• Berlin Start and KMU-Fonds, Investitionsbank Berlin, Berlin	• Kooperationsvereinbarungen mit lokalen Akteuren der Wirtschaftsförderung, Savings Bank Düsseldorf, Düsseldorf

Source: EVERS & JUNG (2007).

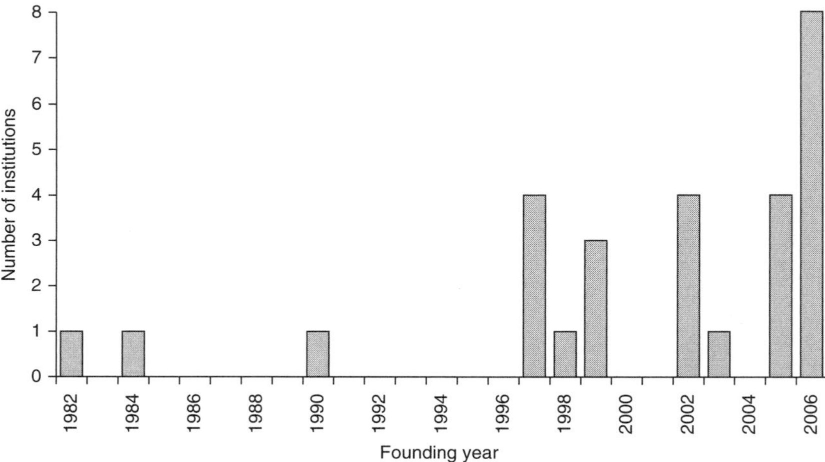

Source: Own data collection.

Figure 8.4 Age of German microcredit programmes

almost always limited in time and/or have conditions attached in respect of target groups. This applies in particular to resources from EU Structural Funds and the EU EQUAL programme. When the promotional funding ends, few projects manage to acquire follow-up funding for themselves by means of income, own resources or further promotional funding. They do not succeed in building up sustainable business models. This can be due to the brief length of the promotional funding scheme, wrong focuses set during the scheme, or indeed to the actors themselves. But it is a fact that massively hinders developments in the microfinance sector.

5 Disbursement of loans: number, terms and conditions, amount

In Germany, the microfinance sector is still young: its programmes are on average only 6.3 years old. Still, six years is certainly a long enough period in which to log successes in the number of loans granted per year and the consequent rise in earnings from interest. To what extent have the German microlenders succeeded in this?

The number of loans granted dropped from 6335 in 2003 (4665 in 2001) to 5983 in 2006. On average, 199 loans are disbursed per year and provider. The statistical spread, however, is very wide for the various programmes. The high average value is due to the participation of KfW and the individual regional promotional banks (Landesförderinstitute), which make between several hundred and several thousand commitments each

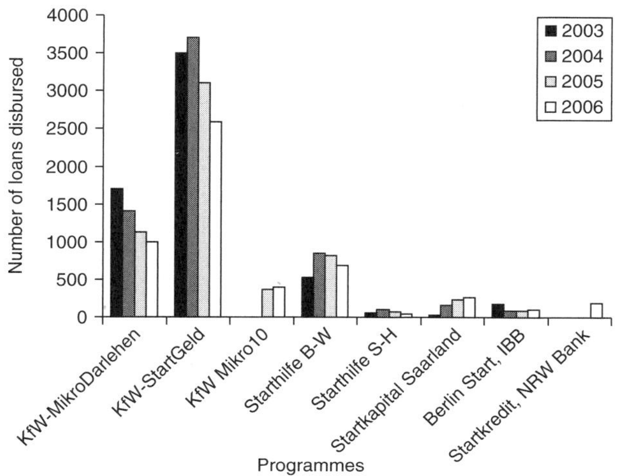

Source: Own data collection.

Figure 8.5 Evolution of the number of loans disbursed by development banks (2003–2006)

year and thereby markedly push up the average lending level of German microlending programmes. Figure 8.5 shows the programmes from the federal and regional promotional banks.

Figure 8.5 reveals that the number of commitments by the Investitionsbank Berlin has stayed fairly constant while it has risen both in the Saarland and under the new programmes Startkredit NRW and KfW Mikro10. The larger established programmes, namely KfW's StartGeld and MikroDarlehen and Baden-Württemberg L-Bank's Starthilfe, in contrast, register a drop, which more than counterbalances the above rises.

Figure 8.6 looks at the remaining programmes separately. Most of the programmes managed to push up the number of loans disbursed. Publicly funded programmes in Hamburg and Bremen appear to have reached a reasonably steady commitment level with total disbursements varying just slightly per year. Only the microloan programme in Mecklenburg-Vorpommern (Mikrodarlehen M-V) shows a sharp drop from 2005 to 2006 – although this was after a first year in the microlending business that outshone all the others. On the whole, then, there was an average rise in commitments in 2004 and 2005 with a decrease in 2006.

Setting aside the programmes of KfW Bankengruppe and the regional promotional banks (Landesförderinstitute), the average credit commitments per year and provider look much less encouraging for the remaining

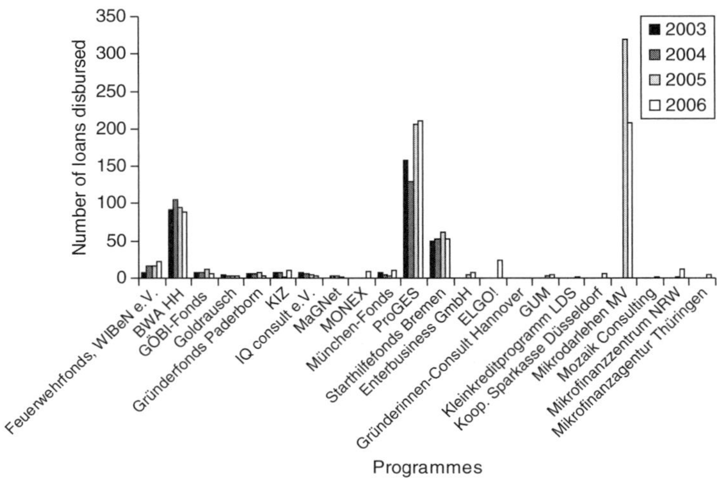

Source: Own data collection.

Figure 8.6 Evolution of the number of loans disbursed by public programmes, DMI accredited programmes and other microfinance programmes (2003–2006)

programmes. As a rule, fewer than 50 commitments are made per provider. The average here stood at 49 in 2005 and 31 in 2006. At this low level, it is hardly possible to cut unit costs to an economically efficient level – the survey waived questions about a precise unit cost analysis in order not to overtax the respondents. At 65 commitments, the European average is also at an unsatisfactory level[14] but in Germany the picture is even more disappointing as far as the number of commitments for the programmes of non-Landesförderinstitute (regional promotional banks) is concerned.

The programmes certified by the German Microfinance Institute (DMI) largely reveal low loan commitments (see Table 8.4). Individual new members such as the Mikrofinanzzentrum NRW at least show high rates of increase between 2005 and 2006. Along with the new members, the DMI can increase the number of disbursed loans from 12 in 2005 to 49 in 2006. If these growth rates can be maintained, the DMI could become a relevant institution regarding impact in two to three years – at present in the authors' opinion its level is not satisfactory.

Neither of the programmes linked directly to a savings bank, GÖBI-Fonds, and the cooperation agreement of the Sparkasse Düsseldorf are succeeding in reflecting the broad client base of the savings banks in the number of their commitments. The programme ELGO! set up in 2006 in

Table 8.4 Number of loans disbursed by DMI accredited programmes

DMI Microlenders	2005	2006
KIZ Mikrofinanz, Offenbach	2	10
Enterbusiness GmbH, Berlin und Brandenburg	5	7
Gründerinnen-Consult Hannover, Hannover	–	–
GUM-Mikrofinanzierung, Bayern und Sachsen	3	4
Mikrofinanzzentrum Nordrhein-Westfalen/ Niedersachsen	2	12
Mikrofinanzagentur Thüringen	–	5
MONEX Mikrofinanzierung Baden-Württemberg e.V., Baden-Württemberg	–	9
Mikrofinanzierung für MigrantInnen, Mozaik Consulting, Bielefeld	–	2
Total	12	49

Source: Own data collection.

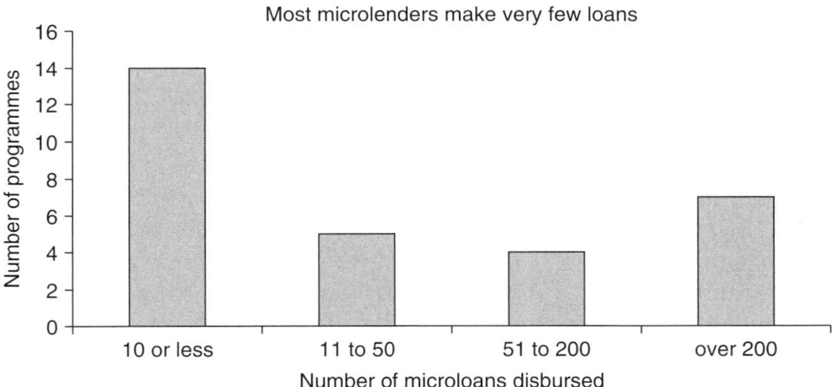

Source: Own data collection.

Figure 8.7 Number of microcredit programmes in relation to loans disbursed by microcredit programmes

the region Emscher Lippe collaborates with several savings banks and is showing a good start with 24 loans disbursed in the first year.

Figure 8.7 analyses the distribution of the programmes grouped according to the number of disbursements.

Of the 29 programmes surveyed, 14 disbursed 10 or fewer loans in 2006,

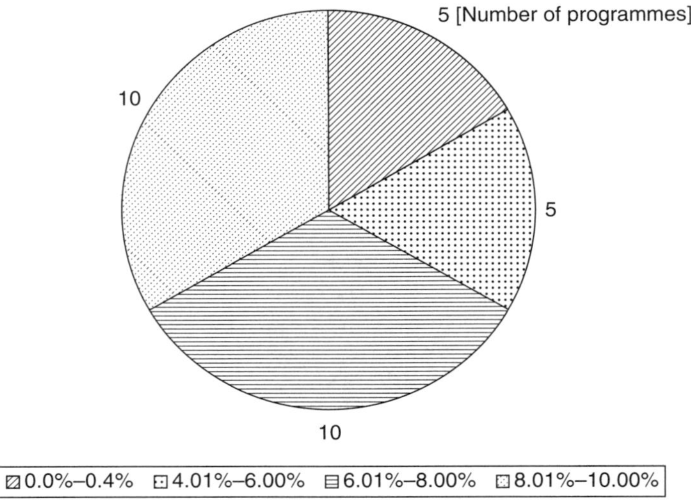

Source: Own data collection.

Figure 8.8 Interest rate ranges in relation to programmes

five disbursed 11 to 50, four disbursed 51 to 200 and seven programmes disbursed more than 200 loans. Five of these seven programmes belong to the group of business promotion institutions.

6 Loan interest and terms

Compared with the last survey in 2003, interest rates have risen by about 2 per cent to an average of 6.64 per cent. Most lie between 4 per cent and 8 per cent; the highest is 10 per cent (see Figure 8.8). The number of programmes which do not charge interest has fallen from six to three. Real borrowing costs are increased through fees such as application, administration or monitoring charges. An example here might be handy. Twelve programmes stated that they charged further fees in connection with the loan disbursement.

Higher interest rates and charges improve the sustainability of the programmes, since they generate earnings which can go at least some way towards meeting risk and handling costs. In the discussion of the results of the previous surveys, it was highlighted that interest levels from German microlenders were too low, and there was a discussion of whether market interest rates contradict social objectives. The change in practice and individual feedback testify to the convincing force of the argument that 'lending rates above market rates of interest prevent bankable borrowers from becoming free-riders in the programmes and at the same time they enable those target groups to be reached which are particularly worthy of support'. It can further be noted that the gap between German and European programmes, which charge an average interest rate of 10 per cent, has narrowed.[15]

The reduction in loan interest charged by leading promotional microlenders is a move in the opposite direction. A possible reason is an attempt to encourage start-ups. The extent to which this succeeds remains to be seen. Be that as it may, the reduced interest charges could possibly make it more difficult for microlending institutions to have higher lending rates accepted on the market and thereby improve their internal financing.

When it comes to loan maturities, the picture is encouraging. Short-term loans are regarded as good practice internationally. Although terms of up to ten years are still occasionally offered, possible loan periods have become shorter, dropping from 62 months on average in 2003 to 55 months in 2006.

7 Cooperation

At the German microlenders' workshop discussions in 2002, and in the preceding survey, microlenders registered a keen interest in cooperating with business promotion institutions (88 per cent) and financial institutions (76 per cent). This is increasingly being implemented. Cooperative relationships exist in 19 of the 29 programmes, with the cooperation relating to individual procedures in the disbursement of the loan.

Under present legislation, commercial lending in Germany is restricted almost exclusively to financial institutions. Cooperating arrangements between microfinance providers and financial institutions are therefore often necessary. Thus, based on Guidelines worked out by KfW Bankengruppe with microlenders and start-up initiatives and associations as well as banking federations,[16] a series of cooperative agreements have been reached between financial institutions, in particular savings banks and advisory centres. Sparkasse Düsseldorf, for instance, cooperates in the microlending disbursement process with several local actors in the local business promotion sphere while the ELGO! start-up network cooperates with several local savings banks. Both cooperation schemes state that the Guidelines were the starting point for their cooperating processes, but that they are the exceptions among the institutions surveyed.

A further eight initiatives have entered into cooperation agreements on the model developed by the DMI. Under this microcredit disbursement model, four partners (microlender, DMI, Microfinance Fund Germany and the bank) cooperate with each other to disburse microloans. Put in simplified terms, the work involved is handled by the individual partners as follows: (1) the microlender attends to checking creditworthiness and monitoring the microloan; (2) the Fund acquires and administers the risk capital; (3) the bank (formally) handles the loan disbursement; and (4) the DMI accredits the microlender and accompanies and advises the partners in matters relating to the disbursement of the microloan.

A far-reaching model of division of work is exemplified by the microcredit programme offered by the BWA, the Ministry for the Economy and Labour, in Hamburg. The BWA has outsourced several procedural stages within its microcredit programme to external service providers. One service provider largely takes over the pre-selection and the appraisal of the creditworthiness examination. Another attends to post-disbursement support and monitoring of the borrowers. Outsourcing the tasks to specialized providers keeps costs low for the credit disbursement process as a whole (including the externally provided services) compared with the programmes of other microcredit actors; as regards the BWA, the programme can in principle be operated and administered by one person with a half-day job for about 100 loans granted per year.

Cooperation between microlenders is a model which is still in its infancy. One opportunity for cutting unit costs, especially for the small German credit programmes, would be a division of tasks in the form of a central back office, as the English microlender Street UK presents as part of its StreetServe offer.[17] Local partners can concentrate more closely on marketing and thereby increase the number of loans. This could possibly be a development path for DMI, where work is already in progress on central database functions. The biggest potential for cost reductions would arise from the DMI offering its members a standard product.

According to the majority of responses from the survey, cooperation between microlenders and financial institutions is still not functioning convincingly. Reasons for this are, for example, poor communication between the partners and the lack of commitment on the part of the principal banks. Above all, there is a call for major projects to be jointly financed, for the cooperating partners to show more willingness to share risks, to raise the number of credit commitments and to cut handling costs. These causes require further and closer investigation, but the topic is of particular importance in that KfW Bankengruppe's Mikro 10 product aims for just such cooperation.

Legal framework for microfinance providers

In Germany the status of the banks is legally defined along the practice of credit allocation, so a banking licence is needed to give loans. The conduct of banking business without a licence leads to the risk of fine and imprisonment. The only way non-banks may facilitate loans for microenterprises is by cooperating with banks. Other providers are public authorities, where the legal status is somehow unclear.

Interest rate levels are limited by a usury law that forbids charging more than double the average interest rate in the sector (for example real estate, loans), or exceeding the average interest rate in the sector by 12 percentage points or more. Still, this regulation would leave enough freedom for German MFIs to charge their loans on a financially sustainable level. But for reasons unknown they do not use this freedom, as shown in Figure 8.8.

So overall, the legal framework for microfinance providers in Germany is very restrictive, the bottleneck being the bank status regulation.[18]

8 Summary and evaluation

In Germany the number of microcredit programmes has risen from 24 to 33. This clear sign of a dynamic process is not reflected in the number of loans disbursed, which is disappointingly low in practice. It makes sustained business development almost impossible: 14 of the programmes surveyed disburse only up to 10 loans and a further five programmes disburse up to 50.

After several regional promotional banks (Landesförderinstitute) and the KfW Bankengruppe launched their programmes, the average number of loans disbursed was 199 in 2006 (although without these the average is 31). This average distinctly exceeds the average figures from 110 surveyed Western European microlenders. Nevertheless, this German approach denotes progress only for the *bankable and nearly bankable microenterprise* target groups defined above. In the *inclusion lending* sector, which targets the integration of disadvantaged groups into the economic process and which is a key aspect in Western European microlending, the target group is not being successfully reached. There are some other elements of the programmes of the regional promotional banks (Landesförderinstitute) and KfW Bankengruppe that could be improved: elements of credit design and processes focus on the traditional way to start a business. Marketing policy could leave broader room for the presentation of the great variety of living situations and business models of microborrowers. In addition, elements of credit design/process which have proven to be successful in many countries (for example, monthly constant rates for loan redemption and interest or step-lending) could be realized. The often obligatory involvement of principal banks lengthens application periods and increases expenses. All too often programmes are largely designed for start-ups and young enterprises requiring application for the loan before the project gets off the ground. Operational funding for already existing enterprises is rarely available through any of these programmes. The rise in recent years in funding demands from the part-time and low-budget start-up target groups – partly financed via own funds or those of acquaintances – and from start-ups from unemployment[19] can scarcely be met with 'traditional' start-up loans. Here lies perhaps the most important reason for the overall decrease in disbursement numbers by KfW Bankengruppe and regional promotional banks (Landesförderinstitute) in 2006. The rising average level of loans and NBank's withdrawal from offering microcredits indicate that the major business promotion institutions have their problems with small clients.

In the inclusion lending sphere, a growing number of activities by local joint ventures (ARGEs) are emerging. The city of Kassel has had a pioneering role here since 1997, with its successfully functioning ProGES-Programm. The opportunities offered to the ARGEs in this sphere by the Social Code (SGB II) are currently being intensively analysed and exploited in, for instance, Hamburg, Frankfurt am Main and Münster.

So far, the establishment of the DMI has had no effect on the number of loans disbursed by its members. In fact, they have the lowest number of disbursements compared with the other groups (excluding 'Other microcredit programmes'). In the past three years, the investments directed towards the establishment of a multiplicative model have meant that a series of new participants have joined the microlending scene and are profiting from the expertise of the DMI network – although the programmes are not so far achieving a satisfactory number of borrowers, either individually or in total. This may be due to the complex structures required under German banking law – the loans are disbursed via the GLS Bank, securitized by capital stock and looked after by microlenders – or again, it may be due to a suboptimal focus in the institution's structure. It may simply be that the model still needs more time to establish and prove itself. It will be interesting to see the outcome of the analysis of the type of DMI member organizations that survive in practice: those offering loans as a secondary line of business in their start-up consultancy service or those concentrating on microlending as the sole business focus. Of interest here is MONEX, which separated the credit business from the start-up context and now offers loans through its own sponsoring organization.

Increasing account is being taken of the changed or better known funding demands of microenterprises: 18 programmes concentrate on founders and existing enterprises, with only 11 geared solely to start-ups. The empirical results from Kritikos et al. (2006), which are still quite recent and require further confirmation, point to challenges in the marketing sphere which can be met through adaptations in marketing operations.[20] This may well apply equally to publicly funded programmes, programmes in the DMI scheme, and programmes from the regional promotional banks (Landesförderinstitute) and KfW Bankengruppe. The changing patterns in start-up procedures call for changing responses not only to the level of loans required but also in timing, loan terms and application targets as well as the processes.

The promising strategy of setting small, flexible marketing units as interfaces with the client, as the American microlender ACCION advocates and practises,[21] is difficult to locate on the German market. Mikro 10, with its attractive commission and promotion of local cooperating ventures, is a first step in this direction. The low number of loans it has placed possibly points to a lack of interest in the proposed target groups on the part of the principal banks, which have to be involved, or to sub-optimal support systems.[22] A conceivable next step would be to develop Mikro 10 further into a wholesale product analogous to easy credit in the consumer sphere; it could then be disbursed locally without loan support systems. This might prove to be an especially promising model for the structures specific to Germany.

A look at other Western European countries reveals that three models in particular have proved to be relatively successful.

Finnvera, Finland's state business-promotion bank, in consultation with the commercial banks for microloans, decided on the direct disbursement of loans, and it implements the creditworthiness examination and support in its branches in key regional locations. The Finnish entrepreneurial base is less than one-tenth that of Germany, but Finnvera achieves 3000 loans every year, which is considerable in comparison with the numbers achieved by the microfinance programmes of the German regional promotional banks (Landesförderninstitute) and KfW Bankengruppe, which work in conjunction with the principal banking system. The Finnish banks, according to Finnvera, agreed to the direct disbursement because, at the next stage, Finnvera then again funds the small but established clients in conjunction with the banks. However, it has to be taken into account that the regional promotional banks (Landesförderninstitute) as well as the KfW Bankengruppe grant smaller loans up to 25 000 euros also within other 'conventional' business promotion programmes which are not 'explicitly' focused on microcredits.

In Spain, a series of savings banks have invested massively in microlending structures in the past four years and they are recording high growth rates. Their strategies vary. La Caixa, for instance, is the largest savings bank and it deals with clients in its own branches. The third-largest savings bank, Caixa Catalunya, has set up a separate foundation for its microcredit business, Un Sol Mon. Wholesale models, where marketing, preparation of the creditworthiness examination and follow-up support are structured into local partners on a commission basis, are at a pilot stage. All the models, however, have one thing in common: special structures are set up – at least for the back office – which then integrate the borrowers back into the standard business in the course of repayment. These examples could perhaps serve as models that might boost the number of microlenders in cooperation with German savings banks.

The French microlending organization Adie, with more than 6000 loans disbursed in 2005, also cooperates closely with French banks, which so far have funded some 80 per cent of the loans. Adie likewise functions as a local marketing partner. It has more than 100 branches and locations in France, and with its specialized know-how it handles the creditworthiness examination and support for inclusion lending and then passes successful clients on to its bank partners. The dynamic rise in lending commitments which the French microcredit organization Adie has been demonstrating for years now, and which the microcredit initiatives of the Spanish savings banks have been emulating in the past few years, is nowhere to be seen on the German market.

In conclusion it must be said that things are indeed moving in Germany, but not sufficiently. The breakthrough in microfinancing is still not in sight. Yet there are clear signs of a dynamic development emerging. Microfinance will only become significant if more players accept responsibility and really look at the demands of micro-entrepreneurs and -enterprises, develop and implement lean processes, and enter (aggressively) the current financing market in order to make microfinance a core business.

Notes

1. See Sternberg et al. (2007: 12ff).
2. Sternberg et al. (2007: 29).
3. Source: Flash Eurobarometer No. 160 (Question 12).
4. Sternberg et al. (2007: 22–4).
5. Source: Flash Eurobarometer No. 174 (Question 14 and 4h).
6. See Wisniwski, S. (2004: 1).
7. A detailed description of the European situation commissioned by the European Microfinance Network was published at the EMN Conference in April 2007 (Evers et al., 2007).
8. See Lehnert (2003: p. 19 ff).
9. See KfW Bankengruppe (2005b).
10. See Kritikos et al. (2006: 23–5).
11. See Habschick et al. (2004: 43).
12. See FACET BV and EVERS & JUNG (2005).
13. Budapest Conference of the EMN and MFC (June 2006).
14. See Underwood (2007), and the analysis of the results by Evers et al. (2007) as quoted above.
15. See Underwood (2007).
16. See KfW Bankengruppe (2005).
17. See Copisarow (2004: 40).
18. FACET BV and EVERS & JUNG (2005: Part 4, p. 19).
19. More than one million start-ups over the past four years were funded by the German

Federal Employment Agency, of which some 70 per cent were still on the market after two years.

20. Kritikos et al. (2006) point out in the study quoted above, 'Is there a Market for Micro-Lending in Industrialized Countries?', that there is a substantial, albeit small demand which is, however, not being reached due to inadequate demand studies by the micro-finance providers. The consequences were a mistaken target group focus and wrong lending products (p. 24). The authors also see as the background a delimitation of the target groups because of the link to support from public funds (p. 3) and an inadequate demarcation from the Alternative Bank (p. 25) in respect of speed and customer-friendliness.
21. See Rhyne and Lopez (2003).
22. See Evers (2002).

References

Copisarow, R. (2004), *Street UK – A Micro-finance Organisation: Lessons Learned from its First Three Years' Operation*, Birmingham: Street UK.

Evers, J. (2001), 'Microlending als Modell effizienter gewerblicher Kleinstkreditvergabe und seine Anwendung für Banken', in W. Fischges et al. (eds), *Banken der Zukunft – Zukunft der Banken*, Wiesbaden: Betriebswirtschaftlicher Verlag Dr. Th. Gabler GmbH.

Evers, J. (2002), *Kredite für Kleinunternehmen, Effiziente Betreuungssysteme von Banken*, Frankfurt am Main: Bankakademie-Verlag.

Evers, J., S. Lahn and M. Jung (2007), 'The status of microfinance in Western Europe', Paris: EMN issue paper.

Habschick, M., J. Evers and M. Jung (2004), *Finanzierung im Kleinen: Praxishandbuch zur Entwicklung innovativer Mittelstandsförderinstrumente*, Norderstedt: BoD GmbH.

KfW Bankengruppe, Institut für Mittelstandsforschung (Bonn), Rheinisch-Westfälisches Institut für Wirtschaftsforschung, Verband der Vereine Creditreform, Zentrum für Europäische Wirschtschaftsforschung (eds) (2005), *Mittelstandsmonitor 2005. Den Aufschwung schaffen – Binnenkonjunktur und Wettbewerbsfähigkeit stärken*, Frankfurt am Main: KfW Bankengruppe.

KfW Bankengruppe (ed.) (2005a), *Existenzgründer und junge Unternehmen gemeinsam stärken. Ein Leitfaden für regionale Kooperationen zwischen Kreditinstituten, Beratungs- und Wirtschaftsförderungseinrichtungen*, Frankfurt am Main: KfW Bankengruppe.

KfW Bankengruppe (ed.) (2005b), *Mittelstandsmonitor 2005: Jährlicher Bericht zur Konjunktur- und Strukturfragen kleiner und mittlerer Unternehmen*, Frankfurt am Main: KfW Bankengruppe.

Kritikos, A.S., C. Kneiding and C.C. Germelmann (2006), 'Is there a market for microlending in industrialized countries?', Discussion Paper No. 251, Frankfurt an deroder.

Lehnert, N. (2003), 'Ergebnisse des DtA-Gründungsmonitors 2002: Schwerpunktthema: Gründer im Voll- und Nebenwerwerb', DtA report, Deutsche Ausgleichsbank, Bonn.

Rhyne, E. and C. Lopez (2003), 'The service company model: a new strategy for commercial banks in microfinance', ACCION's InSight Series, No. 6, Boston.

FACET BV and EVERS & JUNG (2005), 'Policy measures to promote the use of micro-credit for social inclusion', study conducted on behalf of the European Commission DG Employment, Social Affairs and Equal Opportunities, Unit E/2, Zeist.

Sternberg, R., U. Brixy and C. Hundt (2007), *Global Entrepreneurship Monitor – Unternehmensgründungen im internationalen Vergleich: Länderbericht Deutschland 2006*, Hannover/Berlin: Sigma.

Underwood, T. (2007), 'Overview of the Microcredit Sector 2004–2005: covering EU 15, EFA and New Member States', EMN Working Paper 4, European Microfinance Network, Paris.

Wisniwski, S. (2004), *Developing Commercially Viable Microfinance*, Frankfurt am Main: Bankakademie-Verlag.

9 The microlending sector in Hungary: microlending to SMEs

*István Kovács**

1 National environment

The economy of Hungary[1]

Hungary has been a member of the OECD since 1996, NATO since 1999, the European Union since 2004 and is one of the founding members of the organization called Visegrad Co-operation. Hungary covers an area of 93 036 square kilometres with a population of 10 067 000 (as of the end of November 2006). The population density is 108 /km^2, the population is constantly decreasing (by 23 000 people annually) due to the high mortality rate and low birth rate.

According to its constitution Hungary has a social market economy based on fair market competition and a basic economic security for everyone, guaranteed by the state. Within the European Union Hungary is considered to be a rather poor country.

The GDP has been steadily growing; in 2006 it amounted to HUF 23 752 billion (95 billion euros), GDP per capita: 9360 euros. Compared to the European Union average wages are low in Hungary, whereas labour costs and duties are high. The average gross monthly wage was HUF 178 000 (712 euros) in 2006. The rate of unemployment has been rising slightly since 2001, despite the fact that the number of employees increased; it was at 7.5 per cent in 2006. Like industrially developed countries, Hungary has an ageing population. The activity rate of about 53–54 per cent can be considered particularly low.[2]

Hungary's finances are in the red; in 2006 its deficit was the largest among European Union countries. The level of national debt increased to 66 per cent of GDP.[3] The convergence programme designed by the government and approved by the EU was radically decreasing the deficit in 2007, which brought significant restrictions and tensions. Because of the convergence programme – at a cost of great effort and social tensions – the level of national budget deficit proportional to GDP decreased from 11 per cent to 6.8 per cent in 2007. The service sector is becoming stronger and stronger in the Hungarian economy; the economic structure can best be described as a developed industrial country. Processing, engineering and the car industry are dominated by transnational corporations. Hungary lacks natural resources, so its economy requires imports and the balance of payments as well as its balance of foreign trade are both in the red.

The role of SMEs in the Hungarian economy and resources available for SMEs

Micro, small and medium-sized enterprises play an important role in the economic life of the country: they employ 65 per cent of all employees, they produce half of the gross added value and they account for 36 per cent of all export sales. The majority of them operate with a high labour force and low capital intensity; they take a much higher share from employment than from sales income or income generation. In an international comparison the difference between Hungarian small and large companies is rather large.[4] Including the number of individuals carrying out economic activities with a separate tax number, the number of registered enterprises exceeds 1.2 million,[5] the number of active enterprises however does not reach 800 000.[6] The number of enterprises without employees is decreasing, while the number of enterprises with several employees is constantly growing. However, it is true that microenterprises with one employee are the greatest in number. Micro, small or medium-sized enterprises comprise 99.9 per cent of enterprises operating in Hungary.[7] Within this, the proportion of microenterprises, that is, those employing no or 1 to 9 employees is high (95.1 per cent of all active enterprises[8]), whereas in an international comparison the proportion of medium-sized enterprises is particularly small. One of the biggest problems is that the performance, capital and assets of Hungarian microenterprises are far behind the average of the EU 15 countries.[9] Also, the absence of notable entrepreneurial traditions, experience or knowledge, and absence of necessary accumulated capital significantly hindered the development and efficient operation (or simply the survival) of the enterprises. Even today a notable under-capitalization and lack of resources in micro and small enterprises still remains a problem. The evolved entrepreneurial group does not have an entrepreneurial past, which could have enabled capital accumulation. On the other hand, profit-oriented actors of the financial market are averse to financing entrepreneurs because:

- Small volume loans have high expenses and significantly high risks due to higher failure rates.
- The fact that the majority of these enterprises do not have a significant entrepreneurial past raises the level of risk.
- The business policies of lending organizations are over-cautious as a result of their bad experiences in the early 1990s.

According to the analysis of the Hungarian Financial Supervisory Authority for 2006, the profit-oriented financial sector is characterized by 'increasing competition, increasing hunger for profit, willingness to take greater risks, deteriorating loan portfolio, slowing business expansion, increasing competition for resources and deteriorating assets profitability'.[10] This is indicated by the number of market actors as well: there are 37 banks, 8 specialized lending institutes, 156 savings cooperatives, 5 lending cooperatives, 238 financial enterprises as well as 321 lending institutes servicing areas outside the borders, 22 598 lending institute agents and 8669 agents representing financial enterprises.[11]

Some experts are rather concerned by the widening gap between the rich and the poor, which generates notable social tensions.[12] Surveys show that to date there are 2.7 million people living below the subsistence level[13] in Hungary, 100 people freeze to death annually and the number of homeless people exceeds 100 000. Up to half a million people are undernourished, 300 000 of whom are children. The number of unemployed people reached 312 000 in late 2006 and the unemployment rate is 7.5 per cent.[14] The former traditional social benefits shrank due to the decrease in government expenditures, and private savings have virtually been eroded by inflation. All in all, there is quite a wide range of enterprises and private individuals with a chance of self-employment in Hungary. The development of these enterprises is socially necessary and viable economically but their requirements regarding development resources are not yet being met by financial service providers. This range of enterprises will be the potential target group of state-supported microfinance programmes for a long time.

2 The origin of microfinance in Hungary

The National Microcredit Scheme (MCS) was launched by the European Union Commission and the Hungarian Government in the framework of the small and medium-sized enterprise promotion programme of PHARE in 1991.[15] The main aim of the PHARE SME programme was to promote employment and economic restructuring through the promotion of the SME sector. On the verge of the political change in 1990, both the Hungarian Government and the European Union, found it important to increase the number and the influence of small and medium-sized enterprises, as well as to establish the institution of enterprise promotion. In order to achieve these goals the European Union – using PHARE resources – provided significant financial and professional help for the establishment of enterprise development foundations in the counties, the capital city and their operational organizations, called Local Enterprise Agencies (hereafter referred to as LEAs), as well as for the training of their staff and for the launch and operation of enterprise support programmes run by the foundations. The national network of enterprise promotion foundations in the counties and Budapest had covered the whole country by 1996. (In the initial experimental programme, LEAs were formed in six counties, then as a result of successful operation, LEAs were established in all the 19 counties and the capital city.) In accordance with the EU norms, the members of the network are: sector-neutral, operating by the principles of decentralization and regionalism, built on extensive local support and cooperation. The basic activities of the LEAs are counselling, training, properties (business incubators, industrial parks) and providing microcredit, as well as generating development programmes.

The concept of the National Microcredit Scheme was formed in 1991, reflecting the fact that most micro- and small enterprises were not credit-worthy for profit-oriented lending institutes. The solution of this problem is in the interest of the national economy, and required and justified government intervention. To finance the start-up programme, the European Commission allocated ECU 1.15 million from the ECU 21 million of the Hungarian PHARE budget designated for the SME sector in 1990. The first microfinance institution in Hungary, and among the first in Europe, began in 1992 with the enterprise development foundations of the counties and Budapest (LEAs) under the professional coordination and financial interposition of the Hungarian Foundation for Enterprise Promotion (MVA). The resources for the scheme were provided by PHARE (and the Hungarian Government as partner in finance) in the form of targeted support with conditions. The amount of funds available for microcredit has been continuously growing, and by 2006 amounted to about EUR 60 million euros.[16]

The development of the microcredit programme is the result of an integral improvement, which in certain periods of time did not lack regulatory, financial or operational shortcomings (see below in Section 4, especially subsection 4.2).

3 The major actors of the microfinance sector

A summary of the organizations described here is shown in Table A9.1 (see Appendix).

3.1 Government actors

It is the government's role to develop the policy and programme of SME promotion as well as to establish the necessary legal background, institution and the creation and provision of resources. Within all this, it is important to promote the access of SMEs to resources. The establishment of the legal and institutional background in Hungary has mostly been achieved; it only requires to be refined, and the current programmes to be properly configured and operated. Regarding the government management of microfinance, the role of the Ministry of Economy and Transport (GKM) is central because it supervises the majority of the national organizations that have direct relations to microfinance (such as MVA, MFB, MAG).[17] Furthermore, it is the Minister of Economy and Transport that oversees the owner's rights regarding microcredit funds as well as exercising government supervision of the National Microcredit Programme on the basis of Government Decree No. 2163/2004 (5 July).

3.2 Organizations with national authority and with direct relation to microfinance

3.2.1 Hungarian Enterprise Promotion Network Consortium This nonprofit Plc was created by the enterprise promotion foundations. A study about the network commissioned by the European Union (and carried out by the international consulting organization, DFC, in 1999–2000), recommended closer cooperation of the enterprise promotion foundations by establishing a consortium which would operate on market terms. The advisors claimed the operation of several LEAs to be of European standards, and they identified the main problems as being shortcomings in management, regulation and network cooperation.[18] Having accepted this recommendation, the foundations established the Hungarian Enterprise Promotion Network Consortium, as an organization without legal entity on 28 April 2000. Later in December 2003, the foundations established the National Enterprise Promotion Consortium as an NGO, which changed its name and organizational form to the Hungarian Enterprise Promotion Network Consortium non-profit Plc in 2007. This way the network can submit applications independently for programmes and tasks, as well as doing the formerly neglected work of network management and development from a common fund. In order to strengthen cooperation among the members of the Consortium, a web-based closed-communication Management Information System (VIR) was set up, which has been used successfully by the members for several years now. It has also been extended with an Internet-based service system for the clients. The consortium also registered the trademarks and the logo of the network as well as the product called 'microcredit' through the Hungarian Patent Office. The procedures of the Local Microcredit Programmes, which are operated under regulations of the network, have been drawn up by internationally trained experts of the consortium based on their 15 years of microlending experience. Under the name of Hungarian Microfinance Network ® the network became a member of the European Microfinance Network

– (EMN). Only the members of the network are entitled to independently carry out full-range microlending activities without being restricted by law.[19]

3.2.2 The Hungarian Foundation for Enterprise Promotion: non-profit organization (MVA) Since 2001 it has been the Hungarian Foundation for Enterprise Promotion (MVA) that has relayed the professional and financial support of PHARE for the creation and operation of the LEA network and the development of the microcredit programme. It is also responsible for the National Microcredit Fund. It operates under supervision of the Ministry of Economy and Transport, assisted by the National Microcredit Board. The MVA does not deal with the applicants directly, this is done by the local enterprise agencies (LEAs) in the counties and Budapest that are contracted by MVA. The entire process of loan assessment is carried out by these organizations. The MVA currently concentrates on the preservation of the National Microcredit Fund, that is minimizing lending losses in the National Microcredit Programme, as required by the Ministry. In order to increase the efficiency of returns it hires specialized companies to collect problematic loans.

3.2.3 Hungarian Development Bank (MFB) The entirely state-owned MFB, which operates on the basis of a separate law, was not engaged in lending small amounts to microenterprises. Its basic task was to operate the preferential loan constructions supported by the state for enterprises and local governments, which was done by refinancing commercial banks. It started to develop the so-called 'Microcredit Plus' programme in cooperation with the Hungarian Enterprise Promotion Network Consortium in 2005, then to operate the programme with the involvement of the LEA network. The main motive for the programme was the lack of resources and regulatory problems in the National Microcredit Programme.

3.2.4 Creditguarantee Ltd (HG Zrt) Creditguarantee Ltd, which was founded by the state and financial institutes, is experienced in the field of strengthening the security of commercial loans. The guarantee of HG Zrt became a key factor in the Microcredit Plus programme. The guarantee provided by HG Zrt is also associated with some PPP loan constructions developed recently by the Hungarian Enterprise Promotion Network Consortium and its members.

3.2.5 Hungarian Centre for Economic Development and Subsidy Intermediation Ltd (MAG Zrt) MAG Zrt was created by the government by merging former subsidy intermediary organizations. MAG Zrt became a major subsidy intermediary agency responsible for the Economic Development Operational Programme financed with EU Structural Funds.

3.2.6 Hungarian Enterprise Finance Ltd The company was established in 2007 in order to become the holding fund of the JEREMIE programme,[20] which was initiated and financed by the EU. One of the main aims of the JEREMIE programme is to promote larger and more extensive microcredit. In October 2007, the company issued the call for applications from potential microfinance organizations. The members of the Hungarian Microfinance Network are organizations with the potential to become microfinance intermediaries. Nine organizations from the 10 winning institutions are members of the Hungarian Microfinance Network / MVHK Ltd, who made a contract with the Hungarian Enterprise Finance Corporation in May 2008.

3.2.7 Public Employment Service (ÁFSz) The Public Employment Service is not considered to be a microfinance institute; however, the support promoting the unemployed to become entrepreneurs given by its offices, belongs to the category of microfinance due to its amount and objectives. The support is available from state funds at seven regional centres and 23 district offices. The service operates under supervision of the Ministry of Social Affairs and Labour.

3.2.8 Actors on the financial market Banks, specialized lending institutes, cooperative lending institutes and financial enterprises cannot be considered as microfinance organizations; however, we mention them here because due to the increasing competition among them they tend to offer their entrepreneurial loan products more and more often to micro and small enterprises, thus taking a higher risk and in the race for resources, the financial institutes frequently aspire to the public funds intended for microlending. In Hungary it is important to emphasize that the small-volume loans provided to microenterprises by financial institutes cannot be considered microcredit. Microcredit finances enterprises that are not bank-worthy, those that can not be provided with loans in the classic way from commercial banks. Therefore we do not cover the construction called Széchenyi Card in this study in detail since it provides short-term loans for circulating capital to already bank-worthy enterprises and those with a high turnover, and thus does not belong to the area of microlending; in the same way, the chambers or the offices of the National Association of Entrepreneurs and Employers (VOSZ), which promote the Card, are not microcredit institutes either.

In Hungary the business size of financial mediators and lending institutes has increased rapidly, and their profitability reflected on assets and capital has also reached unprecedented heights.[21] In the last year, however, while business size continued to grow at a relatively fast pace, profitability fell back, and the quality of the loans declined. This contrasted with the entire EU, where the opposite was seen last year.

3.2.8.1 Banks Table 9.1 shows that the sum of bank loans provided to microenterprises continued to increase dynamically after the halt in 2004. However, it must be noted that the growth increase can mainly be attributed to loans repayable within the year, and it is a significantly smaller increase in the category of loans repayable beyond that timeframe. Concerning the development of microenterprises, it is worrying that despite the strong increase in 2006 and 2007 the total number of loans for longer than a year is still much lower than it was in 2002 and 2003, and it is considered to be infinitesimal compared to the number of microenterprises (even if we take into account that a significant part of microenterprises consists of entrepreneurs who are self-employed from necessity, and who do not want development or expansion).

3.2.8.2 Savings cooperatives Savings cooperatives[22] are not considered as microfinance institutes either, their activities rather matching those of commercial banks; however, they are more willing to lend small amounts. Their lending activities range from personal and consumer loans to housing and entrepreneurial loans. Through their network of over 1600 branch offices the savings cooperatives are present in every other settlement in Hungary, and they provide financial services to more than 1 million clients. Ninety per cent of the branch offices are found in villages and hamlets where financial services are provided almost exclusively by savings cooperatives.[23] In the lending activities of savings cooperatives – in a similar way to banks – the total volume of short-term loans to microenterprises increased significantly; at the same time the number of loans with a duration of over a year decreased. However, it is noteworthy that the National Federation of Savings Cooperatives (OTSZ) and the Hungarian Enterprise Promotion Network Consortium signed a cooperation agreement in 2007 in order to strengthen the 15-year collaboration of the microlending of LEAs and the lending activities of the savings cooperatives.

3.2.9 Other non-profit organizations The professional and financial development of microenterprises is also promoted by a number of non-profit organizations that are not microfinance institutes, despite the fact that they often have remarkable resources, activities or achievements. Some of the most important ones are: Agricultural Credit Guarantee

Table 9.1 Loans to microenterprises granted by the banking sector (number of loans and million euros)

	2001		2002		2003		2004		2005		2006		2007	
	No.	Gross value	No.	Gross value	No.	Gross value	No.	Gross value	No.	Gross value	No.	Gross value	No.	Gross value
Total loans granted in the period	23724	1531	34841	1652	79084	1922	71940	1899	55209	2498	114701	3163	130479	4945
Total loans with duration > 1 year	10351	740	16947	936	18268	976	8176	804	10036	984	14005	1384	15721	2326
HUF loans with duration > 1 year	9982	550	16540	763	15436	647	5141	373	5055	419	7424	549	7107	788
Development loans out of the above	1988	127	3532	183	2233	154	1251	112	1193	91	1574	201	1461	242
Foreign currency loans with duration > 1 year	369	190	407	173	2832	329	3035	431	4981	565	6581	834	8614	1537
Total loans with duration < 1 year	13373	791	17894	716	60816	946	63764	1095	45173	1514	100696	1780	114758	2620
HUF loans with duration < 1 year	12730	650	17497	609	60073	792	61350	656	39672	1213	90026	1287	105317	1688
Export pre-finance loans out of the above	3	1	7	1	16	1	17	1	10	1	8	0	7	2
Foreign currency loans with duration < 1 year	643	142	397	106	743	153	2414	439	5501	301	10670	492	9441	1001
Total volume of loans (end of period)	41049	1667	36247	2103		2724		2989	67107	3591	104754	3582	121831	5127

Source: Hungarian Financial Supervisory Authority (www.pszaf.hu/engine.aspx?page=pszafhu-idosorok).

Foundation; National Employment Foundation (OFA); Life Career Foundation.

3.3 Microfinance institutions operating at local level

3.3.1 Enterprise development foundations in the counties and capital city (LEAs) The local enterprise agencies in the counties and Budapest that make up the Hungarian Microfinance Network are the most important actors of the Hungarian microfinance sector.[24] In 1992 the members of the network, for the first time in Hungary and among the first in Europe, started their microfinance activities with professional and financial support from the PHARE SME programme. As practical executors of the National Microcredit Programme in Hungary, these organizations have 15 years' experience and practical knowledge of microlending. The foundations are independent organizations with legal entities and were selected following a tender process. The business plans prepared by the LEAs were approved and also financed by the EU delegation and audited quarterly by international advisory or auditing firms. After the establishment of the network, the 19 centres operated through 150 sub-branches or offices, delivering business development services to a singularly wide range of enterprises at a high standard and cost-efficiently across the nation. In 1996 EU experts and politicians claimed the Hungarian microcredit programme to be a success story not only in terms of the Hungarian programme but in terms of all the Eastern-Central European PHARE programmes. In May 1998 in the framework of South-Eastern European Cooperation Initiative (SECI) and together with USAID, the UNO-EEC organized an Expert Meeting for the Best Practice of Microlending, with the participation of 12 Central-Eastern European countries. According to the British 'Bannock Consulting' firm, the Hungarian practice of the time was the best microlending programme in the region.[25]

In 1998 the PHARE support of the enterprise promotion foundations began to be scaled back with the intention that its role would be taken over by the finance of the Hungarian Government and supplemented by income from the sustainable programmes. Unfortunately this did not take place, probably due to network management shortcomings. When the programme-leading PHARE experts left, the professional standards of national coordination declined, and the staff of central management became over-politicized. From 1999, there was a tendency for Network programmes to be taken away from the LEA network. Despite all this, the LEA network did not weaken notably and they all continued. The network itself managed to remain operational. In achieving this, the following factors must have played an important part: knowledge, which

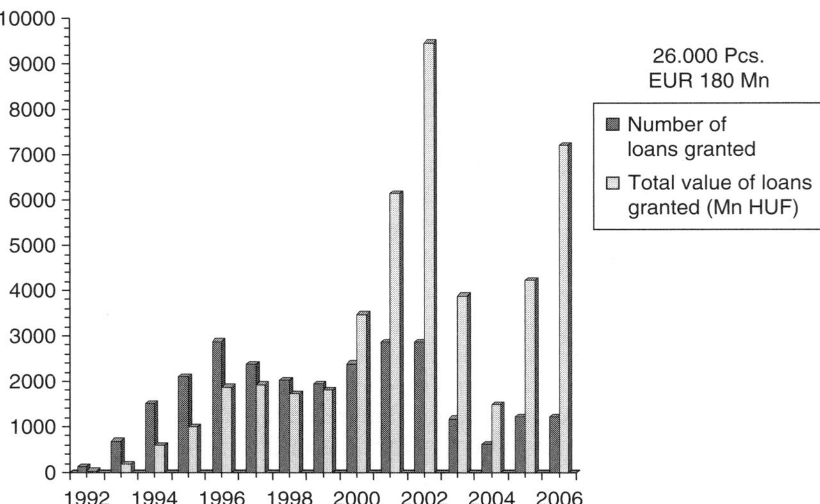

Source: From presentation by István Kovács.

Figure 9.1 Microloans granted by the LEA Network in Hungary between 1992–2006

became marketable; activities that became self-sustainable due to incomes from services; the microcredit totals of LEAs and probably their cooperation established with the creation of the consortium in 2000.

From the beginning to the end of 2007 the LEA Network made over 27 000 loan contracts and provided over HUF 50 billion (about 200 million euros) worth of microcredit and Microcredit Plus for the microenterprises, while permanent lack of resources and shortcomings in central regulations hindered their operation.

The explanation for the cycles seen in Figure 9.1 is the following: as long as the local funds were provided with PHARE resources (between 1992 and 1996), the number of loans granted increased. After that the number of loans decreased; new loans could only been granted from the already repaid amounts. In 1999 and 2000, when new funding arrived, the total amount granted grew again, especially as the upper limit of a single loan was increased to HUF 3 million (12 000 euros) and later to HUF 6 million (24 000 euros). Owing to the operational shortcomings of the centralized fund, the National Microcredit Fund (OMA) was spent by August 2002, and the programme halted. The inflexible operation and the lowering of the grantable amount from HUF 6 million (24 000 euros) back to HUF 3 million (12 000 euros) resulted in the near failure of the programme, as enterprises were unable to apply for the loans. Consequently, by 2004, ungranted amounts of HUF billions (about 8–12 million euros) were accumulated in the fund. As the terms became more favourable for the enterprises, the programme re-ignited, so that the reserves of the Fund were exhausted again by 2006.

3.3.2 Other non-profit microfinance institutes Apart from the LEAs operating the microcredit programme, there are some more non-profit organizations (for example Life Career Foundation) that also carry out microfinance activities. However, their individual role and success in enterprise promotion are dwarfed by the lending work of the LEAs in terms of the number of financed enterprises and volume of loans.

4 The operational models of the individual microfinance programmes

Due to their importance and performance we provide more detailed descriptions of the models of microcredit constructions originating from way back in 1991–92 run by the enterprise promotion foundations.

4.1 The model of the basic construction operating between 1992 and 2000
The local enterprise agencies received microcredit funds as targeted grants with conditions from the EU PHARE programme. The funds operated in a decentralized way; each county enterprise promotion foundation managed its own fund, which was separated from its other resources. The terms and operational regulations of the programme were written by international and Hungarian experts (staff of LEAs, among others). In order to operate the programme each foundation created its own microcredit division, and appointed a microcredit manager to run it. The microcredit managers obtained the expertise to handle the funds from qualifying courses and in international exchange programmes.

The entire process of loan assessment and portfolio handling in microlending was done by the microcredit divisions of the foundations. The approval of loan applications was made by Microcredit Boards created by each foundation. In the work of these boards economists, lawyers, bank experts, entrepreneurs and foundation staff participated in the form of social contribution. Preparation of the approval process meant the examination of the business plan presented on the application form and also a site visit in each case. Then on the basis of the preparation work done by the microcredit division, the Microcredit Board decided on the approval of the loan application.

In accordance with the legal regulations of the time, each foundation contracted a financial institute – mostly a savings cooperative – chosen in a call for tender to grant and collect the loans. The financial institute granted the loans for a fee from the local microcredit funds deposited at the institute making loan contracts with the clients, then collected repayments and interests as well as making records of the loans. It was the duty of the microcredit division of the foundation to supervise the credit portfolio, to carry out follow-up check-ups and manage legal procedures of occasional dead loans.

The procedures were characterized by fast and flexible operation, and the foundations exercised maximum tolerance towards enterprises with financial difficulties. In the first period the foundations were not allowed to ask for more collateral than the assets purchased from the loaned amount, so that the social aims could be achieved. The financial accounts of the programmes were checked quarterly by international auditing firms. Central coordination tasks were carried out by a manager and a clerk. From the beginning, related counselling and training activities were important elements of the microcredit programme. These were also entirely financed from PHARE funds in this period, in a way scheduled and detailed in the annual business plans of the LEAs. There was continuous professional consultation between the national coordinator and the practical experts (national professional meetings, exchange events). Suggestions for modifying the manual, which described the programme operation, could be implemented only after having been approved in Brussels, which was usually a long process, but it ensured professional control.

4.2 The centralized model introduced in 2000

The success of the decentralized programme and the build-up of the local funds surprised and raised the interest of many in both a positive and negative sense. Between 1998 and 2000 a number of revisions, assessments and concepts were made about the programme's present and future. In 2000, a contract was signed, creating the National Microcredit Fund (OMA) by centralizing the formerly decentralized funds. The centralized operation of the microcredit programme had a number of drawbacks. The processes became sluggish, less flexible and the central apparatus significantly expanded, thus making programme operation more expensive. Plus, the professional consultation between the practical experts and the centre management has not been sufficiently developed to compensate the abovementioned deficits. However, the centralization of funds did allow for the amount of microcredit that could be granted in the programme first to HUF 3 million (12 000 euros) then soon to HUF 6 million (24 000 euros) as urged by the LEAs previously, and to significantly improve the terms of the credit construction. It was, however, a major mistake – according to the regional microfinance organizations – to 'harden' the previously flexible collateral assessment regulations. This significantly detached the programme from its original aim, and even today excludes the neediest group of the population that does not have the necessary collateral to apply for microcredit.

4.3 Constructions currently operated by the Hungarian Microfinance Network

In December 2005, after several years of professional debate, the economic minister, who was supervising the programme, approved of most of the initiatives of the Hungarian Enterprise Promotion Network Consortium regarding the re-establishment of the Local Microcredit Funds and the rationalization of the National Microcredit Programme. Thus in 2006–2007 the Local Microcredit Funds were re-established. The Hungarian Enterprise Promotion Network Consortium developed the system of multi-stage microcredit constructions, which are built on each other and are still operated by the members of the network. The general aims of the programmes are to:

1. provide financial support and business consultation;
2. support microenterprises that are not credit-worthy for commercial banks but viable for development;
3. complement the services of commercial banks;
4. serve groups of society with disadvantages (minorities, large families, women, the young, the unemployed and so on), as part of the fight against poverty, promoting the process of becoming an entrepreneur or self-employed, and making them bank-worthy.

The basis of all these elements was the successful decentralized model run before 2000. They are all offered by the LEAs in an integrated service package, the elements of which are the counselling and training programmes run by the LEAs.

4.3.1 Local microcredit programme from the resources of the re-established Local Microcredit Funds The model of this programme is almost identical to the one run before 2000, with the exception that today there is no need to involve a participating bank due to the legal authorization (see the details below in section 9, first paragraph). The LEAs make the microcredit contracts in their own names, and they may transfer the sums approved by the microcredit boards directly from their bank accounts to the enterprises. Keeping records of the loans is also undertaken by the foundations with help of an Internet-based record-keeping service, which has been developed by one of the members of the network: Fejér Enterprise Agency. This enables the clients to send their applications and to access data about their debts through the Internet, and enables the donors to track the financial usage of the loan funds handled. Lending is supplemented by a consultation service.

4.3.1.1 Local Special Programmes from the resources of other donors Knowing the success of the Local Microcredit Programme, in some cases outside donors (such as IBM) provided resources to an LEA for the purpose of microlending in the interest of helping redundant employees to become entrepreneurs.

4.3.2 National Microcredit Programme from the resources of the National Microcredit Fund In the arrangement that became more rational and flexible from 2006, it is still the LEAs that receive the microcredit applications, assess the business plans, make site visits (and also carry out related counselling). The decisions are made by the Microcredit Boards of the LEAs but they must also be approved by MVA. In the central model the contracts today are not made by the local branch offices of the central bank, but by the LEAs on behalf of MVA. Money transfers are also made by authorized staff of the LEAs but only after approval by MVA and from MVA's bank account. Consequently, some of the problems that arose from the centralized operation still exist.

4.3.3 Microcredit Plus Programme from the resources of the Hungarian Development Bank (MFB) The Microcredit Plus programme was developed jointly by experts of the Hungarian Enterprise Promotion Network Consortium and the Hungarian Development Bank. The target group of the Microcredit Plus Programme is a slightly more prepared, viable group of microenterprises. In this programme the LEAs (or companies owned by them) receive microcredit applications, make assessments and site visits (and carry out related counselling). The decisions are made by the MFB with the help of forms completed electronically by the LEAs. The approved contracts are signed by the staff of the LEAs authorized to do so by MFB. The sums are transferred to the enterprises by MFB on the basis of the withdrawal advice made by the LEAs. The original documents need not be sent to MFB.

4.3.4 Small enterprise loan arrangements with the involvement of the resources of the Local Microcredit Funds and financial institutes (PPP-like constructions) There are several elements in the network that are operated by the LEAs together with banks or mostly savings cooperatives using the resources of local funds. In recognition of this work in 2001 a member of the network called Budapest Enterprise Promotion Public Foundation was awarded the Innovative City Strategies Award of EUROCITIES, an organization of European Cities, for the Budapest Small Enterprise Loan provision.

In these arrangements the savings cooperative and the microcredit board of the LEA make a simultaneous decision about the finance of a microenterprise. The contract is also made simultaneously by signing one or two parallel contracts (for example: 50 per cent of the required credit is given by LEAs on the rate of the Central Bank as microcredit, and the other 50 per cent is given by savings on market rates).

4.3.5 New Hungary Microcredit Programme (JEREMIE) Half of the LEAs could connect to the New Hungary Microcredit Programme, which is launched on the JEREMIE Programme initiative and promoted from EU funds in the frame of Economic Operative Programme (GOP). By June 2008, 11 LEAs had won refinancing funding from the Hungarian Enterprise Finance Corporation (nine LEAs also had a contract) and they started to grant microloans. In the frame of conditions given by the Hungarian Enterprise Finance Corporation, LEAs had the opportunity to decide freely about the loan construction and the details of actuation.

4.3.6 Microfactoring arrangements The consortium already suggested years before that a microfactoring programme should be added to the microfinance provision. The Ministry of Economy and Transport announced the Lanchid Factoring Programme in 2003, in which it granted support to microenterprises. The programme was later suspended and subsequently restarted, but without interest rate support for SMEs taking factoring services. The consortium suggests continuing the programme in a more efficient way, so that factoring companies provided with cheap funding would be able to offer low-cost factoring services in connection with consulting and educational services of the LEAs.

5 Microfinance target groups

The entrepreneurs and their enterprises that apply for the financial support of either the National Microcredit Programme or the Local Microcredit Programme, which are operated by the Hungarian Microfinance Network, must meet the following general requirements:

- The applicant must be either an enterprise having already been listed in the company registry or an entrepreneur with an entrepreneurial licence or one who is entitled to one.
- The number of employees of the enterprise must not exceed nine.

Table 9.2 Microloans granted from National Microcredit Fund (2000–2006)

Microcredit loans granted from the National Microcredit Funds after centralization, broken into sectors (million euros)							
Year	Industry	Agriculture	Tourism	Services	Commerce	Other	Total
2000–2006 altogether	19840	11832	5990	42322	39971	2511	122465
Share	16.2%	9.7%	4.9%	34.6%	32.6%	2.1%	

Source: Hungarian Microfinance Network®.

- The annual turnover of the enterprise can be up to a maximum of HUF 200 million (800000 euros).
- The enterprise must fulfil its tax-paying duty towards the state and the municipality, it must not owe any duties or social security contributions or have an overdue debt to another bank.
- The firm must not be bankrupt or be in liquidation.

The Hungarian microcredit regulations and practice do not differentiate between 'social microcredit' and 'entrepreneurial microcredit', with the latter more targeted at enterprise development; nevertheless the wide range of programmes run by the Hungarian Microfinance Network are able to serve both aims with regionally different emphasis. Previously the microcredit arrangements did not show preferences and did not prohibit the investment in certain sectors or target groups (except for some marginal prohibited activities). In periods of resource shortages the LEAs tended to give preference to manufacturing enterprises rather than services or trade.

The share of industries in the loans actually granted from the National Microcredit Fund is shown in Table 9.2.

After the re-establishment of the Local Microcredit Funds, the Hungarian Enterprise Promotion Network Consortium and some of the LEAs developed several loan products serving the needs of specific target groups, such as the arrangements serving the finance of female entrepreneurs, which was designed based on a programme initiated by the European Microfinance Network.

6 Financial terms and conditions

Because of their significance, we focus on the microcredit programmes operated by the Hungarian Microfinance Network with the help of the Table A9.2 (see Appendix).

7 The promotion of involving other financial products for inclusion

The members of the Hungarian Microfinance Network have always argued that they provide the microenterprises with the best possible service customized to the clients' needs. In order to realize this they have continuously sought for various innovative ways to involve alternative financial resources in microfinance. Several elements that blend supported microlending with bank loan arrangements in a PPP form have been developed (see above in Section 4.3. – taking together the credits given by merchant banks and credits using public money). In addition to the two arrangements shown in Table A9.2, the following became registered schemes of the network:

- Budapest Small Enterprise Loan designed by Enterprise Promotion Public Foundation in Budapest
- IBM Restarting Microcredit developed by the Regional Enterprise Promotion Foundation in Szekesfehervar
- 'Aranyhomok' Microcredit Programme designed by Enterprise Promotion Foundation in Bacs-Kiskun County

These successful programmes provide a good base to involve resources from further financial institutions or other donors (such as large companies carrying out major downsizing). Hopefully, the resources from EU Structural Funds' JEREMIE programme will soon be available for the microcredit programme of the network.

8 Government support

There have been many debates on the government's policy related to microfinance support in the last decade. Sometimes there are some very innovative moves independent of the governments; however, several decisions hint that the Ministry of Economy and Transport (GKM), which is responsible for enterprise promotion, did not always give proportional weight to the microcredit programme. Many times one gets the feeling that they fail to sufficiently appreciate the indirect ways of supporting enterprises and the significance of mediating and service-providing institutions. For example, the importance of the microcredit programme was realized by the Ministry only after the EU had launched the JEREMIE programme. Also, even today it is still necessary to emphasize that microcredit does not mean commercial bank loans given to microenterprises. In their rhetoric all governments so far have emphasized the support of the SME sector and the improvement of finance terms; however, it has not entirely been realized in practice or at least not to the required extent.

However, there have been some innovative and positive decisions in microfinance:

- Act XXXIX/2003 on the modification of Act CXII/1996 on lending institutes and financial enterprises. On the basis of Article (1) h. in §2 of the Act, microlending activities of the enterprise promotion foundations are exempt from the action of this law, that is the foundations can provide microcredit with much more favourable conditions than market actors.
- The Minister of Economy's decision in 2005, which enabled the re-establishment of the Local Microcredit Funds and the rationalization of the National Microcredit Programme.
- Act LXXVI/2007 about the modification of Act XX/2001 on the Hungarian Development Bank (MFB). §1 of the law enables MFB to take part in the finance of loans needed for the microlending activities of the enterprise promotion foundations.

9 Regulation: financial handling, regulating microenterprises

The most important Hungarian regulations are as follows:

- Act XXXIX/2003 on the modification of Act CXII/1996 about lending institutes and financial enterprises: this defines operational rules and conditions for profit-oriented actors of the financial market. On the basis of Article (1) h. in §2 of the Act, lending from the National Microcredit Fund of MVA and the microlending activities of the enterprise promotion foundations are exempt from the action of this law.
- Government Decree No. 2163/2004 (5 July) to settle the operation of the Microcredit Programme, Microcredit System realized by utilizing the rights and funds relating the revolving regional and national credit funds financed by PHARE, and their connecting credit guarantee funds: this authorizes the Ministry of Economy and Transport to practise the owner's rights relating to the state-owned Microcredit Funds on behalf of the Hungarian Republic. Financial settlement of the funds with the EU had not been accomplished before the preparation of this study. (We have not any information in June 2008 whether the project has been finished or not.)

Table 9.3 Some details of National Microcredit Programme 1992–2000

Total sums of microcredit loans in the first decentralized period of the National Microcredit Programme 1992–2000.
(Preliminary orientating data before closing audit)

Funds provided (euros)	Granted loans (euros)	Volume of credit funds at the end of period (euros)	Average turn	Increase of nominal value
15663456	44288517	23862446	2.8	1.5

Note: The network was established in several stages gradually in this period. The maximum loan amount was raised gradually from HUF 300000 to HUF 1300000 (1200 to 5200 euros). Average turn: total dispersed amount/total funds provided (that is, the multiplier calculated as the ratio of total dispersed credits and total funds provided).

- Act LXXVI/2007 about the modification of Act XX/2001 on the Hungarian Development Bank: §1 of the law enables MFB to take part in the financing of loans needed for the microlending activities of the Hungarian Enterprise Promotion Foundation and the enterprise promotion foundations on the basis of a government decree.

Other regulations include:

- The National Microcredit Programme is operated on the basis of the 'Microcredit Manual' as approved by the Ministry of Economy and Transport.
- The common Local Microcredit arrangements of the Hungarian Microfinance Network are operated by the members of the network in a procedure approved by the National Microcredit Professional Committee and developed on the basis of the Microfinance Regulation approved by the presidency of the network.

10 Financial and operational sustainability

During the past 15 years of the Hungarian operation of microfinance programmes, a great deal of positive experience has been built up in the field of financial and operational sustainability. The Microcredit Programme, which was launched by the PHARE Programme and modified several times, has been running effectively to this day, however with uneven levels of success. In the first eight years of operation, in the entirely decentralized period, financial sustainability was achieved nationwide, and the nominal value of the received funds increased by 50 per cent (see Table 9.3).

In that period the decentralized microcredit funds were directly handled and managed by the organizations that granted the loans. The costs of central coordination were negligible because the tasks could be carried out by one manager and one clerk. It is important to see, however, that financial sustainability was correlated with the magnitude of the handled fund, portfolio, the transaction interest of the loans and the losses on loans. This last factor is largely affected by the magnitude of risks taken upon granting the loans as well as the magnitude of the legal collateral required for loan security.

Since the centralization of the programme in 2000, income now had to cover the expenses of three participants (LEA, MVA and participating bank), and the share of received commissions was not in proportion with the work done. Thus the costs of central apparatus increased significantly. In 2002 experts from the Hungarian Microfinance Network set out the conditions for sustaining the nominal value of the NMF. Some of its elements were accepted by the Ministry of Economy and Transport in 2005 (eliminating the bank actor and slightly reducing the central role of the MVA).

Some professional arguments regarding financial sustainability

In our opinion in the case of starting a programme financed by public funds and serving the interests of the national economy (like a microloan) it is not completely necessary to consider financial returns and sustainability to be of primary or exclusive importance. The necessity of government intervention and finance in these programmes can be justified on the basis of reducing market failures. For reasons previously stated, money market actors cannot or do not want to provide the resources needed by a wide range of existing or potential microenterprises; therefore government intervention is needed in order to improve this group of enterprises. We believe that substantive support of the microcredit programme (covering losses, periodically supplementing the capital funds) is a much more effective solution than the alternative of providing non-repayable grants and benefits to the needy.

We believe that in the case of microcredit promoting the unemployed to become entrepreneurs, the increase of fund self-sustainability should not be considered as a primary or exclusive objective. From society's point of view, an outcome of the programme is that the participating unemployed no longer queue for unemployment benefit for months, they support themselves and perhaps their families, and last but not least, they get a chance to avoid mental and psychological breakdown associated with unemployment. When you consider these aspects, it is not so unambiguous to assess the relative merits of prioritizing financial sustainability. It is very important to contemplate the economy's level of development as well as the social and cultural background, which may show a remarkable variety even within the given country.

11 The challenges faced by the sector

The greatest challenges that the Hungarian microfinance sector faces are:

- enforcing the professional arguments more effectively and further rationalization of the national Microcredit Programme;
- creating arrangements more suitable for the target group of social and entrepreneurial microlending;
- creating more effective national coordination, training, monitoring and marketing;
- accessing alternative resources for the operation of the Local Microcredit Programmes;
- raising the efficiency and professional standards of the individual microfinance institutes onto a unified, homogeneous level;
- developing the JEREMIE Microcredit Programme as professionally as possible: instead of allowing market aspects and the idea of 'let a 100 flowers flourish' to prevail. Above all, the programme should promote the strengthening of the enterprise promotion institution and its strong bond to counselling programmes.

Acknowledgement

Dr Antal Szabó, Dr Péter Szirmai, Ákos Almási and Dr Gyula Szegedi offered their help and their studies to making this report.

Notes

* With use of studies written by Tibor Szekfu.

1. Figures in the study are converted to euros at an exchange rate of Hungarian forint (HUF)250/euro and are rounded.
2. http://portal.ksh.hu/pls/ksh/docs/hunxftp/idoszaki/fmf/fm20612.pdf.
3. http://www2.pm.gov.hu/web/home.nsf/portalarticles/9CE71763C9C1ECB1C125727C0048022C/$File/Fobb%20makrogazdasagi_jelzoszamok%20_eves%20adatok.xls.
4. The source of this information is the data of the Economic Development Operational Program of the New Hungarian Development Plan (2007–2013) with the complement of the data of KSH (Hungarian Central Statistical Office) and contains the drawn conclusions from this document.
5. http://portal.ksh.hu/pls/ksh/docs/hun/xstadat/xstadat_eves/tabl3_02_01ic.html.
6. http://portal.ksh.hu/pls/ksh/docs/hun/xstadat/xstadat_eves/tabl3_02_02i.html.
7. http://portal.ksh.hu/pls/ksh/docs/hun/xstadat/xstadat_eves/tabl3_02_03i.html.
8. http://portal.ksh.hu/pls/ksh/docs/hun/xstadat/xstadat_eves/tabl3_02_03i.html.
9. The source of this information is the data of the Economic Development Operational Program of the New Hungarian Development Plan (2007–2013) with the complement of the data of KSH (Hungarian Central Statistical Office) and contains the drawn conclusions from this document.

10. http://www.pszaf.hu/engine.aspx?page=pszafhu_publikaciok (http://www.pszaf.hu/engine.aspx?page=pszafhu_publikaciok&switch-content=pszaf_ujdonsagok_20070801_1&switch-zone=Content%20Zone%204&switch-render-mode=full).
11. http://www.pszaf.hu/engine.aspx?page=pszafhu_publikaciok.
12. See Antal Szabó (2006), 'Microcredits in the World', lecture and study, 26 June, Budapest.
13. According to the definition of the Central Statistics Office (KSH), in 2006 it was HUF 60 128 (240 euros).
14. http://portal.ksh.hu/pls/ksh/docs/hun/xstadat/xstadat_eves/tabl2_01_05ia.html?136; http://portal.ksh.hu/pls/ksh/docs/hun/xstadat/xstadat_eves/tabl7_02_03ib.html.
15. PHARE is the acronym of the Poland–Hungary Assistance for the Reconstruction of the Economy.
16. Rated amount from the summarized information reported by the MVA and LEAs.
17. For a more detailed introduction of these organizations, see section 3.2.
18. 'Evaluation of the SME sector in Hungary', strategic study by the DFC (2000), Budapest.
19. Article h.) in § 2. (1) of Act CXII/1996 about lending institutes and financial enterprises.
20. JEREMIE is a joint programme of the European Commission, the European Investment Bank and the European Investment Fund, which aims to help micro, small and medium-sized companies obtain funding from the Structural Funds of the European Union (http://www.eif.org/jeremie/, http://209.85.135.104/search?q=cache:veavb8eg8PgJ:www.eif.org/jeremie/+Jeremie&hl=hu&ct=clnk&cd=1&gl=hu).
21. http://www.pszaf.hu/engine.aspx?page=pszafhu_publikaciok/2007.
22. http://www.takarekszovetkezetek.hu/.
23. Data of the PSZÁF (Hungarian Supervisory Authority); see Table 9.1.
24. http://www.hungarian-microfinance.org.hu/.
25. Alan Doran, Matthew Gamser and Jacob Levitsky: Background paper on financial policies and programmes for strengthening SMEs, through micro-credit, credit guarantee schemes and other intermediaries. See Antal Szabó (2006), 'Microcredits in the World', lecture and study, 26 June, Budapest.

Table A9.1 *The major actors of the Hungarian microfinance sector*

1. Government level	The Government of the Republic of Hungary (Ministry of Economy and Transport)							
	Organizations with national authority and with direct relation to microfinance					Organizations with national authority and with indirect relation to microfinance		
2. National level	2.1.MVHK (Hungarian Enterprise Promotion Network Consortium);	2.2.MVA	2.3.MFB	2.4. Credit-guarantee Ltd	2.5. - MAG Zrt. (Hungarian Centre for Economy Development, Subsidy intermediation Ltd)	3.2.7. Other state organizations	3.2.8. Other actors financial market:	Other non-profit organizations:
	former OVK Kht. (National Enterprise Promotion Consortium Public Utility Company)	(Hungarian Foundation for Enterprise Promotion)	(Hungarian Development Bank)			Public Employment Service	a) banks	– Life Career Foundation
					Hungarian Enterprise Finance Ltd		b) savings co-operatives	– Agricultural Enterprise loan Guarantee Foundation
3. Local implemen-tation level	3.3.1. foundations for enterprise promotion in 19 counties and the capital city (LEAs)					branch offices, agents, other organizations		
				3.3.2. other non-profit microfinance institutions				
				3.3.3. other microfinance organizations				

Source: Constructed by István Kovács.

Table A9.2 Conditions of microcredit programmes

Description	HMA arrrangements			National Micro-credit for develop-ment/ circulating capital	Micro-credit Plus	PPP arrangements run jointly with financial institutes		New Hungary Micro-credit Programme (JEREMIE)
	For develop-ment	For circulating capital	Micro-credit for female entrepre-neurs			Small enterprise loan	Golden Sand for develop-ment/ circulating capital	
Maximum loan amount (in million HUF)	6.350	6.350	5	6.350	Loan aim 'A': 15; Loan aim 'B': 5	15	39 192	6000
Maximum loan period (months)	96	12/36	96	96/36	Loan aim 'A': 120; Loan aim 'B': 84	60	36/48	60
Maximum moratorium (months)	9	6	6	6	24	6	6	24
Interest rate	Variable, central bank base rate + 1% (8.75%)	Variable, central bank base rate + 1% (8.75%)/+2% (9.75%)	Varying, central bank base rate – 1% (6.75%)	Variable, central bank base rate (7.75%)	Variable, central bank base rate (7.75%)	Base interest rate: 10.75%	Central bank base rate / 3 months BUBOR +3%	6.5%
Credit guarantee	Not available	Not available		Not available	Max. 80% of loan amount with interests	Max. 80% of loan amount with interests	–	Available

Credit guarantee fee	–	–		–	Fee to be paid by MFB	Annual 1% of the guaranteed amount (to be paid in one payment)	–	0.5 %
Minimum own funds	10% of loan amount	10% of loan amount	–	20% of loan amount applied for	15% of total net value of development	20% of loan amount applied for	20%/0%	20 %
Client centre	LEA	LEA		LEA	LEA	LEA	LEA	LEA and other organizations
Provided by	LEA	LEA		MVA	MFB Rt.	LEA and financial institute	LEA/savings co-op	LEA and other organizations
Manual, network software	Available	Available		Available, can be expanded	Available	Available/can be expanded	Available	Available
Programme development experience	5 years	5 years		16 years	2 years	6 years	1 years	0.5 years
Service experience	2 years	2 years		15 years	1.5 years	6 years	0.5 years	0.2 years

Notes:

a) The chart does not contain all details of regulation.

b) The individual loan arrangements are built on each other and enable the finance of both weaker and stronger enterprises.

c) It is also possible to combine the individual loan arrangements.

d) The interest rate of microcredit is set to be within a range of the central bank's base interest rate ± 3% by the decision of the Minister of Economy and Transport made in 2005.

Source: Constructed by István Kovác.

10 Microcredit in Slovakia*

*Allan Bussard and Beata Dobova***

1 National context

Slovakia (formerly part of Czechoslovakia) went through a radical socio-economic transformation beginning with the Velvet Revolution in November, 1989. In January 2003, Slovakia became an independent state. During the 1990s, the governments alternated between what could be broadly termed 'nationalist/reform Socialist' and 'Right wing liberal'. However, the broad direction (with some uncertainty during the years when Vladimir Meciar was Prime Minister) was toward a market economy, integration into the EU and NATO. The general outcome of these reforms was achieved, and in May 2004 Slovakia entered the EU, together with its immediate neighbours, Poland, the Czech Republic and Hungary.

Slovakia's population in 2006 was 5 447 000, and is basically stable. The largest cities are Bratislava and Kosice, with populations of approximately 450 000 and 250 000 respectively. Thus, most people live in small centres and rural areas. The country's rural character affects the general economic indicators, primarily the stubborn nature of unemployment, which is mainly a rural phenomenon. However, despite the uncertain path of economic reform, and the persistent unemployment, general economic indicators are increasingly favourable (see Table 10.1). Slovakia's GDP growth remains high, at 9.2 per cent in the second quarter of 2007 (up from 9.0 per cent in the first quarter) (Slovak Statistical Office online database). This continues to confirm the country as the fastest-growing economy in central Europe, and analysts say the growth remains healthy and not inflationary (EBRD, 2006).

Slovakia is on track to adopt the euro in January 2009, and may do so ahead of its Central European neighbours (ECB, 2007), each of which has struggled to fulfil the Maastricht criteria in the lead-up to euro adoption. This strong economic performance has gained momentum in recent years. Unemployment, though high, has fallen the past five years from over 17 per cent to 11.5 per cent (Slovak Statistical Office, 2007). The gap is closing between Slovakia and living standards in the EU15 countries, but still has a far way to go. Average wages have increased almost threefold since 1994, growing from a national average of SKK (Slovak Koruna) 6300 (€200) to a current average of SKK 18 760 (€548). GDP per capita in Bratislava now exceeds the EU average, with GDP/capita in Bratislava at 120 per

Table 10.1 Basic economic statistics

GDP per capita	€7318 (2006)
GDP per capita growth in 2006	6.46%
Inflation	2.5% (2007 est.)
GDP growth	9.2% (second quarter 2007)
Unemployment	11.5% (first quarter 2007)
Average monthly wage	SKK 18 761 (2006 €548)
Population living below poverty threshold	21% (2006)

Source: Slovak Statistical Office, 2007.

cent the EU average, compared with 64 per cent for the country as a whole (Eurostat, Slovak Statistical Office, 2007).

Slovakia continues to struggle with high unemployment in rural areas previously dependent on a single industry, which closed after the collapse of communism. Long-term unemployment rates remain high. There are currently 303 000 registered unemployed in Slovakia, of which 176 000 are long-term (more than 12 months). (Slovak Statistical Office, 2007). Unemployment is the main contributing factor to the relatively high rate of people at risk of poverty. This is currently 21 per cent, one of the highest rates in the EU (Eurostat, 2007). In addition, Slovakia has a relatively large Roma population[1] (8–10 per cent, depending on statistical method) which as a community faces extreme rates of poverty and unemployment. Generally, as one travels east across the country, poverty and unemployment increase. The Roma population is higher in the east, but also Eastern Slovakia is increasingly rural and distant from the economically strong region centred on Bratislava, which is in the extreme west of the country. Slovakia has made solid progress in reducing relative poverty[2] through increasing employment rates. Employment in Slovakia has increased in the past three years from 2.128 million to 2.337 million people (Slovak Labour Office online database). In the long term, improving education and reducing the negative impact from a low socio-economic background on education will be critical in order to sustain economic growth and reduce income inequality (EBRD, 2006).

Starting a business in Slovakia has become steadily easier, meeting World Bank averages. Slovakia currently ranks 72 in ease of doing business in the world (out of 180 countries surveyed). This process currently takes 25 days involving nine separate procedures. This puts it in the middle range of comparative transition economies (World Bank, 2008). The government has recently introduced a 'one-stop shop' approach to starting a new business, which should reduce barriers even more once implemented. Market opportunities are changing rapidly for entrepreneurs. Former, relatively simple access to local markets has been affected by a very rapidly changing retail landscape. The entrance of modern retailing (shopping malls, hypermarkets, international and local retail chains, consumer credit) has all but eliminated traditional market access (local shops, markets) and made market opportunities difficult for emerging entrepreneurs who produce domestic products. However, the introduction of a flat tax of 19 per cent in 2005 has significantly increased business investment.

Access to microfinance has generally been very limited in Slovakia, particularly for start-up entrepreneurs. Most enterprises have been started by private funding. There are currently 390000 registered enterprises in Slovakia, the vast majority of which are sole proprietorships (Slovak Statistical Office, 2007). In addition, venture capital investments, as a percentage of GDP, are the lowest of all OECD countries (OECD, 2006).

2 The origin of microfinance in Slovakia

The first attempt to set up a microfinance programme in Slovakia was in September 1992 with a visit from Ken Vanderweele, the East European Director of Opportunity International (a global MFI,[3] and currently the largest MFI in Central and Eastern Europe). However, this was not successful, owing mainly due to tension between the then government of Vladimir Meciar and the US Agency for International Development (USAID), which was the main funder for microfinance in the region at the time. USAID proved unwilling, given the political climate at the time, to provide significant funding for microfinance, and Opportunity International chose not to enter Slovakia at that time (author's discussion with OI Director).

In 1997, the US-based ACDI/VOCA network[4] (Agricultural Cooperative Development International and Volunteers in Overseas Cooperative Assistance) began activity, and has been operating in rural areas of Slovakia since 1997. Among other activities, it carries out a modest rural entrepreneurship programme, including microcredit. In 1999, the Integra Foundation,[5] with support from the Canadian International Development Agency (CIDA), began a microenterprise development programme for women at risk, which includes access to microcredit. Beginning in 1999, the National Agency for Small and Medium Enterprise (NADSME) Development initiated a microcredit programme, which it delivers through its network of Regional Advisory and Information Centres (RAIC) and Business Incubation Centres (BICs) in selected parts of the country. The National Agency is a branch of the Slovak Ministry of the Economy.

3 Main actors within the microfinance sector in Slovakia

The National Agency for SME Development,[6] a branch of the Ministry of the Economy, has been active in the support of entrepreneurship for some years. Among other programmes in support of small business, it manages a microloan programme in partnership with local banks. Since 1999, the National Agency has made 114 microloans for a total of €1 703 000. The National Agency also manages RAIC (Regional Advisory and Information Centres) in 14 cities of Slovakia. There are also five BICs (Business Innovation Centres) plus a network of business incubators (NADSME, 2006).

VOKA (Rural Organization for Community Activities) has operated in rural areas since 1997 and, among other activities, carries out the following two projects related to microcredit:

- A rural entrepreneurship programme which incorporates training and microcredit. They offer training in business basics, starting a business, case studies in rural entrepreneurship and agro-tourism. Through this programme VOKA provided 11 loans in 2005.
- A youth entrepreneurship programme. In 2005, this programme conducted 22 training courses and received 41 loan applications. Of this number, 29 loans were approved.

VOKA focuses exclusively on rural development, and its microfinance programme complements a range of other programmes, such as: Rural Capacity Building, Sustainable Development Training, Rural Youth Programmes, Rural Employment Training and Institutional Development for Villages.

Integra Foundation: Integra provides training, mentoring, market access and microcredits for start-up women entrepreneurs. To date, 808 clients have completed the entrepreneurship training programme and 161 loans have been disbursed for a total of €371 526. Integra works through four centres: Bratislava, Ruzomberok, Lucenec and Michalovce. Integra's 'Happy Hand' programme provides a range of microenterprise support initiatives for women, within which the microfinance element works.

The Slovak Guarantee and Development Bank:[7] this bank is totally owned by the Slovak Government, and is the only chartered bank that provides microcredit for enterprise in the country. It launched three new microloan products for micro-entrepreneurs in 2005 and has since emerged as the dominant player in microfinance in Slovakia. Since inception, there have been 581 microloans given within these programmes (SZRB, 2006). The three microloan products are:

1. MicroLoan: Credits from SKK 100 000 to SKK 1 500 000 (€3000 to €30 000) for existing or start-up businesses with up to 50 employees. These loans can be for working capital or investments in equipment or real estate. The loans can be for up to five years, with the availability of a grace period. This product is supported by KfW (Germany) and the Council of Europe Investment Bank. These loans carry a reduced need for guarantee or collateral.
2. Women's Entrepreneur Loan: this loan programme carries virtually identical conditions as the 'MicroLoan' programme above, except that it is offered exclusively to women. It offers loans from €3000 to €30 000, at interest rates beginning at 4.8 per cent, for terms of up to five years. These loans are available for start-up entrepreneurs, subject to adequate guarantees. To date, 581 women clients have received loans through this programme, making it the most significant player in providing finance for women's enterprise.
3. Youth Enterprise Loan: again, this loan carries the same conditions, except that it is designed for young people under 30 years of age.

4 Model of microcredit granting in Slovakia: general description of the model

The use of the word 'model' is misleading, as there is no single model of microcredit in Slovakia. Of the four main players, the following main characteristics emerge:

1. National Agency for SME Development: credit is supplemented with the availability of enterprise development counselling in any of the Regional Advice and Information Centres. There are a range of credit and business development services offered.
2. VOKA: VOKA offers a range of training programmes, some of which are connected with enterprise development. They have a small micro-credit programme.
3. Integra: Integra has a training-based model. Clients register (normally in partnership with the local Labour Office) for an enterprise training course that will take place in their location. This typically consists of 40 hours of training in basic business start-up skills, after which the participants are invited to submit a business plan and credit application. About 30 per cent of the training clients end up successful in their loan applications.
4. Slovak Guarantee and Development Bank: this bank offers no additional business development services in addition to the provision of credit on the basis of an approved business concept. However, it has

developed a partnership with Integra who provide business development services for clients who go on to take larger loans from the Bank.

Other Support structures (though none provide microcredit) for entrepreneurship are:

- the Slovak Association of Crafts;
- the Slovak Business Association;
- the Slovak Chamber of Crafts;
- the Slovak Commercial and Industrial Chamber;
- the Slovak Business Alliance;
- the Slovak Association of Production Cooperation;
- the Slovak Association of Small Enterprises.

These groups typically provide association with other entrepreneurs, though are not normally designed for starting business people.

5 Target groups in Slovakia

Each of these programmes target entrepreneurs. Of the four programmes, only Integra specifically adds social criteria to the selection process. While all seek to support start-ups as well as existing enterprises, often the lack of business experience means that it is very difficult to provide a loan with acceptable risk to these start-ups. Women are targeted exclusively by The Integra Foundation, as well as within the Woman Entrepreneur programme of the Slovak Guarantee and Development Bank. Young people are also targeted by this bank, in a programme similar to the women's product.

6 Financial terms and conditions

Table 10.2 gives an overview of the terms and conditions of the main programmes.

7 Other financial products for inclusion

The Slovak Guarantee and Development Bank also offer a guarantee product to SMEs, with loans being disbursed by a local bank. This facility can guarantee up to 60 per cent of a loan. The loan amounts can be up to SKK 15 million (€440 000) for over seven years (SKK 30 000 000 over 10 years in the case of partnership with another guarantor). However, these amounts in most cases exceed the €25 000 defined limit of microcredit established by the EU (SZRB, 2006).

Table 10.2

Agency	National Agency for SMEs	VOKA	Integra	Slovak Guarantee & Development Bank
Date founded	1999	1998	1999	2005
Number of clients	114	600	900	581
Number of loans	114	40	161	581
Total value of loans	€1 703 357	€28 532	€371 526	n/a
Loan size:				
minimum	€1500	€900	€300	€3000
maximum	€45 000	€6000	€3000	€33 000
average	€ 14 941	€706	€2307	n/a
Typical interest rate	6.25%	8–12%	9.5%	From 6.5%
Typical loan term	6–48 months	6–24 months	24 months	60 months
Available for start-up?	Yes	Yes	Yes	Yes
Collateral type	Physical property, real estate or 3 co-signers	Notarized declaration or 2 guarantors	Physical property or guarantor	Must be collateralized by real estate
Grace period available	Yes	Yes	Yes	Yes
Number of offices	44	1	4	11

Note: Exchange rate used €1 = SKK 33.4.

Source: Annual reports of these four agencies.

8 Government support

Government support generally relates to policy initiatives with respect to administrative burdens, tax regulation, ease of hiring and firing and generosity of bankruptcy legislation. One could say that for the last 15 years the Slovak Government has undertaken a constant reform process, in the transition period from socialism. As such, the policy environment for entrepreneurship is constantly improving, though unevenly. During the period 1998–2006, there was a strong pro-business government, which introduced a wide range of measures (flat tax, bankruptcy law, attraction of foreign investment, employment law, and so on) aimed at supporting, if not specifically micro-entrepreneurship, business in general. More recently, with the election of a more centre-left government (June 2006) there have been some modest moves to strengthen labour laws in a way that could be seen as somewhat anti-business. This is because of the government's declared intention to reintroduce more restrictive labour laws, with a greater focus on the rights of workers. However, the current Slovak government remains committed to creating a positive environment for business, including entrepreneurship.

High social insurance costs remain a burden to entrepreneurs, and restrict labour flows. As well, the indirectly related issue of labour mobility is a barrier, as housing and mortgage availability make it difficult for workers to move in search of jobs. Furthermore, the sharp price differences for housing between cities (where unemployment is low) and rural areas (with high unemployment) make labour mobility very difficult. Slovakia has the second-lowest volume of mortgages as a percentage of GDP in the EU. One now finds people commuting 80–100 kilometres or more daily to work in Bratislava.

In October 2007, a new law for sole proprietors was passed by parliament and will be implemented throughout the country. The main feature of this law is the provision of a one-stop-shop which will allow entrepreneurs to conduct all business registration formalities in a single location.

9 Regulation: fiscal treatment, regulation of microenterprises, and so on

There is no specific law in Slovakia regulating microenterprises. They operate within the normal commercial code. Most microenterprises operate within the bounds of the law on sole proprietorship or the law governing limited liability companies.

There is no provision in the law either for microfinance institutions. Of the four main actors, only the Slovak Guarantee and Development Bank has a banking licence. The National Agency delivers microcredits in partnership with several local banks. VOKA provides loans under the conditions of the Citizenship Law, which allows such financial transactions between legal or physical persons if it does not become the prime business activity, which for VOKA is not the case. Integra works as two organizations, the Integra Cooperative, which serves as the financial delivery arm of the Integra Foundation. Members who wish to take a loan join the Coop, within which there is the right to mutual financial help in the form of loans and other instruments.

10 Financial and operational sustainability

Each of the main actors adopted different sustainability models. The Slovak Guarantee and Development Bank operated as a commercial bank, though the 100 per cent shareholder is the Slovak Government. It uses a range of guarantee and other financial facilities from within the EU, Council of Europe or agencies like KfW to enable it to manage a higher than normal risk profile for its microcredit products. The National Agency is chartered under the Slovak Ministry of the Economy, and as such is not faced with issues of financial sustainability. Since it manages its microloan products through local banks, which retain the earnings from the programme, the National Agency can only function as a government programme.

VOKA's loan programme is modest, and as an organization is financed mainly through a range of private and public donors, including the EU (Sapard, Socrates, Leonardo), the Open Society Foundation, the Children of Slovakia Foundation and the UniCredit Foundation. In addition, VOKA has succeeded in attracting a number of local donors and businesses in its support. Integra is financed by a range of sources. Like VOKA, Integra has managed and continues to manage a wide range of projects funded by public sources such as the EU (EQUAL, Leonardo, CARDS), SlovakAid, CIDA, USAID, and so on. Moreover, private foundations have been a major source of funding for the women's microcredit programme, particularly Citigroup Foundation and Shell Foundation. As noted above, while the Integra Foundation delivers training and other business development services, the Integra Coop delivers microfinance services, and receives financial returns. In addition to microcredit, the Integra Coop invests in larger SMEs, and some of the profits from these investments serve to support the costs of the microenterprise programme.

11 Challenges for the sector in Slovakia

Many of the challenges that microfinance and microenterprise development face in Slovakia are similar to those faced by other countries in the EU: competitiveness and the difficulty of breaking into a market with a new product or service. The microfinance institutions (MFIs) can only be as strong as the clients they lend to. However, due to the recent past and the challenges of climbing out of the legacy of communism, there are some particular challenges faced in Slovakia. For microfinance as a poverty alleviation strategy, the geography of the Slovak economy is such that while parts of the country are economically booming, there remains pockets of underinvestment, high unemployment and economic inactivity. This is partly due to the legacy of communism and the artificial and unbalanced nature of its economic policy. In terms of attitudes, for a range of reasons, entrepreneurship does not normally present itself as a first choice for those who are unemployed or socially excluded.

- In the urban context of low unemployment and high economic growth, skilled and motivated people can find jobs, which is often preferable to the risk of entrepreneurship.
- Start-up capital for small business is still very difficult to access for a person with no experience of running her own business.
- In areas of high unemployment, the risk of entrepreneurship is high as well, as the lower economic activity in a local area may mean weak markets for the goods or services intended.
- Many Slovaks still have no experience of entrepreneurship directly (family or acquaintance) and so their default response is to seek a job.
- There exists a high barrier to entry for those seeking to start a business from unemployment, as unemployment benefits cease as soon as a business is registered.
- For those women on unemployment or maternity leave, entrepreneurship is not attractive as they lose their benefit when they form a new company, even though they may not have significant income for a long period (Varbanova, 2006)
- For women on maternity leave, the legal obligation of their former employer to hold their job open means that, after a period of inactivity and reduced income, most women prefer to return to their previous employment.

One problem peculiar to the National Agency is that it administers its microloan programme through local banks, which add their own criteria to the borrower; at times these loans are generally out of reach for small or start-up entrepreneurs. VOKA and Integra, as private agencies, do not have loan portfolios large enough to allow for complete financial self-sustainability, and thus must depend on (at times uncertain) donor or public funding.

It is unlikely that any of the MFIs noted in Slovakia will attain the scale of those seen elsewhere in Central and Eastern Europe. Due mainly to a late start and a strong economy this sector is likely to remain small, sharing characteristics with agencies in the more developed countries in the EU, rather than a developing world microfinance model. However, the roughly 1000 micro-entrepreneurs who have been helped through these programmes, and the jobs which have been created, do provide reason to believe that this sector can continue to grow, even if at a relatively slow pace.

Notes

* Microcredit is defined as a loan for business creation.

** Experts: Anka Rajska, Iveta Erlichova, Lenka Surotchak, Monika Smolova, Jela Tvrdonova and Mario Vircik.

1. Roma (also known as Gypsies in English) are an ancient people, with their own language and culture, and comprise a significant minority in all Central European countries.
2. Relative poverty follows the most commonly used definition of poverty by the EU (used by Eurostat) which defines those at risk of poverty below a threshold of 60 per cent of national median equivalent income.
3. MFI: Microfinance Institution.
4. www.voka.sk.
5. www.integra.sk.
6. www.nadsme.sk.
7. www.szrb.sk.

Bibliography

Applica (2005), *Poverty in the EU: European Observatory on the Social Situation*, Brussels: Network on Social Inclusion and Income Distribution.

EBRD (2006), *Strategy Document for Slovakia*, London: EBRD.

ECB (2007), *European Central Bank October 2007 report on Slovak Euro Accession*, Frankfurt: European Central Bank.

EUROSTAT (2007), data for the Slovak Republic, http://epp.eurostat.ec.europa.eu.

Integra (2006), *Integra Foundation 2006 Annual Report*, Bratislava: Integra.

NADSME (2006), *National Association for the Development of Small and Medium Enterprises 2006 Annual Report*, Bratislava: NADSME.

OECD (2006), *Policy Brief, Financing SMEs and Entrepreneurs*, Paris: OECD.

Slovak Statistical Office online database, www.statistics.sk.

SZRB (2006), *Slovak Guarantee and Development Bank 2006 Annual Report*, Bratislava: SZRB.

Varbanova, Asya (ed.) (2006), *The Story Behind the Numbers: Women and Employment in the Central and Eastern Europe and the Western Commonwealth of Independent States*, Bratislava, Slovakia: UNIFEM.

VOKA (2006), *VOKA 2006 Annual Report*, VOKA, Slovakia: Banska Bystrica.

World Bank Group (2008), *Doing Business Slovakia, A Project Benchmarking the Regulatory Cost of Doing Business in 178 Economies*, Washington: World Bank Group.

11 Microcredit in Luxembourg

*Véronique Faber**

National context

The Grand Duchy of Luxembourg is a constitutional monarchy. With a population of 469 100 inhabitants,[1] it covers an area of 2586 km^2 and shares borders with France, Belgium and Germany. The GDP per capita of 58 000 euros is the highest in Europe.[2]

Forty per cent of the population are foreign nationals, mainly emigrants from Portugal. Asylum seekers are allowed to work after nine months of registering their application, which does not automatically qualify them for a residence permit.[3] Forty per cent of the labour force are trans-border workers from neighbouring countries. An additional characteristic of the labour market is the high percentage (98.6 per cent) of Luxembourg nationals working in the public sector as you need to be a Luxembourg national to be employed full-time.[4] This creates the unique situation of having a higher foreign labour force in the private sector than a national one.

Generally, countries with a low percentage of workers who have given less than one year's service also tend to have a significant percentage of workers who have given many years' service (over 10 years). Luxembourg falls within this group, which also includes Japan, Italy, Greece and Belgium. The other end of the scale includes the United States, the United Kingdom and Denmark. Within the context of globalization and liberalization of the economy, the persistence of forms of lasting employment is often considered unfavourable to labour market flexibility and growth. However, the stability of labour relations also helps maintain a largely peaceful social environment, which is clearly attractive to investors.[5]

Part-time work is less common in Luxembourg than in most other European countries. In 2001, the proportion of part-time work was 10.3 per cent in Luxembourg, but 17.9 per cent in the fifteen EU countries. This situation is not positive in itself. A labour market in which part-time work is underdeveloped may exclude certain categories of people, such as those bringing up children. The low frequency of part-time work is more indicative of the persistence of traditional forms of labour relations (piecework and stability of labour relations) and social relations in Luxembourg.[6]

Poverty and unemployment

Clearly, the favourable objective data on unemployment (only 4.5 per cent[7]), social relations and the standard of living do not have the positive impact referred to above if the population's subjective judgement of their material situation is negative. Comparison of European data on the percentage of the population living below the monetary poverty threshold, which is 60 per cent of the national median income, and the percentage of people who consider themselves poor and claim that they do not have the necessary income to enjoy a decent standard of living clearly shows that the subjective judgement and the objective material situation may well differ.[8]

The risk-of-poverty indicator, which shows the percentage of people living below the threshold of 60 per cent of the national median income, does not indicate differences in the standard of living in absolute terms between countries, given that this threshold is higher in a rich country (such as Luxembourg) than in a poor country. It does, however, provide an indication of the 'relative' risk of poverty in a country, a risk that is smaller in Luxembourg than in most other European countries. Comparison with the subjective poverty indicator provides additional information. Together with Denmark, Germany, Austria, the Netherlands and Ireland, Luxembourg is one of the countries in which subjective judgement and objective data are very close (see Table 11.1).

(Micro-)entrepreneurs

Because of this distinct labour market structure, it is not surprising that only 26 per cent of entrepreneurs have Luxembourg nationality. A very high percentage are of French or Belgian nationality and 44 per cent are non-residents; 82 per cent of entrepreneurs are male, and 89 per cent have experience in the particular business line – either through previous business or employment.[9]

The self-employment rate is 8 per cent, which is below the EU 25 average of 15 per cent.[10] Self-employment is generally perceived, especially by Luxembourg nationals, as a poverty trap rather than a way out of poverty as it does not guarantee stable income levels and clearly defined working hours.[11] This is usually explained by the lack of a national entrepreneurial spirit believed to be another characteristic of the labour market in Luxembourg.

The majority of enterprises in Luxembourg employ fewer than 10 people and thus qualify, by European Commission (EC) standards, as microenterprises.[12] In the Luxembourg context, this definition does not apply, as a small country such as Luxembourg represents quite a limited market, and enterprises usually employ fewer than 10 people.

Table 11.1 Objective poverty and subjective poverty(EU 15)

	Risk-of-poverty indicator: % of households living on incomes below 60% of the national median income (1999)	Subjective poverty indicator: % of people who consider themselves poor (2001)*
Belgium	16	32
Denmark	9	9
Germany	16	14
Greece	22	54
Spain	19	34
France	18	30
Ireland	17	24
Italy	20	41
Luxembourg	12	8
Netherlands	12	18
Austria	13	16
Portugal	20	66
Finland	8	30
Sweden	10	20
United Kingdom	21	27

Note: * People who consider their net income below what they consider essential to have a decent standard of living.

Source: Eurostat and Eurobarometer, 56.1 (October 2002).

Main actors

SMEs (Small and Medium-Sized Enterprises) are regarded in national policies as an important motor for the creation of employment, and a range of financial instruments exist that are geared towards SME start-up and expansion. These instruments, which are aimed at entrepreneurial sector development rather than at social inclusion of the unemployed, are offered by the SNCI (Société National de Crédit et d'Investissement), the Mutual for Craftspeople and the Mutual for Trade and commercial banks.

The SNCI is a public banking institution owned by the Luxembourg state. Among other instruments, the SNCI provides, in collaboration with the Ministry for Middle Classes, Tourism and Housing, start-up loans and equipment loans for SMEs. These loans are to be seen as complementary to other state aids and personal investments described in this section.

The SNCI also grants start-up loans to newly incorporated SMEs. It may also finance investments of Luxembourg companies abroad.

The SME Start-up Loan is the only support that does not require a bank guarantee but does require personal or group collateral, a business plan and a financial plan. Further, the entrepreneur must provide 15 per cent of the capital plus legal licences and authorizations, which in the majority of cases come from personal savings. According to the 2006 Annual Report, 16 SME Start-up Loans have been approved out of only 24 requests, for a total amount of 1 million euros.[13]

This loan product only covers costs related to the development of the business plan covering such items as production licences, rent, stock and tools. The loan amount ranges from 5000–250 000 euros with a market rate of 5.25 per cent per year (as of 2007) without additional fees or commissions. The SNCI reduced the minimum loan volume to 5000 euros to target smaller business start-ups in 2005. There is only one disbursement, and repayments are made on a quarterly basis after a maximum five-year grace period with a 10-year loan period.

The SME Equipment Loan generally has a subsidized interest rate of 2.5 per cent per year and can be used by start-ups and existing businesses. For start-ups, this loan amounts to 75 per cent of the total investment with a minimum investment of approximately 12 500 euros with a repayment period of at most, 10 years, with quarterly repayments. According to the 2006 Annual Report, 126 loans have been approved for a total amount of 37.5 million euros, of which 21.8 million went to the craft sector.[14] It is not specified how many loan applications were made.

Although the SME Equipment Loan only requires a personal or group bond as guarantee, the loan application has to be made via a commercial bank, which in turn will ask for bank guarantees.

The Mutual for Craftspeople and the Mutual for Trade, although organized differently, both provide guarantees ranging from 15–20 per cent for credit lines from the SNCI and from commercial banks, these being added to guarantees provided by the applicant. In 2004, the Mutual for Craftspeople approved 66 out of 103 applications and the Mutual for Trade approved 9 out of 31.[15] The requirement is to be a member of one of the two mutuals.

Most commercial banks do not operate an SME department and only provide general information for start-ups and on available credit lines on their website. For confidentiality purposes and as they don't differentiate between SMEs and other enterprises, banks do not or cannot provide data on how many microenterprises and start-ups they have financed. Required guarantees for a start-up credit are usually 100 per cent. This could partly explain why less than 5 per cent of business start-ups have received a commercial credit line and 89 per cent have invested personal resources.[16]

Although most commercial banks do not have a minimum loan amount and thus consider that they are providing small credits, an 'SME and Commercial Banks Observation Lobby' was created for better and more appropriate bank credit lines and conditions for SMEs.

Regulation and role of government

No special regulation for microcredit exists as microcredit, as such, does not exist in Luxembourg. Bank loans to SME customers and state credits are covered by the Consumer Credit Law.[17]

The government provides subsidies that address specific investment needs for the creation or expansion of businesses. These aids are principally available through the Ministry for Middle Classes' SME Action Plan with the goal of promoting economic growth and job creation.[18]

Most government entrepreneurship programmes aim at informing and supporting new entrepreneurs with respect to legal and administrative requirements and procedures, as well as available subsidies and credit lines. The Chamber of Commerce,[19] for example, publishes information,[20] provides training and is involved in initiatives such as the interregional entrepreneur programme 1,2,3, GO, which aims at improving the quality of business plans; poor business plans are often cited as the main reason why commercial banks do not finance new projects.[21] These initiatives provide information and training only.

Future for microfinance in Luxembourg?

There are no microfinance institutions based or active in Luxembourg at the moment. In 2008, the alternative financing NGO Etika,[22] which collaborates with the BCEE (Banque et Caisse d'Epargne de l'Etat), plans to launch the first microcredit project in Luxembourg that targets financial inclusion rather than enterprise development. As the instrument is in development at the moment, information has not yet been made public.

Some Business Development Services (BDS) projects are in process. The immigrant support organization ASTI[23] has set up catering and crafts microenterprises that train and employ immigrants. Objectif Plein Emploi[24] supports local microenterprises that promote a higher quality of life and reinforce communities through funding. The employment agency ADEM (Administration de l'emploi) offers, in collaboration with the Ministry of Work and Employment, a subsidy programme for the creation of enterprises for the unemployed.

In a research paper on a potential microfinance market in Luxembourg, its author Orlandi (2005) concludes that it would not be possible to introduce a long-term sustainable national microcredit institution based on the following realities already discussed in this section: limited market;

low self-employment rates; and risk-averse attitude of Luxembourg nationals.[25]

A solution could be a regional cross-border approach that would link Luxembourg to existing microcredit networks in neighbouring countries, such as ADIE in France or Crédal in Belgium. This could be achieved through bilateral agreements, as those microcredit organizations are partly financed by local governments and/or *communes* in the context of local employment programmes.

Notes

* Collaborator: Tom Theves.

1. Statec (2006).
2. The GDP per capita includes non-resident revenue, Statec (2005).
3. There have been only 523 new applications in 2006 (39.5 per cent from Serbia and Montenegro), (www.mae.lu).
4. Statec (2001).
5. www.portrait.public.lu.
6. www.portrait.public.lu.
7. ADEM 'Bulletin Luxembourgois de l'emploi', No. 5, May (2007).
8. Statec (2006).
9. For a detailed profile of entrepreneurs in Luxembourg see Ries (2006).
10. Eurostat Yearbook 2005: Europe in Figures.
11. European Commission (2004).
12. Fewer than 10 staff members, not more than 2 million euros annual turnover and/or on the balance sheet.
13. http://admin.mum.lu/users/images/snci/Downloads-NewsUpdater/rapp_ann_snci_2006.pdf.
14. http://admin.mum.lu/users/images/snci/Downloads-NewsUpdater/rapp_ann_snci_2006.pdf.
15. Orlandi (2005: 39).
16. Ries (2006: 19).
17. Since 1993. See European Commission (2007: 51), available at www.european-microfinance.org/data/File/the_regulation_of_microcredit_in_europe.pdf.
18. www.mcm.public.lu/fr/plan/index.html.
19. www.cc.lu.
20. For example, Chambre de Commerce (2006).
21. www.123go-networking.org.
22. www.etika.lu.
23. www.asti.lu.
24. www.ope.lu.
25. Orlandi (2005: 48).

References

ADEM (2007), 'Bulletin Luxembourgeois de l'emploi', No. 5, May.

Chambre De Commerce (2006), *Challenging Entrepreneurship: Everything You Need to Know about Setting up a Company in Luxembourg*, Luxembourg: CDC Luxembourg.

European Commission (2004), *L'esprit d'entreprise*, Flash Eurobarometer report no. 160.

European Commission (2007), *The Regulation for Microcredit in Europe*, Expert Group Report.

Eurostat (2005), *Eurostat Yearbook 2005: Europe in Figures*, Luxembourg: Office for Official Publications of the European Communities.

Orlandi, Andrea (2005), 'Microfinance in a Microcountry? The existence of a "finance gap" in the access to capital by microenterprises and possible intervention: The case of Luxembourg', MA Dissertation, University of Warwick.

Ries, Jean (2006), *Une Typologie des Entrepreneurs Luxembourgeois*, Cahier économique No. 103, Luxembourg: Statec.

SNCI (Société National de Crédit et d'Investissement) (2006), *Annual Report 2006*, Luxembourg: SNCI.

Statec (2001), *Annuaire Statistique du Luxembourg*, Luxembourg: Statec.

Statec (2005), *Annuaire Statistique du Luxembourg*, Luxembourg: Statec.

Statec (2006), *Annuaire Statistique du Luxembourg*, Luxembourg: Statec.

Website references

www.123go-networking.org.

www.asti.lu.

www.cc.lu.

www.etika.lu.

www.mae.lu.

www.mcm.public.lu/fr/plan/index.html.

www.ope.lu.

www.portrait.public.lu.

www.statec.lu.

12 Microcredit in Norway

Elisabet Ljunggren and Trude Emaus Holm

National context

Norway is a small country in northern Europe with approximately 4.5 million inhabitants. Its economy is largely dependent on export of oil and gas as well as fisheries and fish farming. Norway is ranked as one of the wealthiest nations in Europe; it is not an EU member. It has a history of independence since 1905 when it seceded from Swedish governance. During World War II it was occupied by nazi Germany, but with exile government and troops, Norway fought on the allied side. This led to a tight connection to the USA in the post-war period and to NATO membership. The Norwegian economy has been strong since the 1970s when the income from oil and gas export increased. The strong economy has led to a growth of the public sector and a strong welfare state. Some key figures are shown in Table 12.1.

The employment distribution between the public and private sector shows that 66 per cent of the employees in the public sector are women while the number of male employees in the private sector is 63 per cent (OECD, 2001). Among immigrants born abroad,[1] six out of ten were employed, but fewer female immigrants than men. Non-western female immigrants have lower incomes compared to immigrant women and men from western countries and in relation to men with non-western backgrounds (Henriksen, 2006). Norway has, despite being perceived as one of the most gender-equal countries in Europe and in spite of being rated as one of the most entrepreneurial countries in Europe (Bullvåg et al., 2006), a low share of women entrepreneurs: 21 per cent of Norwegian men are business owners, whilst the number for women is 9 per cent (Allen, Langowitz and Minitti, 2007). There are approximately 300000 active businesses in the private sector in Norway (Statistics Norway, Ownership in Norway). In 2006, 51374 new business entities were registered in Norway (Statistics Norway, Ownership in Norway). Two out of three entities are small businesses with the owner as the only employee (Statistics Norway, Ownership in Norway).

There are significant differences in the types of businesses men and women start. Women tend to be concentrated in social and personal services where 53.3 per cent are women, and within health and social services where 48.7 per cent are women. Men meanwhile dominate construction (98.5 per cent) and transport and communication (91.1 per cent) (Statistics

Table 12.1 Key data (Norway)

GDP	• GDP growth in 2007: 3.7%[(1)]
	• GDP/inhabitant 60465 euros
Employment	• 2005[(2)]: employment rate for women 72% and men 78%
	• 43% of women work part-time
	• 13% of men work part-time
Unemployed	• 2.1%[(3)] women 2.0% and men 2.1%
Risk of poverty	• Men 10% and women 13%[(4)]
Immigrants	• 8.3% (415000) of the population (2007)[(5)]

Sources:
1. Statistics Norway (2008).
2. Statistics Norway (2007b).
3. Statistics Norway (2007b).
4. Eurostat (2003).
5. Statistics Norway (2007c).

Norway, 2001). This is due to the gender-segregated education system in Norway (Statistics Norway, Women and men in Norway). Many young girls select education enabling them to work in the public sector. For example 94 per cent of nursery school teachers, 90 per cent of nurses and 70 per cent of teachers are women. On the other hand 82 per cent of engineers, and 94 per cent of electricians, plumbers and mechanics are men, and are therefore trained to work in the private sector (Statistics Norway, Women and men in Norway). This gender-divided education pattern gives men an advantage in market knowledge necessary for entrepreneurship, as it is extremely rare to start up businesses within the public services such as nursing homes and schools (Alsos and Ljunggren, 2006).

Norway's main strategy in achieving gender equality has been to strengthen women's economic independence by increasing their labour market participation. The welfare system is seemingly gender-neutral and guarantees most basic needs. The Norwegian welfare system ensures child care and parental leave. These measures have been crucial for the dual career family policy.

Microfinance in Norway

The microcredit finance system (Grameen Bank) was introduced in Norway in 1992. It was introduced explicitly as a means to support women entrepreneurs financially and to give advisory support. Today, Norway has two main microcredit organizations: Network Credit Norway – NCN (Nettverkskreditt BA) and Innovation Norway (IN). Their activity appears to overlap. Innovation Norway reported 220 microcredit groups throughout the nation in 2005; some of these were organized by county administrations. In sum, these groups had more than 1150 active members. The loan capital was 44 million Norwegian Krone (NOK) (5.5 million euros). Average turnover in the businesses was 500 000 NOK (62 500 euros), while 12 per cent had a turnover of more than 1 million NOK (125 000 euros). Eight new groups were established in 2006. Each group has 5–7 members. The Innovation Norway microcredit groups apply for funding for loan capital of up to NOK 200 000 (25 000 euros). A maximum 95 per cent of required finance can be lent, which is administered by the group. Each group has a process leader approved and paid by Innovation Norway.[2]

While Innovation Norway's main target group for microcredit is women, although they offer the service to men as well, Network Credit Norway (NCN) mainly target immigrants, men and women, and in 2006 immigrants represented 90 per cent of the members. NCN's first groups were formed in Oslo in 1997 and expanded to Bergen in 2000. Their programmes gradually evolved, and in April 2003 the institution was established as an independent social cooperative enterprise. The NCN loan products are a result of a partnership with Foundation Microinvest and Cultura Bank who administer the loans and savings. It is also guaranteed by the European Investment Fund, and in total the guaranteed capital is 4.8 million NOK (600 000 euros). At present, approximately NOK 950 000 (115 000 euros) is on loan to members. Since 1997, 200 people have been part of network groups organized by this institution; more than 800 have participated in some sort of training or advice activity during this period (information provided by NCN). The organization also has peer loan groups and offers individual loans for existing businesses and linkage loans from banks with or without partial guarantees from Foundation Microinvest. In 2005, the total loan portfolio was 34 loans; in 2006 42 loans were granted and by September 2007, 12 loans were accepted. Each loan can be up to a maximum of NOK 200 000 (25 000 euros), though the average loan is NOK 40 000 (5000 euros). The division of borrowers between groups and individuals (active members) is that three-quarters of the loans are to group borrowers.[3] Of those that are participating in the NCN microlending programme:[4]

- 44% have an income from a job in addition to their business;
- 41% of the businesses are home-based;
- 70% of the loans are lent to single heads of household.

The members prefer to keep their businesses distinct from their private finances, and 82.4 per cent use a separate bank account for their businesses.

Governmental support and policy

In Norway, as in most western countries, financing for new business start-ups has four main sources: personal savings, debt financing, soft loans or grants supported by the government, and equity funding from venture capital (Borch et al., 2002). Norwegian banks offer debt financing, but without personal savings or property it is difficult to gain such financing, and this is an uncommon source of business start-up financing regardless of the entrepreneur's background and gender. The government entrepreneurship support funding is mainly offered by Innovation Norway with different types of grants. Some municipalities also offer grants to entrepreneurs, but the extent of this type of funding is limited (Pettersen et al., 1999). Also, business angels are a source of financing, but they invest relatively small amounts (Borch et al., 2002). The most common source of financing is personal savings (Borch et al., 2002).

In addition to their microcredit funding Innovation Norway has four different public subsidies for entrepreneurs:

1. The entrepreneur grant.
2. The BU-entrepreneur grant.
3. The incubator grant.
4. The inventor grant.

The entrepreneur grant, the BU-entrepreneur grant and (to some extent) the incubator grant are also regional policy means, and thereby give priority to business start-ups in rural areas. This makes it difficult for entrepreneurs in larger cities to access these grants (Alsos et al., 2006b).

The entrepreneur-grant measure distributes about 600–700 grants, and approximately 85 million NOK (approx. 11 million euros) is spent each year. Also, Innovation Norway has a rule requiring 40 per cent of the entrepreneur grants to be allocated to female entrepreneurs, although regional governance has made this target more difficult for Innovation Norway to accomplish (Alsos et al., 2006b). The BU-entrepreneur grant is similar to the entrepreneur grant, but the money is reserved for business start-ups related to agriculture. Each year approximately 300 grants are made and 23 million NOK (2.9 million euros) is spent. The incubator grant makes approximately 80 grants a year, accessing a pool of 20 million NOK (2.5 million euros). The money goes to entrepreneurs that are located in a business incubator. The inventor grant is distributed to approximately 100 persons a year, and 8 million NOK (1 million euros) is approved every year. The aim of this grant is to stimulate and contribute to industrial innovation. In total 1100–1200 entrepreneurs receive a grant from Innovation Norway each year. Given that 51 374 new entities were registered in Norway in 2006, the conclusion is that very few have access to public financial support.

In addition to these four grants administrated by Innovation Norway, some municipalities in Norway have local industrial grants. There is no overall public report on these arrangements.

Conclusions

Basic statistics on Norway reveal that the growth rate in GDP is approximately at the OECD average, the unemployment rate is low, the poverty level is fairly low, and the entrepreneurial propensity is high (Bullvåg et al., 2006). Despite these seemingly good scores on a societal level, entrepreneurship and self-employment among Norwegian women is still less common than among Norwegian men – and less than politically desired (Departementa, 2008); this is also true for immigrants (AID, 2003/04). Women still tend to be educated and work in traditional female occupations. These occupations are part-time, lower paid and often in the public sector where private start-ups are rare, as little of the public sector is privatized in Norway. One of Norway's challenges is to make women think and act less traditionally both in choices of education and work, in order to be able to acquire adequate experience for self-employment. Women with non-western ethnic backgrounds are worst off in the labour market. This group is an untapped resource in Norwegian society, and many have both the education and experience to start their own businesses.

But also access to finance is crucial for entrepreneurship. Research has revealed that gender makes an important difference when it comes to the amount of loan and equity capital raised to develop a new business (see for example Cliff, 1998; Alsos et al., 2006a). An overview of policy directed towards promotion of entrepreneurial activities and local measures for gender equality in entrepreneurship (Pettersen et al., 1999) revealed that the support measures are 'gender neutral', but that the industries and activities supported are the industries and activities in which men start up their businesses. The consequence is that they become 'male support schemes'. Hence, the finance issue needs to be addressed.

This makes microcredit financing aimed at women entrepreneurs and immigrant entrepreneurs an important service. As shown, it is a relatively widespread measure which to some extent reaches its target groups. Despite the fact that relatively small amounts are lent out, research has shown that this is quite an effective means for women entrepreneurs (Lotherington and Ellingsen, 2002). There is no evidence of how effective the measure is among immigrants.

This chapter concludes that microcredit funding is a necessary source of funding for groups in Norwegian society that otherwise have problems in acquiring funding for business start-ups. This makes it possible for them to become self-employed and thereby economically independent.

Notes

1. Register based employment statistics for immigrants, 4th quarter 2006: http://ssb.no/emner/06/01/innvregsys/.
2. All information provided by Innovation Norway.
3. Personal communication with Unni Beate Sekkesæter, leader of NCN.
4. Source: www.nettverkskreditt.no.

References

Allen, I.E., N. Langowitz and M. Minitti (2007), *2006 Report on women entrepreneurship*, http://www.gemconsortium.org/download/1189934988477/GEM_2006_Womens_Report_May_07.pdf, accessed 10 September, 2007.

Alsos, G.A. and E. Ljunggren (2006), 'Kjønn og entreprenørskap' (Gender and entrepreneurship), in O.R. Spilling (ed.), *Entreprenørskap på norsk* (Entrepreneurship in Norway), 2nd edn, Oslo: Fagbokforlaget.

Alsos, G.A., E.J. Isaksen and E. Ljunggren (2006a), 'New venture financing and subsequent business growth in men- and women-led businesses', *Entrepreneurship, Theory and Practice*, September, pp. 667–686.

Alsos, G.A., B. Brastad, T. Iakovleva and E. Ljunggren (2006b), 'Flere og bedre bedriftsetableringer? Evaluering av Innovasjon Norges stipendordninger 1999–2005' (More and better business start-ups? An evaluation of Innovation Norways grants 1999–2005), NF-report 11/2006, Bodø: Nordlandsforskning.

Borch, O.J., E.J. Isaksen, S.A. Jenssen, L. Kolvereid, R. Sørheim and L.A. Widding (2002), *Kapitalmarked for Nyetablerte Bedrifter – en Studie av Etterspørsel- og Tilbudssiden* (The finance market for nascent firms – a study of demand and supply), Bodø: Handelshøgskolen.

Bullvåg, E., L. Kolvereid and B.W. Åmo (2006), *GEM: Entreprenørskap i Norge 2006* (GEM: Entrepreneurship in Norway 2006), Bodø: Handelshøgskolen.

Cliff, J. (1998), 'Does one size fit all? Exploring the relationship between attitudes towards growth, gender and business size', *Journal of Business Venturing*, **13**(6), 371–95.

Departmenta (2008), *Handlingsplan for meir entreprenørskap blant kvinner* (Action plan to promote entrepreneurship among women), Oslo: Departementa (The ministries).

Eurostat (2003), http://epp.eurostat.ec.europa.eu/portal/page?_pageid=1996,39140985&_dad=portal&_schema=portal&screen=detailref&language=en&product=sdi_ps&root=sdi_ps/sdi_ps/sdi_ps_mon/sdi_ps1111, accessed September 2007.

Henriksen, K. (2006), 'Women in the immigrant population. Who are they and how are they doing?', SSB, available at http://www.ssb.no/vis/english/magazine/art-2006-12-04-01-en.html.

Lotherington, A.T. and M.B. Ellingsen (2002), 'Små penger og store forventninger. Nettverkskreditt i Norge 1992–2002' (Little money and great expectations. Network credit in Norway 1992–2002), report, Tromsø: Norut Samfunnsforskning.

OECD (2001), *Employment Outlook*, Paris: OECD.

Pettersen, L.T., G.A. Alsos, C.H. Anvik, A. Gjertsen and E. Ljunggren (1999), *Blir det arbeidsplasser av dette da, jenter? Evaluering av kvinnesatsing i distriktspolitikken* (Do you make any workplaces girls? Evaluation of the regional policy and women as target group), NF-report 13/99, Bodø: Nordlands Forskning.

AID (2003–04), *Mangfold gjennominkludering og deltakelse. Ansvar og frihet* (Diversity through inclusion and participation), Oslo: Stortingsmelding nr.49.

Statistics Norway (2001), '*Antall fulførte utdanninger, etter kjønn studieåret 1999/2000*' (Number of completed educations after gender, study year 1999/2000), available at www.ssb.no/emner/04/utdanning_as/200108/vedltab%203.html.

Statistics Norway (2007a), 'Eigarskap i næringslivet' (Ownership in Norway), available at http://www.ssb.no/emner/10/01/ner/, accessed 15 September.
Statistics Norway (2007b), 'Women and men in Norway', available at http://www.ssb.no/english/subjects/00/02/10/ola_kari_en/, accessed 13 September.
Statistics Norway (2007c), 'Largest increase ever in immigrant population', available at http://www.ssb.no/english/subjects/02/01/10/innvbef_en/arkiv/art-2007-05-24-01-en.html.
Statistics Norway (2008), http://www.ssb.no/regnskap/, accessed 25 June.
Statistics Norway (2009), *Likestilling* (Gender equality), available at http://www.ssb.no/likestilling/, accessed 13 July.

13 Microfinance in Sweden

*Ranjula Bali Swain**

1 National context

Sweden has shown a good macroeconomic performance with high rates of growth. Its gross domestic product (GDP) is set to grow by 3.2 per cent in both 2007 and 2008, whereas unemployment is forecast to decline to 4.4 per cent in 2007 and 4.0 per cent in 2008 (Ministry of Finance, 2007). However, joblessness is widespread among immigrants and young people, and combating exclusion in the labour market is a key challenge for policy makers (OECD, 2007). Approximately 800 000 people live below the poverty line, which is 9 per cent of the total population.[1] A large part of these poor are single-parent families, the young and old, and immigrants. Moreover, financial exclusion is a reality for women and people living in sparsely populated areas. To assist them, the National Action Plan against Poverty and Social Exclusion 2003–2005 includes the promotion of starting a business.

In general, there are no major microcredit programmes in Sweden. The nearest similarity to microcredit schemes are some financial institutions established by the government to support small and microenterprises. ALMI is the only (public-funded) company providing loans to established companies and start-ups, complementing commercial loans. The commercial banks have not shown much interest in small and microenterprises (Siewertsen et al., 2005). Between 1000 and 4999 micro-operations were established in Sweden with support from the promotional banks (like ALMI) (European Commission, 2003).

The entrepreneurial environment within Sweden, however, is mainly focused on large companies. On average, people prefer wage employment. Moreover, complicated administrative and tax procedures for microenterprises make it very cumbersome to start and run small businesses. For ethnic entrepreneurs the registration process is even more complicated to understand. About 99 per cent of all private enterprises in Sweden are SMEs, of which 71 per cent are solo entrepreneurs. Compared to other (European) countries, the proportion of entrepreneurs in Sweden is below the average: the proportion of nascent entrepreneurs is 2.03 per cent (global entrepreneurship rate = 5.34 per cent). Immigrants are over-represented in self-employment compared to waged employment, especially in the retailing and restaurant sectors; 13.8 per cent of the self-employed and 9.7 per cent of all employed are foreign born (Siewertsen et al., 2005).

In Sweden, microcredit type support helped create only 1.7 jobs per firm besides the self-employment of the small enterprise founder (European Commission, 2003). In a survey of European businesses, access to finance remains a major constraint for 20 per cent of SMEs (Grant Thornton, 2002). High handling (or operational) costs for credit institutions is one of the most important obstacles according to the Microcredit Working Group. This is about 700 euros for Sweden and this accounts for about 7.5 per cent of the average microcredit amount.

According to the assessment in Siewertsen et al. (2005), the financial sector in Sweden does not show much interest in the issue of supporting self-employment as a career for the unemployed, and the instrument of microcredit is underdeveloped. Many mergers in the 1980s and 1990s have resulted in the existence of four large banks in Sweden, which have more than 80 per cent of the total assets on the banking market. In addition, there are a number of cooperatives, savings banks and foreign banks. There are no partnerships between banks and microfinance institutions, although ALMI cooperates with (local) banks because they give complementary loans to commercial loans.

Even though there are many subsidies and funds available in Sweden for all types of NGOs and programmes funded by the central and local government and the EU, there is no policy and only limited debate in relation to self-employment and microfinance. Most programmes are biased towards wage employment, and the total finance for social and employment programmes is decreasing (Siewertsen et al., 2005).

2 The history of microfinance in Sweden

Researchers have argued that every developed country has its own history of microfinance (Seibel, 2003). Savings banks in Sweden developed in a similar way to the many microfinance institutions (MFIs) of today. The savings banks had a social and philanthropic role, which is very similar to the role of MFIs in Europe today. As the European Commission (2003) also notes, savings banks, along with cooperative banks, remain the main traditional operators in the field of microcredit in Europe.

The microfinance history in Sweden can be traced back to the first savings banks that were established in the 1820s. They were the first financial organizations open to the general public. Sweden was a highly rural country, with less than 10 per cent of the population living in urban areas by the mid-nineteenth century. Initially, urbanization resulted in increasing poverty in the towns. The local governments, comprising the local socio-economic elites, had the responsibility of providing for the poor and offering a minimum standard of living. Hence, there was an obvious and strong incentive to start savings banks that contributed to reducing the costs for poor relief (Sjölander, 2003). A majority of these banks had the local- socio-economic elites as their donors or founders. The focus of the savings banks was to supply labourers with financial services. In such banks the social factors were greater than the financial aspects. The management was even freed from taxes, because the non-profit institutions (banks) were considered to be charity institutions. The founders gave starting capital for these institutions in order to reduce the general costs of care for the poor. The tax relief remained in place until 1910 (Lilja, 2004).

At first the saving banks were limited to the large cities but between the 1850s and the 1870s, many rural banks were established. By the turn of the century, these banks had spread to the less populated and developed regions. Moreover, the well-established savings banks extended their network by opening branch offices on a large scale. By the 1860s, the growth of the working class and the monetization of the Swedish economy had led to increasing deposits in the saving banks.[2] The mechanization and the modernization of Swedish agriculture led to an increasing demand for capital, which also led to an increase in the demand for the savings banks (Morell, 1997). With time, the savings banks became more professional and the rules and procedures became more standardized.

3 Main actors within the microfinance sector in Sweden

3.1 ALMI

ALMI provides microcredit without security to new and existing businesses. Under its Microloan scheme, since May 2007, ALMI has offered loans up to a maximum of SEK 100 000 (€10 700). The loan is given to companies that have the potential to survive in all kinds of fields. ALMI does not take any collateral for this loan and the firms have up to five years to repay it. During the first year, the interest rate is reduced and ALMI's basic interest rate (5 per cent, August 2007) is charged. However, from the second year onwards the market interest rate is charged on the loan.[3]

ALMI helps enterprises with business development, providing financial services for innovations and start-ups and established businesses. Its main objectives are to increase the number of enterprises, ensuring a greater number of innovations reach the market and that enterprises have an enhanced competitive strength. ALMI was founded in 1994 and has branches all over Sweden. It is owned by the state (51 per cent) and is the parent company of a group of 21 subsidiaries. Other owners are county councils, regional authorities and municipal cooperative bodies. It has approximately 450 employees. The boards of the subsidiary companies are made up of politicians, local business representatives and organizations with links to the business world. ALMI's lending activity is self-financed, and the management and day-to-day operation are financed by annual grants from the owners.

ALMI specifically aims to promote the development of competitive, small and medium-sized businesses as well as to stimulate new enterprise with the aim of creating growth and innovation in Swedish business life. The driving objectives are to get a greater number of innovative ideas into the market successfully, to see more viable businesses launched and developed, as well as to increase the competitiveness and profitability of the businesses. Its activities span the full cycle of development of business ideas to profitable businesses. Enterprises at different stages of development have different requirements, therefore at ALMI the activities are organized into three business areas according to client needs – Innovation, New Enterprises and Established Businesses. Within these areas, the two principal services that are offered are financing and business development.

ALMI meets approximately 100 000 SMEs and potential SMEs each year. Of these, about 24 000 become involved in extensive development programmes. It also assists in the evaluation of approximately 3500 new technology concepts and products annually, and contributes financially to some 2400 innovations.[4] At the end of 2006, ALMI had extended credit to nearly 32 500 client companies. In total, ALMI handled 3051 loans in 2006, of which 479 were microloans. Thus, through its new microcredit product (announced May 2007) and financial and non-financial services, ALMI is beginning to make an important contribution towards microfinance.

3.2 PITEM

Partnerskap för Integration, Tillväxt, Entreprenörskap och Mångfald (PITEM, Partnership for Integration, Growth, Entrepreneurship and Diversity) is a project that was started by the Nätverk för Entreprenörer från Etniska Minoriteter (NEEM, Network for Entrepreneurship from Ethnic Minorities) and BalticFem. Its main objective is to promote entrepreneurship among ethnic minorities. PITEM works with women and helps them to develop their ideas into functional business plans. They further contribute by providing knowledge about rules and formalities that are necessary when starting a business. PITEM, with financial support from ALMI, works to provide microcredit to immigrant women entrepreneurs.

3.3 Ekobank

Ekobank is owned by its members, with membership being mandatory for opening an account. It calls itself a social bank as its primary focus is not on profitability, but on the way the borrowers want to use their money. Ekobank's objective is to be the natural partner for Sweden's social economy. Ekobank therefore finances organizations and projects that work for the renewal of society in a wider sense and at the same time have sound finances and organization structures.[5] It thereby activates local capital in order to support sustainable development at local level. All loans granted from Ekobank must have adequate securities. Guarantors and real estate properties are two common securities used. For instance, when projects that are not able to provide their own security need a loan, people who would like to support the project can serve as guarantors. Group loans are another way in which a cluster of people who want to work together can build up capital for a project. Each person takes out a loan and at the same time serves as a guarantor for the other loanees in the group for the same amount they have been loaned. In this way, the entire group takes responsibility for a larger loan, and no single person needs to take on the entire loan. If a group member is unable to pay his/her loan, the amount is divided among the other members in the group. This is secure for the bank and the loanees. In addition, there are interest-free savings accounts that enable Ekobank to grant loans to needy projects with a low interest rate that just covers the bank's administrative costs.

Ekobank also offers various types of accounts where the savings are used to finance organizations that have a social or ecological value, and some of this money is granted as loans to private persons (members). For instance, its Ecology accounts are used for loans for alternative energy, ecological and biodynamic agriculture, conservation, research and other ecological projects. Health care account savings contribute to financing care of older and/or handicapped people, alternative medicine and therapy forms, drug abuse treatment and social projects. Children up to the age of 18 can earn interest on their savings at a favourable rate. Ekobank is also included in the national deposit guarantee system which means that the state guarantees protection for deposits made in banks up to SEK 250 000 (€27 200) per depositor and bank. Ekobank's innovative microfinance products and its social objectives are yet another example of the flexibility and relevance of microfinance in a developed society like Sweden, and can lead the way for similar MFIs in the rest of Europe.

4 Regulations

In the early 1800s there was no governmental supervision. Informal regulation based on social control in the local communities was possible through the donors voluntary participation and their status and legitimacy as the elites in society. This was also cost-effective for the government, which could obtain key information about the savings banks from the governors who were active in establishing many of the early savings banks. Today there are no direct regulations for the microfinance sector in Sweden. Microfinance activity is regulated within some of the main laws and normative acts. The Legislation for Financial Institutions[6] applies to commercial banks, savings banks and guarantee societies. It regulates how much capital these types of institutions have to raise in order to start their business, and among the other regulations there are very extensive rules, for instance on how to secure the savers money and so on.

There is no usury law in Sweden and it is not possible for non-banks to lend, except for ALMI, which is publicly owned. Outside of the government, lending is not possible. The legislation about government financing by ALMI Företagspartner AB[7] states that ALMI is obliged to charge a higher interest rate than banks, because of the higher risk and so that it does not compete with the banks (European Commission, 2007; ALMI, 2006).

5 Financial and operational sustainability

In several European countries, a below-market interest rate practice (soft loan or even interest-free loan) still exists. According to different sources, such soft loan funds provided by private microcredit institutions should be regarded as being of limited value.[8] Such private funds cannot be self-sustainable, and therefore independent of public subsidies. Using the EU reference rate as the benchmark[9] for Sweden, the average interest rate in relation to reference rate is about 1.7 per cent for loans with a maturity of 3–5 years and 2.36 per cent for loans with a maturity of over five years.

In terms of the general features of the collateral policy of microcredit programmes, real estate is not usually used as collateral, because in the event of bankruptcy, the legal process may last up to five years. In Sweden, the share of typical collateral for specific microcredit programmes are receivables (60 per cent) or no collateral (40 per cent) (European Commission, 2003).

Self-sustainability is a major issue for any microcredit fund. In order to achieve sustainability, microcredit institutions can either charge an above-market interest rate, which is acceptable if the risk is higher, or they may increase the interest rate because of the risk associated with the low survival rates of many businesses.[10] The interest rates can also be high because the 'alternative is either borrowing at even higher rates, perhaps from an informal money-lender, or not borrowing at all'. The relatively high administrative costs of a microcredit, however, need to be addressed. One option for a self-sustainable microcredit activity is to scale up to offset the likely marginal profitability. Another option is to allow the microcredit operators to be fully self-sustainable, charging higher interest rates. Available data suggests, however, that operational sustainability is not obtained immediately and depends on an appropriate application rejection rate by the microcredit institutions: it therefore suggests that there is a need for a substantial injection of capital and/or subsidies, during the early stage of operations. ALMI's experience in Sweden shows that the operational sustainability benchmark of microlending extension seems to evolve to 100 per cent between five and eight years (European Commission, 2003).

Administrative costs associated with microcredit activities are high relative to a microloan amount. Of these, wages are the most important component, as providing microcredit is labour-intensive. However, the ratio of these costs progressively declines with the portfolio size. To mitigate this factor, different forms of partnership have been agreed recently between public promotional banks and retail banks as well as business support providers. As ALMI receives economic support from the government, it can give loans even if they are labour intensive. Banks know this and trust ALMI, so they continue to take a major part in the financing of companies.

6 Challenges for the sector in Sweden

Although there are many initiatives to address unemployment there is no clear policy for using microfinance to help encourage self-employment. Apart from two organizations that are active at national level, self-employment and microfinance is in a development phase in Sweden. In addition, the three systems (financial, employment and social) do not actively cooperate.

The main bottleneck in Sweden, however, seems to be the administrative procedures, the bureaucracy and taxes involved in establishing a business. Although various resources and services are in place to assist entrepreneurs in starting a business, the business environment is unfavourable to the small business sector. Therefore, it is important not only to develop policy measures to support microenterprises but also to create an environment that is small-business minded in terms of entrepreneurial context, legal framework, tax system and cooperation between the different systems. Furthermore, the three systems (financial, employment and social) must cooperate, and there needs to be a debate on microcredit and the role to be played by banks, savings banks, welfare and employment institutions.

Notes

* Expert: Per Jonsson.
1. Source: Siewertsen et al. (2005).
2. Petersson (2001).

3. Source: ALMI lanserar nytt mikrolån, www.almi.se.
4. Source: www.almi.se.
5. It encourages people to take free initiatives to enrich society in the form of a wider variety of forms of health care, educational methods and artistic expression. Ekobank considers money as a social medium through which cooperation among people and groups is made easier. It is also interested in sustainable business which has consideration for the environment and for human beings.
6. Lag om bank- och finansieringsrörelse 2004:297; Förordning om bank- och finansieringsrörelse SFS 2004:329.
7. Förordning om statlig finansiering genom ALMI Företagspartner AB SFS 1994:1100.
8. *The State of Community Development Finance 2001*, Collins et al. (2001).
9. The reference rate used for average calculations for Sweden is 5.68 per cent.
10. Statistically, 50 per cent of all new companies tend to disappear over a five-year period.

References

ALMI (2006), www.almi.se/finansering.html, accessed 31 August 2007.

Collins, Sam, Thomas Fisher, Ed Mayo, Andy Mullineux and Danyal Sattar (2001), *The Sate of Community Development Finance 2001*, Birmingham: NEF.

European Commission (2003), *Microcredit for Small Businesses and Business Creation: Bridging a Market Gap*, Enterprise publications, Brussels: European Commission.

European Commission (2007), 'The regulation of microcredit in Europe', Expert Group Report, Enterprise and Industry, Brussels: European Commission.

Fälting, L., E. Liljefrost and T. Petersson (2006), 'The microfinance revolution revisited: experiences from the savings banks history in Sweden', *European Dialogue*, **36**, 33–48.

Lilja, K. (2004), 'Marknand och hushåll. Sparande och krediter I Falun 1820–1910 utifrån ett livscyckelperspective', *Uppsala Studies in Economic History*, **71**, Uppsala University.

Ministry of Finance (2007), 'The Swedish economy', press release, Ministry of Finance, 20 September 2007.

Morell, M. (1997), 'Family farms and agricultural mechanization in Sweden before World War II', in Lars Jonung and Rolf Ohlsson (eds), *The Economic Development of Sweden since 1870*, Cheltenham, UK and Lyme, NH, USA: Edward Elgar.

OECD (2007), *Economic Survey of Sweden, 2007*, Paris: OECD.

Petersson, T. (2001), 'Framväxten av ett lokalt banksystem. Oppunda sparbank, Södermanslands enskilda bank och stationssamhället Katriasneholm 1850–1916', *Uppsala Studies in Economic History*, **56**, Uppsala University.

Seibel, H.D. (2003), 'History matters in microfinance', *Small Enterprise Development*, **14**(2), 10–12.

Siewertsen, H., J. Evers, S. Forster, I. Heetvelt, P. Ramsden and W. Thomas (2005), 'Policy measure to promote the use of micro-credit for social inclusion', study conducted on behalf of the European Commission DG Employment, Social Affairs and Equal Opportunities, unit E/2.

Sjölander, A. (2003), 'Den naturliga ordningen. Makt och intressen i de svenska sparbankerna 1882–1968', *Uppsala Studies in Economic History*, **63**, Uppsala University.

Grant Thornton (2002), *European Business Survey*, Grant Thornton International.

14 Microcredit in Belgium
*Annika Cayrol and Jean Marchand**

1 National context

Belgium is no exception to recent worldwide interest in microcredit; the national context is favourable to microcredit. Indeed, even if Belgium is considered a rich and industrialized country – number 24 worldwide for its quality of life according to The Economist Intelligence Unit's index[1] in 2005 – poverty still exists.

The figures[2] from 2005 indicate that the poverty risk percentage is at 14.7 per cent, which represents more than 1.5 million Belgians. The sectors of the population that are more at risk seem to be women (15.5 per cent versus 14 per cent men) and elderly people over 65 years old (20.6 per cent). Moreover, single parents (35.1 per cent) tend to be more at risk than families or couples.

Finally, being employed appears to be a clear parameter in helping to avoid poverty. Indeed, employed people only have a poverty risk percentage of 3.9 per cent, while the unemployed are at 30.7 per cent and the retired at 18.4 per cent.

Compared to the European average, which lies at 16 per cent[3] according to the DG Employment, Social Affairs and Equal Opportunities, Belgium has slightly fewer people at risk of poverty (15.2 per cent).

According to Prof. Dr Rainer Trinczek (Trinczek, 2007) from the Technical University of Munich, 'it is a proven fact that employment not only reduces the poverty risk but also the general risk of social exclusion, as work is a major means for social integration'.

Therefore, one way to include people who are socially excluded from the system is through employment. This is where the possibility of microcredit, may it be to become an independent worker or to help launch or maintain a Small and Medium Enterprise (SME), can change someone's situation in order to reduce the poverty level.

2 The origin of microcredit in Belgium

2.1 Inception to present

Microfinance is a broader concept than microcredit. It can include other financial services such as insurance, savings, pension plans and so on. The Development Centre from the OECD defines it as 'loans, savings, insurance, transfer services and other financial products targeted at low-income clients' (Wegner, 2006). With regard to Belgium, microfinance is almost equivalent to microcredit.

In Belgium, the roots of solidarity-based finance are deep. Microcredit sees its origin with the creation of a 'Mont de Piété' in 1618,[4] influenced by an Italian monk who started a piety credit, in Italian 'monte pietà'. The idea is to lend money at a low or zero rate of interest to poor people in need. This institution still exists today.

In 1892, the first 'Gilde d'épargne et de credit' (saving and credit guild) inspired by the Raffeisen system in Germany was initiated in Rillaar by the Abbot Mellaerts (Vanhuslt and Vanderhasselt, 2007). At that time, the social purpose of the guilds was also combined with religious and political considerations; nonetheless, by collecting deposits, it offered local credit activities to needy farmers exposed to usury practices. Then, these guilds gathered around the 'Caisse Centrale de Crédit' during the twentieth century, whose activities are no longer considered as microcredit.

Even though two out of the three current organizations promoting microcredit (Fonds de Participation and Crédal) were created as early as 1984, the historical beginning of microcredit was carried out as a five-year pilot project by the King Baudouin Foundation from 1997 to 2002 (Bayot, 2001–02).

Indeed, the 'microcredit business line' of the Fonds de Participation only started in 2002 when they took over the 'Prêt Solidaire' (Solidarity loan) from the King Baudouin Foundation. This was done because the latter did not wish to become a credit institution.

In 1984, the cooperative microfinance institution Crédal was born. Since then, it has been providing ethical savings to its members, and to its credit clients (social-economy organizations) low interest rates as well as management advice. In 2000, it initiated a microcredit programme for those who wish to become self-employed called 'MC2', which is growing steadily (Crédal, 2006). It offers loans for starting and developing businesses as well as adapted support services to the financially excluded self-employed.

Finally, Brusoc, a branch of the 'Société Régionale d'Investissement de Bruxelles' (SRIB) created a microcredit product in 2001 aimed at those wishing to start their own business in the Objective 2 zone[5] of the Brussels-Capital Region.

2.2 Microcredit: a tool to invest ethically and combat poverty

Microcredit materialized in Belgium as a result of different influences such as the creation of the Grameen Bank and the Year of Microcredit. However, a decisive influence – at least in the creation of Crédal – has been in the 1980s when people started to wonder where their money was invested.

The public's attention was drawn to the fact that some banks were supporting the racist regime of apartheid in South Africa. Creating Crédal ensured that the money invested was reinvested in social-economy projects.

Another reason for these organizations to come up with this initiative is that it increases the chance of reducing poverty. For financially marginalized people, these institutions can be a way to become reintegrated into the economic system. Also, since the amount of credit these institutions grant is generally smaller, they answer a different need from that met by mainstream banks. Finally, one common goal microcredit institutions share is the promotion of self-employment.

2.3 The creation of microfinance institutions

As mentioned earlier, microcredit appeared in Belgium first as a pilot project from the King Baudouin Foundation. The market is now divided between three main actors, Fonds de Participation, Brusoc and Crédal. These players offer microcredit to underprivileged people in two ways:

- public or semi-public for the Fonds de Participation (public credit agency) and Brusoc ('société anonyme' stock company – in which shares are held by seven public and private organizations, with the Brussels-Capital Region being the major shareholder)
- limited liability cooperative company with social purposes for Crédal

Although their products are different (as detailed in section 6), their goal is similar in the sense that they aim to fill a gap left by mainstream banks, that is to address a financially excluded population that wishes to start up an economic activity.

3 Main actors within the microcredit sector in Belgium

3.1 Main actors

In this section, three main actors are identified, described and exemplified: the microfinance institutions (MFIs), the support structures and the public authorities.[6]

According to the Development Centre of the OECD (Wegner, 2006), MFIs are defined as 'a broad range of financial sector organisations such as banks, non-bank financial institutions, financial cooperatives and credit unions, finance companies and NGOs specialising in serving people who lack access to traditional financial services'.

In Belgium, there are three main MFIs matching the historical entities mentioned above: the Fonds de Participation, Crédal and Brusoc.

Table 14.1 Presentation of main actors in Belgium

	Fonds de Participation	Crédal	Brusoc
Activity area	Belgium	Brussels & Wallonia Regions	Brussels Region (Objective 2 Zone)
Legal form	Federal public company	Limited liability cooperative company with social purpose (SCRL FS)	Subsidiary of the SRIB stock company – in which shares are held by 7 public and private organizations with the Brussels-Capital Region being the major shareholder
Products	'Prêt Solidaire' – Solidarity Loan 'Prêt Lancement' – Start-up Loan[a]	MC2: microcredit	Microcredit 'Fonds d'Amorçage' – Starters' Loan[b]
Programmes	'Plan Jeunes Indépendants' – Young Independents Plan	'Affaires de femmes, femmes d'affaires' (AFFA)	

Notes:

a The amounts granted by the start-up loan can go up to €30 000. This product has still been included here because the average amount granted is below €25 000; it averages €23 955 with support services, and €24 110 without in 2006.

b The starters' loan ranges between €5000 and €95 000 and averaged €30 578 in 2006. It is included in this table as its loan range also includes credits below €25 000, and is often mentioned in the microcredit sector, but it will not be presented in more detail in this study.

Sources: www.fonds.be, www.credal.be and www.srib.be (2007).

All microcredit products and programmes shown in Table 14.1 refer to 'small loans to financially and socially excluded people for self-employment projects that generate income, allowing them to care for themselves and their families, and to SMEs', where the term 'small' means below €25 000. There are two exceptions which are explained in notes.

From this table, one can observe that Brusoc is the only MFI that does not have a targeted programme. The reason is probably that their target group is already quite specific. Indeed, it focuses on people who wish to start a business in the Objective 2 zone of the Brussels-Capital Region.

Another organization that it is important to mention here is Hefboom. In September 2007 this organization started to offer microcredits up to €12 500 in the Flemish and Brussels-Capital Regions. Its aim is to become the counterpart of Crédal. Currently, Hefboom combines financial products, such as investment credit, short-term credit, guarantees or loans, with support services.

The second group of main actors is support structures. MFIs work in close collaboration with support structures such as local enterprise counters or 'one-stop-shops' for businesses, social secretariats[7] and enterprise centres. There are quite a few support structures in Belgium, such as UCM, Unizo, GroupeOne, Job'in, HDP, SD Worx, Securex . . .

Thirdly, there are the public authority actors that work on a transnational, federal or regional level.[8]

3.2 Description

3.2.1 MFI: Fonds de Participation The Fonds de Participation is a federal public agency that supports and encourages entrepreneurship. It delivers its missions under the umbrella of three ministries: Middle Class, Finances and Employment.

The Fonds de Participation has the following main objectives (www.fonds.org):

1. To maximize the impact of the granted credits/interventions to support SMEs and to help fight unemployment, keeping an open spirit and partnership attitude regarding other players in the field;
2. To share the Fonds de Participation's know-how with other organizations, namely the goal of facilitating access to professional credit, while providing them with the best technical and financial services;
3. To act as a 'knowledge centre' known for its expertise, to spread and coordinate best practice on financing SMEs.

Among the different types of financial tools offered by the Fonds de Participation, is the microcredit business line, which includes three microcredit mechanisms:

- Start-up Loan which comes with an optional professional support service.
- Young Independents Plan is a programme to support an application

Table 14.2 *Selected figures from the Fonds de Participation's annual report 2006*

	Approved credits		Amount (€)		Average granted amount (€)
Solidarity Loan	26	2%	299 857	0.4%	11 535
Start-up Loan (with support services)	464	40%	10 475 737	14.1%	23 955
Start-up Loan (without support)					24 110
Start-up Loan (Young Independents Plan)					23 175
Other loans	659	57%	63 670 920	85.5%	
Total	1149	100%	74 446 514	100%	

Source: Fonds de Participation (2006b).

for a Start-up loan aimed at young people – less than 30 years old – who have a business project.

- Solidarity Loan aimed at underprivileged people who start up an independent activity.

The target groups for these products are the unemployed or those who can not easily obtain credit from mainstream banks and who wish to launch their own economic activity.

In 2006, the total amount of all approved credits and microcredits owned by the Fonds de Participation was €74 446 514 (see Table 14.2). Together, the Solidarity Loan and the Start-up Loan products amount to €10 775 594. The Fonds de Participation's microcredit activity represents 42 per cent of the credit production in terms of approved loans and 14.5 per cent in terms of amounts in euros.

Adding the Solidarity and Start-up Loans together shows that the Fonds de Participation is the principal provider in the microcredit sector in Belgium in terms of amounts and number of approved credits.

3.2.2 MFI: Crédal Crédal was created in 1984 as a cooperative organization whose aim is to collect funds to lend money to associations helping the underprivileged. At first, only associations (solidarity-based credits) were targeted, but the loans Crédal now grants are more diverse.

One product and one programme match the microcredit definition proposed in this study. These are MC2: microcredit, which targets people setting up their own business, and the AFFA programme, launched in 2005, which aims to improve participation of women as self-employed workers.

All the loans are made in an ethical manner, with stable interest rates that are not directly linked to the market nor to the applicant's credit risk. Also, there is a pedagogical dimension, with support services being offered all through the introductory phase of the loan and often during the whole period of the loan (www.credal.be).

Crédal has three objectives that come from the vision of its founding members (www.credal.be):

1. To support social projects that do not have access to bank credit, on the one hand, thanks to moderate rate loans in Wallonia and Brussels, and on the other hand through management advice.
2. To offer solidarity-based investments by supporting initiatives concerning the underprivileged, the excluded, Belgians or foreigners, in short, those projects tackling the causes and not only the effects of marginalization.
3. To offer to the communities and private individuals a form of alternative saving whose output is not initially financial, but is above all social and human. That is, to build a trusting relationship based on transparency.

At the end of 2006, Crédal had 1121 shareholders and a total fund of €9 471 456. During 2006, 49 requests for microcredits were granted for a total amount of €320 107 (see Table 14.3).

3.2.3 MFI: Brusoc Created in 2001, Brusoc is a subsidiary of the SRIB, whose role is to help and guide self-employed people and small enterprises. In short, Brusoc aims to develop the social and local economy in the Brussels-Capital Region (www.srib.be).

Brusoc has three credit products of which only one matches the definition and scope of this study. The first two, the 'Fonds d'Amorçage' (Starters' Fund) and the 'Prêt Subordonné' (Subordinate Loan) do not meet the definition exactly.[9] The 'Microcrédit' (Microcredit) product is targeted at people living in precarious conditions who would like to start or to develop an independent economic activity.

All products have in common the following conditions:

- they target people wishing to develop an activity in the Objective 2 zone of the Brussels-Capital Region;

Table 14.3 Selected figures from Crédal's annual report 2006

	Approved credits		Amount (€)		Average granted amount (€)
Crédit social accompagné	112	38%	355705	3%	2800
Microcredit	49	16%	320107	3%	8585
AFFA[a]	1		10000		10000
Other loans	137	46%	10620743	94%	
Total	298	100%	11296555	100%	

Note: a. The only microcredit given to a woman participating in the AFFA programme was granted by Hefboom to a candidate entrepreneur residing in the Flemish Region. Crédal is clearly an important player on the microcredit market in Belgium.

Source: Crédal, Annual Report (2006).

Table 14.4 Selected figures from Brusoc's annual report 2006

	Approved credits		Amount (€)		Average granted amount (€)
Microcredit	13	21%	164111.17	9%	13055
Starters' Fund	42	69%	1188724.05	69%	30578
Subordinate Fund	6	10%	380000.00	22%	
Total	61	100%	1732835.22	100%	

Source: Brusoc, Annual Report (2006).

- the target group has trouble obtaining a mainstream bank loan;
- the candidate is ready to bring a minimum contribution.

At the end of 2006, 17 microcredit cases had been finalized for a total amount of €194780. Table 14.4 shows the distribution per type of credit at Brusoc.

3.2.4 Business support structures Support structures are essential links between the target groups and the MFIs. They advise and inform potential borrowers about the possibility of accessing microcredit to start up an economic activity.

Created in 2003, there are now ten registered business one-stop-shops in Belgium.[10] The idea behind these structures is to simplify the administrative procedures[11] for start-ups and established SMEs. They usually have their headquarters in Brussels and branches in other Belgian cities. Their legal status is 'association sans but lucratif' which is a type of not-for-profit organization.

They guide entrepreneurs through the administrative formalities but can also be the ones to direct the candidates to the right organizations that can help them finance a project. They are an important intermediary institution between the target groups and the MFIs.

Social secretariats provide assistance and support for companies, the self-employed and private individuals in all fields of social regulation and human resource management. Sometimes, these entities are combined with a business one-stop-shop.

Another support structure called 'enterprise centres' help to create and develop businesses. They make available a series of services ranging from administrative help, office rental and business planning to training. They can also be combined with other business services such as a 'guichet d'entreprise local' (local company counter; see for example: https://www.go-start.be/gostart/frameset.htm?lang=fr), which performs eligibility studies and gives information on legal issues.

3.2.5 Public authorities Public authorities are involved at two levels in the microcredit sector in Belgium. There are the regional governments, namely Wallonia, Flanders and Brussels-Capital, and the Federal government which support different microcredit initiatives or act as guarantees.

3.3 Main microcredit actor functions

In most cases in Belgium, MFIs are the motors of microcredit, support structures are the key intermediaries between MFIs and potential customers, while private institutions and public authorities usually provide funds and/or guarantees. These relationships are illustrated in Figure 14.1.

4 Model of microcredit granting in Belgium

In Belgium, MFIs have different juridical statuses, operating modes and objectives, as explained previously. Financial strategies, fund dispensers and beneficiaries vary according to the rules of each microcredit institution. The same goes for granting conditions, granted amounts and interest rates, which are detailed below.

4.1 Guarantees

Concerning microcredit, none of the main Belgian MFIs asks for an obligatory guarantee, for the simple reason that it is, in most cases, too much of a constraint for the applicant.

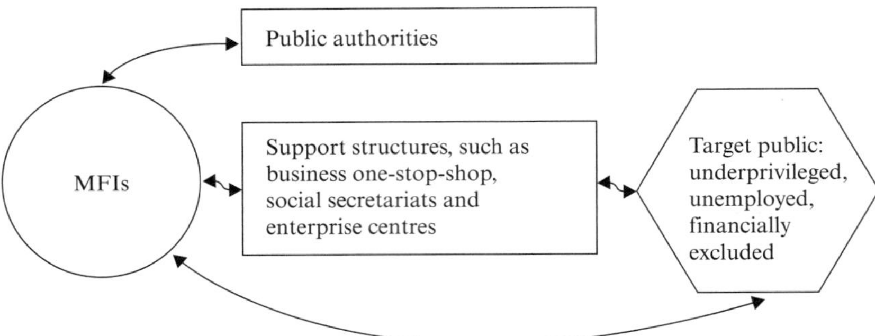

Source: Réseau Financement Alternatif.

Figure 14.1 Main microcredit actor functions and mechanisms

However, Crédal lowers its interest rate (from 5 per cent to 3 per cent) if one or more people close to the beneficiary guarantee(s) 50 per cent of the amount of the loan.[12] There are also two other possible ways to reduce the interest rate; by providing, in cash, 25 per cent of the amount granted or by subscribing for cooperative shares for 20 per cent of the amount obtained.

Indeed, it is only since October 2006 that Crédal decided to cancel the compulsory condition that stated that 'one or more people close to the beneficiary must guarantee 50% of the obtained amount' (Proximity Finance Foundation, 2007).

4.2 Interest rates

The interest rates proposed by the MFIs range from 3 per cent to 8 per cent (8 per cent occurring only in one case), most of them being at 3 per cent or 4 per cent. Although there are no laws limiting the interest rates for self-employment and SME microcredits, there is a usury law in Belgium that limits the interest rate for consumption credit and therefore for microcredit consumption.[13]

It is interesting to note that some people, generally because of their religious beliefs, refuse to borrow money that they will need to pay back with interest (Proximity Finance Foundation, 2007).

4.3 Support services

Support services are another essential aspect of the way MFIs operate. There are two types of support services: before and after the microcredit is granted. The structures can be business one-stop-shops, social secretariats, enterprise centres or one of the following:

- 'Coopérative d'activités' (activity cooperative): support service organization that allows for people who wish to set up their own business to do it in a secure framework that facilitates the start-up as well as helping the entrepreneur to learn how to manage a company on a day-to-day operational basis (http://www.coopac.be/spip.php?rubrique4). The candidate has an employed status.
- 'Couveuse d'entreprise' (Enterprise incubator): an integration tool to assist self-employment projects of the would-be self-employed who are currently unemployed (http://emploi.wallonie.be/THEMES/SOCIO/couveuses.htm). This structure allows the candidate to keep his/her social allowances by having a trainee status.

4.4 Amounts granted

The amounts that can be granted by Belgian MFIs range between €1250 and €30 000. If the definition is strictly followed, the maximum amount should be €25 000, but as mentioned earlier, this study includes the Start-up Loan from the Fonds de Participation, which offers loans that can go up to €30 000.

Average amounts granted vary between €8585 (Crédal; MC2) and €24 110 (Fonds de Participation; start-up loan without support services).

4.5 Repayment period

The repayment period for microcredit in Belgium ranges from 1 to 10 years. The average seems to be around 3–4 years. More details for each microcredit product or programme are provided in section 6.

5 Target groups in Belgium

In Europe, there are two major groups that are targeted by microcredit programmes: the people at risk of poverty (unemployed, inactive), and micro-entrepreneurs who are usually excluded from mainstream bank credit (Guichandut, 2006). This remains true for Belgium.

Within the scope of this study, only microcredit for self-employment and SMEs is considered. Table 14.5 details the target groups for the three main MFIs in Belgium, per product or programme.

As shown in the table, the target groups for the products are quite broad, usually the unemployed and those who have been refused credit from a mainstream bank. However, looking at the programmes, target subgroups emerge. These subgroups are women and young people under 30 years old. The reasons behind targeting these subgroups differ.

Crédal took the decision to especially target women with AFFA since, according to statistics,[14] only 33 per cent of self-employed persons were women in 2005.

Table 14.5 Target group per microcredit product / programme

MFI / Product	Target group
Brusoc / Microcredit	People living in precarious conditions: recipients of a social allowance, unemployed and refugees[a] in the Objective 2 zone of Brussels-Capital
Crédal / MC2	(Future) micro-entrepreneurs who have difficulty accessing mainstream bank credits
Fonds de Participation / Solidarity Loan	People not having access to mainstream bank credit and who have difficulty obtaining starting capital because of their financial situation. It can thus be people receiving social help from the Public Centre of Social Action (CPAS) of Belgian municipalities, recipients of 'integration income', asylum seekers or recipients of unemployment allowance
Fonds de Participation / Start-up Loan	Unemployed fully compensated, inactive unemployed for at least 3 months, recipients of a 'waiting allowance' or 'integration income'
MFI / Programme	**Target group**
Fonds de Participation / Young Independent Plan	People under 30 years old, inactive unemployed becoming self-employed for the first time
Crédal / AFFA	Women wishing to become self-employed

Note: a See Bracke (2002).

Sources: www.fonds.be, www.credal.be and www.srib.be (2007).

The Fonds de Participation launched its programme because the Global Entrepreneurship Monitor classified Belgium as coming last – among 49 countries – in 2006 in terms of entrepreneurial activity (only 2.7 per cent[15] of adult population 18–64) (Fonds de participation, 2006b). They decided that the most efficient way to stimulate entrepreneurship would be to interest the younger unemployed.

Finally, Brusoc aims its products at a geographical subgroup. The beneficiaries have to create their economic activity in the Objective 2 zone of the Brussels-Capital Region. Objective 2 zones are defined by the EU as 'all areas facing structural difficulties, whether industrial, rural, urban or dependent on fisheries. Though situated in regions whose development level is close to the Community average, such areas are faced with different types of socio-economic difficulties that are often the source of high unemployment.'[16] For the Brussels-Capital Region, it translates to the following neighbourhoods; Saint-Gilles, Anderlecht, Brussels, Molenbeek, Forest, Schaerbeek and Saint-Josse, which is also named the 'North–South axis'[17] of Brussels.

6 Financial terms and conditions

For this section, the best way to present the information is in a table, showing the product and programmes on one axis and the different financial terms and conditions on the other.

As mentioned previously, there is no particular regulation for investment credit but only for consumption credit. Therefore, interest rates can vary. Of course, for microcredits, they are not especially high, since this would not correspond to the target groups' requirements.

Table 14.6 gives a summary of commonly used financial terms and conditions per product or programme available in Belgium. It includes interest rates, grace periods, loan amounts, repayment periods, collaterals and main business services provided, but also objectives, target groups, reimbursement instalments and excluded sectors, among others.

The characteristics of Brusoc's Starters' Loan are not shown, since this product does not fully fit the microcredit definition. Even though the Start-up Loan of the Fonds de Participation does not fully fit the microcredit definition, it has been included for the following reasons:

- the loan is only €5000 higher than the official limit of the definition (€30 000 instead of €25 000);[18]
- the average amount of its loans is below the €25 000 upper limit (see point 3.2.1 above);
- the Fonds de Participation includes it in its 'microcredit business line';
- the target group is in line with the one defined by the European Union.[19]

7 Other financial products for inclusion

7.1 Consumer microcredit: 'crédit social accompagné'

The 'credit social accompagné' is a consumer credit, provided by Crédal, for people on the road to social inclusion.[20] This type of credit aims to improve the applicant's living conditions by enabling them to pay for useful goods (such as energy saving systems, items for disabled people) or by supporting specific needs (health expenditure, driving licence fees, special insurance and so on).[21]

Some conditions are required to benefit from this type of loan:[22]

Table 14.6 Financial terms and conditions

Microfinance institution	**Fonds de participation**		
Product / programmes	**Solidarity Loan**	**Launching Loan**	**Young Independents Plan**
Interest rate	3%	4% but 3% if coaching is followed for first two years	
Grace period (postponing the reimbursement of the capital)	3 months	1 to 3 years depending on the structure	
Amount	up to 12.000€	up to 30.000€	up to 30.000€ and possibility of interest-free loan of 4.500€ that can be reimbursed in the 6th and 7th year of the project
Repayment period	4 years	5, 7 or 10 years depending on project	
Collateral - guarantee - personal savings - peer group	No guarantee but personal collateral is regarded as a positive element	No guarantee	
Own contribution	None	25% of loan amount	
Main business services provided	Free professional follow-up services before and after (18 months) credit granted	Free professional follow-up services for 18 months after credit granted	If a project is accepted, the candidate receives a 3–6 months support service, 375€/month if she/he has no income which can be combined to an establishment or a waiting allowance from the NEM - free professional support services for 24 months after credit granted

<table>
<tr><th colspan="3">Crédal</th><th>Brusoc</th></tr>
<tr><th>MC2 investment microcredit</th><th>MC2 treasury microcredit</th><th>AFFA</th><th>Microcredit</th></tr>
<tr><td>5% but 3% under certain conditions, please see point 4.1</td><td>8%</td><td>5%</td><td>4%</td></tr>
<tr><td colspan="2">3 or 6 months possible depending on the case</td><td>None</td><td>None</td></tr>
<tr><td>up to 12.500€</td><td>up to 10.000€</td><td>up to 10.000€</td><td>1.250€–25.000€</td></tr>
<tr><td>Maximum 4 years</td><td>Maximum 1 year</td><td>3 years</td><td>1–5 years; average 3 years</td></tr>
<tr><td colspan="2">No guarantee. 125€ of administrative costs if the credit is accepted by the committee, but finally refused by the client</td><td>No guarantee</td><td>No guarantee</td></tr>
<tr><td colspan="2">Refundable 5% of credit amount in a guarantee fund if microcredit <12.500€ but 10% of loan if >25.000€ through co-financing</td><td>Refundable 3% of credit in a guarantee fund (2% as individual contribution and 1% as collective contribution)</td><td>620€ minimum</td></tr>
<tr><td colspan="2">Support services provided by support structures before credit granted and Crédal expert available upon request after the credit is granted</td><td>240 hours over 4 months free training / 3 to 5 women ‘support circles’ - peer coaching/ technical adviser and trainer available during the first year</td><td>Free support services before and after the credit is granted during the whole repayment period*</td></tr>
</table>

Table 14.6 (continued)

Microfinance institution	**Fonds de participation**		
Product / programmes	**Solidarity Loan**	**Launching Loan**	**Young Independents Plan**
Loan decision-making criteria	Project's financial, economical and technical success chances - Professional and management competency as well as candidate's honor - Quality and policy of enterprise - Viability and financial structure of enterprise - Reimbursement capacity		
Reimbursement	45 constant monthly instalments	Monthly instalments	
Excluded sectors	All sectors except some restrictions on agriculture, transportation and exportation, according to EC 1998/2006 regulation 15/12/2006, art. 87 & 88		
Co-financing possibility	No	Yes, with Starteo, Crédal MC2, Brusoc loans or a mainstream bank loan	
Subordination	Yes, "quasi capital" status		
Target group	People not having access to mainstream bank credit and that have difficulties obtaining starting capital because of their financial situation	Unemployed fully compensated, inactive unemployed for at least 3 months, recipients of a "waiting allowance" or an "integration income"	Under 30 years old inactive unemployed becoming self-employed for the first time
Objective	Start up an independent economy activity	Create or start up an independent activity or SME	Prepare potential candidates for the launching loan

- being employed under Articles 60 or 61, i.e. receiving from the CPAS 'Centre Public d'Action Sociale' either unemployment or social benefits;
- proving his/her ability to repay the loan as well as existing charges;

Crédal			**Brusoc**
MC2 investment microcredit	**MC2 treasury microcredit**	**AFFA**	**Microcredit**
- No access to mainstream bank credit - Start or develop a viable economic activity - Commit to the solidarity process programme - Accept follow up services - Have a mature project enterprise		– Respect the support circle rules - Have a planned business plan - Answer all questions and pass on requested information	- Difficulty accessing mainstream bank credit - Need to develop activity in Objective 2 zone of Brussels-Capital
Constant monthly instalments			Constant monthly instalments
Pure import-export, call centres, messaging services or politically incorrect businesses			None
Yes, with Launching Loan (Fonds de participation), Brusoc loans or a mainstream bank loan			Yes, but rarely
No			No
(Future) micro-entrepreneurs who have difficulty accessing mainstream bank credit		Women wishing to create self-employment	People that wish to launch or develop their economic activity, that are unemployed in the Objective 2 zone of Brussels-Capital and have trouble accessing mainstream bank credit
Create or expand an independent activity	Finance temporary cash flow needs	Train and eventually grant a microcredit to become self-employed	Support local economy by helping and coaching the creation or development of activities, self-employed or SMEs

- proving that no other less costly solution exists – or it should be preferred;
- making sure the candidate is resident in Brussels-Capital or in Wallonia.

The amount of this credit can vary from €500 to €7500 and the loan period can be 12, 18, 24, 30 or 36 months, depending on the loan amount. Concerning the annual interest rate, the law requires that it represents the total cost of the credit,[23] which is 6.5 per cent for loans up to €2000 and 5.5 per cent[24] for loans from €2001 and upwards.

This financial product differs from the scope of this study because it does not apply to self-employment projects or SMEs. However, this consumer credit is still microcredit, because:

- It is another way to fight poverty, since this credit can allow someone to access employment (for example by purchasing a vehicle to be able to work in remote locations);
- It refers to small loans;
- It targets those at risk of poverty or marginalized people.

7.2 Guarantee mechanism: measure to promote microcredit access to micro-entrepreneurs[25]

Since the International Year of Microcredit in 2005, a new initiative has emerged from the Walloon government. The idea is to facilitate the granting of credit under €25 000 to entrepreneurs with mainstream banks through a system of guarantees.

In concrete terms, it consists of a first 80 per cent guarantee from the mutual guarantee company[26] for a microcredit[27] provided by a bank to a microenterprise.[28] Then, the 'Société des Cautions Mutuelles de Wallonie' (SOCAMUT) insures 75 per cent as a counter-guarantee for the first security provided by the MCA. It can also finance up to €500 of the administrative costs to help the application for microcredit.

In Belgium, the following mainstream banks have signed an agreement with the Société Wallonne de Financement et de Garantie des Petites et Moyennes Entreprises (SOWALFIN): Banque du Crédit Professionnel, CBC, CPH, Crédit Agricole, Banque du Brabant, Crédit Professionnel Interfédéral, Delta Lloyd Bank, Dexia, Fortis, KBC and ING. Moreover, the MFI Crédal is currently in negotiations to sign a 50 per cent guarantee scheme with SOWALFIN.

With this mechanism, the SOCAMUT wishes to foster the development of microenterprises that have no access to investment credit because they do not have a guarantor.

To benefit from this system, the applicants must fulfil the following requirements:

- They must have no financial difficulties.
- They must not work in the following sectors: banking–

finance–insurance, real estate promotion, energy production,[29] health, culture,[30] agriculture–fishing–aquaculture, naval construction and transport.[31]

This initiative does not completely fit in with the microcredit definition adopted in this study because it does not offer loans, but a guarantee; however, this is still important if the number of possible microloan applicants is to be increased.

8 Government support

Public support for microcredit in Belgium is organized at three levels:

- Transnational level:[32] European organizations such as the European Social Fund (ESF), the European Investment Fund (EIF) and the European Regional Development Fund (ERDF);
- Federal level: the federal public service of employment, work and social consultation;
- Regional level: Wallonia, Flanders and Brussels-Capital.

The general trend shows that public administration is becoming more and more inclined to support microcredit institutions. Moreover, this tendency is expected to intensify in 2007 with the launching of new European programmes.[33] Indeed, microcredit has gained a lot of interest in recent years because member states are increasing their efforts 'to modernise their welfare states' (Evers and Jung, 2007) as well as to implement new strategies[34] to fight unemployment and poverty (Evers and Jung, 2007) and to increase economic development.

Government support happens in three ways: by direct or indirect intervention, through a guarantee system or by participating in different programmes.

Public institutions invest directly or indirectly in the capital of an MFI. Brusoc and Fonds de Participation can be used as an example of this type of investment. Indeed, the ERDF funds Brusoc directly to the tune of €2 500 000 to support its activity in the Objective 2 zone of Brussels-Capital.[35]

In the same way, the Brussels-Capital Region funds Brusoc directly, via the SRIB. The Fonds de Participation is a financial public institution and as such all its capital is totally financed by the Federal government.

The guarantee system (Independent Expert Group, 2005) allows banks to reduce their risk while granting loans. The Walloon Region intervenes in this way by financing the SOWALFIN.[36] A similar system exists with the EIF.

A third way for governments to support microcredit is by financially backing programmes promoting independent employment activity regarding a specific group. An example would be the programme AFFA. This programme is supported by the three Belgian Regions (Flemish, Walloon and Brussels-Capital), but also by a transnational player, the ERDF (http://www.credal.be/affa/liens.html#1).

9 Regulation

The legal framework of the Belgian microcredit sector applies to two levels: microcredit institutions and self-employed entrepreneurs. It is dependent on both the European and Belgian juridical systems. Indeed, no specific legislation applies concerning the size of the enterprise; therefore microenterprises are treated just like regular enterprises. The regulation depends more on the nature of the organization or the sector in which it operates.

9.1 Microfinance institutions granting microcredit

This section will examine how different MFIs are influenced by the European and Belgian legal framework.[37]

The Belgian legislation differs according to the type of credit granted, that is, whether it is an investment loan or a consumption loan. For this study, only the first case will be examined. Interestingly enough, in Belgium, as in the United Kingdom and Poland (Underwood, 2006), investment loan providers do not have to comply with any particular restrictions[38] limiting their interest rates. Nonetheless, Belgian legislation does not especially favour MFIs in terms of self-financing.

A first way for MFIs to obtain finance would be for them to collect money deposits, just as credit unions in the UK and in Ireland, as well as some structures in Lithuania and Latvia do (Lynch, 2004). However, collecting money on deposit is not allowed in Belgium for institutions that do not have banking status, and it is not easy of Belgian MFIs to fulfil the conditions necessary to acquire that status (Disneur, 2006). Indeed, the method of evaluating credit risk and capital required by the 2006 European directive[39] issued from the 2004 Basel II agreements (Bayot, 2006) often mean that banking status remains out of reach for MFIs. Therefore, since it is compulsory to have this status in order to collect money deposits, this method of financing is directly eliminated.

A second option for MFIs to obtain finance is by selling shares to the public. This is the most interesting way for MFIs to collect savings and raise capital. However, public issue of shares is strictly regulated by European and national laws, and a number of restrictions make this practice complex. The law requires the publication of a leaflet when the public issue of shares concerns more than a hundred people and if the amount is more than €100 000 (Bayot, 2006).

The regulation regarding the publication of a leaflet is quite inappropriate for smaller MFIs in the sense that it is an expensive formality, and in that the requirements regarding the leaflet are too strict and can be difficult to satisfy (Bayot, 2006). However, MFI cooperatives that have asked to be certified by the National Council of Cooperation (CNC), such as Crédal, can be exempt from the requirement to produce a leaflet (Disneur, 2006) if the shareholder benefits from the services rendered by the cooperative and if the total amount of the operation does not exceed €2 500 000 (Disneur, 2006). The conditions regarding this exemption are, however, the subject of difficult arbitration by the control authority, the Commission Bancaire, Financière et des Assurances.

Another advantage for cooperatives that have received CNC certification is that the dividend paid to their shareholders is exempt from tax up to a total value of €160 (Disneur, 2006). However, cooperatives do not benefit from more favourable taxation regarding corporation tax.

Finally, MFIs can also raise funds by means of donations. Moreover, but only if they have ASBL[40] status, they can ask the Ministry of Finance to authorize them to allow individual donors to obtain tax relief on their gifts. Once this has been granted, donations from individuals higher than €30 allow for a deduction of the same amount on the donor's net taxable income.[41] However, donations cannot exceed 10 per cent of the donor's net taxable income, and also, when they are higher than €250 000 in the same tax year they are no longer tax deductible.

To finance their operational needs, MFIs cannot rely only on income coming from donations and share subscriptions because they are too unpredictable, so obviously other means of finance are needed.

9.2 Self-employed entrepreneurs

9.2.1 The self-employed activity

9.2.1.1 Registration with the Crossroads Bank The registration is done at the Crossroads Bank for the entrepreneur to receive a registration number. This organization verifies that the person or entity has the 'entrepreneurial capacities' necessary to become self-employed.

'Entrepreneurial capacities'[42] are defined as basic management knowledge and professional competencies.[43]

9.2.1.2 Demonstration of 'entrepreneurial capacities' Entrepreneurial capacities can be proven by recognized diplomas and sufficient practical

Table 14.7 Social security contributions

	Quarterly contribution amount
Activity starts between 1 April and 31 December 2007 included	€501.29
If 2007 corresponds to your 2nd complete calendar year of activity	€582.18
If 2007 corresponds to your 3rd complete calendar year of activity	€659.43

Source: UCM (2007): 'Vos cotisations sociales pendant la période de début d'activité', http://www.ucm.be/ucm/ewcm.nsf/_/594EE6C8ADD61997C1256C67004685A1?opendocument.

experience (Fonds de Participation, 2006a). Under certain conditions,[44] such as a widow taking up the activity of a deceased partner, or some regulated intellectual professions, among other examples, applicants may be exempt from proving basic management skills and professional experience.

9.2.1.3 A rule in favour of immigrant workers In 2003, the federal government modified the legislation with regards to employees and self-employed work access for foreign people. For example, the rule that foreigners must have resided in Belgium for at least 10 years before being eligible to obtain the self-employed worker's card has been rescinded.[45]

9.2.2 Self-employed status

9.2.2.1 Social security contributions Any self-employed worker who starts up an economic activity must pay contractual and provisional social security contributions at the end of each quarter (Proximity Finance Foundation, 2007). These contributions will be levelled three years after the business has started according to the effective assessed income (see Table 14.7).

However, there are exemptions, exonerations or reductions relating to social security contributions,[46] allowing 'any person having the social status as a self-employed worker whose income does not reach a certain amount to follow, under certain conditions, a more favourable scale.'[47]

9.2.2.2 Tax system The self-employed workers who started up a business for the first time in 2004, 2005, 2006 in a principal self-employed profession are exempt from paying the tax increase.[48]

9.2.2.3 Social security system The self-employed worker needs to register with a social insurance fund within the previous six months or within the 90 days following the start of the business. In exchange for the contributions paid, the self-employed worker obtains some social rights:[49] family allowances, pension, complementary pension, sickness and disability insurance, continued insurance,[50] bankruptcy insurance.

A move towards a better social security system for the self-employed has been observed in recent years (Proximity Finance Foundation, 2007):

- increase in the minimum pension for self-employed workers, which is now €12 065.74;[51]
- increase in disability allowances;
- increase in family allowance and maternity benefits.

9.2.2.4 Unemployment benefits The usual rule is that when an unemployed person wants to launch an independent business he/she loses his/her rights to unemployment benefits. This rule can be a first and important obstacle to starting up a business.

However, if the would-be entrepreneur informs the unemployment office in writing, he/she will be able to keep, under certain conditions,[52] his/her unemployment benefits for a period of up to six months. This period of time is considered an appropriate preparation time to launch an independent business (Fonds de Participation – Département études, 2006a).

If the activity is discontinued, the rule stipulates that any entrepreneur can again benefit from unemployment allowance if the termination of the independent activity happens within nine years of its beginning (Proximity Finance Foundation, 2007). On the other hand, if the business ends within six months, and the entrepreneur was previously employed, he/she must prove that his/her former employer is not ready to re-hire him/her.

It is clear that the loss of unemployment allowance while launching a business does not encourage underprivileged people to try this activity (Fonds de Participation – Département études, 2006a).

9.2.2.5 New regulation on self-employed status from September 2007 As of 1 September 2007, two major changes will take place concerning access to self-employed status (UNION&ACTIONS, 2007).

Primarily, on a positive note, the recognition of practical experience can be demonstrated going back up to 15 years, whereas currently the timeframe is only 10 years. However, a second change is that the minimal level of education required for certain professions will be increased (six years of education instead of only four previously).[53]

To conclude this section, it is interesting to note that Belgian legislation, by means of its methodical and maybe severe way of analysing candidates, allows only the most motivated and qualified entrepreneur candidates to continue. This procedure can, however, be considered less simple and open than other countries, such as the UK, require.

10 Financial and operational sustainability

'Operational self-sustainability refers to the lender's ability to cover through operating revenue (interest and fees) operational expenses, the cost of borrowing and loan loss provision' (Underwood, 2006).

The operational sustainability of a public or para-public organization is hardly predictable, since most of its resources are made up of public funds. Indeed, interest rates set by Brusoc and the Fonds de Participation do not allow them to reach sustainability.

Moreover, political risks significantly threaten the sustainability of a public federal structure such as Fonds de participation. Indeed, uncertainty about the political context in Belgium might mean that its current federal management is shifted towards regional authorities. The latter would then have the opportunity to redefine their future (continuity, development or suppression).

Regarding private MFIs, Crédal, which is the only example in Belgium, has clearly not yet reached operational and financial sustainability.[54] Indeed, the income provided by interest charged amounts to more or less 5 per cent of total operational costs. The rest comes from cooperative shares, subsidies, donations and financial products.

The Belgian context is peculiar because there is no maximum interest rate applicable to investment loans. Therefore, MFIs are free to increase their interest rates on investment loans to cover all their costs, and to become sustainable if they wish.

Belgian MFIs decide not to increase their interest rates because they are strongly attached to their social goal,[55] and the availability of public funds allows MFIs to offer loans with lower interest rates.

Moreover, the feared consequences that might arise from an increase in interest rates on investment loans could be:

- difficult access to loans for low-income and socially excluded people;
- renouncing their social goal;
- activities might be funded by consumer loans and credit card debt (Evers and Jung, 2007).

Furthermore, as a recent study asks: 'would an interest rate [. . .] above 40 per cent be politically and morally acceptable to the public, to policy makers, to MFIs and to clients in Western Europe?' (Evers and Jung, 2007).

As far as Belgian MFIs are concerned, the social goal has precedence over operational sustainability, at least as long as the political climate is favourable.

11 Challenges for the sector in Belgium

The challenges for the microcredit sector in Belgium lie in the respective roles of public authorities and MFIs.

11.1 The role of public authorities

In recent years, public authorities have focused on improving the status of the self-employed worker. They have mainly developed protection against medium or long-term risks (family allowances, pensions, disability allowance and so on). Nonetheless, it could be interesting to encourage this status by creating incentives that have an immediate effect.

One idea would be to facilitate the change from an inactive status to that of a self-employed worker by maintaining unemployment allowances during the start-up phase, as the government in Ireland has done (Proximity Finance Foundation, 2007). Another suggestion would be to reduce social security contributions during the launch phase of the business.

In the same way, to support the development and financing of MFIs, the Belgian public authorities could clarify the conditions relating to exemption from publishing a leaflet for CNC approved cooperatives (see point 9.1.1).

Another idea for public authorities to help MFIs is through guaranteeing their risks. This is already underway, but it could still be developed further (refer to Crédal's example in section 7.2).

In addition, since government subsidies are usually given out punctually, they are an important but quite unstable source of finance. A suggestion that would be a real improvement in this area would be to establish a type of 'management contract', which, in exchange for set objectives, would guarantee recurring funding to MFIs on a longer term (ideally 3–5 years).

Furthermore, since MFIs take care of target groups that mainstream banks marginalize, there could be a type of legislation that helps them financially: mainstream banks could be required by a government law to pay a certain sum to MFIs, as a type of 'Universal banking service'.

Lastly, in the light of current trends, the support and interest focused on microfinance projects by public authorities is strong and increasing, which is a good omen for the future of this sector.

11.2 The role of microcredit-granting microfinance institutions

MFIs will continue their efforts to keep on meeting the needs that are not satisfied by mainstream banks. Some potential developments are identified as beneficial, both for the target public and the MFIs:

- promoting the MFIs directly among target groups through adapted communication means;
- improving the time spent dealing with microcredit cases by simplifying the procedure.

Two other points are interesting to mention. First, it is important for MFIs to continue to think about how to reach operational and financial sustainability, or at least to gain more independence from public subsidies. Secondly, it is suggested that more microcredit impact studies be carried out so that concrete results may be shown to public or private financiers. This initiative could help to convince them to renew or initiate subsidies and to obtain statistics on the social role of microcredit as a complementary or palliative system to structures implemented by the federal government.

Another important challenge, at the European level, which interests credit cooperatives, is to access the advantages promised by banking status without its constraints. Indeed, banking status allows money to be collected on deposit and thus is an interesting method of finance. Credit cooperatives have trouble accessing this status since the rules have been set by the Basel II agreements, except the special status being reserved for credit unions and some Central European structures.

Notes

* External Microcredit Expert: Michel Genet.

1. The Economist Intelligence Unit's quality-of-life index (2006), 'The world in 2005, Quality-of-life index', available at http://www.economist.com/media/pdf/QUALITY_OF_LIFE.pdf.
2. Economie – SPF Economie, classes moyennes et énergie (2005), 'Revenus et conditions de vie', Indicateurs EU-SILC 2005, available at http://statbel.fgov.be/figures/download_fr.asp#lfs.
3. DG Employment, Social Affairs and Equal Opportunities (2007), 'Tackling social exclusion: people experiencing poverty have their say', available at http://ec.europa.eu/employment_social/emplweb/news/news_fr.cfm?id=233.
4. Mont-de-Pieté (2007), 'Presentation de l'institution', available at http://www.montdepiete.be/fr/present.htm.
5. The Objective 2 zone comprises industrial and socio-economically fragile neighbourhoods. For the Brussels-Capital Region they include: Anderlecht, Brussels, Forest, Molenbeek-Saint-Jean, Saint-Gilles, Saint-Josse and Schaerbeek.
6. Another main actor is of course the target groups, which are dealt with in detail in section 5, and therefore only briefly mentioned here.
7. The Belgian social secretariat is an 'organization that, in the name of and on behalf of

the employer, completes compulsory formalities, namely regarding social security legislation, related to the hiring and managing of human resources.', http://creation-pme.wallonie.be/demarches/engagementpersonnel/PER8/PER08.htm.

8. More details in section 8.
9. The first because, although it targets SMEs having trouble getting a mainstream bank loan, the size of loans can climb up to €95 000, which is not considered a small amount, and the second, for a similar reason, because the loans can amount to €75 000.
10. Economie – SPF Economie, classes moyennes et énergie (2007), 'Guichets d'entreprises agréés – Liste', available at http://mineco.fgov.be/enterprises/crossroads_bank/bce_kbo_fr_006.htm.
11. Economie – SPF Economie, classes moyennes et énergie (2006), 'Agrément des Guichets d'entreprises', available at http://mineco.fgov.be/enterprises/crossroads_bank/terms_and_conditions_fr.htm.
12. Crédal (2007), 'Le microcrédit pour entreprendre', available at http://www.credal.be/pdf/mc2/me-clients.doc.
13. Economie – SPF Economie, classes moyennes et énergie (2007), 'Modification des taux annuels effectifs globaux', available at http://mineco.fgov.be/protection_consumer/Credit/credit_fr_001.htm.
14. INASTI (2005), 'Evolution du nombre des assujettis (travailleurs indépendants + aidants) selon le sexe (situation au 31 décembre)', available at http://www.rsvz-inasti.fgov.be/fr/tools/statistics/gender_05.htm.
15. Global Entrepreneurship Monitor (2006), 'Global Entrepreneurship Monitor 2006: Global Summary Results', available at http://www.gemconsortium.org/about.aspx?page=global_reports_2006.
16. Regional Policy Inforegio (2006), 'Objective 2: Revitalising areas facing structural difficulties', http://ec.europa.eu/regional_policy/objective2/index_en.htm.
17. Région de Bruxelles-Capitale (2007), 'Objectif 2', available at http://www.bruxelles.irisnet.be/fr/region/region_de_bruxelles-capitale/ministere_de_la_region_de_bruxelles_capitale/competences_et_organisation/secretariat_general/cellule_de_coordination_des_fonds_structurels_europeens/objectif_2.shtml.
18. Enterprise and Industry (2007), 'Access to Finance: Microcredit', available at http://ec.europa.eu/enterprise/entrepreneurship/financing/microcredit.htm.
19. Enterprise and Industry (2007), 'Access to Finance: Microcredit', available at http://ec.europa.eu/enterprise/entrepreneurship/financing/microcredit.htm.
20. DG Employment, Social Affairs and Equal Opportunities, Social Inclusion (2006), 'Rapport conjoint sur la protection sociale et l'inclusion sociale 2006', available at http://ec.europa.eu/employment_social/social_inclusion/docs/2006/annex_fr.pdf.
21. Crédit social accompagné (2007), 'A quoi peut servir le crédit?', available at http://www.credal.be/creditsocial/index.html#3.
22. Crédit social accompagné (2007), 'Respectez-vous une des conditions d'accès suivantes?', available at http://www.credal.be/creditsocial/index.html#3.
23. Economie – SPF Economie, classes moyennes et énergie (2007), 'Informer et protéger les demandeurs de crédit – Prévenir le surendettement', http://mineco.fgov.be/protection_consumer/complaints/Credit.
24. The interest rate can be updated on a three-monthly basis (Ibid.).
25. Sowalfin presentation (2007): LA SOCAMUT, http://www.sowalfin.be/content01.php?documentDocNo=189.
26. In French: SCM (Société de Cautionnement Mutuel).
27. Up to €25 000 in this case (http://www.sowalfin.be/content01.php?document DocNo=189).
28. Up to 10 people employed and annual turnover up to 2 million euros, http://www.sowalfin.be/content01.php?documentDocNo=189 (accessed 27 July 2007).
29. 'except renewable energy sector', http://www.sowalfin.be/content01.php?document DocNo=189.

30. 'except audiovisual production', http://www.sowalfin.be/content01.php?documentDocNo=189.
31. 'except inland water shipping and multimodal goods transport' http://www.sowalfin.be/content01.php?documentDocNo=189.
32. European Microfinance Network (2007), 'EU and microfinance', available at http://www.european-microfinance.org/microfinance_unioneuropeenne_en.php.
33. European Investment Fund (2007), JEREMIE, available at http://www.eif.org/jeremie/index.htm.
34. 'Funding can make economic sense for member states because the costs for job-creation via self-employment are lower than the costs of unemployment benefits' (European Commission, 2007, p. 27).
35. Région Bruxelles-Capitale (2007), 'Micro-crédit Programme Objectif 2', available at http://www.quartiers.irisnet.be/contenu/content.asp?ref=169.
36. Subsidies granted to the SOWALFIN, http://www.ejustice.just.fgov.be/cgi/api2.pl?lg=fr&pd=2005-10-05&numac=2005027369.
37. For further information on the links between European and Belgian legal frameworks, please refer to http://www.european-microfinance.org/microfinance_unioneuropeenne_en.php.
38. 'In many member states substantial micro-lending activities are carried out by non-banks, in particular so-called microfinance institutions [. . .] These activities are not governed by special legislation but do not require a banking licence, either' (Expert Group Report, 2007).
39. European Parliament and Council Directive 2006/49/CE issued on 14 June 2006 on the adequacy of equity funds from investment companies and credit organizations, OJ L 177.
40. ASBL: Association Sans But Lucratif, a type of not-for-profit association.
41. Fédération Royale du Notariat Belge (2007): 'Les Dons et Legs', http://www.dons-legs.be/gdl_avn02.asp.
42. Hoge Raad voor de Zelfstandigen en de KMO (2007), 'Loi-programme pour la promotion de l'entreprise indépendante', available at www.hrzkmo.fgov.be/Portals/hrzkmo/fr/Legislation/Generalites/Loi-programme/Loi-programme%20generale.pdf.
43. Guichet des Chambres de commerce (2007), 'Mon diplôme est-il suffisant?', available at http://www.leguichet.be/xml/categorie-IDC-3684-.html.
44. Economie – SPF Economie, classes moyennes et énergie (2007), 'Connaissances de base', available at http://mineco.fgov.be/ministry/formalities/detail_formalities_fr.asp?idformalite=147.
45. Economie – SPF Economie, classes moyennes et énergie (2007), 'Commerce ambulant', available at http://mineco.fgov.be/SME/travelling_trade/travelling_trade_fr.htm#Textes_l%E9gaux.
46. Caisse d'Assurances Sociales de l'UCM (2006), 'Note d'information de l'Indépendant – Le Statut Social des Travailleurs Indépendants', available at http://www.ucm.be/C1256C0D003C8BF5/_/D27CB0B07766FA95C1256D06003151F7/$file/STI0106b.pdf?OpenElement.
47. Caisse d'Assurances Sociales de l'UCM (2007), 'Note d'information de l'Indépendant – Exonération et Réduction des cotisations sociales sur base des articles 37&40 de l'arrêté royal du 19 décembre 1967', available at http://www.ucm.be/C1256C0D003C8BF5/_/D46904BBFF16B7FCC1256D06002EE348/$file/A400007a.pdf?OpenElement.
48. Service Public Fédéral Finances (2007), 'Versements Anticipés – Exercices d'Imposition 2007', available at http://fiscus.fgov.be/interfaoiffr/publicaties/gratis/pdf/VA2007.pdf.
49. INASTI (2007), 'Welcome at the National Fund', available at http://rsvz-inasti.fgov.be/en/helpagency/index.htm.
50. An insurance that 'guarantees you rights under the social statute for a maximum term of 2 years. The maximum term can be extended up to 7 years if it will make you reach retirement age' (http://www.rsvz.be/en/selfemployed/continued insurance/index.htm).

51. Questions Capitales (2007), 'Du nouveau pour les indépendants!', available at http://www.questionscapitales.be/node/617.
52. ONEM (2007). 'Quelle est l'incidence d'une activité indépendante sur le droit aux allocations de chômage?', available at http://www.onem.be/D_opdracht_zelfstandige/default.asp?MainDir=D_opdracht_zelfstandige&Language=FR&IndexDir=Regl/Werknemers&Button=1.
53. Union des Classes Moyennes du Hainaut (2007), 'Accès à la profession: nouvelle régle-mentation à partir du 01er septembre 2007', available at http://www.ucm-hainaut.be/association/news.php?Id=1.8239584294299.
54. '[. . .] in 2006, the total subsidies amount granted to Crédal was €804.361' (Crédal, 2006).
55. '[. . .] offering credit in an ethical and transparent way, with stable and independent interest rates from the market, and from credit risk.' (Crédal, 2006); '[. . .] as a public institution of credit, has carried out its social aim by granting attractive loans for its target groups.' (Fonds de participation, 2006); 'BRUSOC, a SRIB subsidiary, finances, supports independent, small enterprises and social economy projects, by granting loans with preferential interest rates', (http://www.brusoc.be).

References

Bayot, B. (2001–2002), *Elaboration d'un service bancaire universel, Deuxième partie – L'accès au crédit et l'exemple du Community Reinvestment Act*, Brussels: Réseau Financement Alternatif.

Bayot, B. (2006), *L'Europe réglemente l'activité des banques*, Cahier FINAncité N°3, Brussels: Réseau Financement Alternatif.

Bracke, J. (2002), Rapport FEIRA: 'Rapport de mise en oevre 2002 pour la Belgique relarif à la Charte européenne des petites enterprises', available at http://www.mineco.fgov.be/enterprises/best/best_report_feira_2002_fr.pdf.

BRUSOC, (2005), *Rapport Annuel*, Brussels.

Caisse d'Assurances Sociales de l'UCM (2006), 'Note d'information de l'indépendant: le statut social des travailleurs indépendants', Brussels.

CEFIP, Centre de Connaissance du Financement des PME (2006), 'Transmission des PME Belges: le Financement: Rapport Intermédiaire', Brussels, available at http://www.cefip.be/FILES/Documenten/FR/Transmissions%20des%20PME%20Belges_FR_28_11_2006.pdf.

Crédal (2006), *Rapport Annuel*, Brussels.

Disneur, L. (2006), 'Recherche juridique relative aux financiers alternatifs', unpublished study, Réseau Financement Alternatif, Brussels.

European Commission (2007), 'The regulation of microcredit in Europe', Expert Group Report, April, available at http://ec.europa.eu/enterprise/entrepreneurship/financing/publications.htm.

European Parliament and Council Directive (2006), '2006/49/CE issued on 14 June 2006 on the adequacy of equity funds from investment companies and credit organisations', OJ L 177 (30/6/2006), pp. 201–55, Brussels.

Evers, J. and M. Jung (2007), 'Status of microfinance in Western Europe: an academic review', European Microfinance Network Issue Paper, Hamburg, available at http://www.european-microfinance.org/data/File/Librairy/ISSUE%20PAPER.pdf.

Expert Group Report (2007), 'The Regulation of microcredit in Europe', European Commission, DG Enterprise and Industry, Brussels, available at http://www.europeanmicrofinance.org/data/File/the_regulation_of_microcredit_in_europe.pdf.

Independent Expert Group (2005), 'Guarantees and Mutual Guarantees', report to the Commission, Brussels, available at http://ec.europa.eu/enterprise/entrepreneurship/financing/docs/guarantees_best_report.pdf.

Fonds de Participation – Département études (2006a), 'L'entreprenariat immigré en Belgique – Etats des lieux et perspectives d'avenir', study carried out for the INTI programme

'Integration and nationals from third countries', 2005–2006, European Commission DG Justice, Liberty and Security, Brussels.
Fonds de Participation (2006b), *Rapport Annuel*, Brussels.
Guichandut, P. (2006), 'Europe occidentale et reste du monde: parle-t-on des mêmes pratiques?', *Finance and Common Good*, no. 25, Finance Observatory, Geneva, Switzerland.
Lierman, F. (2007), 'Banks and microfinance: for business or just for CSR?', Dexia Bank Belgium, paper presented at 4th European Microfinance Conference 2007 24–26 April, Berlin.
Lynch, M. (2004), 'La régulation des banques d'économie sociale au sein de la communauté européenne', Interface no. 22, Brussels, available at http://www.financite.be/ma-documentation/ma-documentation-accueil/la-regulation-des-banques-d-economie-sociale-au-se,fr.html.
Mathot, F. (2005), 'Le Micro-crédit fête 20 ans d'existence en Belgique: bref rappel du concept. . .', asbl Job'in, Brussels, available at http://www.econosoc.be/?rub=actualite&page=news&id=744.
Proximity Finance Foundation (2007), 'L'impact de la microfinance en Belgique', in partnership with the CeFiP, SME Financing Knowledge Center, with the aid of the King Baudouin Foundation, Brussels.
Reifner, U. (2002), 'Micro lending: a case for regulation', Institut Für Finanzdienstleistungen, Hamburg, available at http://www.european-microfinance.org/pays.php?pild=19.
Rico Garrido, S., M. Lacalle Calderón, J. Márquez Vigil and J. Durán Navarro (2006), *Microcredit in Spain*, Foro Nantik Lum de Microfinanzas, European Microfinance Network, Madrid.
Service Public Federal Finance (2007), 'Versements anticipés: exercices d'Imposition 2007', Brussels, available at http://fiscus.fgov.be/interfaoiffr/publicaties/gratis/pdf/VA2007.pdf.
Trinczek, R. (2007), 'Income poverty in the European Union', Technical University Munich, Munich, available at http://www.eurofound.europa.eu/ewco/surveyreports/EU0703019D/EU0703019D_4.htm.
Underwood, T. (2006), *Overview of the Microcredit Sector in Europe 2004–2005*, Paris: European Microfinance Network.
UNION&ACTIONS (2007), 'Le secteur des services aux personnes', *Hebdomadaire*, no. 22, Brussels.
Vanhuslt, J. and W. Vanderhasselt (2007), 'Aspects de l'histoire et du fonctionnement de la banque Cera', Belgian Raiffeisen Foundation, available at http://www.cera.be/brs/fr/about/history/raifbelgium/.
Wegner, L. (2006), 'Microfinance: how bankers could buy back their soul', OECD Development Center, *Policy Insights*, no. 31, available at http://www.oecd.org/dataoecd/58/10/38272013.pdf.

Recommended websites

BRUSOC: www.srib.be.
CREDAL: www.credal.be.
Europe Investment Fund: http://www.eif.org/jeremie/index.htm.
European Microfinance Network: www.european-microfinance.org.
Fonds de Participation: www.fonds.org.
SOWALFIN: http://www.sowalfin.be/content01.php?documentDocNo=189.

Interviews

Marion Cahen, Analyst, Brusoc, 16 August 2007.
Christine Henaut, Microcredit Advisor, Crédal, 16 August 2007.
Cédric Deschamps, Microcredit Advisor, Crédal, 16 August 2007.

15 Microcredit in Spain: the role of savings banks[1]

Silvia Rico Garrido, Maricruz Lacalle Calderón and Bárbara Jayo Carboni

The purpose of this chapter is to analyse how microcredit loans are currently disbursed in Spain and to illustrate the unique role played by savings banks in promoting this new financial instrument geared towards society's most underprivileged members.

1 National context

Economic and social context[2]

Since the transition to democracy in 1975, Spain has undergone rapid economic modernization. With its admittance into the European Union in 1986, Spain's economic policies have evolved and its economy has transformed into one of the most dynamic in Europe, growing at an average annual rate of 5 per cent up to 1990. In the beginning of the 1990s, the Spanish economy went into a four-year recession and has since entered a period of expansion that has persisted uninterrupted to today. In light of this trend, GDP growth registered 3.9 per cent from 2005 to 2006 (the highest in the last six years).

The extraordinary dynamism of the Spanish economy can be attributed to a diverse set of factors, which capture not only the changes in the macroeconomy of Spain as a result of the process of convergence and integration in the European Monetary Union, but also several important structural components such as demographic shifts, principally driven by an influx of immigration. Since 2000, Spain has experienced one of the highest rates of immigration in the world (three or four times greater than the average rate of the United States, eight times greater than that of France, and dwarfed only in relative terms by Cyprus and Andorra in Europe). According to the Padrón Municipality, 9.26 per cent of the population of Spain is of a foreign nationality.

The effects of these demographic changes are significant, affecting economic growth potential by introducing greater flexibility in various structural elements, especially in the labour market. The most important indicators have been an increase in productivity, expansion of supply-side growth opportunities, and a simultaneous increase in job creation coupled with a decrease in unemployment from 15 per cent in 1996 to 9 per cent in 2006.

Another important element to highlight is the relevance of services in the economy and society, which is illustrated in the sector breakdown of GDP. In 2004, services comprised 67 per cent of GDP and 65 per cent of total employment.

Poverty in Spain

Despite great advances in the industrial economy, in 2005, 20 per cent of the population of Spain lived below the poverty line (Eurostat, 2007). This percentage is significantly greater than the average of the European Union, which was 15 per cent (Eurostat, 2001).

The most common form of poverty, affecting approximately 85 per cent of those households that are defined as poor, is relative poverty. Households are said to be in relative poverty if they have the capacity to cover basic necessities, but lack the goods and services that are common to other households in the area. Although the incidence of severe poverty is rare, a small sector of households and individuals are categorized as extremely poor (Adiego and Moneo, 2004; Fundación FOESSA, 2005).

The accelerating increase in the number of young people who live in poverty is particularly relevant. Young people under the age of 25 comprise 44.1 per cent of the poor and 65 per cent of the extremely poor. When analysing the poor in Spain, the groups most strongly disadvantaged are gypsies and immigrants. In addition, relative poverty due to unequal salaries and a marked increase in low-salary jobs have disproportionately affected women.

Finally, it is important to consider that the great majority of people affected by unemployment, illiteracy, drug addiction, delinquency, and general exclusion are the poor.

Financial system

In Spain, financial policy lies in the realm of the government, which operates through the Ministry of Economy and Treasury, which, in turn, conducts activity through five executive agencies, of which the Bank of Spain plays a primary role.

Many financial institutions depend on the Bank of the Spain, which grants the credit necessary for their operations.

- Instituto de Crédito Oficial (ICO);
- Private banks;
- Public banks;

- Credit cooperatives;
- Savings banks.

Savings banks play a unique role because while they are private institutions subject to market forces and with limited social objectives, they have nonetheless reinvested a substantial percentage of their assets in the social fabric. Some savings banks have specialized in providing savings services for the general public and the financing of small and medium enterprises. Combining their financial operations with intense social activity has become an essential management strategy of savings banks. The social work funds aim to address the demands of the population, especially towards integrating excluded populations into cultural activities.

Currently, 46 savings banks exist throughout Spain, investing more than half the resources of Spanish families and businesses. Today, savings banks grant 47.44 per cent of all loans and 56.95 per cent of all mortgages.

Business structure

According to Bárcenas López (2006), small and medium enterprises in Spain are an important element of cohesion and dynamism in the local environment, essential to growth and employment in both Spain and the European Union.

The Spanish business structure is classified by the number of employees in the organization. Under this classification system, microenterprises employ 1 to 10 employees, small and medium enterprises (SMEs) employ 10 to 250 employees, and large businesses have more than 250 employees. From this perspective, it is important to point out the great importance of microenterprises in Spain. According to the Institute of Fiscal Studies (2007), microenterprises represented 93 per cent of Spanish enterprises and 17.7 per cent of total employment, which, when combined with SMEs comprising 6.8 per cent of all businesses and 46.0 per cent of employment, constitute the backbone of the economy.

2 The origin of microfinance in Spain: when, why and how

As in other countries, interest in microcredit has grown among the Spanish public and private organizations, media, and scientific community. Over the last seven years several financial institutions, along with the government and various non-governmental organizations (NGOs), have entered the field of microcredit with the aim of directly addressing the issue of poverty and social and financial exclusion.

Data from Eurostat (2007) reveals that 20 per cent of the Spanish population lives below the poverty threshold, significantly higher than the European Union's average of 15 per cent. Further, the rate of financial exclusion in Spain, defined as the percentage of the population that does not have access to a bank account, is 9.4 per cent – slightly lower than the European Union's average of 10.1 per cent (Carbó Valverde and López del Paso, 2005).[3]

To address these rates of social and financial exclusion, some financial institutions have started to grant microcredit loans in Spain. Specifically, the estimated volume of microcredit loans has risen from 1.1 million euros in 2001 to a total of 62.1 million euros in 2005.[4]

In Spain, a microcredit is defined as an individual loan granted to people at risk of social and financial exclusion. Microloans are made on the basis of the trustworthiness of the applicant and the feasibility of the projects to be financed. Vulnerable groups are offered a financial alternative to set up economic initiatives or small businesses – microenterprises – which allow them to generate a regular source of income through self-employment. Hence, microcredit loans serve as a tool for social integration and the enhancement of living conditions.

Originally, during the 1990s, certain NGOs (such as Women's World Banking in Spain) began granting microloans in Spain. These organizations financed their programmes by setting up specific agreements with government agencies or financial institutions to grant loans or guarantee funds.

However, major growth in the use of microloans began at the turn of the twenty-first century as a result of the support of the government and the financial system, mainly through the savings banks.

More precisely, in 2001 and 2002, the Spanish government launched two national microcredit programmes that partnered with (or involved / sponsored / worked through) financial institutions and not-for-profit Social Microcredit Support Organizations (SMSOs). Both programmes are backed by institutions of the European Union: the European Investment Fund and the European Social Fund. This reflects the public support for microcredit at both a European and national level, as a mechanism to promote employment and social inclusion in a context characterized by the weakening of the welfare system.

Similarly, in 2001, Caixa Catalunya, through its Fundació Un Sol Món, became the first savings bank to grant microcredit loans through a proprietary programme. Other savings banks have since followed suit with their own programmes and/or programmes affiliated with the government agencies. Now, most Spanish savings banks offer microcredit, reaching approximately 10 000[5] citizens through 3921 microcredit loans by the end of 2005.

We can therefore identify two main types of microcredit programmes in Spain (see Table 15.1).

Table 15.1 The main microcredit programmes in Spain

I. Financial institutions' proprietary programmes	Savings banks launched their own programmes at the beginning of this decade as part of their social function to prevent financial exclusion and promote economic development and social progress.	
II. Financial institutions' programmes affiliated with the government agencies on a national scale	*i). The Microcredit Line of the Instituto Crédito Oficial (ICO)*	The ICO Microcredit Line was set up in 2002 under the motto 'your word is your bond'. The European Investment Fund collaborates with the ICO to improve financing conditions by partially covering the risk.
	ii). Microcredit Programme for Entrepreneurial and Business Women	This programme, aimed exclusively at women, has been implemented by the Spanish Women's Institute since 2001. This organization answers to the Ministry of Labour and Social Affairs, in collaboration with the Directorate of Small and Medium Sized Enterprises and the National Organisation for Innovation, which in turn answers to the Ministry of Industry, Tourism and Trade. The savings bank 'la Caixa' participates as the financial institution. This programme is co-financed by the European Social Fund.

Source: Rico et al. (2004).

3 The Spanish microcredit model

The Spanish microcredit model is based on the existence of SMSOs, which serve as a liaison between the lenders who supply the microcredit (in Spain, lenders are limited to official financial institutions: commercial

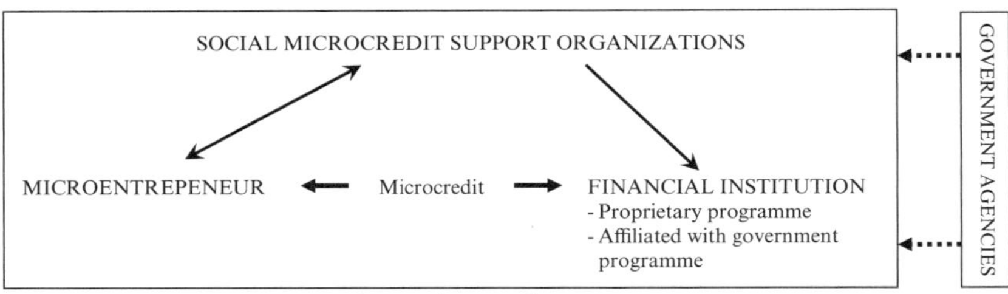

Source: Authors.

Figure 15.1 How microcredits are granted in Spain

banks, savings banks and credit cooperatives) and the microentrepreneur. SMSOs, which may be private or public institutions, are recognized for their close contact with vulnerable groups and their experience in social/labour integration through promoting self-employment.

As Figure 15.1 demonstrates, microloans are usually granted in the following way: i) The microentrepreneur contacts an SMSO for information; ii) the SMSO identifies the potential beneficiaries, provides them with the necessary help to complete a microcredit application, and forwards their application to the financial institution; iii) the financial institution then makes a credit rating based on the project's feasibility, and if the assessment is positive, formalizes the microcredit agreement. This agreement is signed directly by the financial institution and the micro-entrepreneur; iv) in addition to the above, the SMSOs are also responsible for follow-up work, providing the necessary support to micro-entrepreneurs throughout the duration of the loan.

We shall now provide a more in-depth analysis of each of these actors involved in the implementation of microcredit programmes: government agencies, financial institutions and SMSOs. The clients will be analysed in the section on target groups.

4 Main actors implementing microcredit programmes in Spain: government agencies, financial institutions and Social Microcredit Support Organizations

4.1 The Spanish government

As mentioned, since the beginning of the present decade, the Spanish government has launched several microcredit programmes at a national, regional and local level. For the purpose of this chapter, we will analyse the two main programmes with a national scope, that is, the ICO Microcredit Line and the Microcredit Programme for Entrepreneurial and Business Women of the Women's Institute.

4.1.1 The ICO Microcredit Line Created at the end of 2002 and operative since then, it has 'your word is your bond' as its motto. The programme objectives include:

- promoting self-employment, creating microbusinesses and reducing unemployment;
- easing access to finance;
- supporting the 'financially excluded' so that their business ideas can be made into reality.

The agents involved in the ICO Microcredit Line and their functions are as follows:

- The European Investment Fund (EIF) working alongside the ICO to improve financing conditions by covering 80 per cent (during 2003) and 50 per cent (in subsequent years) of default risk.
- Private financial institutions channel and manage microloans. In 2003, 39 financial institutions, both commercial banks and savings banks, were active. At this stage, the Spanish commercial banks played an important role: three of the main banks (BBVA, Grupo Santander and Banco Popular) granted 60 per cent of the 15.1 million euros channelled through this public initiative (805 microloans). However, the banks have recently abandoned microcredit activity because of the increased percentage of risk required by the ICO Microcredit Line. This percentage – originally 20 per cent with the remaining 80 per cent covered by the ICO and the FEI – increased to 50 per cent in 2005. Unlike the savings banks, which can resort to social work funds[6] to cover the risk of non-payment in microcredit operations, commercial banks have much tighter budgets for corporate social responsibility activities, thus limiting their ability to cover losses. As a result, according to ICO (2005) and CECA (2005) data, the volume of microloans disbursed through the ICO Line declined to 4.7 million euros in 2004 and 0.5 million euros in 2005 (see Figure 15.2).[7]
- Social work institutions *(Instituciones de Asistencia Social)* comprise institutions, associations, foundations and public or private organizations geared towards bolstering the creation of microbusinesses, creating self-employment and providing incentives for entrepreneurial activities. In 2003, 67 institutions took part, although

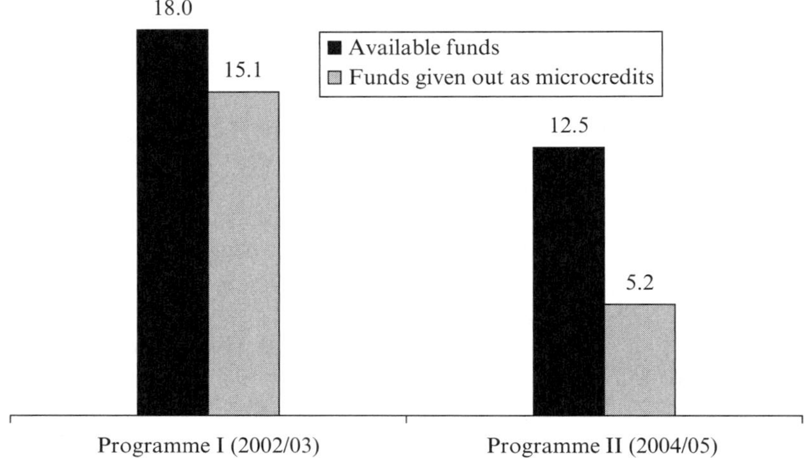

Sources: CECA (2005); ICO (2005).

Figure 15.2 Microloans granted through the ICO Microcredit Line (until October 2005) (in millions €)

their numbers were drastically reduced to five in 2004 and to none[8] by the start of 2005. These institutions are what we call SMSOs, whose functions and characteristics will be examined in depth later on in this section.

- The ICO Foundation provides funds for technical assistance.

Figure 15.3 summarizes the model of the ICO Microcredit Line.

4.1.2 The Microcredit Programme for Entrepreneurial and Business Women of the Women's Institute was launched in 2001 by the government and exclusively geared towards women. This other major microcredit programme is jointly promoted by the Women's Institute, the Ministry of Industry, Tourism and Trade, the savings bank 'la Caixa' and several SMSOs interested in gender issues.

This programme is co-financed by the European Social Fund, and its line of credit is injected annually with 6 million euros from 'la Caixa'. The programme's chief objective is to support enterprising businesswomen in their commercial projects, providing them with access to funding under favourable conditions with no need for guarantees.

The amount of microloans granted through this programme is included in the overall figures for microloans issued by 'la Caixa' (Table 15.2).

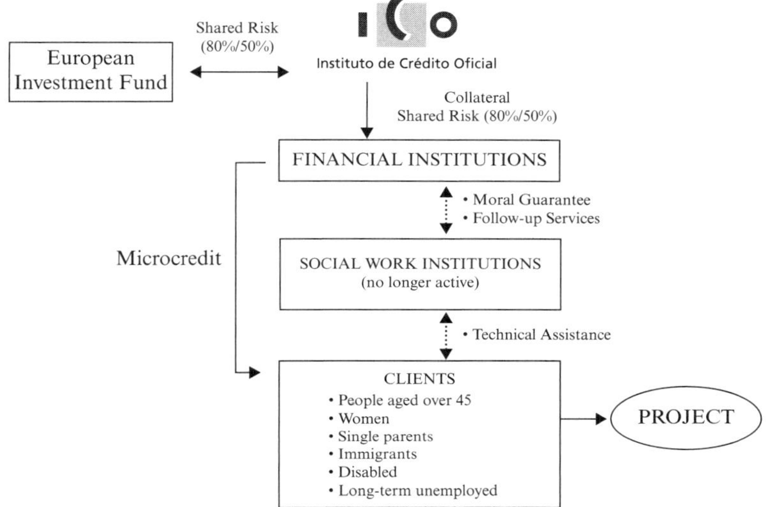

Sources: Authors; ICO (2005).

Figure 15.3 Model of the ICO Microcredit Line

This programme is aimed chiefly at women who meet the following selection criteria.

- The recipient must be a female entrepreneur or businesswoman who is starting up a business or who has started it within the previous year.
- The recipient must present a business plan designed according to an established format, as well as obtain a validation certificate issued by one of the women's business organizations involved in the programme.
- More than 50 per cent of the company must be owned by women.

The significance of this programme is that it represents a positive plan of action to counter the long-standing disadvantage women face in the job market.

4.2 Financial institutions: savings banks' proprietary programmes

According to data provided by the Spanish Confederation of Savings Banks (CECA, 2005), nearly all 46 savings banks grant microcredits. Seven of them, however, are the most active in this field and have carried out a

Table 15.2 Microcredits granted in Spain by the seven main savings banks (from the start of their microcredit lines until December 2005)

Savings bank	Finance granted (Mill. €)	No. operations
A	20.90	1472
B	7.33	786
C	5.69	704
D	2.69	534
E	2.09	220
F	1.85	205
G	1.23	307
Total	41.8	3921

Note: a This data comes from the survey undertaken in collaboration with the EMN during the first six months of 2006, and it is the most recent data on the sector. For reasons of confidentiality, we cannot reveal the identity of the different savings banks, and so we will refer to them as Savings Banks A, B, C, D, E, F and G. They include the following institutions: BBK, CAI, Caixa Catalunya (Un Sol Món), Caixa Galicia, CajaGranada, Kutxa and 'la Caixa'.

Source: Survey (2006).[a]

greater number of operations through their proprietary programmes, as shown in Table 15.2. More specifically, since the beginning of the decade, these banks have carried out 3921 operations worth 41.8 million euros.

Currently, the financing sources for microcredit come from the mandatory reinvestment of post-tax profits in social work. Hence, Spanish savings banks (with few exceptions)[9] offer microcredit based on an off-balance sheet model.[10] In some cases, the funds come from public subsidies. For example, the microcredit programme of CajaGranada is partly financed by the European Union EQUAL programme.[11] Since microloans are subsidized, two potentially negative outcomes may occur:[12]

1. The lack of financial risk for savings banks in their microcredit operations may mean that due diligence on the loans is more lax. As a result, clients may interpret the relaxed vigilance standards as reduced responsibility for loan repayment. Consequently, a significant rise in arrears and default levels may occur, with the end result being a weakening in programme sustainability and the jeopardizing of the borrowers themselves.
2. Savings banks will fail to promote truly social and ethical banking. However, some socially responsible savings products have already been

launched, such as the BBK's solidarity deposit and CajaGranada's solidarity bank card. The BBK's solidarity deposit devotes a percentage of the profits to finance: 1) microcredit programmes for small business start-ups; 2) loans for family needs (housing rental, debt cancellation in an immigrant's country of origin, etc.); or 3) funding of social organizations. As for CajaGranada's *Tarjeta Solidaria* (Solidarity Bank Card), 0.7 per cent of fees are devoted to the microcredit programme.

4.3 Social Microcredit Support Organizations (SMSOs)

As mentioned, the main purpose of the SMSOs is to serve as a link between the end client and the financial institutions by offering a moral guarantee and technical support for the financed projects and monitoring the progress of the approved business plan. In 2001, the Fundació Un Sol Món of Caixa Catalunya pioneered this model for granting microloans. Since then, this model has been increasingly used by other financial institutions and by the government agencies. Although the ICO Microcredit Line originally used a similar model with support from social work institutions (*Instituciones de Asistencia Social*), the system has been abandoned. In the Microcredit Programme for Entrepreneurial and Business Women, seven women's business organizations collaborate as SMSOs.

The advantages of this model are evident given its widespread use. For example, 'la Caixa' or Caixa Catalunya's Fundació Un Sol Món use a network of nearly one hundred SMSOs. Table 15.3 details the main features of these institutions.

The importance of SMSOs in microcredit activity in Spain is attributed to the functions they fulfil as intermediaries, jointly responsible to financial institutions and microentrepreneurs alike. Table 15.4 reveals these specific functions.

Some SMSOs provide potential microcredit clients with training and preparatory courses in business management, negotiation, and/or banking processes. In some cases, attendance at these courses constitutes a prerequisite for applying for microcredit. This training period guarantees better technical preparation for the client. Likewise, it works as a natural selection process in identifying clients who demonstrate entrepreneurial spirit and skills.

SMSOs are responsible for assessing the suitability of the client as a future entrepreneur, especially since microenterprise failure may exacerbate social and financial exclusion. However, if a client abandons a successful small business to accept a job as an employee in a larger company, this is not considered a failure of the microcredit. On the contrary, SMSOs and microcredit entities consider that the microcredit has fulfilled its objective of social, labour and financial integration.

Table 15.3 Main features of the SMSOs

Types	• Public: organizations run by regional or local councils (employment agencies, local development agencies, employment enterprise centres, etc.). • Private (generally non-profit organizations): chambers of commerce, unions, NGOs, administrative agencies and consultants, among others.
Requirements	• Experience in social integration: organizations whose main activity is to foster employment and self-employment amongst the social strata with the greatest difficulty in gaining a stable job. • Thorough knowledge and work experience with vulnerable groups, such as the unemployed, immigrants, ethnic minorities, vulnerable women or the disabled. • With social and institutional influence in the targeted geographical or social area in coordination with other organizations and the local government agencies. • Training and business management skills in order to follow up on and mentor entrepreneurs. Managers of SMSOs must be capable of advising microcredit clients on accounting, commercial and administrative issues, etc. • Transparency and good communication with the financial institutions. Given the joint responsibility that exists between the financial institution and SMSOs, enormous importance is attributed to communication, mutual understanding and the appropriate allocation of tasks. Financial institutions provide the money and assume the credit risk, whereas SMSOs are responsible for selecting the beneficiaries and remaining close to them during the business launch and throughout the term of the microloan.

Source: Rico et al. (2005).

Apart from playing the role as a link and mentor between financial institutions and clients, SMSOs promote the distribution of microcredits. SMSOs enable financial institutions to gain access to collectives that they have not traditionally dealt with, especially since many of these population segments reside in remote or marginalized areas with little financial profitability potential. Likewise, SMSOs compensate for the lack of social work experience among the financial institution employees who process the microloan. SMSOs therefore offer financial institutions a means of extending microcredit coverage.

Table 15.4 Functions of the SMSOs

For the microentrepreneur	• Identification of potential beneficiaries. • Assistance, information and advice for the microentrepreneur and his/her business idea. • Training of the microentrepreneur in the preparation of his/her business plan and other business matters, including marketing, taxes and legal counsel. • Revision of the business plan and of the necessary additional documentation. • Presentation of the documentation required by the financial institution for the microcredit. Provision of moral endorsement or guarantee of the beneficiary and his/her business plan to the financial institution. • Training and technical assistance throughout the term of the microcredit. • Control and monitoring of the microenterprise for at least one or two years in order to guarantee its feasibility and the repayment of the credit.
For the financial institution	• Selection of the micro-entrepreneurs on the basis of: – Exclusion from any other type of ordinary credit. – Potential for business success due to an enterprising spirit. • Evaluation and selection of the projects in terms of economic sustainability. • Monitoring and control of the business in order to ensure credit repayment.

Source: Rico et al. (2005).

5 Target groups

The groups identified by the main microcredit schemes are those who have difficulties in accessing traditional financing methods due to their socio-economic and employment status. The microcredit schemes allow these groups to exercise their right to credit to transform their business ideas into reality. The main microcredit beneficiary groups in Spain are:

- vulnerable women;
- immigrants;
- long-term unemployed;
- single-parent families;
- people over 45 years of age;
- people with disabilities;
- ethnic minorities.

Table 15.5 Estimate of potential microcredit clients in Spain

Women	979.3 thousand unemployed women[a]
	(Rate of female unemployment of 10.5%)
Immigrants	3.8 million persons of a working age[b]
Unemployed	1.76 million persons[a]
	(25% are long-term unemployed, i.e. seeking employment for over a year)
	(25% are under 25 years old)
	(56% are women)
Single-parent homes	405 500 homes[c]
	(87% headed by a woman)
People with disabilities	1.34 million persons with disabilities of a working age[d]

Sources: Data drawn from:
a 2nd quarter of 2007 of Survey of the Active Population (INE, 2007a).
b 4th quarter of 2006 of Survey of the Active Population (INE, 2007a).
c 2nd quarter of 2007 (Instituto de la Mujer: Women's Institute, 2007).
d Survey on Persons with Disabilities, Deficiencies and State of Health, 1999 (INE, 2007b).

Table 15.5 provides an estimate of the potential microcredit clients in Spain.

Next, we will analyse the vulnerability of the two main beneficiary collectives: women and immigrants.

Women

As highlighted by the Fundación FOESSA and Cáritas (1999), difficulties in accessing the labour market and the increase in single-parent households headed by women explain the increased vulnerability of women to social exclusion.

At the beginning of this decade, the mass incorporation of women into a volatile labour market led to high levels of female unemployment relative to that of men, reaching 20.4 per cent in 2000 as compared to 9.5 per cent for men. While the female unemployment rate has dropped over recent years (10.5 per cent in the second quarter of 2007), it remains notably higher than male unemployment (6.1 per cent for the same period). These results show persistent employment discrimination by gender (see Figure 15.4).

Due to the rising number of divorces and single-parent households headed by women, the vulnerability of women has increased as they assume responsibility for both household care and income generation. Although the number of single-parent households in Spain remains low at around 2.5 per cent of all total households, 87 per cent of the total single-

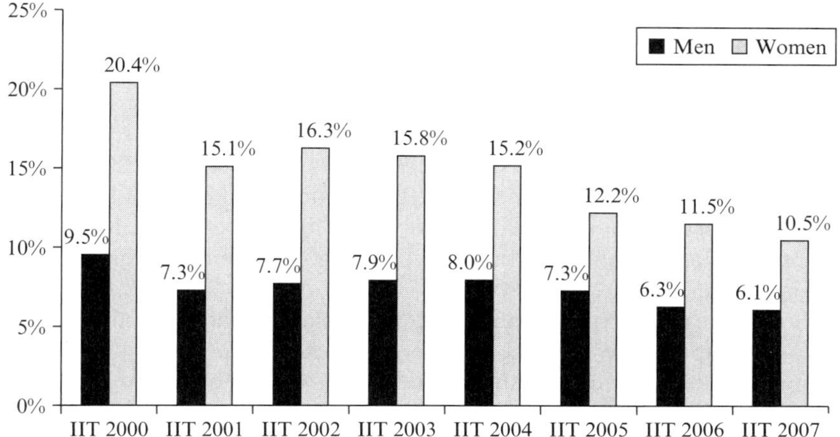

Sources: Authors; INE (2007a).

Figure 15.4 Unemployment in Spain by gender, 2000–2006

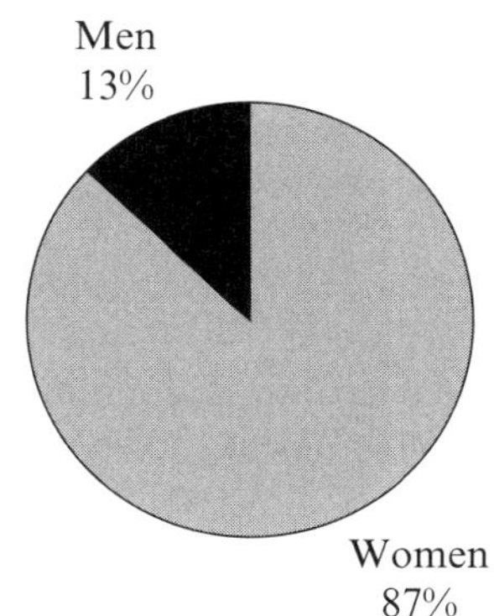

TOTAL: 405 500 households headed by one adult

Sources: Authors; Instituto de la Mujer (2007).

Figure 15.5 Breakdown of single-parent households by gender, 2nd quarter of 2007

parent households are headed by women (Instituto de la Mujer, 2007) (see Figure 15.5).

These factors (high female unemployment and a high percentage of households headed by women) justify the estimates of the Women's

Institute (Instituto de la Mujer, 2006) which, on the basis of data supplied by the European Union Household Panel (EUHP), states that 23 per cent of women were at risk of social exclusion in Spain in 2001.

Immigrants

According to a study by the National Statistics Institute (INE, 2007a), the number of immigrants registered in the Municipal Registrar of all cities on 1 January, 2006 was 4 482 568, representing 9.9 per cent of the total population and almost five times higher than the number of immigrants registered in 2000.

Several reasons explain immigrants' exclusion, including: i) the lack of resources upon arrival in the country; ii) lack of knowledge of the language; iii) difficulty in obtaining a formal job, due to absence of necessary documentation and/or lack of professional experience; iv) the need to send wages home to support relatives; and/or v) the rigidity of the legal framework and problems in accessing social protection services. As shown in Figure 15.6, the immigrant population at risk is becoming increasingly acute due to accelerated population growth.

5.1 Scope of microcredit in Spain

Although the spectrum of potential microcredit clients is wide, in light of the phenomenon of the feminization of poverty in Spain, women are one of the main targets of microcredit programmes. Based on data supplied by Lacalle et al. (2006b) and ICO (2005), women receive between 50–60 per cent of all microloans, while immigrants also obtain a significant percentage in the range of 38–55 per cent.

A breakdown of clients in microcredit programmes devised by the Savings Banks and the ICO Microcredit Line is shown in Figures 15.7 to 15.10.

5.2 Analysis of the depth of outreach of microcredit amongst the most disadvantaged

In line with the definition adopted in the Microcredit Summit in Washington DC, in February 1997, microcredit refers to 'small loans to very poor people for self-employment projects that generate income, allowing them to care for themselves and their families'.

On this basis, it is important to assess whether the work of SMSOs, the Spanish government agencies and financial institutions has benefited the population segments at greatest risk of social and financial exclusion. With this objective, the Foro Nantik Lum de MicroFinanzas, through its field work,[13] has carried out a preliminary analysis of the client and project selection criteria used by SMSOs and financial institutions.

According to the Survey (2005), practically all SMSOs agreed that since

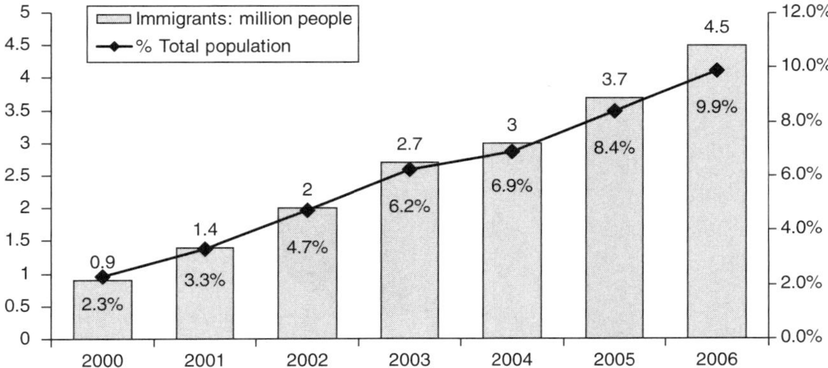

Source: INE (2007a).

Figure 15.6 *Immigrant population in Spain 2000–2005*

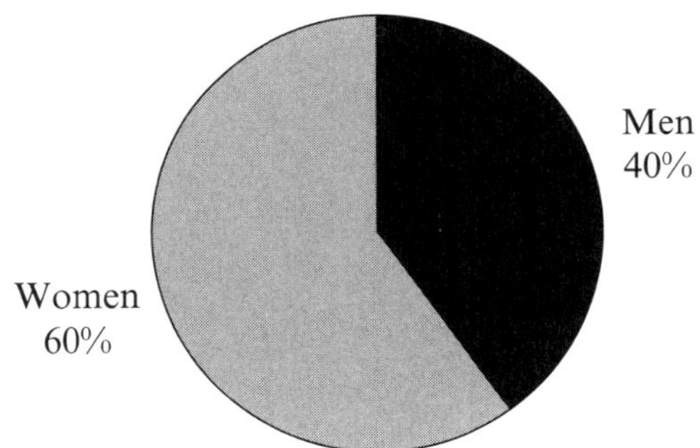

Note: Includes data from BBK, Caixa Catalunya, Caixa Galicia, CajaGranada, Colonya Caixa Pollença and 'la Caixa'.

Source: Survey (2006).

Figure 15.7 *Microloans granted to women by savings banks' proprietary programmes (2005)*

microloans are not subsidies, demonstration of project feasibility and client entrepreneurial character is required. Nevertheless, according to SMSOs, these two selection criteria should not exclude social indicators such as unstable family conditions, the suffering of a disease or lack of education.

Yet in practice, SMSOs pay less heed to social criteria than to economic feasibility criteria, mainly due to the large responsibility involved in supporting a client and his or her project. A wrong decision could have a seriously adverse effect. If, for example, an infeasible project were approved,

Source: ICO (2005).

Figure 15.8 Microloans granted to women by the ICO Microcredit Line (2002–2004)

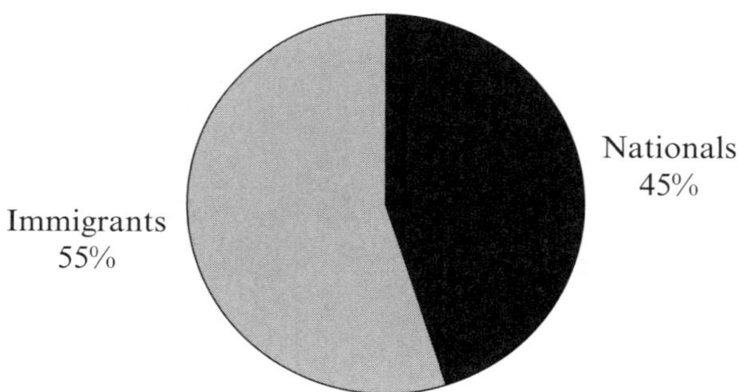

Note: Includes data from BBK, Caixa Catalunya, Caixa Galicia, CajaGranada, Colonya Caixa Pollença and 'la Caixa'.

Source: Survey (2006).

Figure 15.9 Microloans granted to immigrants by savings banks' proprietary programmes (2005)

bankruptcy would not only lead to default, but the client would be further excluded from the financial system, including access to credit lines targeted at disadvantaged groups.

In sections 5.2.1 and 5.2.2, this phenomenon is illustrated by the results obtained in the Survey (2005).

5.2.1 Client selection criteria Microcredits in Spain enable groups at risk of social and financial exclusion to exercise the right to credit to

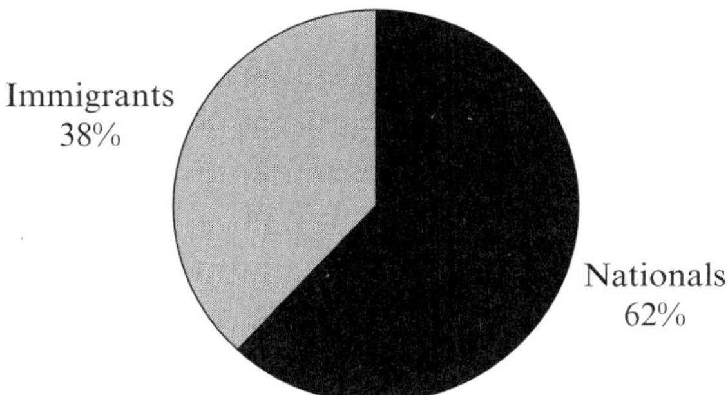

Source: ICO (2005).

Figure 15.10 Microloans granted to immigrants by the ICO Microcredit Line (2002–2004)

convert their business ideas into profitable microenterprises, capable of generating income used to improve living standards. As shown in Figures 15.7 to 15.10, microcredit primarily reaches two priority groups: women and immigrants.

With the objective of quantifying the depth of outreach of Spanish microfinance institutions, the Foro Nantik Lum de MicroFinanzas carried out the Survey (2005), in which SMSOs and financial institutions were asked to grade the relevance (high, medium or low) of the following client selection indicators.

i. Economic indicators:
   - income level;
   - alternative income sources in household;
   - savings;
   - size of the household;
   - number of dependants;
   - size of the dwelling or number of rooms;
   - recipient of public subsidies.
ii. Training and employment situation indicators:
   - level of education;
   - technical skills;
   - previous profession or activity;
   - months of unemployment;
   - instability of current job.
iii. Health indicators:
   - chronic illnesses affecting them or their family;

RARELY USE

- Size of the dwelling or the number of rooms
- Relationships with neighbours
- Recipient of public subsidies
- Months of unemployment

SOMETIMES USE

- Level of education
- Number of dependents
- Previous business experience
- Household size
- Instability of current employment
- Lack of chronic illnesses affecting them or the family
- No addiction to drug or alcohol
- Lack of emotional problems
- Business training

USE OFTEN

- Entrepreneurial spirit
- Income level
- Technical skills
- Alternative income sources in the household
- Savings
- Previous profession or activity
- Family stability
- Social ties

Source: Survey (2005).

Figure 15.11 Degree of use of the selection indicators for clients

- emotional problems or failure;
- addiction to drugs or alcohol.

iv. Social stability indicators:
- family stability;
- relationship with neighbours;
- social ties.

v. Indicators of business aptitude:
- entrepreneurial spirit;
- previous business experience;
- business training.

The results show that SMSOs and financial institutions favour potential clients with an entrepreneurial profile, alternative economic possibilities, specific technical skills, previous work experience, and family and social stability. A more detailed analysis of the results is provided in Figure 15.11.

These results were compared to the opinions of experts who participated in the Foro Nantik Lum de MicroFinanzas workshops, who unanimously stated that microcredit mainly reaches people capable of running a microbusiness successfully. Thus, in Spain, there is a reluctance to disburse microloans to 'the poorest of the poor'. To access the poorest strata, mentoring and training in business management prior to the granting of the microloan is required. The cost of providing these services and the inherent credit risk are still perceived as very high by financial institutions and SMSOs.

Unlike the trend in the developing world, the microcredit system in Spain considers it more appropriate to care for the poorest strata through subsidies as opposed to accepting the challenge and opportunity of sustainable development provided by microcredit.

5.2.2 Project selection criteria The Survey (2005) carried out on SMSOs and financial institutions by the Foro Nantik Lum de MicroFinanzas also incorporated an assessment of the degree of use of the following four project selection parameters:

1. project viability;
2. client's state of social and financial exclusion;
3. job creation potential of project;
4. trust in the SMSO presenting the project.

From the results obtained, the criterion of project feasibility was clearly the most important factor in the financing decision, followed by the client's state of social and financial exclusion and the project's capacity for creating employment. For financial institutions, trust in SMSOs shares second place with the beneficiary's social exclusion status (see Figure 15.12).

The high priority given to project feasibility in comparison to criteria of a more social nature can be considered as further proof that the most vulnerable population segments are excluded by the current microcredit system. At present, the system may not be fully confident in the ability of the poorest strata to repay a microcredit, and thus prefers to offer non-returnable subsidies.[14]

6 Financial terms and conditions

Across all Spanish microcredit programmes, a microcredit is defined as an individual loan which is granted to set up small businesses or microenterprises that generate self-employment and jobs. The main requirements of the target segment are:

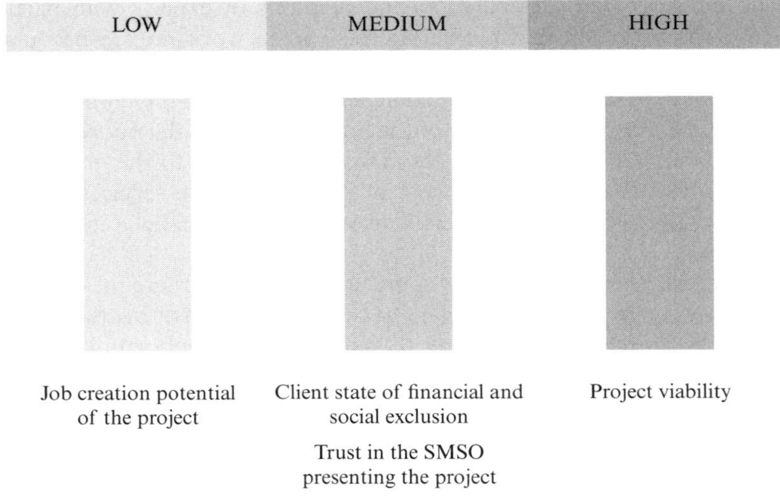

Source: Rico et al. (2005).

Figure 15.12 Degree of use of project selection criteria

a. to form part of a disadvantaged social group with particular difficulties in finding employment;
b. no access to a formal financial system due to lack of collateral;
c. to possess entrepreneurial skills and a feasible business initiative.

The terms and conditions of the loan also tend to be similar across the programmes, as shown in Table 15.6.

7 Government support and regulation

As analysed in section 4, the Spanish government is playing a significant role in the promotion of microcredit. This support is backed by a cost–benefit rationale. As in the rest of Europe, Spanish microloans have the potential to become an effective tool in creating jobs and driving down public spending on unemployment benefits. Data released by the European Commission (2003) show that the subsidies granted by European governments to each start-up microenterprise cost in the range of 2000 to 5000 euros, significantly lower than the 18 000 euros paid out in benefits to an unemployed individual. Similarly, microcredit can achieve cost savings in the provision of social benefits to unemployed and/or vulnerable people. If the Spanish government were to devote part of its budget to microcredit programmes designed to create microbusinesses and new jobs, it would not only boost its

Table 15.6 Terms and conditions of microcredit programmes in Spain

	Savings banks' proprietary programmes	ICO Microcredit Line	Microcredit Programme for Entrepreneurial and Business Women
Loan size	From 6000 to 25000 euros[a]	25000 euros	15000 euros
Grace period	From 0 to 6 months[b]	None In the 2007/08 phase, grace periods can be agreed	6 months (optional)
Repayment term	From 2.2 to 6 years	2 or 3 years (2003) 3 or 4 years (2004) 5 years (2005/06) 1 to 7 years (2007/08)	5 years
Current rate of interest	Between 3.25% and 6%	6% (2003) 5.5% (2004) 5.5% (2005/06) ICO interest rate for 7-year loans with a grace period of 2 years (2007/08)	5% fixed rate over duration of loan
Guarantees	No guarantees (in most cases)[c]	No guarantees	Not required
Fees	No fees (in most cases)[d]	No fees	0.50% up-front fee; 0.25% for feasibility study; 0% early amortization
Maximum financing	Up to 100% of project	95% of project (2003–2006) 100% of the project (2007/08)	95% of project

Notes:

a The BBK microcredit programme offers up to 50000 euros.

b The BBK microcredit programme offers up to 24 months.

c Some institutions require guarantees based on personal savings or group guarantees.

d Some institutions charge up-front or delinquency fees.

Sources: Rico et al. (2004), Survey (2006), ICO (2004), ICO (2005), ICO (2007) and Ministerio de Trabajo y Asuntos Sociales (2007).

public revenues, since the new workers would pay taxes and social security contributions, but also reduce social assistance-related costs.

Currently, no specific laws exist to regulate the microcredit industry in Spain in either the financial markets or the establishment of microbusinesses. All the financial institutions that are currently providing microcredit loans are doing so in a 'legal' manner. As a result, financial institutions have pushed for regulation by the Bank of Spain, which oversees the credit of all banks. In December 2007, Spanish savings banks and their industry organization CECA launched the Spanish Network of Microfinance with the objective of promoting debate and lobbying to create necessary financial regulation in the microcredit industry. Similarly, no specific regulation governing the initiation of microenterprises currently exists. Consequently, micro-entrepreneurs face the same bureaucratic obstacles and benefits as any other small business owner.

8 Financial and operational sustainability

Due to the scarcity of programme cost information, there are very few rigorous studies on the financial and operational sustainability of the microcredit sector in Spain. According to CECA (2005), the default rate reached 34 per cent in 2002–2003, falling significantly to 2.12 per cent in 2004. In the case of the proprietary programmes of the savings banks, the default rate was between 0.13 per cent and 7.01 per cent between 2002–2005. Since savings banks often do not disclose their methods for calculating the default rate, it is difficult to compare and evaluate the overall loan repayment rate in Spain, thus hindering an analysis of the overall sector sustainability.

On the other hand, it is important to recognize that savings banks utilize social work funds for supporting their microcredit programmes. These funds are non-refundable, thus enabling the savings banks to sustain losses in the short to medium term. Nevertheless, in many industry forums, Spanish savings banks have emphasized their efforts to reduce costs to increase the development and scope of microcredit. In short, although social work funds may alleviate concerns about financial sustainability in the medium term, long-term industry viability is contingent on improvements in operational efficiency and effectiveness.

9 Challenges and conclusions

Spanish savings banks offer the vast majority of microloans through funds reserved for their social work. It is difficult to find a private institution capable of covering the financial and operational costs of disbursing microloans. In all cases, microcredits are either directly or indirectly subsidized through savings bank social work funds or covered by national public organizations (for example, ICO) or European institutions (for example, the European Social Fund or the European Investment Fund).

Microcredit institutions should not require any type of collateral since microcredit was created precisely to provide access to credit to those who have no resources or guarantors/co-signers. The only guarantee that should be required is an individual moral guarantee. That is, clients are trusted with loan repayment because of a conviction in their capabilities or in the financial viability of the project. In Spain, financial institutions substitute collateral with a moral guarantee that SMSOs provide in their selection of feasible business plans and trustworthy clients.

Even though Spanish microcredit programmes are still relatively new, based on the analysis performed in this chapter, we have drawn up the following conclusions and recommendations to be considered by all agents involved in microcredit programmes in the Spanish context:

- Savings banks play the most important role in the growth of microcredit through their proprietary programmes and/or government initiatives. Savings banks combine their experience in financial brokering with their traditional social vocation. Their programmes rely on Social Microcredit Support Organizations (SMSOs), which link credit providers and micro-entrepreneurs. The partnerships between savings banks and SMSOs are a unique feature of microfinance provision in Spain.
- The distribution of microcredit depends on SMSOs, which have connections to groups traditionally excluded from the financial sector. The SMSOs work alongside the micro-entrepreneur and the financial institutions to promote fulfilment of the business plan and repayment of the microcredit. The SMSOs' experience in social work, integration of vulnerable groups, and proper selection of feasible projects facilitates the provision of credit to marginalized collectives ignored by the formal financial sector. Hence, SMSOs can provide a larger customer base for offering other financial products in the future.
- To better service both clients and financial institutions, SMSOs must either possess or internally develop professional expertise in the field of social integration and business management. Boosting the professional capacity of the SMSOs requires increasing both technical and financial support from financial institutions and the government.
- Two criteria are currently considered priorities in the granting of microloans:
  - business plan viability;
  - entrepreneurial attitude.

These criteria can put the poorest population segments in a disadvantageous position, given that the poorest of the poor require a substantial investment in training and support before microloans can be disbursed. Thus, this issue should be the focus of further research on the Spanish microcredit system to determine the depth of outreach of microloans in the funding of projects of the poorest segments.

- Moreover, although the savings banks' commitment to the microfinance sector has helped the excluded exercise their right to credit, the focus on financial feasibility over social criteria may mean that the most attractive, 'almost' bankable, individuals benefit most. The depth of outreach of programmes, that is, their ability to aid the most vulnerable, may remain limited as long as social criteria remain subordinate.
- In Spain, microcredit loans are a useful tool to reduce the unemployment rate through self-employment. Microcredit represents an alternative financial tool for the integration of women and immigrants into the labour market.
- Additionally, microcredits increase public funds by cutting unemployment-related costs, boosting social security contributions and reducing spending on social assistance for the unemployed immigrants. The biggest challenge that lies ahead is the creation of a 'solidarity network' among the various organizations working to integrate vulnerable people into our society – financial institutions, SMSOs and public organizations – with the aim of ensuring that microcredit, as a tool to fight exclusion and poverty, is accessible to the most impoverished.

Amongst the challenges facing the microcredit sector in Spain, two should be especially emphasized: 1) development of an adequate regulation which speeds up the granting of microcredits by financial institutions while eliminating bureaucratic obstacles confronted by micro-entrepreneurs; and 2) enhancement of open and transparent information regarding the programmes' costs in order to attain financial and operative sustainability in the microcredit sector through improved appropriate analysis.

Notes

1. This chapter is based on a previous book titled *Microcredit in Spain*. The book was jointly published in 2007 by the Foro Nantik Lum de MicroFinanzas (Madrid) and the European Microfinance Network (Paris). The authors are co-directors of Foro Nantik Lum de MicroFinanzas.
2. This section is based on the data available in the following references: Banco de España (2007), Central Intelligence Agency (2007), Malo de Molina (2007), Viñals (2007) and INE (2009).

3. Data collected from the Eurobarometer and the Blue Book on Payment and Security Settlement Systems drafted by the Central European Bank.
4. Figures come from:

   - A data survey carried out by Foro Nantik Lum de MicroFinanzas during the first half of 2006 (referred to as Survey 2006) in collaboration with the European Microfinance Network (EMN). This survey was sent out to 47 financial institutions and 70 Social Microcredit Support Organisations (SMSOs); responses were received from 11 and 22 organizations, respectively, representing a significant sample of all institutions working with microcredits in Spain today.
   - A data survey sent in February 2005 (referred to as Survey 2005) to 8 financial institutions and 7 SMSOs, representing the main microcredit institutions in Spain at that time.
   - Several workshops held at the Universidad Pontificia Comillas (Madrid), in which experts from financial institutions, SMSOs and academia took part with the purpose of debating and exchanging experiences.

   Secondary sources have also been used, mainly annual reports from savings banks and commercial banks, data from the Municipal Register, socio-demographic indicators from the Spanish National Statistics Institute (INE), Social Security statistics, reports and publications from the Bank of Spain and the Microcredit White Book drawn up by the Savings Bank Foundation (FUNCAS) in 2005.
5. Assuming two jobs per microenterprise.
6. Savings banks have to mandatorily reinvest their post-tax profits in social work.
7. Among the potential reasons that lie behind this decline are:

   i. The small loan size entails a high per-unit transaction cost for financial institutions, thus causing a negative impact on profitability.
   ii. Financial institutions lack experience in this type of operation. The ICO Microcredit Line does not provide additional funds for loan follow-up.
   iii. The strict conditions of the microcredit loan – without a grace period or flexible repayment terms – could have a negative impact on arrears and defaults, which Martínez Estevez (2005) estimates at 35 per cent.

   Another reason may presumably be that savings banks are choosing not to participate in the ICO Microcredit Line. Remarkably, in the new 2007/08 phase of the programme, only four savings banks are affiliated.
8. At the beginning of the programme, tension existed among the ICO Microcredit Line and the financial and social institutions that offered support and follow-up services for micro-entrepreneurs. In some cases, these institutions believed that the ICO Microcredit Line failed to consider the high costs of providing the necessary services and that the remuneration provided was merely symbolic. On the other hand, the ICO Microcredit Line sometimes disputed the quality of services provided. As a result, many institutions left the programme. Currently, the responsibilities of providing follow-up services for the micro-entrepreneurs is left to the financial institutions.
9. The most relevant exception is 'la Caixa', which is in the process of setting up a Microcredit Bank with its own banking licence.
10. This means that profit and losses resulting from the microcredit operations are not consolidated in the bank's financial statements.
11. EQUAL is an EU labour initiative promoted by the European Social Fund. Its aim is cross-national cooperation to promote new ways of fighting against discrimination and inequality in the labour market.
12. These outcomes have not been verified due to the short lifespan of microcredits in Spain.
13. See note 4.

14. Due to the complexity and relevance of this issue, we recommend that all involved agents jointly conduct further research on social, political and economic impacts.

References

Adiego Estella, M. and C. Moneo Ocaña (2004), 'Pobreza y pobreza persistente en España 1994–2001', INE, available at www.ine.es.

Banco de España (2007), 'Informe Anual 2006', August, available at www.bde.es.

Bárcenas López, J. (2006), 'Intervención del presidente de CEPYME en el día Europeo de las Pymes', August, available at www.cepyme.es.

Carbó Valverde, S. and R. López del Paso (2005), 'Exclusión financiera: un panorama', *Perspectivas del sistema financiero*, no. 84, Madrid: Fundación de las Cajas de Ahorros.

Central Intelligence Agency (2007), *The World Factbook*, August, available at www.cia.gov.

Confederación Española de Cajas de Ahorros (CECA) (2005), 'Situación del microcrédito en las cajas de ahorros españolas', in FUNCAS (ed.), *El Libro Blanco del Microcrédito*, Madrid: FUNCAS.

Confederación Española de Cajas de Ahorros (CECA) (2007a), ¿Qué son las Cajas?, August, available at www.ceca.es.

Confederación Española de Cajas de Ahorros (CECA) (2007b), 'Datos Básicos Cajas de Ahorros', August, available at www.ceca.es.

European Commission (2003), 'Microcredit for small businesses and business creation: bridging a market gap', Report, November, Brussels: Enterprise Publications.

Eurostat (2005), *Europe in Figures. Eurostat Yearbook 2005*, Luxembourg: Office for Official Publications of the European Communities.

Eurostat (2007), 'At-risk-of-poverty rate after social transfer', available at http://epp.eurostat.ec.europa.eu/portal/page/portal/living_conditions_and_social_protection/data/database.

Foro Nantik Lum de MicroFinanzas (2005), 'Los Microcréditos en España: Principales Magnitudes 2004', I National Conference on Microcredit organized by the Obra Social 'la Caixa', 9–10 March 2005, Madrid.

Fundación FOESSA (2005), 'La Pobreza en España', Informe Sociológico sobre la situación social en España, available at http://www.entornosocial.es.

Fundación FOESSA and Caritas (1999), 'La Pobreza en España', Informe FOESSA, available at http://www.entornosocial.es.

Fundación FOESSA and Caritas (2005), 'La Pobreza en España', Informe FOESSA, http://www.entornosocial.es (updated version).

Guzy, M. and T. Underwood (2006), 'Immigrant participation in microloan programmes in Western Europe', Paris: European Microfinance Network.

Instituto de Crédito Oficial (ICO) (2004), 'Línea de microcréditos del Instituto de Crédito Oficial', November 2004, available at www.ico.es.

Instituto de Crédito Oficial (ICO) (2005), 'Microcréditos nacionales. Programa impulsado por el Instituto de Crédito Oficial', Dirección General de Negocios.

Instituto de Crédito Oficial (ICO) (2007), 'Línea ICO-Microcréditos para España 2007–2008', August 2007, available at www.ico.es.

Instituto de la Mujer (2007), 'Las mujeres en España', Estadísticas, September 2007, available at www.mtas.es/mujer.

Instituto Nacional de Estadística (INE) (2007a), 'Demografía y Población, Mercado Laboral, Encuesta de Población Activa', September 2007, available at www.ine.es/inebase.

Instituto Nacional de Estadística (INE) (2007b), 'Sociedad, Salud, Encuesta sobre Discapacidades, Deficiencias y Estado de Salud 1999', October 2007, available at www.ine.es/inebase.

Lacalle, M. (2002), *Microcréditos. De pobres a Microempresarios*, Barcelona: Ed. Ariel.

Lacalle, M., S. Rico, J. Márquez and J. Durán (2006a), 'Glosario básico sobre microfinanzas', Cuadernos Monográficos no. 5, Madrid: Foro Nantik Lum de MicroFinanzas.

Lacalle, M., S. Rico, J. Márquez and J. Durán (2006b), 'Microcréditos e Inmigración: Inserción sociolaboral en España y Reducción de los flujos migratorios irregulares', Cuaderno Monográfico no. 7, Madrid: Foro Nantik Lum de MicroFinanzas.

Malo de Molina, J.L. (2007), 'Los principales rasgos y experiencias de la integración de la economía española en la UEM', *Documentos Ocasionales*, no. 0701, Madrid: Banco de España.

Martínez Estévez, Aurelio (2005), 'El programa de microcréditos del ICO', *Perspectivas del Sistema Financiero*, no. 84, Madrid: FUNCAS.

Ministerio de Economía y Hacienda (2007), 'Síntesis de Indicadores Económicos', August 2007, available at www.meh.es.

Ministerio de Trabajo y Asuntos Sociales (2007), 'Programa de microcréditos para mujeres emprendedoras y empresarias', August 2007, available at www.mtas.es/mujer/programas/empleo/apoyos_financieros.html.

Moya Arjona, F. (2007), 'Sistema financiero Español', August 2007, available at www.monografias.com.

Rico, S., M. Lacalle, J. Durán and C. Ballesteros (2004), 'Los Microcréditos: alternativa financiera para combatir la exclusión social y financiera en España. Descripción de las principales iniciativas', Cuaderno Monográfico no. 1, Madrid: Foro Nantik Lum de MicroFinanzas.

Rico, S., M. Lacalle, C. Ballesteros and J. Durán (2005), 'Las entidades sociales de apoyo al microcrédito: su papel fundamental en la concesión de microcréditos en España', Cuaderno Monográfico no. 3, Madrid: Foro Nantik Lum de Microfinanzas.

Survey (2005), Data survey on microcredit activity in Spain carried out by the Foro Nantik Lum de MicroFinanzas. The survey was sent out to 8 financial institutions and 7 SMSOs.

Survey (2006), Data survey on microcredit activity in Spain carried out by the Foro Nantik Lum de MicroFinanzas in collaboration with the European Microfinance Network. The survey was sent out to 47 financial institutions and 70 SMSOs.

Viñals, J. (2007), 'La economía española: tendencias recientes y retos para el futuro. Intervención en el encuentro hispano-ruso', *Intervenciones Públicas*, Madrid: Banco de España.

16 Microcredit in Romania

Maria Doiciu and Diana Bialus

1 National context

After the fall of Communism, the Romanian economy went through a transition period from a centralized system to an open market economy and started to grow, increasing business opportunities for entrepreneurs of all sizes.

Macroeconomic summary

Disciplined monetary and fiscal policies pursued over recent years have improved the macroeconomic picture considerably. During this period, domestic consumption has taken the lead role in the growth of the economy. Household consumption has continued to grow strongly, partly driven by the effects of 2005 income tax[1] cuts and largely driven by the boom of household loans for current consumption (they recorded a 89.4 per cent increase in 2006 compared to 2005).[2] However, structural constraints on the domestic production side of goods and services continue to co-exist with exchange rate pressures (the Romanian leu, RON had the largest appreciation against the euro and US dollar in 2006 compared to any other emerging markets' currencies). As a consequence, the persistence of excess demand has fuelled import growth, widening the current account gap further (see Table 16.1).

The fastest growth has been among the expansion in numbers of microbusinesses. As can be seen from Table 16.2, microenterprises represent almost 90 per cent of the total number of Romanian enterprises.[3]

Commercial banks traditionally operate on a walk-in client basis. If they seek direct contact with enterprises, it is those having fixed locations, buildings and equipment. This is not the case for the Romanian MSMEs market segment, and those located in remote rural areas in particular are unlikely to approach banks for loans. The existing microfinance sector, represented by the Non-Bank Financial Institutions (NBFI),[4] is unable to cover the growing demand for financial services from SMEs.

The gap in demand for financial services for micro and small enterprises was estimated for 2007 at 700 million euros.[5,6] The small enterprise gap is an approximation, derived from the demand analysis model, better suited for microenterprises. Thus, the small enterprise gap is most likely greater than shown.

This analysis shows the continuing need for microfinance in Romania and justifies the development of the sector.

Table 16.1 Selected macroeconomic indicators

Macroeconomic indicator	2003	2004	2005	2006	2007f
Real GDP growth (%)	4.9	8.4	4.1	7.7	6.5
CPI inflation – Dec., annual change (%)	14.2	9.3	8.7	4.8	4.5
Current account balance (% of GDP)	–6.2	–8.6	–8.7	–10.5	–10.5
Trade balance (% of GDP)	–7.8	–8.9	–9.9	–15	–15
Exchange rate (e.o.p., RON/EUR)	4.11	3.97	3.68	3.4	3.5
Unemployment rate – year end (%)	7.4	6.2	5.8	5.5	5.5
Government budget balance (% of GDP)	–2.4	–1.0	–0.9	–1.7	–2.8
Public debt (% of GDP)	27.0	22.4	18.9	20.3	21
NBR reserves in months of imports	4.6	5.9	6.6	6.8	7

Note: f: forecasts of the National Prognosis Commission (NPC), National Bank of Romania (NBR).

Sources: NBR and National Statistics Institute (NSI).

Table 16.2 Romanian MSME sector structure

Size / year Number of enterprises	2004	2005	2006	2007 (est.)
Micro	358 242 (89%)	372 930 (88%)	410 763 (89%)	451 839 (89%)
Small	36 080 (8%)	37 559 (9%)	43 419 (10%)	47 760 (10%)
Medium	8 674 (2%)	9 030 (3%)	9 322 (2%)	10 254 (2%)
Total	402 996 (100%)	419 519 (100%)	463 504 (100%)	509 854 (100%)

Source: Data drawn from: Annual report on the SMEs sector in Romania (National Agency for SMEs, 2007).

2 The origin of microfinance in Romania

2.1 When?

The Romanian Credit Union (CU) System, one of Europe's oldest, is in a critical phase of its evolution, with the diversified financial needs of its members: individual employees requiring major changes in operating systems. During 2002–2006 the process of adapting Romanian legislation to EU regulations continued, and this impacted on the activity of the employees of CUs. The number of members decreased and the consolidation of the small CUs led to stronger organizations. At the end of the financial year 2006, 2695 credit unions were registered with the National Bank affiliated to 39 territorial unions which reported 1 115 633 members.[7]

Microfinance activities in Romania, mainly targeting microenterprises and SMEs, began 15 years ago when the first international microfinance institution (MFI), 'Opportunity International', launched its programme for the financing of SMEs in Romania, establishing the Izvor Foundation. Set up in 1995 as a not-for-profit organization and re-registered as an NBFI, Opportunity Microfinance Romania (OMRO) helped small entrepreneurs develop their businesses and contributed to the creation of new jobs.

The Romanian microfinance sector developed fast, with other MFIs entering the market. For example, Community Habitat Finance International (CHF) established CHF Romania; World Vision founded CAPA[8] Foundation; and Open Society Foundation were the sponsors of the Centre for Economic Development (CDE).

2.2 Why?

During the 1990s, Romania went through a period of transition from a centralized economy to a market economy, but also through a process of economic growth. Such an economic environment brings opportunities for small entrepreneurs, but also an increased demand for finance. As most of the existing financial institutions present on the market at that time were focused on medium or large enterprises, there was a need for microfinance to be fulfilled by the microfinance sector.

2.3 How?

All the microfinance institutions that contributed to the creation of the microfinance sector in Romania were set up with help and assistance from international organizations with extensive experience in the sector. All these institutions were initially established as non-governmental organizations (NGOs), and throughout their existence they were transformed according to the changes in the legislative framework affecting the microfinance sector in Romania.

3 Main actors within the microfinance sector in Romania

3.1 Who are the actors?

Romanian MFIs share a common purpose: to provide access to finance of less than €25 000. The microloans are extended in addition to other financial services, specially designed for entrepreneurs who are unable to access the finance they need to develop, beyond the capital generated within their business.

In Romania, there is a large geographical area to cover, with varying economic environments in which development and practices of MFI are at different stages. Currently, there are 21 microfinance institutions operating in Romania, according to statistics provided by the National Bank of Romania (NBR). However, these institutions are very different and can be segmented into several groups.

3.1.1 Institutional type: legal structure of the MFIs In Romania, the new legal framework GO 28/2006 requires the registration and licensing of the MFIs as NBFI microfinance companies by the NBR. CDE, as a microfinance foundation, is excepted as long as they are exclusively administrating public funds. The segmentation map (Figure 16.1) is a comprehensive picture of the Romanian MF sector. The MFIs are represented to show their maturity/age (number of years of operation); legal status of NBFI or NGO; the size of their portfolio, Gross Loan Portfolio (GLP); and the social or commercial orientation based on their missions.

3.1.2 MFI mission, targeted market and service offered Due to increased competition, commercialization is the strategy of almost all medium and large MFIs. However, there are a number of more targeted initiatives that may take a different, more focused path, for example the support for women entrepreneurs (Integra), farmers (LAM, FAER and CAPA Finance), and former miners (CDE and CHF-Express Finance).

One of the most significant factors affecting the performance of the Romanian MFIs is the market or type of customers they serve. This, in turn, is affected by the MFI's mission and orientation. These factors are strongly connected to and influence the MFI's size and its average loan size, both having a bearing on its financial and social performance.

Therefore, the Romanian MFIs were divided into three categories: social oriented; social and commercial oriented; and commercial oriented (see Table 16.3).

3.1.3 MFI fund size and maturity As global microfinance practice has developed, it has become clear that the age of an MFI is a crucial factor in understanding its relative performance. In Romania, due to the new legal framework which lowered the barriers of registration and licensing, 13 new MFIs, some of them with significant resources, registered in 2006–2007. Therefore, the sector is divided into mature MFIs and new ones. The

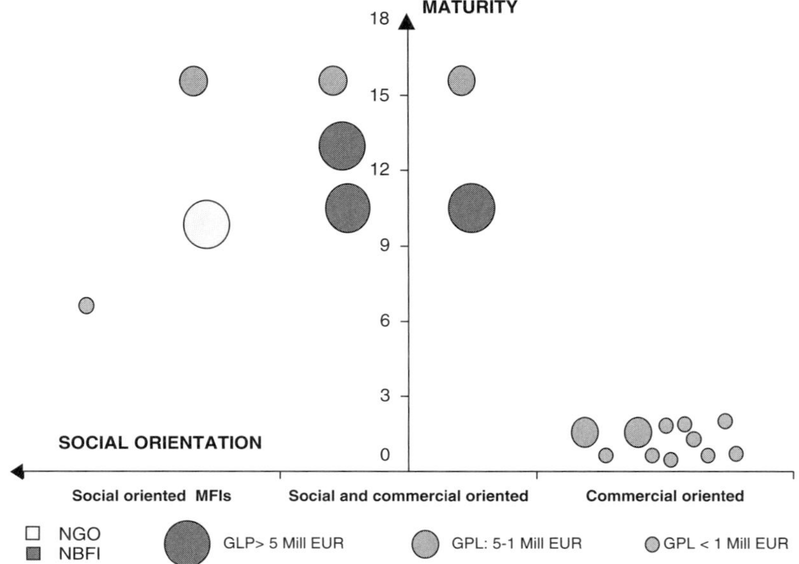

Note: The first MF segmentation exercise was developed under the EU funded project: *From Exclusion to Inclusion Through Microfinance: Learning From East to West and West to East* – Working Group 4 Benchmarks and performance measurement implemented by Micro Finance Center (MFC), EMN and Community Development Finance Association (CDFA).

Source: Report Benchmarking Microfinance in Romania 2005–2006.

Figure 16.1 Romanian MF sector's segmentation map

former have a fully developed lending methodology, internal mechanisms and controls, and develop new ones, if and when required.

As Table 16.3 demonstrates, the industry consists primarily of mature, large and medium-sized microfinance organizations trending towards continued growth.

3.2 Description of main Romanian Micro Finance Institutions (MFIs)

For the purpose of this chapter, below is a description of the most mature MFIs in Romania, established more than six years ago. These are: CAPA Finance, Express Finance, Opportunity Microfinance Romania (OMRO), ROMCOM, Integra, LAM, FAER, Centre for Economic Development (CDE) and UNCAR.

3.2.1 CAPA Finance[9] CAPA Finance has offered credit in Romania since 1996. Created initially as a programme of World Vision International,

Table 16.3 Romanian microfinance sector segmentation

Peer groups	Romanian MFIs
All Romanian	CAPA Finance, CDE, Express Finance (CHF), FAER, Integra, LAM, OMRO, ROMCOM, Aurora, Tomis, Interomega, Pozitiv, 10 new
Age	
1 – 3 years	Aurora, Tomis, Interomega, Pozitiv, + 9 other new MFIs
4 – 6 years	–
7 – 9 years	CDE, Integra
10 – 12 years	CAPA Finance, Express Finance (CHF)
13 – 15 years	OMRO, ROMCOM, LAM, FAER
Fund size	
Large Gross Loan Portfolio > €5 000 000 Target: High-End	
a) in 2005	CAPA Finance, Express Finance (CHF)
b) in 2006	Express Finance (CHF), CAPA Finance, OMRO, CDE
Medium Gross Loan Portfolio = €1 000 000 – €5 000 000 Target: Broad	
a) in 2005	OMRO, ROMCOM, LAM, FAER, CDE
b) in 2006	LAM, FAER, ROMCOM, Interomega, Pozitiv
Small Gross Loan Portfolio < €1 000 000 Target: Low-End	
a) in 2005	Integra
b) in 2006	Integra, Aurora, Tomis, 10 new
Legal structure	
NBFI	CAPA Finance, Express Finance (CHF), FAER, Integra, LAM, OMRO, ROMCOM, Aurora, Tomis, Interomega, Pozitiv, + 9 other new MFIs
NGO/Foundation	CDE
MFI mission, targeted market and services offered	
Social oriented	Integra, ROMCOM, CDE
Social and commercial oriented	CAPA Finance, Express Finance (CHF), LAM, FAER, OMRO
Commercial oriented	Aurora, Tomis, Interomega, Pozitiv, + 9 other new MFIs

Source: Report Benchmarking Microfinance in Romania 2005–2006.

with lending capital from the Romanian-American Enterprise Fund, CAPA became a separate organization in 1999. A social orientation combined with a high operational performance made CAPA a major microfinance organization in Romania. Initially set up as a foundation, CAPA managed in 2004 to register as a joint-stock company with CAPA Foundation as majority shareholder and other participations from World Vision and MEDA. Currently, CAPA Finance is in the process of registering as a Non-Bank Microfinance Institution.

- *Gross Loan Portfolio (2006)*: €18 340 930.
- *Number of Active Borrowers (2006)*: 6981.
- *Target Borrowers:* households, microbusinesses, entrepreneurs in rural areas.

3.2.2 Express Finance (EF)[10] After 11 years working through CHF International, Express Finance is the institutional successor for the operations for business and housing loans to the micro, small and medium-sized enterprises (MSME) sector and individuals in Romania. Express Finance started with a modest €115 000 (USD 150 000) in Timisoara 12 years ago to start its 'Model Project for NGO Development'. EF was the leader of the consortium that implemented the complex project 'Enterprise Development and Strengthening' financially supported by USAID, consisting of concerted activities to improve the legal and regulatory environment, increase the competitiveness of selected sectors such as rural tourism and information technology and computers (IT&C) and increase access to credit, and to administer emergency assistance projects for floods in 2005. During these years the institution disbursed more than 12 500 loans totalling USD 50 million (€38.5 million).

- *Gross Loan Portfolio (2006)*: USD 10 781 750 (€8.3 million).
- *Number of Active Borrowers (2006)*: 2366.
- *Target Borrowers*: underserved, unserved business and housing markets principally in Romanian urban areas.

3.2.3 Opportunity Microfinance Romania (OMRO)[11] Opportunity Microcredit Romania begun in 1995 with the creation of the Izvor foundation, a non-profit organization. Because of legal requirements, the structure and the name of the institution were changed on three occasions: Banca Populara Izvor in 1995, Opportunity Microcredit Romania Microfinance company in 2000, and in 2006 Opportunity Microcredit Romania as an NBFI. OMRO's purpose is to support SMEs' development in the central regions of the country. In 2007, the 12th year of trading, they have exceeded 10 000 loans which have actively contributed to the creation of more than 4000 new jobs.

- *Gross Loan Portfolio (2006)*: €9 660 671.
- *Number of Active Borrowers (2006)*: 2155.
- *Target Borrowers*: individual and authorized people, whose activity is in production, commerce, services or agriculture.

3.2.4 ROMCOM Microfinance[12] The ROMCOM programme started in 1992 at the initiative of Christliche Ostmission, a Christian charity organization in Worb, Switzerland, with the purpose of encouraging private initiative in Romania in the sectors of production, services and agriculture. Since 1992, ROMCOM has financed 882 projects, amounting to some 11.3 million CHF (€6.73 million), which led to the creation and support of 5300 jobs. The loans are released through the ROMCOM Foundation, from funds allocated by Christliche Ostmission and the Swiss Agency for Development and Cooperation.

- *Gross Loan Portfolio (2006)*: €2 392 125.
- *Number of Active Borrowers (2006)*: 287.
- *Target Borrowers*: entrepreneurs and SMEs in urban and rural areas.

3.2.5 Integra[13] Integra Romania was founded in June 2000 as a Romanian non-profit organization, with offices in Oradea and Brasov. It is a member of the Integra Network, a group of community economic agencies in Central and Eastern Europe, with offices in Slovakia, Bulgaria, Russia and Serbia and a support office in the USA. On 22 June 2007, the legal entity which serves as a vehicle for the activity of microlending, Integra Microfinantare IFN SA, was registered with the National Bank of Romania.

- *Gross Loan Portfolio (2006)*: €313 222.
- *Number of Active Borrowers (2006)*: 135.
- *Target Borrowers*: microenterprises, entrepreneurs in rural areas, and women at risk.

3.2.6 LAM[14] Founded in 1992, LAM Foundation developed its activity as a regional development project in Covasna, Harghita and Brasov counties. The financial support necessary for the development of the Foundation's activities came mainly from the Swiss Confederation and from HESK/EPER Organization (Organization to Help the Evangelic

Churches in Switzerland). Their main objective is to enlarge the agricultural sector and to create and promote a long-term development programme in the private agriculture sector.

- *Gross Loan Portfolio (2006)*: €2 417 648.
- *Number of Active Borrowers (2006)*: 608.
- *Target Borrowers:* at the beginning loans were offered exclusively to farmers and SMEs in the agricultural field from the rural areas; currently, LAM also offers loans to SMEs in the production and services sector.

3.2.7 Foundation for the Promotion of Agriculture and Regional Economy (FAER)[15] FAER foundation from Reghin – Mures was registered in December 1992 and was created with support from the Swiss Confederation Government and from HEKS/EPER (Organization to Help the Evangelic Churches in Switzerland). Its global objective is to support and sustain private agriculture and small and medium-sized enterprises, in order to promote regional economy in the Maramures, Bistrita and Suceava counties.

- *Gross Loan Portfolio (2005)*: €1 432 000.
- *Number of Active Borrowers (2005)*: 609.
- *Target Borrowers:* rural farmsteads and farmers, small and medium-sized agricultural enterprises, SMEs and rural tourism lodgings in the villages where there is limited access to the banking system.

3.2.8 Centre for Economic Development (CDE[16])[17] Centre for Economic Development (CDE – Centrul pentru Dezvoltare Economica) is a Romanian non-governmental organization, dedicated to assist the development, investment, growth and success rate of businesses. The centre is a member of the Soros Open Network (SON). The mission of the centre is to promote the economic development of micro, small and medium-sized enterprises, by providing entrepreneurs with a one-stop source of business information, support (through training sessions and consultancy services) and financial products, in order to address the needs of an expanding market and to enhance the clients' ability to make a profitable use of the economic activities they run.

- *Gross Loan Portfolio (2006)*: €6 760 419.
- *Number of Active Borrowers (2006)*: 3498.
- *Target Borrowers:* entrepreneurs from rural areas, who undergo an activity that generates income, are between 18 to 65 years

old and prove the ability to develop and maintain a sustainable business.

3.2.9 National Association of the Romanian Credit Unions (UNCAR)[18] One of the oldest European systems, the Romanian CUs are solid financial institutions which offer a large variety of financial products and services to their targeted beneficiaries. It is planned that new CUs will be created within the territorial unions and UNCAR will be developed by attracting external funds at competitive costs.

Credit unions are social oriented and are organized based on market principles. Their members can be employees with reduced incomes who have restricted access to loan and saving services from a bank's portfolio or other financial institution. The credit unions' network promotes the services to employees at non-credit union companies.

- *Gross Loan Portfolio (2006)*: 1 013 530 RON (307 million euros).
- *Number of Active Borrowers (2006)*: 782 511.
- *Target Borrowers:* individual employees, members of the CUs for personal needs, housing (consumer loans).

4 Model of microcredit granting in Romania: general description of the model

There are three main microlending models utilized by the main MFIs.

4.1 Individual lending to MSMEs, farmers and individuals

Most of the Romanian MFIs are focused on delivering loan products geared to specific business purposes: merchandise, raw materials, agriculture and investment in equipment and machinery. In addition, microloan products serve more general needs such as working capital and personal consumption.

Once an application is received, the client's request can be evaluated based on use of funds: investment, working capital, inventory, seasonal credit, and so on. Amounts vary between €2000 to €25 000; average loan size in 2006 was €7000. Interest rates are lower for agricultural borrowers and/or repeat clients. In addition, the MFIs charge service fees that contribute to their operational self-sufficiency but also add to the overall cost of the loan.

Usually a loan to a new client is limited to between five and 12 months, with monthly payments. The maximum increase in loan size is 60 per cent for the next loan. Collateral is most often in the form of an endorser statement, bill of exchange, cheque or mortgage.

4.2 Individual lending with Group guarantee (IL-GG)

This methodology was created and used by CDE within the World Bank-funded programme for economical development in the depressed former mining areas. 'Peer Groups' (PGs) are created, consisting of between 7–10 individuals. The members of the PG are involved in the assessment of each individual loan application of the PG's members, and guarantee each other's loans. This lending methodology facilitated the creation of a pressure group whose main purpose is to ensure the reimbursement of credits on time. Additionally, the crediting of informal groups by the CDE extended the concept of partnership at the level of the individuals in the mining communities whose main aim is to access, use and reimburse the microloans.

4.3 Individual lending through Business Services Organizations (BSOs[19]) (IL-BSOs)

This methodology was created by CHF-EF with the financial support received from the United States Agency for International Development (USAID). BSOs received training from CHF-EF on credit policies, procedures and implementation.

BSOs' capacity-building programme focuses on marketing and promotion techniques, identification of good business clients, technical assistance in completing loan applications, maintaining and tracking programme indicators and data, client assessment, and business monitoring and evaluation. BSOs identify, pre-screen and recommend the potential clients to CHF-EF. After the loan application analysis, performed by the CHF-EF's credit officer, the loan is disbursed (see Figure 16.2).

The CHF-EF's credit officers are based within a branch office or within the offices of BSOs. They are equipped with a laptop computer, fax, internet access and a mobile telephone. They are highly mobile finance professionals who conduct business evaluation and loan application analysis of the clients identified by local BSOs. They serve rural, isolated or otherwise difficult-to-serve communities.

4.4 Advantages of the IL-GG and IL-BSO lending models

The integration of the provision of financial services for income-generating activities into an association-based peer-group structure has proven to be a viable tool for organizing partner BSOs, PGs and MFIs; it has also promoted their role as active participants in the development of Romanian civil society. Client-driven demand promotes BSO awareness that their products/services must be market responsive and affordable.

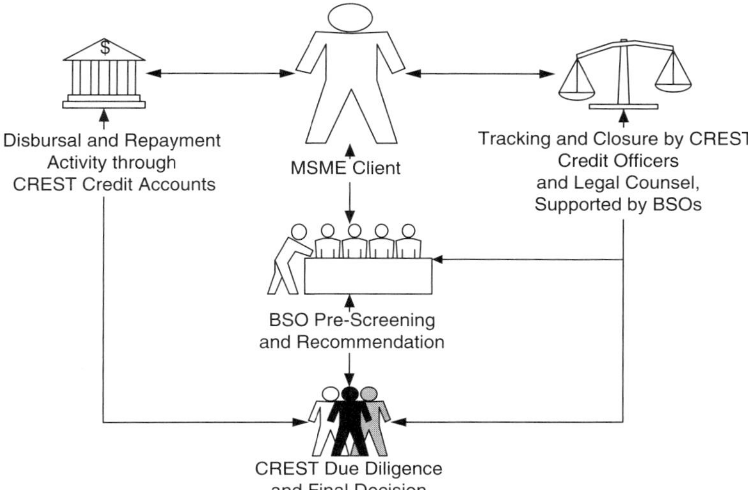

Source: CHF–EF presentation to the 4th ENM's MF conference – Berlin 2007.

Figure 16.2 Loan disbursal and repayment

1. Access to local markets: the BSO-PG's ties to the local business community give the microfinance provider exceptional access to formal and informal information about the local market, conditions and client history. This can provide an invaluable edge in minimizing risk and ensuring a successful lending operation.
2. BSO membership growth: membership size is a direct function of the diversity and quality of its services, and by offering access to financial services, a BSO can increase its membership and retention. This results in higher revenues, a more sustainable operation and expanded capabilities for mobilizing business constituencies on key policy issues.
3. Sustainability: the provision of a valued product to their members enables the BSO to charge for the service, supporting its efforts to become operationally sustainable. In addition, larger membership serves as the foundation for achieving operational economies of scale.

4.5 Non-financial services

All MFIs provide basic advice to their clients on business planning, and assist new clients in writing of applications. These services reduce the amount of time spent by the credit officers on analysing loans while increasing the micro-entrepreneur's capacity to manage the credit and the business. These non-financial services and credit monitoring activities contribute to the overall quality of the portfolio, because entrepreneurs are better educated about gaining access to credit and completing loan applications, about cash flow and managing their investment projects.

Some MFIs (Integra, ROMCOM, FAER and LAM) provide specialized training services for business planning. They also provide vocational training, consultancy and assistance in a project's application development for EU co-funded programmes in the rural areas for women entrepreneurs, the unemployed and farmers.

5 Target groups in Romania

The Romanian microfinance institutions target five main groups:

- micro and small entrepreneurs (start-up enterprises);
- farmers/entrepreneurs in rural areas;
- unemployed;
- women at risk;
- micro and small entrepreneurs.

The general objective of all Romanian MFIs is to finance micro and small entrepreneurs, either from urban or rural areas, operating in different fields of activity. The development of the Romanian economy has increased opportunities for micro and small businesses, but has also amplified their need for financing. However, most of the banks are not willing to lend money to these enterprises because of the high administrative costs involved. Therefore, the microfinance institutions are those that focus on this important segment of the market.

Farmers/entrepreneurs in rural areas: another important group that is not reached by banks either because of their remote location or because their business are too small are the farmers or small entrepreneurs in rural areas. Two of the Romanian MFIs, FAER and LAM, are specialized in lending to farmers, agricultural enterprises and generally clients located in remote rural areas. Apart from these two organizations, the CHF International, CAPA Finance and Centre for Economic Development also have programmes for rural areas.

The unemployed are targeted mainly through governmental programmes implemented through the Romanian MFIs. An example of such a programme is the Mine Closure and Social Mitigation Project funded by the World Bank and implemented by the Ministry of Economy and Commerce.[20] The two microfinance institutions partnering in this project are CHF International Romania (now Express Finance) and Centre for Economic Development. The project targets miners who have been laid off after restructuring of this sector, but also other residents in the mining communities who have been affected by the related downturn in the local economy.

A smaller group, but with a high need for financing, is women at risk. The most active Romanian MFI in this area is Integra Foundation who target women at risk: single and divorced mothers, unemployed women, widows, handicapped women and gypsy women. Integra's microfinance activities are usually implemented through the Microenterprise Development Programme for women, which includes: training, microcredit, market access and other business development services.

6 Financial terms and conditions

6.1 Interest rates

The Romanian microfinance sector is regulated by Law 240/2005 and Ordinance 28/2006. These two regulations set the general legal framework for microfinance institutions and the terms for the extension of microloans. Law 240 stipulates that microfinance institutions can only extend loans of up to €25 000, for a maximum period of 60 months. However, the legislation on microfinance does not impose any limitation on the interest rate that the MFIs can collect for the loans they extend. On average for a standard loan, the current interest rate is between 10 per cent and 18 per cent.

6.2 Others: grace period, amount, repayment period, collaterals

As mentioned in the first paragraph of this section, the amount and repayment period for the microloans are set by the Microfinance Law 240. The loan amounts go up to €25 000 and can be as small as €500 in rural areas. The repayment period depends on the type of loan extended. For lines of credit it can be as low as one month for covering the working capital requirements, while for investment loans it can be up to a maximum of five years.

Romanian microfinance institutions allow for grace periods in long-term loans, according to the type of business. The type of collateral required also depends on the nature and size of the loan. For small loans, of up to €2000, some of the Romanian MFIs do not require any collateral. In the case of higher loan amounts, the collateral can be production equipment, vehicles or real estate.

6.3 Main business services provided

Most of the Romanian MFIs offer not only financing, but also business development services for their clients. Most of these services are limited to training clients in drawing up a business plan and in efficient business management. However, some MFIs have rather targeted business development programmes. An example of such an institution is Integra, with its Market Access Programme. By working with its existing clients, Integra is trying to open new marketing and sales channels, establish networking opportunities and support them through training.

6.4 Example of a typical microfinance product
Start-up loan product offered by OMRO:

- Loan's beneficiary: micro and small enterprises, family businesses, registered persons (individual entrepreneurs, professionals) (in the commerce, services, manufacture or agriculture sector), start-up companies, or companies with less than three months' trading history.
- Loan's designation: financing of expenses, both for investments and working capital, according to the business plan presented.
- Loan's value: between 1000 RON (€300) and 25 000 RON (€7600).
- Repayment period: between three and 36 months.
- Evaluation and approval of the application: up to seven days.
- Guarantees: guarantors, mortgage, personal guarantees.

7 Government support
The Romanian Government (GOR) has contributed to the development of the microfinance sector through the creation of a coherent and enabling legal framework for microfinance activities and microfinance institutions and through provision of financial sources and technical assistance. The Micro Finance companies law 240/2005 was the initiative of the Romanian MFIs, sponsored and supported by the SME Agency and Ministry of Economy and Finance.[21]

The Romanian Micro Credit Scheme (RMCS)[22] is a €82.5 million financial facility launched by the European Bank for Reconstruction and Development (EBRD), the European Commission, the Romanian Government and a syndicate of commercial banks. It provides loans – in the local currency or euros – to local banks and non-bank microfinance institutions to on-lend to micro and small enterprises (MSEs), including the financing of start-up MSEs. The facility is being created to address the issue that entrepreneurs in Romania, especially in remote and rural areas, have little access to finance other than from sources beyond the financial sector that can charge very high interest rates. Currently the RMCS is being implemented by OMRO, CHF-EF and Transylvania Bank.

The mine closure and social mitigation project, implemented by CHF-EF and CDE, is available for SMEs located in cities from mining regions and is implemented through the National Agency for the Implementation of Mining Regions Reconstruction Programme, based on World Bank support for the Romanian Government. The project started in November 2004 and the granting period initially ends in 2007, with repayment of loans scheduled to begin after July 2007. Nevertheless, the financing scheme is being continued under a revised project. By end September 2006, 4367 microcredits had been granted, amounting to approximately €9.8m.[23] The average microcredit size was about €1500 for individuals applying for consumer loans and €5200 for self-employed entrepreneurs or a microenterprise. According to the Progress Report prepared for the Ministry of Economy and Commerce, by end September 2006, 96 per cent of microcredits had been granted for start-ups. By sector distribution, 45 per cent were for agriculture, 32 per cent for retailing, 17 per cent for services, and 6 per cent for small-scale production.

The Rural Development Programme – Micro-credit component[24] started in 2001. It is funded by the International Fund for Agricultural Development – FIDA/IFAD, and it covers 15 counties. By end 2006, it had financed 1108 projects, mounting to about €15.4m [25] (average value per project was about €13 900). Most disbursements were made in 2006 (about €5m). By sector distribution, the highest disbursements were in the areas of animal breeding (26.5 per cent), mechanical equipment (19.5 per cent) and agro-tourism (15.1 per cent).

The micro-credit programme for the unemployed[26] is funded through an agreement of the Ministry of Labour and Social Solidarity (National Agency for Labour Force Employment (ANOFM)) made with International Bank for Reconstruction and Development (IBRD) in 2001, and is implemented through the CDE.

The European-funded project, Technical Assistance to develop the SMEs sector in Romania – Access to finance component,[27] implemented by the Ministry of SMEs and Ministry of Development Public Works and Housing (MDPWH), provides training, networking and technical assistance to develop project proposals for EU funds.

8 Regulation

The regulatory framework for microfinance activities in Romania is as follows.

Government Ordinance 40, in force since 2000, provides for licensing of credit organizations (other than banks) to administer public funds (for example World Bank loan guaranteed by the Romanian Government for the economic development of the former mining areas, and microcredits for the unemployed engaged in economic activities).

Micro Finance Companies (MFC) Law no. 240, adopted by the Romanian Parliament in July 2005, created an enabling environment for the MFIs to grow and expand their portfolio of products and support services. According to Law 240, microcredits up to €25 000 are granted to entrepreneurs and micro and small enterprises to finance economic activities and business development.

Government Ordinance 28, in force since January 2006, regulates the conditions for non-banking financial institutions to grant loans in order to ensure and maintain financial stability. The National Bank of Romania is the supervisory authority of all Non Bank Financial Institutions (NBFIs): leasing, mortgage, credit unions, including Micro Finance Companies. GO 28 is expanding the range of beneficiaries through the inclusion of individuals and consumer loans.

The existing legal framework recognizes the microfinance sector as part of the Romanian financial sector. The drafting of the current microfinance legislation was based on general microfinance principles, at the same time taking into account the Romanian legal, economic and cultural background:

- Minimum capital designed to ensure self-sustainability of microfinance companies and to enhance market legitimacy and reputation. The legal framework imposes a minimum share capital of €200 000. Specifically, this minimum share capital is warranted by the economies of scale in microfinance, as below this threshold a microfinance entity may find it challenging to support the minimum necessary infrastructure and still operate profitably unless it operates with donors' funds. As such, by imposing this minimum share capital, microfinance companies are forced to be more efficient in their activities and achieve the desired self-sustainability.
- Limited regulatory barriers for market entry of microfinance companies, as 'finance-only' entities – absence of limitations on foreign ownership, management and sources of capital. This is especially true since the recent European Union integration of Romania and anticipated economic development will most likely determine a decrease or termination of donor-granted funds and force current microfinance entities to seek non-donor sources for funds on-lent to micro-borrowers.
- Consumer protection by truth-in-lending requirements. Two consumer protection issues are particularly relevant to microfinance and warrant attention:
    1. protection of borrowers against 'abusive' lending and collection practices, and

2. 'truth in lending' – providing borrowers with accurate, comparable and transparent information about the cost of loans.

Generally, the different combinations of transaction fees and interest calculation methods make it difficult for borrowers to compare interest rates of microfinance lenders when choosing a microfinance lender. This is the reason why the law requires microfinance companies to disclose their interest rates and other material terms and conditions of the microcredit contract to microfinance applicants prior to conclusion of the microcredit contract. This is designed to be an efficient tool to help applicants evaluate the true cost of microfinance, and should promote price competition within the microfinance market. Finally, the requirement to disclose interest rates should encourage microfinance companies to focus on the necessary steps to increase efficiency and thus lower interest rates.

- Credit information. The legal framework clearly provides for the right of microfinance providers to exchange and share information on the credit history of borrowers, either with the Central Banking Risks Office, the Credit Bureau or other credit agencies: public or private. The experience in other countries suggests that when microfinance companies begin to compete with each other for customers, over-indebtedness and default will rise sharply unless microfinance companies have access to a database that captures relevant aspects of their clients' credit history. Credit information services offer important benefits both to financial institutions and to their customers. By collecting information on clients' credit history, lenders can have more sophisticated risk-based pricing. Similarly, entrepreneurs and individuals may use their good repayment record with one lender as a means to gain access to another credit from another microfinance company or from banks. At the same time, available credit history may allow microfinance companies to be much more aggressive in lending without collateral requirements and may also have a beneficial effect on competition among lenders. The combination of credit bureaux and statistical risk-scoring techniques has expanded lower-income groups' access to credit.

In addition, the first eight Micro Finance Institutions created, with the support of international donors, around 20 new MF Companies under the new legal framework; these are in the process of registering and licensing with the National Bank of Romania.

The existing legal framework recognizes that the microfinance sector is part of the Romanian financial sector. One of the lessons learned by the Romanian MFIs from the lobby effort for the legal framework was the importance of a clear, coherent and supportive legal framework. In less than two years, the Romanian MF sector changed from not being regulated at all, to the other extreme of overregulation. It was considered crucial to engage in continuous lobbying to make stakeholders aware of the sector's main characteristic: efficient financial services with positive social and developmental impact.

9 Financial and operational sustainability

It is nevertheless vital to the health of the sector to be able to evaluate its products, service delivery and impact. This section presents the main findings of the Romanian microfinance sector benchmarking performed under the project Technical Assistance to Develop the SME sector in Romania.[28] Eight of the largest and most mature Romanian MFIs participated in this survey. The performance indicators were drawn from an EU-funded project, 'From Exclusion to Inclusion through Microfinance: Learning from East to West and from West to East'.[29] It designed a tool to measure sector performance and impact. Practitioners across the sector must be able to understand and improve their own performance. Additionally, they must be able to measure their progress against that of their peers, as well as to demonstrate to stakeholders the viability and value of MFIs within a social and economic context.

Operational self-sufficiency is defined as the point at which the MFI can meet its operational costs with its operational income. This is interest earned from the operational loan portfolio. In Table 16.4 the average operational self-sufficiency for all Romanian MFIs, as well as for its three peer groups, is greater than 100 per cent.

Thus, at present, the eight Romanian MFIs that took part in this survey are self-sufficient, covering their administrative costs with client revenues. In Figure 16.3 it can be seen that all Romanian MFIs managed to increase their operational self-sufficiency over the past four years.

A financially self-sufficient MFI has enough revenue to pay for all administrative and operational costs, loan losses, potential losses and fund costs. As is the case for operational self-sufficiency, the main Romanian MFIs are currently financially self-sufficient (see Figure 16.4). This transforms the ability of an MFI to operate at a certain level of profitability and allows it to provide quality services with no dependence on donor inputs. Being financially self-sustainable is essential for the Romanian MFIs as donor funds are becoming less available. As such, they will need to

Table 16.4 Profitability and sustainability indicators

Indicators	All Romanian MFIs		Large Romanian MFIs		Medium Romanian MFIs		Small Romanian MFIs	
	2005	2006	2005	2006	2005	2006	2005	2006
Operational self-sufficiency (%)	120.23	139.86	110.67	153.51	123.94	125.82	111.44	109.72
Portfolio yield (%)	16.53	14.94	11.90	15.29	16.23	11.71	27.27	23.21
Financial self-sufficiency (%)	118.50	135.47	113.48	150.20	121.92	124.25	111.44	110.17

Source: *Benchmarking Microfinance in Romania (2005–2006).*

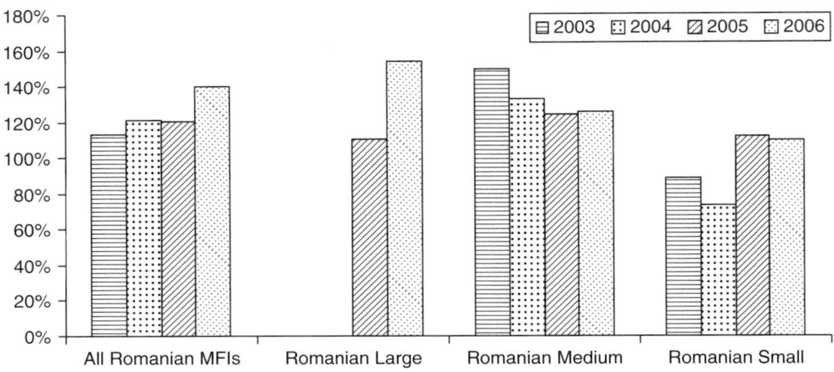

Source: *Benchmarking Microfinance in Romania (2005–2006).*

Figure 16.3 Romanian MFIs: operational self-sufficiency

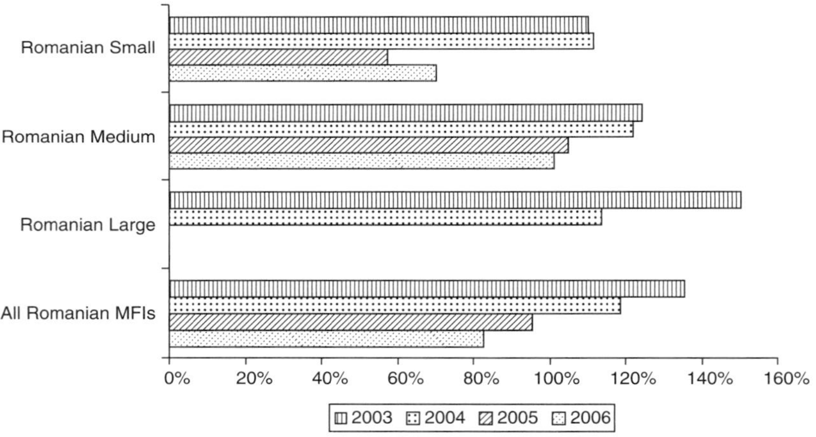

Figure 16.4 Romanian MFIs: financial self-sufficiency

continue shifting to a more commercial orientation, which will allow them to support their activity and further develop these commercial funding sources.

11 Challenges for the sector in Romania[30]

The Romanian MFI sector is entering a new stage of development. Legal, economic and financial changes will continue to reshape the opportunity landscape for MFIs individually and as a whole. While commercialization is the strategy of almost all medium and large MFIs, there are a number of more targeted initiatives that may enable them take a different, more focused path towards maintaining their social mission.

For the commercialization strategy MFIs are focusing on:

i. improvement of performance indicators, especially operational and financial sustainability;
iii. increase of portfolio capital through borrowing from investors and banks;
iii. diversification of financial products offered to clients.

Innovative projects that combine financial services with community development support activities and training are ensuring that the Romanian microfinance sector is a bridge between commercial lending and socio-economic development. These include:

- Market access for women entrepreneurs, project developed by Integra Foundation.
- Access to financial services of private farmers and former miners from depressed rural and mountainous areas or the redundant workers from former state-owned enterprises, projects funded by World Bank and Swiss Confederations, project implemented by CAPA finance, Express Finance, LAM and FAER Foundations.
- Economic development of Roma (Gypsy) communities, project funded by Open Society Foundation and implemented by CDE.
- Micro-entrepreneur clubs and training programmes, projects implemented by OMRO and ROMCOM.
- Recently RMCS for microenterprises and start-ups financial facility funded by EU, GOR and EBRD.

To provide financial services for unmet demand (that is 30 per cent of total demand for microfinance) means that the existing amount disbursed by MFIs needs to be tripled to reach almost 50 per cent (€350 million) of the market within the next few years in order to maintain the social economic mission. This is the challenge for the Romanian microfinance sector.

Notes

1. Since 2005 the Romanian Government introduced in the fiscal code a flat income and profit tax of 16 per cent.
2. National Bank of Romania.

3. SME Definition

Enterprise Category	Number of Employees	Turnover	Or	Total Assets
Medium-sized	< 250	< EUR 50 million		< EUR 43 million
Small	<50	< EUR 10 million		< EUR 10 million
Microenterprises	<10	< EUR 2 million		< EUR 2 million

4. NBFIs as defined by Government Ordinance (GO) 28/2006 are: microfinance companies, leasing companies, mortgages companies and credit unions.
5. Estimates provided by *Benchmarking Microfinance in Romania (2005–2006)*, a report of the project Technical Assistance to Develop the SME sector in Romania (funded by PHARE and the Romanian Government).
6. Estimates provided by Richard Crayne, expert of the PHARE Project – Technical Assistance to Develop the SME sector in Romania.
7. Report of the Board of Administration of the National Association of Credit Unions, presented to the annual National Conference of the Romanian Credit Unions, Romania, June 2007.
8. CAPA is the Romanian abbreviation of Business Consultancy and Training for Entrepreneurs.
9. Source: annual report of CAPA Finance.
10. Source: annual report EF.
11. Source: OMRO annual report.
12. Source: ROMCOM's annual report.
13. Source: Integra's annual report.
14. Source: LAM's annual report.
15. Source: FAER's annual report.
16. CDE is the Romanian abbreviation of Centre for Economic Development.
17. Source: CDE's annual report.
18. Source: Report to the National conference of UNCAR – June 2007.
19. BSOs are the territorial Chambers of Commerce in industry, trade associations, local business and farmers' associations, NGOs, community development associations, and so on.
20. Currently the Ministry of Economy and Finance.
21. The USAID Programme Economical Development and Strengthening – Microfinance Coalition Component provided technical assistance to the Romanian MFIs in drafting and promoting Law 240. Source: assessment of the impact of USAID's ten years for assistance in micro-lending, rural credit, mortgage, and equity investment: Romania's unique financial mechanisms were assisted by USAID.
22. Source: press release, Ministry of European Integration and BESD, December 2006.
23. Credits are given in USD.
24. Source: progress report of the Rural Development Programme prepared by the Ministry of Economy and Finance, presented at the project's closure conferences.
25. Credits are given in USD.
26. Source: ANOFM's progress report.
27. Source: MDPWH's progress report.
28. Technical Assistance project funded by the GOR and the PHARE programme of the European Union. The project report is published as *Benchmarking Microfinance in Romania (2005–2006)*.
29. EC-funded project implemented by the Microfinance Center for Central and Eastern Europe and the New Independent States, European Microfinance Network and the community development finance association.
30. Based on the report of the RMCS's exit route.

17 The state of microfinance in Poland

*Agata Szostek**

1 National context

The first partially free elections in Poland after World War II took place in 1989; since that time Poland became the first country in the former Eastern bloc to re-establish democracy and embark on an economic and social transition to a market economy.

The so-called 'shock therapy' programme implemented during the early 1990s enabled the country to transform its economy into one of the most dynamic and robust in the region.[1]

Today, Poland's economy is by far the largest among the new EU member states. It accounts for over 50 per cent of the cumulative population of the 12 new member states and also about 50 per cent of their cumulative GDP.[2]

The initiation of Poland's transition in the early 1990s was marked by remarkably difficult macroeconomic conditions comprising high inflation, a large legacy of external debt, and a high black market foreign exchange premium.

At that time in the Polish economy, a large part of the enterprise sector was considered 'value subtracting' (the final output was worth less than the sum of the inputs), and the Polish policy makers took huge risks by making the Polish currency (zloty: PLN) convertible, fixing the exchange rate, and lowering import barriers.

Microfinance in Poland was introduced into an environment which was undergoing an economic transformation, trying to satisfy the demand of different levels of 'entrepreneurs'. There was a lack of personal savings (probably resulting from high inflation), lack of assets, and lack of access to financial capital from regular banks.

Furthermore, many rural inhabitants were forced to move to towns or move into the manufacturing or service sectors due to inefficient and over-developed agriculture offering decreasing revenues.

2 The origin of microfinance in Poland

Agriculture Foundation (currently FWW) represented the first attempt to fill this gap, providing lending services to the low-income population to stimulate a spirit of enterprise and to create off-farm employment opportunities. With the loan capital borrowed from the Ministry of Agriculture

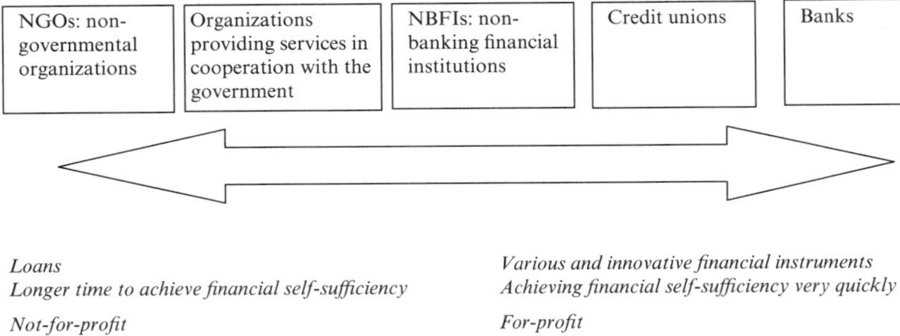

Figure 17.1 The microfinance continuum in Poland

and Food Economy, FWW started its first small loan programme in 1991, and the following year, thanks to a partnership with the Ministry of Labour and local governments, a well organized microloan programme began to operate.

Credit Unions (CUs), today the most active and flourishing organizations in the Polish microfinance industry, followed soon after. As a matter of fact, the first CU in the renewed Poland was established in 1992 in Gdansk, from a group of workers of the Electric Heating Company. Despite an initial series of legal constraints, CUs quickly spread, helped in part by the international funds from the World Council of Credit Unions and USAID. One year later in 1993, another institution set up a new microfinance programme: the Foundation for the Development of Polish Agriculture with its REP (Rural Entrepreneurship Programme). At the end of 1994, Fundusz Mikro, currently the largest non-bank microloan provider in Poland was registered, granting its first loan in February 1995. Inicjatywa Mikro, which received the initial funds for its loan capital from Fundusz Mikro, was created in 1996 and started its operations in the south of Poland.

The third operational model of microfinance in Poland (apart from the above-mentioned credit unions and traditional microfinance institutions) is the network of loan funds. These were variously financed (partly from governmental sources, partly from international donors and the European Union through the PHARE programme) and were only recently grouped into a national association.

3 Main actors within the microfinance sector in Poland

The current microcredit providers in Poland include commercial and cooperative banks, credit unions, specialized non-bank financial institutions, and microloan programmes (see Figure 17.1). The banks' market share is 98 per cent (in terms of the value of loans).[3]

Even though the banks seem to be the only significant player, they have interest in the market segment and have sufficient infrastructure to physically reach the consumers, there are several constraints, which make their role in market development questionable. Firstly, their offers for start-ups younger than two years old are limited, due to high requirements for business plans and guarantees. Secondly, they are not able to manage microenterprise lending risks, which are very different from those for small and medium enterprises. Thirdly, they still do not understand the microenterprise segment, applying an SME lens during the interactions, and they do not take low-scale and non-expanding enterprises seriously. This limits banks' intervention to mature microenterprises (a small fraction of the total market).

On the other hand, specialized non-bank financial institutions and microloan programmes have the market intelligence and know-how to work with disadvantaged groups. They also know how to manage risks of working with start-ups and many of them integrate business development services to prepare their future clients.[4]

Since the banks serve only the mature microenterprises, this chapter will not discuss banks.

3.1 Providers of microfinance services, financial and non-financial, supported by the government[5]

3.1.1 The Polish Agency for Enterprise Development (PAED) PAED is a governmental agency subordinate to the Minister of the Economy. It was established by the Act of 9 November 2000, on the establishment of the Polish Agency for Enterprise Development. Its task is the management of funds assigned from the State Budget and European Union for the support of entrepreneurship and the development of human resources, with particular consideration given to the needs of small and medium-sized enterprises (SMEs). PAED is among the institutions responsible for the implementation of activities financed from the Structural Funds.

The objective of the agency is the implementation of economy development programmes, in particular with respect to the support of:

- SME development;
- export development;
- regional development;
- application of new techniques and technologies;
- creation of new jobs, tackling unemployment and human resources development.

This objective is carried out through:

- The provision of grants to SME sector companies, institutions supporting the development of SMEs, training institutions and labour market institutions;
- the rendering of advisory and expert services;
- the facilitation of access to knowledge, economic information, studies and analyses to entrepreneurs;
- the organization of undertakings of an informative and promotional nature.

3.1.2 PAED Programmes for Small and Medium-sized Enterprises The Polish Agency for Enterprise Development participates in the implementation of a policy entitled 'Government Policy Guidelines for Small and Medium-sized Enterprises in the years 2003–2006', Sectoral Operational Programmes: Improvement of Enterprise Competitiveness and Human Resources Development, as well as pre-accession PHARE programmes. Within the scope of the above-mentioned programmes, the agency conducts numerous SME-oriented activities; *inter alia*, it provides support both to the development of the business environment and directly to companies.

Direct assistance provided to small and medium-sized companies takes the form of grants allocated to information and advisory services as well as to investment (for example purchases of machinery and equipment). Entrepreneurs may obtain grants, *inter alia* with respect to activities associated with the following:

- company development;
- export development;
- implementation of quality systems;
- introduction of new technologies and innovations;
- acquisition of financing;
- occupational safety and health.

In addition, PAED conducts intermediary activities seeking to match economic partners.

Indirect assistance for the SME sector comprises, above all, the following activities:

- the expansion and enhancement of the microloan system and guarantee and seed capital fund system for SMEs through the increase of the capital of these institutions;
- the provision of financing to the network of consultation centres, ensuring free access to information for entrepreneurs;

- cooperation with regional and local governments in the field of preparation and evaluation of programmes for the development of the SME sector; and
- support of the existing and developing centres of technology transfer, science and technology parks and technology incubators.

3.1.3 Regional financing institutions The Polish Agency for Enterprise Development does not maintain regional offices. However, PAED cooperates with institutions chosen through competitive selection procedures – Regional Financing Institutions (RFIs) – which act as the Agency's partners in the process of implementation of policies towards SMEs (like commerce chambers, foundations). The RFIs are for the most part regional development agencies or other institutions that have an established record in the field of SME development. Every RFI runs a consulting and advisory centre.

3.1.4 Non-financial services for microenterprises

Consultation centres Consultation centres (PK) function as first-contact institutions for small and medium-sized enterprises. In 2007, around 190 were in service. PKs provide free information services with respect to issues associated with entrepreneurial activities and enterprise management. The role of a PK advisor is to identify the available assistance programmes and to provide detailed information as to the conditions for the granting of assistance. Among PKs, an important player is the National System of SME Services.

The National SME Services Network (KSU)[6] The National SME Services Network (KSU) has been in operation since 1996. After ten years, it comprises over 180 cooperating outlets in 190 localizations in Poland. The network consists primarily of regional and local development agencies, business support centres, chambers of industry and commerce, and local non-profit foundations and associations, which render services directly to the SME sector. These outlets have implemented a quality assurance system, which ensures that a high standard of advisory services is rendered, typically of a general and pro-innovative character, on training, informational and financial topics (loan-granting and loan guarantees). This is an open system in which new centres join each year. Institutions interested in joining the KSU are invited to pursue the registration requirements specified by the ordinance of the Minister of the Economy and Labour on KSU. Not all of the organizations registered in KSU provide specific services targeted only at microenterprises. On the other hand, there are organizations which target these clients and are not members of the KSU. Organizations providing non-financial services for microenterprises or the self-employed and not listed are non-governmental organizations usually operating in the form of foundations.

3.2 Non-governmental organizations and non-banking financial institutions

3.2.1 Polskie Stowarzyszenie Funduszy Pożyczkowych (Polish Association of Loan Funds) The Polish Association of Loan Funds represents the interests of the loan funds from all over Poland and supports their activities to develop regions and the micro, small and medium enterprise sector. The Polish Association of Loan Funds was established in 2002 by representatives of 50 loan funds operating as non-governmental and non-profit organizations. The goal of the association is to create and expand a strong and independent system of loan funds in Poland and thus to ensure effective financing of the start-up and growth of micro, small and medium enterprises.

On the basis of a survey conducted by the association in the period February–April 2007,[7] there were 69[8] institutions with 75 loan funds, whose goal was to provide financing to micro, small and medium enterprises.

In 2006, the group of the largest funds (five as shown in Figure 17.2) was the most active. This group granted 17 800 loans (91.2 per cent of the total disbursed by all the loan funds) of the value of PLN 283 500 000 (approx. € 71m), which was 76.5 per cent of the total value of all disbursed loans.

Apart from loan funds that are members of the association, in Poland there are also 'closed' loan funds which provide financing only to their members. An example of these is Zrzeszenia Prywatnego Handlu i Usług (Association of Private Trade and Services) located in Olsztyn, which has been in operation since 1997. Unfortunately there is no data available in order to map such initiatives.

Among the identified loan funds, members of the Polish Association of Loan Funds, only a few concentrate on providing loans to microenterprises.

The identified *leading* microcredit providers are as follows (see Table 17.2):

1. Fundusz Mikro Sp. z o.o. (FM): registered as a limited liability company, de facto a non-banking financial institution.
2. Inicjatywa Mikro Sp. z o.o. (IM): registered as a limited liability company, de facto a non-banking financial institution.

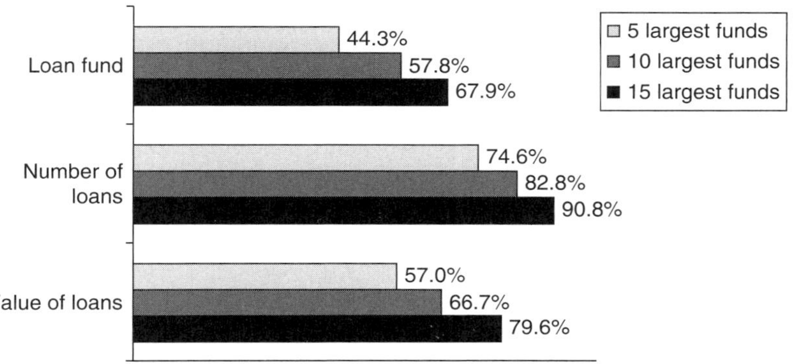

Source: Report no. 7/2007 Fundusze Po'yczkowe w Polsce, Szczecin, kwiecien 2007, available on: http://www.psfp.org.pl/raporty/raporty.html.

Figure 17.2 Share of the largest 5, 10 and 15 loan funds in the total loan capital and the number/value of loans granted by all the funds (31 December, 2006)

Table 17.1 Division of loans by value offered by members of the Polish Association of Loan Funds

Division of loans by value	Number of loans in the period 1 January 2006–31 December 2006	Value of loans in the period 1 January 2006–31 December 2006
a) up to 10 000 PLN (€ 2628)	a) 59.2%	a) 17.6%
b) 10 000 PLN – 30 000 (€ 2628> 7885	b) 27%	b) 22.9%
c) 30 000 PLN – 50 000 PLN (€ 7885 – 13142)	c) 4.8%	c) 10.6%
d) 50 000 PLN – 120 000 PLN (€ 13142 – 31543)	d) 8.6%	d) 44%
e) 120 000 PLN – 300 000 PLN (€ 31 543 – 78 858	e) 0.4%	e) 4.4%
f) >300 000 PLN (>€ 78 858)	f) 0.0%	f) 0.4%

Source: Report no. 7/2007 Fundusze Po'yczkowe w Polsce wspierajace mikro, małe i srednie przedsiębiorstwa według stanu na 31 grudnia 2006 roku.

Table 17.2 Ranking of loan funds selected on the basis of average loan amount and outreach (based on data as of 31 December, 2006)

Name	Place in ranking	# of loans disbursed from inception	Average loan amount PLN/euro	% of participation in the total loan fund of loans in the association
Fundusz Mikro Sp. z o.o	1	92 754	7 700/2024	70.88%
FWW	2	8624	11 700/3075	6.59%
Inicjatywa Mikro Sp. z o.o.	3	5328	11 600/3049	4.07%
FDPA	4	4498	17 400/4573	3.4%
Fundacja Rozwoju Gminy Zelów	5	773	19 900/5230	0.59%
Pomorski Fundusz Pożyczkowy Sp. z o.o.	6	427	19 500/5125	0.33%
Stowarzyszenie 'Ostrzeszowskie Centrum Przedsiębiorczości'	7	298	18 500/4862	0.23%
Stowarzyszenie Wspierania Małej Przedsiębiorczości z/s w Dobiegniewie	8	265	19 300/5073	0.2%
Stowarzyszenie 'Radomskie Centrum Przedsiębiorczości'	9	187	17 400/4573	0.14%
Fundacja 'Przedsiębiorczość'	10	156	15 900/4179	0.12%
Nidzicka Fundacja Rozwoju 'NIDA'	11	128	20 300/5336	0.1%
Bieszczadzka Agencja Rozwoju Regionalnego Sp. z o.o.	12	115	11 900/3128	0.09%
Agencja Rozwoju Przedsiębiorczości S.A.	13	72	19 200/5046	0.06%

Source: Report no. 7/2007 Fundusze Po'yczkowe w Polsce wspierajace mikro, małe i srednie przedsiębiorstwa według stanu na 31 grudnia 2006 roku.

3. Fundacja Wspierania Wsi (FWW): Rural Development Foundation.
4. Fundacja na Rzecz Rozwoju Polskiego Rolnictwa: Foundation for the Development of Polish Agriculture (FDPA).

FM is the largest loan fund with 11.4 per cent of the total loan capital of the members of the association; it also disbursed the highest number of loans amongst the loan funds within the association, 92800, which is 70.9 per cent of all loans disbursed. The average loan amount distributed by FM was the lowest, at 7700 PLN (€ 2024). The second in this ranking is FWW with 8600 loans, which represents 6.6 per cent of the total number of loans.

Inicjatywa Mikro Sp. z o.o. follows, with 5300 loans, representing 4.1 per cent of the total granted by the loan funds.

FDPA comes fourth: 4500 loans disbursed, which amounts to 3.4 per cent of the total number of loans.

3.2.2 Fundusz Mikro Sp. z o.o. (registered as a limited liability company, de facto a non-banking financial institution)

Origins and development Fundusz Mikro (FM) was officially registered in December 1994, but disbursed its first loan on 20 February of the following year. It was established under the auspices of the Polish American Enterprise Fund (PAEF), which contributed $20 million (approx. € 18 million) for the primary purpose of promoting the development of the Polish private sector through the issuing of loans to micro- and small-sized businesses. This huge sum had to be maintained as loan capital, while a grant of $4 million (approx. € 3.6 million) was issued by the US Agency for International Development (USAID) to cover the expenses involved in establishing a national network of branches. The pilot project consisted of creating only three representative offices and it was successfully completed in February 1996. During its second full year of lending operations (1996/97), the number of outlets located in Poland's largest towns grew to 15 and FM extended over 5500 loans, while, as of 1 January 1998, the 23 outlets had issued about 10000 loans, showing an impressive growth. This demonstrated the existence of a high unmet demand for capital from micro-entrepreneurs all over the country who, despite running a viable business, could not secure credit from regular banks.

The financial year 1998/99 was the first in which FM achieved operational self-sufficiency, even earlier than planned in original business plans. This goal was achieved largely thanks to a significant improvement in the loan repayment rates and measures directed towards better monitoring of costs. A simple financial service generally focused on offering loans was abandoned in favour of an offer based on ensuring access to long-term financing on conditions increasingly more favourable to enterprises. This new approach meant offering loans with decreasing interest rates for subsequent repeated loans of increasing amounts, rendering the offer more and more attractive for entrepreneurs interested in a long-lasting cooperation with FM.

Products and conditions FM's loans are granted in Polish zlotys (PLN) to microenterprises conducting different kinds of activities: borrowers use the amount either for the purchasing of current assets, such as stock, or for investment purposes, such as the buying of machinery, equipment, or improving premises. There are two types of loans: the individual one and the solidarity-group one. Officially all loans are individual, but within solidarity groups, members guarantee each other and cannot obtain a further loan until the whole group has fully repaid the previous loan cycle. This second type was the most common during the first six years of FM activities, because of advantages both on the borrowers' and on FM's side: for clients it is easier to find co-signers who share their same situation, rather than asking for a guarantee from someone who does not get any return from the agreement, while for FM, group loans require less monitoring and encourage repayment on time.

At this stage interest rates on group loans were kept lower in order to encourage their use. As of today, individual loans are more popular. In the case of individual loans, the collateral takes the form of either personal guarantee of several guarantors or a pledge on fixed assets and/or real estate.

Interests on loans are fixed for the whole period and are set to cover all costs (operating as well as financial and risk) and to maintain the financial self-sustainability of the institution. The average rate is 20 per cent per annum, but this changes according to several factors such as the particular product chosen, the length of the client's relationship with FM, past repayment records and a qualitative evaluation conducted by loan officers on the applicant's motivation, entrepreneurial skills, viability of business and cash flow management. In the best scenario it can be as low as 13.5 per cent. There is also an administration fee, which on average is about 6 per cent of the loan amount; this increases the APR to a maximum of 30.7 per cent. It is impossible to compare FM's interest rates with those of the banks (which are much lower), because the latter usually do not grant such loans concerning risky micro-entrepreneurs. The size of loans ranges from a minimum of PLN 1000 (€ 250)[9] to a maximum of PLN 150 000 (€ 37 500), but the first loan cannot be more than PLN 50 000 (€ 12 000). FM's loan products are summarized in Table 17.3.

Table 17.3 Loan products offered by Fundusz Mikro

	Target client	Amounts	Loan term	Guarantee
Business loan	Addressed to entrepreneurs conducting their own businesses.	For first time borrowers with Fundusz Mikro loan amounts range from: PLN 1000 (€ 250) to PLN 50 000 (€ 12 000). For repeat FM clients, the loans can be in the range: PLN 1000 (€ 250) to PLN 150 000 (€ 37 500).	The maximum loan term is 36 months. With lower loan amounts, the repayment term is consequently shorter.	The number of guarantors (or none) depends on the loan amount and loan term. There is also a possibility of pledge on real estate as loan collateral.
Business loan without guarantors	Addressed to all conducting businesses, no need to present guarantees.	Start from PLN 1000 (ca. 250 ca. euro) to PLN 10 000 (ca. 2500 ca. euro).	Maximum loan term is 12 months.	
Business loan SOLO	Business loan SOLO is addressed to repeat FM clients. This loan does not require any collateral.	From PLN 1000 (€ 250) to PLN 15 000 (€ 4000)	Maximum loan term is 18 months. For loans up to PLN 10 000 (€ 2 500) this period is 12 months.	
Business loan express	Addressed to FM clients who need to borrow a small amount IMMEDIA-TELY. In order to obtain this loan, it is necessary to have repaid at least 6	Up to PLN 3000 (€ 800)	The maximum loan term is 3 months.	This loan does not require any form of collateral.

Table 17.3 (continued)

	Target client	Amounts	Loan term	Guarantee
	instalments of the outstanding loan.			
Starter	Addressed to those who plan to start their own business. A detailed description of the planned enterprise is required.	Up to PLN 7000 (€ 1900)	Maximum loan period is 12 months.	The number of guarantors depends on their income.

Source: Developed by author on basis of information available on FM website: http://www.funduszmikro.pl/produkty.php.

The cost of all the loans consists of interest rate and an administration fee, which depend on the loan amount and loan term. Loan officers play a fundamental and quite autonomous role in the final decision regarding granting the loan to the potential borrower.

Clients' profile In its 12 years of activity, FM has been able to develop a wide network of field offices (37 as of 2006) and loan-officers (around 90), reaching more than 46 350 clients and currently serving over 14 810 borrowers.[10]

Figures 17.3 to 17.5 illustrate the type of businesses served by the institution. Loans for trade businesses constitute half of all loans distributed by FM. In recent years, the purpose of the loan has changed and the majority are for investment. Almost 40 per cent of clients are first-time clients, which can be due to the fact that some of the businesses graduate to the banking sector.

All of these businesses employ fewer than ten people. Most of the borrowers (78 per cent) live and operate in large towns, while only a small 7 per cent come from rural areas.[11] FM's clients run very small business activities, but cannot be considered as socially excluded or poor people. FM's target does not focus specifically on the poorest segments of the population, who they feel should be supported by state institutions, but rather on talented micro-entrepreneurs willing to develop a business activity.

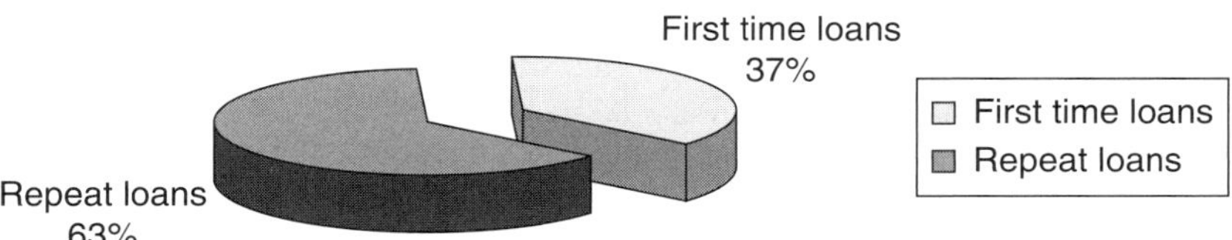

Source: Created by author on basis of data from FM website: http://www.funduszmikro.pl/results.php.

Figure 17.3 FM borrowers by number of loans

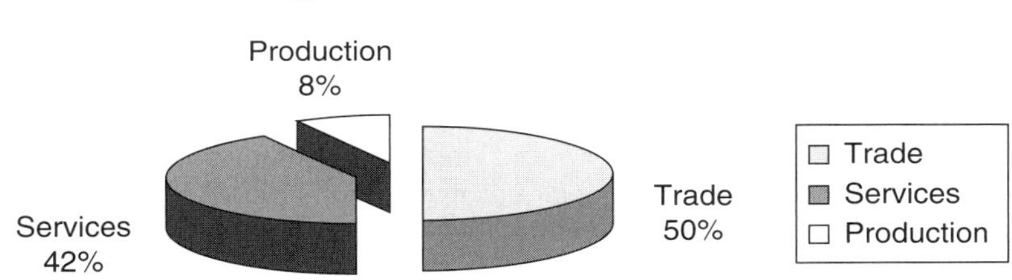

Source: Created by author on basis of data from FM website: http://www.funduszmikro.pl/results.php.

Figure 17.4 FM borrowers by type of business

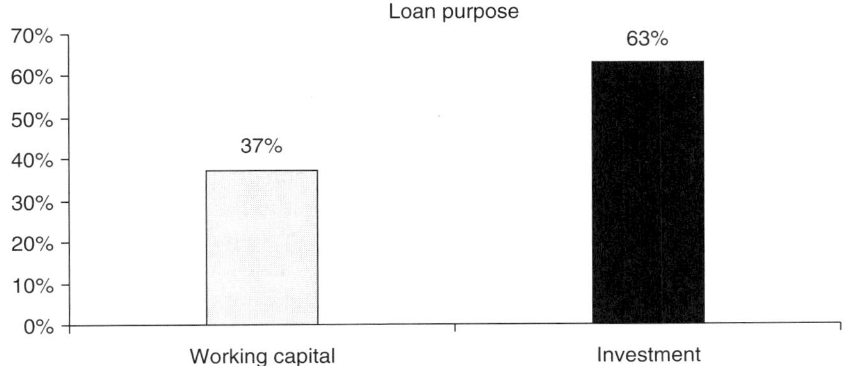

Source: Created by author on basis of data from FM website: http://www.funduszmikro.pl/results.php.

Figure 17.5 Usage of FM loan

Performance FM is the largest MFI operating in Poland and by any measure is one of those achieving the best results (see Tables 17.4–17.6 and Figure 17.6).

The rate of failure to repay (<180 days late) counted as a percentage of the gross outstanding portfolio is 3.82 percent.

3.2.3 Inicjatywa Mikro Sp. z o.o. (registered as a limited liability company, de facto a non-banking financial institution)

Origins and development Inicjatywa Mikro (IM) started operating a loan fund of US$1 million (€ 900 000) from the Polish American Enterprise Fund. Its mission has been to support local microenterprise development in the southern part of Poland. It transformed into an independent MFI, registered as a Limited Liability Company, in February 1996, when its main donor supporter became Opportunity International, which had been invited to Poland to provide technical assistance and to develop adequate standards for the MF industry in the region.

IM operates in southern Poland in the regions of Krakow (the Voivodship of Malopolska), and Katowice (the Voivodship of Silesia) through four branches, with two loan officers for each branch. In this part of Poland there are approximately 8 million people, comprising 21 per cent of the entire population of the country. This region was chosen for its particularly disadvantaged situation in the transition process: under the communist regime great state-owned factories situated near Krakow underwent a heavy restructuring process and led to mass unemployment. Furthermore, outside these industrial areas agriculture is predominant, but not very well developed, and soon after the fall of the planned system it was unable to keep up with the competition generated by a new, open-market economy. The other towns where the remaining branches are located were characterized by the presence of mines and a well-developed metallurgical and chemical industry, which is now restructuring, resulting in high unemployment rates among former miners and manual workers. The attention of IM is focused on supporting the financing of start-up microbusinesses important for the re-birth of a sound economy in the area, generating new income and employment and serving as examples of private successful initiatives to the discouraged population of the two regions.

The mission of IM is to contribute to the transformation of Polish society by providing loans to microenterprises, entrepreneurs and small businesses including start-ups, which have a potential for growth but do not meet the requirements to qualify for bank credit. IM's target therefore includes start-ups and already set up registered activities, employing fewer

Table 17.4 Cumulative results of FM for the period February 1995 – July 2007

Cumulative number of loans	Cumulative number of clients	Cumulative loan amounts
101 810	46 350	282 962 158 PLN (€ 72.5 m)

Source: Designed by author on basis of data from FM website: http://www.funduszmikro.pl/results.php.

Table 17.5 FM financial information

Balance sheet	30 September 2006 PLN/euro
Gross loan portfolio	69 013 373.8/ 18 140 886
Total assets	22 691 356/ 17 357 160.6
Savings	0
Total equity	32 965 166.8/ 8 665 238.5

Source: www.mixmarket.org/demand.

Table 17.6 FM performance indicators

Overall financial performance	31 September 2006
Return on assets (%)	1.93%
Return on equity (%)	3.47%
Operational self-sufficiency (%)	111.23%
Revenues	
Financial revenue ratio (%)	26.83%
Profit margin (%)	10.09%
Expenses	
Total expense ratio (%)	24.13%
Financial expense ratio (%)	2.23%
Loan loss provision expense ratio (%)	0.89%
Operating expense ratio (%)	21.00%
Risk	
Portfolio at risk > 30 days ratio (%)	16.96%
Loan loss reserve ratio (%)	11.35%
Risk coverage ratio (%)	66.95%
Write off ratio (%)	3.87%

Source: www.mixmarket.org/demand.

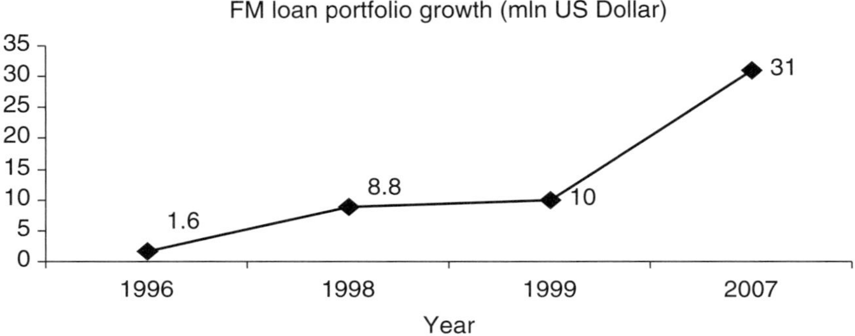

Source: Created by author based on data from FM website: www.funduszmikro.pl.

Figure 17.6 FM: outstanding loan portfolio growth

than 10 people, which could not qualify for a regular bank loan because of lack of adequate collateral, a relative short period of operation or the use of a simplified bookkeeping system.

IM's mission is guided by the Opportunity International Network's four core values:

- respect;
- commitment to the needy;
- integrity;
- stewardship.

In 2005, in recognition of its performance and potential, Inicjatywa Mikro received a grant of PLN 10000000 (€ 2500000) from the Polish Agency for Enterprise Development, out of the EU structural funds for on-lending to small entrepreneurs. IM has at present 20 staff, of whom nine are loan officers.

Products and conditions Inicjatywa Mikro offers individual loans (group loans have been discontinued due to the limited number), to promote business development and job creation.[12]

The loan features are as follows:

- maximum loan amount: 120000 PLN (€ 30000);
- maximum loan term: 60 months (for bigger loan amounts only);
- interest rate: 14–19 per cent depending on the loan amount and timely repayment (12 per cent is offered to a few long-term clients).

Repayment:

- loan with fixed monthly payments;
- balloon repayment loan – the total principal repaid with the last interest payment;
- revolving loan.

Collateral: whilst each application is treated on its individual merits, IM will always take security, and at a level considered adequate in comparison to the risk. Collateral will include some, if not all, of the following:

- promissory note (signed by borrower + spouse);
- vehicles or fixed assets;
- real estate.

Working capital loans are for working capital: purchase of raw materials, stock, services (see Table 17.7). Investment loans are mostly for machines and equipment for enhancing production (see Table 17.8). A credit Line is a credit that can be used according to the client's needs. They can withdraw and repay part or all during the period of the credit line (see Table 17.9). Start-up loans are to be used for entrepreneurs with experience in the business that is being established (see Table 17.10). Car loans are loans specifically for the purchase of a car or vehicle for business use (see Table 17.11).

<u>Clients' profile</u> IM target groups are as follows:

- Start-ups: people with knowledge and skills who see starting their own business as an opportunity;
- Micro and small businesses,
- Micro-entrepreneurs who run mainly stable businesses but who do not meet bank criteria (not enough credit history or collateral, inadequate financial results), are at an early stage of development, in need of bridge financing.

<u>Performance</u> As of 31 December 2006, the portfolio outstanding was PLN 9 200 000 (€ 2 300 000) and the number of outstanding loans was 970 (see Table 17.12).

From the beginning of its operations IM has granted over 5300 loans worth over PLN 61 700 000 (€ 15 425 000).

Figures 17.7 and 17.8 show that working capital stands out as the

Table 17.7 Working capital loan

Rate of interest	Term	Fees
14–19%	Up to 60 months	2–3%

Source: Provided by I. Norek, the CEO of IM.

Table 17.8 Investment loan

Rate of interest	Term	Fees
14–19%	Up to 60 months	2–3%

Source: Provided by I. Norek, the CEO of IM.

Table 17.9 Credit line

Rate of interest	Term	Fees	Additional points
15–19%	Up to 24 months	3.5%	Only for clients with a good repayment history with IM Max loan PLN 75 000 (€ 19 000)

Source: Provided by I. Norek, the CEO of IM.

Table 17.10 Start-up loan

Rate of interest	Term	Fees	Additional points
19%	Up to 36 months	3.5%	Max loan PLN 30 000 (€ 7 500)

Source: Provided by I. Norek, the CEO of IM.

Table 17.11 Car loan

Rate of interest	Term	Fees	Additional points
15%	Up to 60 months	3%	Max loan PLN 50 000 (€ 12 500)

Source: Provided by I. Norek, the CEO of IM.

Table 17.12 IM financial information

Balance Sheet 31 December 2006	PLN/euro
Gross loan portfolio	9 250 249/2 431 524
Total assets	17 022 862/ 4 474 637
Savings	0
Total equity	16 237 386.8/ 4 268 166.7

Source: www.mixmarket.org/demand.

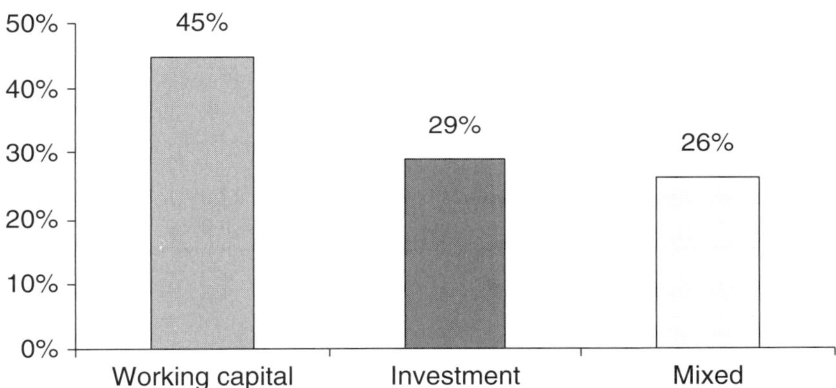

Source: Created by author on basis of data provided by I. Norek, the CEO of IM.

Figure 17.7 Loan purpose

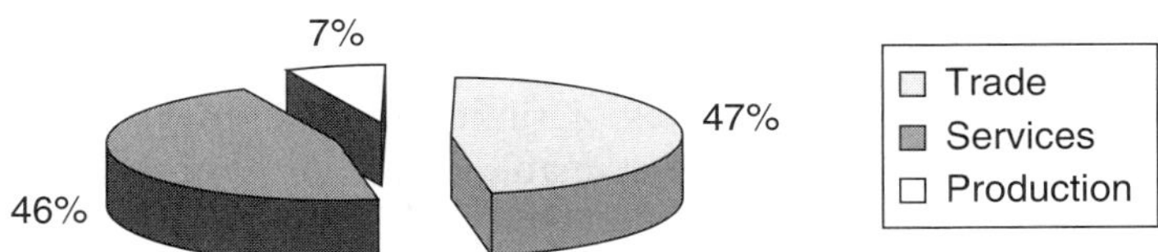

Source: Created by author on basis of data provided by I. Norek, the CEO of IM.

Figure 17.8 IM business types

predominant loan purpose, and loans are equally distributed among trade and service businesses, with only a small number serving production (7 per cent).

Microenterprises comprised 96 per cent of the businesses, employing

Table 17.13 IM performance indicators

Overall financial performance	31 December 2006
Return on assets (%)	4.98%
Return on equity (%)	5.36%
Operational self-sufficiency (%)	144.30%
Revenues	
Financial revenue ratio (%)	16.22%
Profit margin (%)	30.70%
Expenses	
Total expense ratio (%)	11.24%
Financial expense ratio (%)	0.50%
Loan loss provision expense ratio (%)	n/a
Operating expense ratio (%)	11.06%
Risk	
Portfolio at risk > 30 days ratio (%)	12.34%
Loan loss reserve ratio (%)	2.11%
Risk coverage ratio (%)	17.08%
Write off ratio (%)	0.00%

Source: www.mixmarket.org/demand.

up to nine staff, and the average loan amount in 2006 was PLN 15350 (€ 3840). See Table 17.13 for further performance indicators.

3.2.4 *Fundacja Wspierania Wsi (FWW): Rural Development Foundation*

Origins and development[13] The Rural Development Foundation is a private, non-governmental, not-for-profit organization established in 1999. Its mission is 'to support economic, social, cultural, educational and pro-environmental initiatives of rural and small-town inhabitants, thus contributing to all-sided, sustainable development of rural Poland'. The origins of the current institution date back to the early 1980s: the US government wanted to support Polish rural areas, but did not trust the communist regime and did not want to entrust its funds to the state. It was therefore decided to convey the funds to the Polish Catholic Church, which was deeply rooted in the countryside, reaching even the smallest villages. The church hierarchy expressed a favourable opinion on the initiative, but did not want to manage the funds directly and tried to set up an independent foundation. After five years, the 'Water Supply Foundation' was established in 1987 (it turned out to be the first foundation established in this part of Europe after World War II). The activity of the foundation consisted of promoting and financially supporting projects regarding the entire water supply system, purification plans and the improvement of agriculture techniques through the implementation of modern sewerage systems, though the support to rural farmers often went beyond the official mission.

After the change in the political regime, a new foundation was registered: the 'Agricultural Foundation', established in 1991. Its mission was similar to the one carried out by the Water Supply Foundation (that is the development of private initiative and entrepreneurial activities in rural, depressed areas), but it was accomplished through the disbursement of microloans to active rural entrepreneurs; the scale of operation was smaller than the current one and loans were very small. It was only in 1999 that the two, almost twin institutions merged in the 'Rural Development Foundation', which has been continuing the work of its predecessors, addressing the concerns of the rural population and directing its resources to social and economic goals.

The microloan programme was set up at the beginning of the operation of the new institution, in early 1999. The main goal of the project is the prevention and reduction of unemployment and the fostering of private initiative among low-income individuals and groups living in rural areas and small towns.

Financial funds for covering the programme come from three main sources:

1. the foundation's own capital;
2. the governmental 'Rural Agency';
3. a special loan granted by the World Bank to the Polish government.

The microloan programme is delivered through the *Program Mikropożyczki 05*, and its main aim is the prevention of unemployment in rural areas and in small towns (up to 20 000 inhabitants). This is to be achieved through creating access to finance in the form of a loan for starting or developing the business, and especially for creating new work places.

In 2006, FWW cooperated with 14 local advisors in order to deliver the loans under the microloan programme. The local advisors have their own registered businesses, which incorporate financial brokerage. The agreement with FWW is signed between the foundation and the advisor's business. The compensation for providing services to FWW depends on the number of loans granted on the basis of loan applications submitted by the advisor and on their timely repayment.

Products and conditions The maximum loan amount is PLN 10 000 (€ 2500). The loans do not bear interest and are granted for a period of

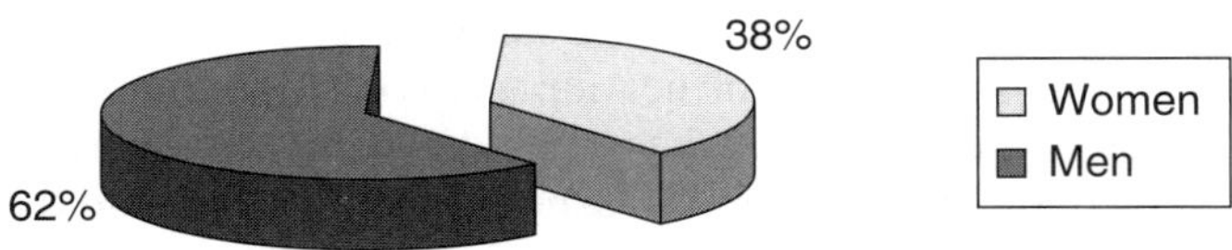

Source: Created by author on basis of data from FWW website: www.fww.org.pl.

Figure 17.9 FWW clients by gender

up to 24 months. The collateral used is the personal guarantee of two co-signers who, with the borrower, sign a promissory note.

Clients' profile The programme is aimed at the population of rural areas (villages and small towns), who conduct their businesses and engage in agro-tourism. In 2006, the target client group has been expanded and now also includes salaried workers and pensioners whose income is not higher then 1.5 of the lowest national pension in the actual year, and who engage in income-generating activities as an extra source of income for the household. From the total number of 1499 loans, 31.35 per cent was granted for those starting their businesses.

Among those who received loans for business development, 296 (28.77 per cent) received a second loan, 32 (2.13 per cent) a third loan and nine clients (0.87 per cent) received a loan for the fourth time. In the previous years the loans were granted under the programme 'Mikropożyczki' (in the period 1999–2003) and/or under the programme of Activation of the Rural Districts (in the period 2003–2004).

Although 62 per cent of the borrowers were men (see Figure 17.9), women applied for start-up loans more often than men. The percentage of women who received loans to start their own business was 32.63 per cent of the total number of granted loans, while the men's part amounted to 30.68 per cent. Among FWW clients, production is represented by a relatively higher number of the businesses than is the case with FM and IM. This is due to the presence of agri-production (honey, cheese, etc.) (see Figure 17.10).

The borrowers are usually quite young. Borrowers up to 30 years of age comprise 28.42 per cent, and those aged up to 45 comprise 74.98 per cent.

In total, 5200 household members profit from the income generated by the businesses using FWW loans.

Performance Timely repayment is very high. In 2005, 97 per cent, and in 2006, 96 per cent of loans were repaid no later than 15 days from the

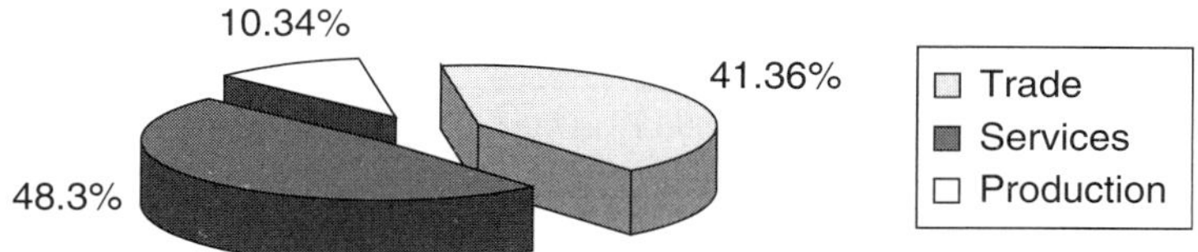

Source: Created by author on basis of data from FWW website: www.fww.org.pl.

Figure 17.10 FWW clients by business type

Table 17.14 Number and values of loans distributed in the years 2005–2006

No. of loan agreements signed		Currency	The cumulative values of loans disbursed			Average loan amount 2005–2006
2005	380		2005	2006	Total	
2006	1119	Amounts in PLN	3 648 500	10 830 700	14 479 200	9659
Total	1499	Amounts in euro	912 125	2 707 675	3 619 800	3864

Source: Created by author on basis of data available from the FWW website: www.fww.org.pl.

repayment date show on the loan contract. From the total number of 1499 loans, 31.35 per cent were granted to start-up businesses.

3.2.5 Fundacja na Rzecz Rozwoju Polskiego Rolnictwa – Foundation for the Development of Polish Agriculture (FDPA) [14]

Origins and development FDPA is a private, not-for-profit institution established in 1988 with the main goal of sustaining the transition to an open market-economy for the Polish food and agriculture sector. It also aimed to promote the development of civil society in rural areas, where 38 per cent of the Polish population reside. At the beginning, FDPA concentrated on the transfer of western agricultural know-how to Poland. In 1993, as a result of the closure of state farms, rural unemployment grew drastically. Therefore, FDPA decided to increase the scope of its activities beyond the agriculture and food sector. FDPA concentrated on programmes supporting integrated rural development, entrepreneurship development (including rural tourism) and the creation of non-agricultural jobs in rural areas.

Table 17.15 FWW data as of 30 November, 2007

	2006 PLN/euro	As of 30 November 2007 PLN/euro
Number of loans distributed (cumulative)	7385	8507
Amount of loans distributed (cumulative)	65 075 500/ 17 105 775	76 100 500
Average loan amount	8812/ 2316	8945/ 2351
Number of loans outstanding	1718	2146
Gross outstanding loan portfolio	9 608 669/ 2 500 304.2	11 291 078/ 2 967 977
Women clients in %	40.3	40
Number of start-ups (cumulative) and as % of all loans	3486 (47%)	3876 (46%)
Loans per business type – trade in %	35.6	35.4
Loans per business type – services in %	52.1	52.7
Loans per business type – production in %	11.4	11.9
Loans per business type – other in %	0.8	0
Number of loans per loan advisor	132	–
Delinquency (PAR-30) in %	1.9	0.97
Default rate %	0.2	–

Source: From the director of the FWW Mikropozyczki Programme, T.M.Steppa.

FDPA runs two main programmes: the 'European Integration Programme' (EIP) and the 'Rural Entrepreneurship Promotion Programme' (REP). The first project is aimed at supporting the integration process of Polish rural areas into the European Union framework, empowering rural people with the instruments needed to diversify economic activities and modernize agriculture techniques, and building a stronger civil society.

The REP programme is a microcredit initiative started in 1993, whose main goal is to sustain and promote local development in rural areas, inspiring entrepreneurship and fostering the setting up of micro and small business activities which provide jobs, develop infrastructures and stimulate economic growth.

REP was the first established microlending programme in Poland, and it is still the only one operating exclusively in rural areas, through its six field offices. FDPA' s support derives from international donors such as the Caritasverband Deutschland, the Polish-American Enterprise Fund, the Levi Strauss Corporation and the British Know-How Fund. The only prerequisite to access the funds of FDPA is that the applicant must live in a rural area, though the Levi Strauss Foundation has established a particular fund for unemployed people also living in urban environments. FDPA lending activities have become more intensive recently thanks to the involvement in the Rural Development Programme (PAOW), financed by the World Bank and grants from the British government, PARP and the Unidea Foundation and European Union (SPO WKP) to increase the microcredit fund.

Products and conditions Initially the loans granted by FDPA could go beyond the amount of PLN 20 000 (€ 5000). Loans are used for purchasing machinery, computers, cars, stocks or whatever small investment is needed for developing the business. They are not consumer loans. The interest rates are not subsidized and are set at the level of 14 per cent to 16 per cent APR, plus a commission of 3 per cent. Clients are able to repay such charges and willing to do so because they realize that FDPA's funds are their only chance to finance their activity, since most of them have no access to bank credits. FDPA's procedures are extremely simple and quick: once the potential borrower gathers the few documents required and finds the two co-signers who guarantee for him or her or sets up a solidarity group, only three to five days are required to receive the money. Furthermore, customers know that they can always count on FDPA's local officers, who provide a friendly, supportive loan service. Loans must be repaid within a flexible period ranging from three months to two years, depending on the amount and loan usage. Repeat loans are very common, even among clients who have already reached a bankable level, as they become accustomed to the foundation's simple procedures and do not want to access the bureaucratic banking system. FDPA is willing to carry on supporting these 'graduated' clients, because they allow the foundation to obtain higher profits through lower risks and costs. This also offsets some of the higher risk lending.

Clients' profile Giving up the original women-only target, FDPA turned to all potential entrepreneurs living in rural areas. Attention has been focused on these areas since the beginning because they have been neglected for many years, yet they have the highest levels of unemployment.[15] Polish agriculture in fact, though very extensive, is not very profitable and farmers often need a second economic activity to make ends meet. Particularly in need of financial support are three categories of people: the unemployed (often former state-farm workers), young people and women, all of them often lacking a reliable credit history and collateral to access the banking system. The programme's goal is also to help individuals who have little chance of finding a job and who need an additional income to provide for their families, as well as to support entrepreneurship among young people from poor families. The programme also supports the creation of new rural jobs outside agriculture. From its experience, FWW believes that it is an effective instrument to counteract unemployment.

Performance In its thirteen years of activity, REP has disbursed 4370 loans worth PLN 74 500 000 (€ 29 800 000). In 2006 through its six field offices, 403 loans were disbursed totalling PLN 1 590 000 (€ 3 900 000), with the average loan amount of PLN 39 500 (€ 9875). The outstanding loan portfolio at year end was PLN 16 818 576 (€ 4 205 000). The quality of the portfolio was maintained at a good level, with delinquency of PAR > 30 days at 4.34 per cent.

The breakdown of clients according to business type in FDPA is similar to that in FM, with the highest proportion being trade businesses (see Figure 17.11). Loans are used in even proportions for working capital and investment (see Figure 17.12).

In 2006, 64 per cent of borrowers were newly established businesses. Also that year, exceptionally, the number of women borrowers fell significantly to 35 per cent (as opposed to 43 per cent in the previous year, 2005). Over 60 per cent of FDPA clients come from villages or small towns (see Figure 17.13).

3.3 Credit unions

3.3.1 SKOK, Krajowa Spółdzielcza Kasa Oszczednosciowo – Kredytowa

Origins and development At Poland's request, the World Council of Credit Unions (WOCCU) provided technical assistance funded by USAID to help create a credit union system after the fall of Communism in Poland. Prior to 1992, there were no credit unions operating in Poland. In addition to the first tier of individual credit unions, WOCCU and its Polish counterpart worked to create many of the secondary-level financial services that are present in most developed credit union movements

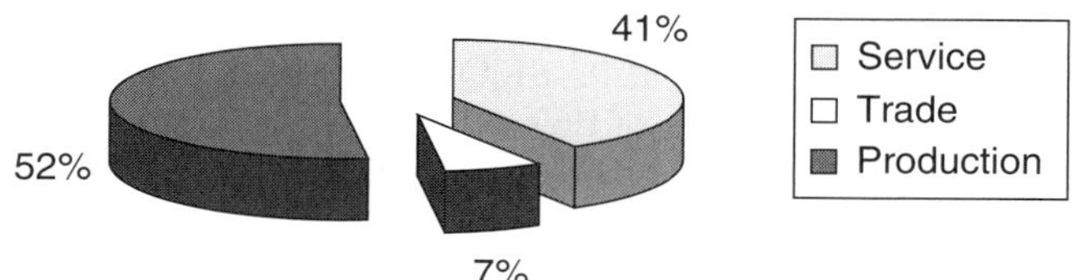

Source: Created by author on basis of data available at FDPA website: www.fdpa.org.pl.

Figure 17.11 FDPA clients by business type

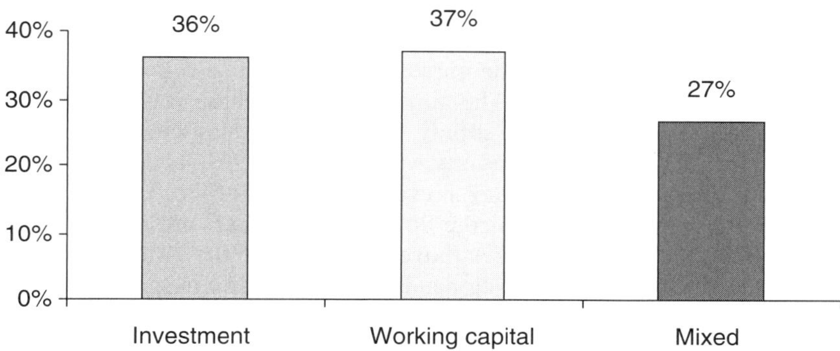

Source: Created by author on basis of data available at FDPA website: www.fdpa.org.pl.

Figure 17.12 FDPA loan usage

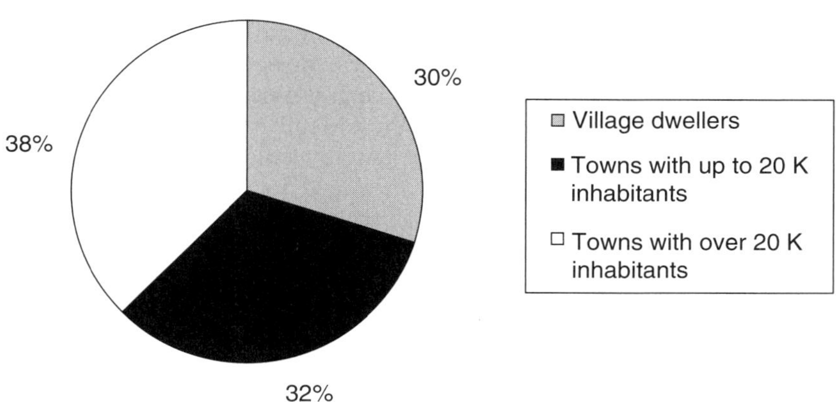

Source: Created by author on basis of data available at FDPA website: www.fdpa.org.pl.

Figure 17.13 FDPA borrowers per location of residence

around the world.[16] The National Association of Cooperative Savings and Credit Unions (NACSCU, or SKOK in Polish) was established in September 1992, with the aim of defending CUs' interests and extending their network. The foundations for development of the Polish movement were laid within a project mostly funded by USAID, which offered US$3.9 million (€ 23000000),[17] and only partly by WOCCU.

Together with the National Association, the Central Finance Facility (CFF), a Stabilization Fund and an Insurance Company, was created, rendering CU financial services more efficient and secure. As a result of the great enthusiasm and commitment in the development of CUs in Poland, in 1993 USAID sponsored a new project entitled 'Building the Polish Savings and Credit Union System' which lasted two years and was then refocused in 1995 with the implementation of a so-called 'Phase II', for another couple of years. The aim of this new phase was to improve CUs' organization and service supply, to train board staff of start-up CUs and to reach financial sustainability within March 1999. The goal of self-sufficiency was reached in 1998. It is estimated that for every US$1 (€ 0.78) spent in the implementation of the Polish CU system from 1992 to 1999, over US$40 (€ 31) of new assets have been generated.[18] The Polish CU network is one of the most developed in the world and surely the only one which has obtained such outstanding results in little more than a decade since its foundation. Table 17.16 illustrates this exceptional growth.

Products and conditions To keep up with the rapid development of the financial market and services, CUs have to supply their members with the latest and most innovative products. Today they offer a wide range of facilities which very much resembles the range available in the banking sector. On the business lending side, they provide both short-term working capital loans and investment loans, while consumer loans are offered to households for their personal expenditures. Members can decide to entrust their savings both to time deposits and to demand/current accounts. Money transfer services have been developed to accommodate clients' needs. CUs have been allowed to issue their own credit cards and ATM cards since 1997. Insurance services are supplied by the affiliated TUW-SKOK Mutual Insurance Company and TU SKOK ŻYCIE SA, which specializes in providing life insurance. Polish CUs constitute an advanced, integrated system able to furnish the most innovative utilities to their beneficiaries and, at the same time, their owners.

Clients' profile Data about the current depth of outreach of CUs are not available; the most recent figures date back to March 1998, when the WOCCU project sponsored a survey conducted on 605 members of 21

Table 17.16 Growth of the CUs in Poland

Years	No of CUs	No of members (in thousands)	Assets (in thousands of PLN)	Savings (in thousands of PLN)	Loans (thousands of PLN)
1992	13	14	4277	3565	2985
1993	32	21	11 173	8528	8697
1994	106	46	35446	29362	25650
1995	137	85	100752	91570	83431
1996	168	138	219443	190446	160843
1997	237	194	368260	312562	280598
1998	290	259	590376	528376	412482
1999	420	306	882727	740056	668386
2000	560	394	1199362	995251	865748
2001	680	525	1752316	1558436	1235554
2002	923	703	2455086	2253906	1659780
2003	1285	924	3343652	3111630	2212939
2004	1461	1169	4228673	3937924	2856265
2005	1553	1395	5329024	4989570	3502929
2006	1589	1551	5967348	5552967	4047325
March 2007	1608	1577	6131571	5701970	4248611

Source: From the SKOK website at: www.skok.pl.

CUs in the country, in order to draw up a profile of CU clients. It turned out that, with an average deposit size of US$437 (€ 399)[19] and a depth of outreach of 12 per cent, CUs represented the largest MF provider in Poland and, above all, the one reaching the poorest layers of the population, although the purchasing of a share is required in order to become a CU member.

The main characteristics of CU members are: 64 per cent are in the age group 30–49 years old, they are almost equally divided between males and females, and only 16 per cent have education level beyond high school. Concerning their income level, more than a third of them indicated their annual income was between US$909–1818 (€ 830–1660), while another 27 per cent reported it to be between US$1819 (€ 1661) and US$2727 (€ 2490), a quite modest level bearing in mind that the World Bank's data registered an average GDP per capita for Poland of US$3590 (€ 3278).

Numbers are significant, but even more are the respondents' declarations: 23 per cent of them stated 'having enough money to buy themselves and their family members only food and clothing, but being barely able to pay the monthly bill', while another 34 per cent declared having an income

Table 17.17 Enterprise lending at SKOK

Members total:	1 550 700
Of these:	
Members conducting their own business	7700
Accounts of business owners	7300
No. of outlets (branches and cashpoints)	1600

Source: GUS, Wyniki finansowe spółdzielczych kas oszczędnościowo-kredytowych w 2006 r.

which enabled them to buy food, clothes and pay the monthly bills, but 'insufficient for buying anything more'.[20] CU members seem therefore to belong to various social layers, from white-collar employees to manual workers, but they are mainly low-income recipients, relying on CUs as their sole source for financial services (52 per cent of those interviewed answered this way).

It is difficult to distinguish which among the business owners – members of SKOK – run a microenterprise, but taking into account the target client of SKOK, these might constitute a high percentage of the total number of members.

4 Government support and regulation

There is no specific regulation for microfinance institutions in Poland. The existing regulation, although it does not directly support microfinance, creates an environment in which it is relatively easy to establish microfinance institutions, and in which they can conduct their activities.

Credit Unions – SKOK – operate under special legislation for credit unions. The legislation is very favourable and has contributed to the very fast development and growth of SKOKs in Poland.

According to the author and microfinance practitioners in the country, the main legal barriers that microfinance institutions encounter are the following:

- Lack of legal title in collecting debts – the banks have the advantage over other non-banking financial institutions in being able to use a short and effective procedure in acquiring the legal title to collect debts. Microfinance institutions provide access to financing for the riskier clients and should also be able to use such a tool.
- Accounting regulations – institutions that are not banks have less favourable regulations concerning the principles of creating and dissolving loan loss reserves; they cannot treat the loan loss reserves as

a cost, and as a result the created reserves do not diminish the basis for taxation.

- Tax regulations – in spite of the fact that the income of microfinance institutions, which are *not-for-profit* institutions, is used only for conducting their statutory activities, they are not tax exempt.
- Interest rate 'statutory' limits – in July 2006, legislation was passed which limits the total cost of credit (interest rates and other manipulation costs charged by the lender). This is especially unfavourable and difficult for microfinance institutions, since operational and risk costs are much higher with their target group.

5 Sources of financing of loan funds[21]

The predominant source of funding for the loan funds is EU structural funds (25.4 per cent as of December 2006). The second largest source of financing is foreign funds (18.9 per cent as of December 2006), while the third source of capital for loan funds for the institutions is the government (17.3 per cent as of December 2006). Own capital has increased and by the end of 2006 consisted of 13.2 per cent of the sources of financing loan funds of the institutions.

6 The future of the sector in Poland[22]

In Poland, almost 2 million low-income households need microcredit to finance their current microenterprises or to realize their self-employment aspirations. Only 3 per cent of them are currently served. The Microfinance Centre for Central and Eastern Europe and the New Independent States (MFC) has conducted comprehensive demand and supply studies, which aimed to answer the following questions:

- Who needs microcredit and what is the market?
- How can effective demand be stimulated?
- Are current supply schemes scalable?
- How can market development be facilitated?

Who needs micro credit and what is the market?

In Poland, 6 per cent of low-income households generate income from formally registered self-employment activities. These add up to 400 000 existing enterprises. Another 28 per cent of low-income households have members who have plans and/or the potential to become self-employed. Lack of capital is an important challenge for almost 40 per cent of current micro-entrepreneurs and those aspiring to self-employment. However, formal credit history of current micro-entrepreneurs is very poor. Only 21 per cent of them have ever used any formal source of microcredit and 15 per cent are now repaying it. Banks are a major source of business loans (94 per cent). There are few potential and current micro-entrepreneurs who are considering external financing of their businesses from a formal source in the next three years. However, when we show them the concept of the microloan the interest in enterprise financing is three times higher than in their previously declared plans.

According to MFC research, the microcredit market in Poland accounts for 29 per cent of low-income households and includes up to 1.98 million low-income microenterprises. Seventeen per cent of the market are existing microenterprises and 83 per cent are potential start-ups (low-income households aspiring to self-employment). Only 3 per cent of them use microcredit at the moment. The rest of the low-income population falls naturally into a group of households which is either not eligible for microcredit or they objectively do not need microcredit. The total value of the market, estimated on the basis of the average loan size of those micro-entrepreneurs who are currently using it (18 250 PLN/€ 4800), is 36.08 trillion PLN (€ 9.5 trillion).

How can effective demand be stimulated?
In order to make the demand effective, three issues are important:

- Increase awareness about the financing options – current and potential entrepreneurs know little about microcredit and are not aware of microenterprise finance providers. Twenty-four per cent of potential entrepreneurs do not mention any source of financing! Current micro-entrepreneurs know about a very narrow range of options, limited mostly to banks.
- Change negative attitudes towards borrowing – one-third of those aspiring to self-employment and a quarter of current micro-entrepreneurs are afraid of borrowing, for cultural rather than economic reasons.
- Provide business development services and incentives for those aspiring to self-employment – there is an evident need to increase knowledge and skills as well as to promote entrepreneurial behaviour among the low-income population in Poland. Only half of those aspiring to self-employment have an adequate background (financial education as well as business skills). Additionally, regulatory and administrative hurdles are still the biggest challenges that the micro-entrepreneurs and start-ups face in Poland. Poland is not very different from its neighbours, but still many things need to be improved to reach the level of more developed OECD countries.

Apart from the strategies already mentioned to stimulate demand, the key issue for microcredit market development in Poland is to scale up the supply schemes. The analysis conducted by MFC clearly indicates the need for linking specialized non-bank financial institutions with commercial and cooperative banks and the network of guarantee schemes. This kind of partnership is a win–win solution that combines strengths of all key actors.

We would argue that it is unlikely that the Polish example is unique in Europe. In the opinion of MFC experts, the huge market gap does not show the failure of microcredit. It demonstrates a need to move from the experiment to the scaling-up phase. This can be done only if there are delivery models that are viable for all the stakeholders, especially for commercial players.

Notes

* Consultant: Grzegorz Galusek.
1. Poznanski (1993).
2. Dugiel (2008).
3. Matul et al. (2007).
4. Ibid.
5. Based on information from PAED website: www.parp.gov.pl.
6. www.ksu.parp.gov.pl.
7. Report 7/2007 Fundusze Po'yczkowe w Polsce, Szczecin, kwiecien 2007, available at http://www.psfp.org.pl/raporty/raporty.html.
8. Polska Fundacja Przedsiebiorczosci from Szczecin, in the years 2004–2005, created six new loan funds.
9. For the years 2005–2006, the conversion of Polish currency to the euro was evaluated on an average 1EUR=4 PLN.
10. http://www.funduszmikro.pl/aktualne_wyniki.php.
11. http://www.funduszmikro.pl.
12. Data provided by I. Norek, the CEO of IM.
13. Information from website: www.fww.org.pl.
14. Information from FDPA Annual Report 2006 available at: www.fdpa.org.pl.
15. Information from Annual Report 2006 available at: www.fdpa.org.pl.
16. Evans and Richardson (1999).
17. The euro–dollar conversion rate in 1992 was: US$1 = 0.75 euro (http://www.x-rates.com/cgi-bin/hlookup.cgi).
18. Evans and Richardson (1999).
19. US$1 = 0.91 euros (http://www.x-rates.com/cgi-bin/hlookup.cgi).
20. Survey results are reported in Evans and Richardson (1999: 9–11).
21. Report No. 7/2007 Fundusze Po'yczkowe w Polsce, Szczecin, kwiecien 2007, available on: http://www.psfp.org.pl/raporty/raporty.html.
22. This section is based on Matul et al. (2007).

References

Bałtowski, Maciej and Maciej Miszewski (2006), *Transformacja Gospodarcza w Polsce*, Wydawnictwo Naukowe PWN.

Dugiel, Wanda (2008), 'Poland's economic position against the background of EU countries – macroeconomic approach (2)', *Gospodarka Materialowa i Logistyka*, No. 4/2008, Polskie Wydawnictwo Ekonomiczne.

Evans, Anna Cora and David C. Richardson (1999), 'Polish Credit Unions Development:

building a sustainable network of financial services to serve low-income masses', WOCCU Research Monograph Series n.17, August, available on WOCCU website, http://www.woccu.org.

Matul, Michał, Justyna Pytkowska and Marcin Rataj (2007), 'Developing the Microcredit Market in Poland', *MFC Newsletter*, No. 2/2007.

Poznanski, Kazimierz (1993), *Stabilization and Privatization in Poland: An Economic Evaluation of the Shock Therapy Program*, Boston: Kluwer Academic Publishers.

Zespol Fundacji Centrum Organizacji Pozyczkowych (2002), *Mikrofinanse w Polsce, Niewykorzystany Potencjal, Finansowanie Najmniejszych Przedsięwzięć Gospodarczych*, Warsaw: Microfinance Center for Central and Eastern Europe and the New Independent States.

Internet sources

http://www.fdpa.org.pl, accessed on 6 August 2007.

http://www.fdpa.org.pl/fdpaen/annualrep.pdf, accessed on 9 August 2007 (FDPA: Annual report 2005).

http://www.funduszmikro.pl, accessed on 5 August 2007.

http://www.fww.org.pl, accessed on 11 August 2007.

http://www.fww.org.pl/polski/sprawozdania/index.htm, accessed on 7 August 2008 (Fundacja Wspomagania Wsi w Warszawie, SPRAWOZDANIE z działalności Fundacji Wspomagania Wsi w roku 2006 [Rural Development Foundation in Warsaw, Activities Report]).

http://www.inicjatywamikro.pl, accessed on 11 August 2007.

http://www.ksu.parp.gov.pl, accessed on 10 August 2007.

http://www.mixmarket.org, accessed on 5 August 2007.

http://www.mixmarket.org/en/demand/demand.show.profile.asp?ett=1077&, accessed on 5 August 2007 (Fundusz Mikro, Limited Liability Company, Financial statements for the year ended 30 September, 2006, including the opinion of an independent auditor).

http://www.parp.gov.pl, accessed on 7 August 2007.

http://www.psfp.org.pl, accessed on 7 August 2007.

http://www.psfp.org.pl/raporty/raporty.html, accessed on 5 August 2007 (RAPORT No. 7/2007 Fundusze Pozyczkowe w Polsce [Loans Funds in Poland], Szczecin, April 2007).

http://www.skok.pl, accessed on 12 August 2007.

http://www.woccu.org, accessed on 12 August 2007.

http://www.x-rates.com/cgi-bin/hlookup.cgi, accessed on 28 October 2007.

18 Microfinance in the Netherlands

*Margot Lobbezoo**

National context

Microfinance has always existed in the Netherlands. By the end of the nineteenth century, the first cooperative banks had become active, focusing on poor farmers, and as early as 1915 the government had started to support small and medium enterprises with a guarantee facility. Microfinance[1] has continued to grow over the years with many initiatives being developed. Examples include a successful government programme supporting people on welfare to start their own company with loans, income support and business development services, the access to overdraft facilities for small enterprises from the general banks and several private initiatives. Moreover, informal rotating saving and credit associations (ROSCAs) have been active for many years in the Netherlands, particularly amongst the migrant community.

Financial inclusion is achieved in the Netherlands through a covenant on basic bank accounts signed by the major Dutch banks (covering 95 per cent of the Netherlands) in 2001.[2] This initiative was taken after the Salvation Army found that many people with a poor history at the national credit bureau could not open a bank account and were thus excluded from access to basic bank services. In 2001, the amount of people without a bank account was estimated by social organizations to be only several thousand people. In 2003, as a result of the covenant this number has decreased considerably. However, this access to basic bank services does not yet give them automatic access to other financial services.

Many of these activities are taking place away from the public eye. There has been little awareness of microfinance in the Netherlands itself. There is, for instance, no unanimous accepted definition of microfinance in the Netherlands. Ironically, although the Netherlands has been sending microfinance experts to developing countries for over 20 years, and there have been many campaigns about microfinance in developing countries by the development NGOs, only recently has there been a growing awareness that something needs to happen to reach more people with microfinance in the Netherlands itself. The promotion of entrepreneurship as a way out of economic exclusion and a tool for social cohesion is gaining momentum in the Netherlands.

The economic and social situation in some neighbourhoods in the

Netherlands has sparked a more active role for the government. The welfare system in the Netherlands has for years been good, but particularly in recent years, due to the high costs and the ageing of the population, many cuts have taken place. According to the CBS in 2004, 9 per cent of all households in the Netherlands were living on a low income.[3] Almost 25 per cent of all people with a low income live in the four large cities of the Netherlands: Amsterdam, Rotterdam, The Hague and Utrecht. The main risk groups for poverty are non-western immigrants, one-parent families and elderly singles. Interestingly, many of these self-employed have a low income. The reason for this low income for entrepreneurs is that their income fluctuates over the year. The risk of a (temporary) low income for entrepreneurs is therefore greater than for those in a regular job.

The government has taken up microfinance in its policy plan for 2007–2011 and has established an advisory council on microfinance. More actors in society have started to embrace microfinance openly. Banks have started to rethink their position in this field, and the first professor focusing solely on microfinance and small businesses in the Netherlands has been appointed.

BACKGROUND TO THE SITUATION IN THE NETHERLANDS

The Netherlands is a constitutional monarchy with a multi-party democracy. Although small in surface (41.500 km^2) the population is dense, with more than 16.3 million people,[4] 19.4 per cent of whom were either born abroad or one of their parents was born abroad. The education level is quite high, with 41 per cent of the population aged between 15 and 64 having graduated from secondary school, and 25 per cent from higher education. In the year 2005, the GNP was 505.6 billion euros. According to the Central Bureau of Statistics (CBS), around 7 per cent of GNP is earned in the grey economy.[5] With an unemployment rate of 5.5 per cent (in 2006), a large part of the especially big city population receives unemployment benefits or welfare.

The origin of microfinance in the Netherlands

History of microfinance

For over a century, microfinance has been present in the Netherlands. At the end of the nineteenth century, the first cooperative banks started in the Netherlands, and in the former Dutch colony of Indonesia, the first municipal credit bank started in 1895.[6] The Dutch government started to offer guarantee facilities for Small and Medium Enterprises (SMEs) as early as 1915. Whilst not focusing on providing finance itself, the government has always tried to support SMEs.

After World War II, banks could be divided into four categories: merchant banks, savings banks, cooperative banks and a Postal and Girobank, each with a clearly defined client profile. Between 1960 and 1980, the structure of the industry changed, with the emergence of many banks focusing on new client groups and products. This resulted in a boom in local branches for the different banks. They also started to include insurance and travel in their product portfolio. Currently, a large concentration is taking place, with banks becoming financial conglomerates. The main general banks are ING, ABN AMRO, Fortis, Rabobank (a cooperative bank), and SNS.[7] A new general bank has emerged in recent years: the DSB bank, which started as a credit bank, has recently received a full bank licence and can now also take savings.

Interestingly enough, micro and small enterprises are often seen as clients of retail banking and not of corporate banking. According to the report 'Microcredits in the Netherlands' by FACET BV,[8] most loans provided by banks to micro and small enterprises are given in the form of an overdraft facility.

Although banks may provide services to small enterprises, these services would not always be considered to be microfinance since they do not comply with the following characteristics of microfinance given by FACET:[9]

- Small credit amounts (for the Dutch context €1000 to €3000/5000).
- Relative short repayment periods (increasing with the loan amount).
- Opportunity to (continually) renew the loan.
- Limited amount of support services predominantly aimed at the effective use of the credit.
- Management Information Systems specific for microcredit.
- Staff only focusing on providing microcredit.
- Strict repayment systems.
- Repayment capacity dependent on family income.

In the last 10 to 15 years, the focus of government has been on promoting (innovative) start-up companies. Under the social welfare support programme for the self-employed (BBZ) the government encourages recipients of social benefits to start their own business. This takes place at municipality level and differs in success between the municipalities. In addition at local level several starters' programmes have been initiated which include a credit facility often with additional funding from the European Social Funds (ESF).[10]

Since the beginning, the first ideas about providing financial services to the poor were developed with the involvement of internationally experienced Dutch experts. Dutch development organizations (NGOs) as well as the Ministry of Foreign Affairs, the Rabobank Foundation and special funds and organizations (Triodos Doen, ASN-Novib, Oikocredit) have been active abroad in the field of microfinance. However, in the Netherlands itself, microfinance was not actively promoted, and lessons learned abroad were not used to develop the microfinance sector further in the Netherlands. This started to change around 2004 when the Ministries of Social Affairs and Economic Affairs started their first research into microfinance in the Netherlands. Dutch individuals, having visited microfinance institutes abroad, during work or holiday visits, became inspired to start programmes and developed activities to promote entrepreneurship amongst vulnerable groups in the Netherlands using microfinance.

Why microfinance

The United Nations (UN) year for Microcredit 2005, during which Her Royal Highness (HRH) Princess Máxima was one of the UN advisors, has created a momentum for change and inspiration for many in the Netherlands. The growing importance of corporate responsibility in the business world (with all related initiatives such as the Global Reporting Initiative and the Financial Times Stock Exchange FTSE4 Good Index) has made banks rethink their social and environmental effect. All these elements came together at the same time and sparked a new movement for microfinance in the Netherlands.

In line with the objectives for microfinance in developing countries, the Netherlands views entrepreneurship as a way out of poverty for vulnerable groups and a way to improve social inclusion. The welfare system is declining because of the high cost involved and is currently the responsibility of municipalities. Dutch society is rapidly individualizing and wants people to become economically independent rather than have the government look after them. Both developments have led to an active stimulation of economic independence for people that rely on welfare. Entrepreneurship is seen as one of the ways to reach that economic independence. The Dutch Association for Small and Medium Enterprises has seen a decline in access to finance for newly established companies and students (those wanting to start a company without having to build up a working and financial history) and has actively lobbied the government for improvement.

According to research carried out by Bureau Bartels for the Ministry of Economic Affairs in 2004, the economic climate for an entrepreneur to obtain a small business credit loan has deteriorated in the past decade.[11] In particular, loan requests below €25 000 are refused more often than larger amounts. They also mention that the government guarantee scheme for loans for SMEs is becoming more and more focused on the larger loan amounts. Since banks are becoming more risk-averse in their investments (based on the Basel II regulations), the market gap between microloans and regular loans has grown rapidly. The government has acknowledged this and has given microfinance some major boosts.

The current status of microfinance

An exponential growth in small projects and funds can be seen. These initiatives can be divided into private, government and corporate initiatives. Some of these initiatives are stimulated by the European Union through ESF or the related fund, Equal Initiative.[12] The number of customers reached with microfinance through those initiatives remains low. During a meeting at INHolland University for Applied Science[13] it became clear that most initiatives have provided between 6 and 25 loans to date. A new one-year pilot project of the Ministry of Social Affairs has just started. It aims to reach 300 micro-entrepreneurs in three cities through a comprehensive programme combining business advisory services with lending by banks (backed with a guarantee scheme). In this pilot, one of the objectives is to involve banks in rendering the financial services, rather than the municipalities that have been involved up until now under the general social welfare programme.

The government realizes that insufficient micro-entrepreneurs have been reached and established the 'Council for Microfinance in The Netherlands'[14] in February 2007. This council consists of members holding high-ranking positions in both government and the private sector, including microfinance experts. This council will promote networking amongst parties who are active in entrepreneurship development and microfinance, it will fulfil an ambassador function within this network, increase the knowledge of entrepreneurs about the financing possibilities, make recommendations to the Minister of Economic Affairs and formulate solutions to provide access to microfinance in the Netherlands (see Figure 18.1).

One of the first indirect results of the work of the council is that microfinance has been included in the policy plan[15] of the present government. This policy plan includes a revival of 40 so-called focus districts. These districts can be found in all major cities of the Netherlands and have many social and economic problems. One of the government goals is to increase the number of enterprises (with personnel). The government has developed several plans to achieve this goal, stating that 'there will be microcredits for starting entrepreneurs with special attention to those in the 40 focus districts'. From the point of view of social cohesion, the government also wants to increase entrepreneurship especially for unemployed people receiving social benefits. By the end of 2007, the council will provide advice

Notes: From left to right: Chairmen of the council Mr D. Laman Trip, HRH Princess Máxima, State Secretary of Economics Mr B. Heemskerk, Senator Mrs J. Sylvester and microfinance specialist Mr N. Molenaar. Not in the picture are council members Mr B. Staal (chairman of Dutch Bank Association) and Mr L. Bolsius (City Councillor Rotterdam).

Source: Picture provided by Senter Novem.

Figure 18.1 Members of the Council for Microfinance in the Netherlands and the State Secretary of Economics, October 2007.

to the government on how to reach an additional 15000 entrepreneurs with microfinance annually.[16]

Description of the microfinance sector in the Netherlands

The microfinance sector has seen growth in recent years. Complex relations have been formed and new players have entered the sector. In order to analyse this sector, more is involved than describing the actors and their functions. The five forces analysis[17] of Porter has been used to assess the present state of the microfinance sector in the Netherlands (see Figure 18.2). Each of the forces and the actors within them are further explained below.

Competitive rivalry within the industry

Traditional providers include banks, NGOs and government. The most common form of microfinance used by general banks is the overdraft

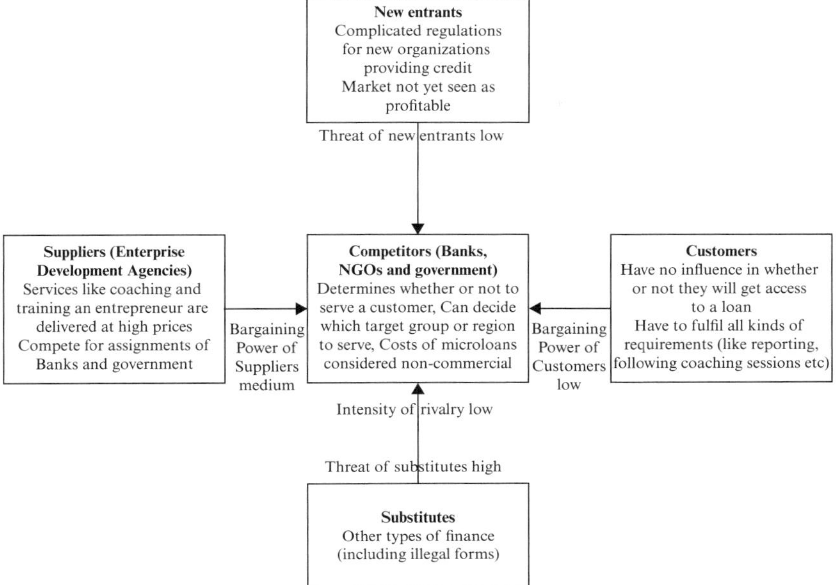

Figure 18.2 Microfinance industry analysis by M. Lobbezoo based on Porter's five forces analysis (July 2007)

facility, where they charge a higher interest rate than for other loans and will be able to review the extension of the overdraft each year. Banks like Rabobank and Fortis Bank feel that microcredit is important and partner with NGOs or universities in special programmes. The costs for reviewing the loan application and assisting the entrepreneurs then often lie with the (subsidized) NGOs. Fortis Bank is an exception and has started its own microfinance programme including loans and insurances.[18] Fortis Bank cooperates with an NGO (SEON) that carrries out a pre-screening of the loan applicants before submitting them to the bank. This NGO has also set up a special training programme for the staff at the bank.

Municipal credit banks (GKBs) have in the past focused mainly on debt restructuring. Their mandate is to focus on a specific target group; only if someone has been refused by several banks can they become a customer.[19] Of late they have started to launch microlending facilities which they consider part of their mandate as well.

Banks are operating in a highly competitive industry. This means that they are competing for customers and trying to bring their costs down. However, when it comes to the product 'microfinance', this competition is very low. Few of them wish to become active, since they consider the costs for a microloan to be high compared to those for a larger loan. Most microfinance activities are carried out from the point of corporate responsibility and are not considered part of the mainstream banking product. These activities are often not even incorporated in the balance sheet.

The ESF of the EU (Equal, Inti and others) have been used to promote entrepreneurship amongst vulnerable groups. Several NGOs and universities started projects which include credit facilities. Women@Work in Action Microcredit in Amsterdam is such a project using peer groups. Since the target group includes many women with a debt situation, they partner with the Municipal Credit Bank.

Municipalities provide loans directly through their BBZ programme; this is a programme where those with social benefits are supported to start their own business. This programme will be described in more detail later.

There are several other providers including credit card companies and mail order companies. Together with supplier credits their loans are used as an indirect form of financing. Informal investors often focus on innovative entrepreneurs at a small and medium level and rarely at micro-level (FACET BV, 2006).

Within the microfinance industry hardly any advertisements are used to attract customers, and providers have a very low visibility. Those providers that want to target microfinance customers seem so far to find it difficult to reach them. A provider can determine whether or not to serve a customer and does not need to give much explanation about the products it offers and the conditions under which they might be made available. They can also decide to stop providing microfinance at any point. Most activities take place at the local level and concentrated only in a few larger cities in the Netherlands. Providers decide themselves which clients to serve and where. They are not yet vying for microfinance clients. One may thus conclude that the competitive rivalry in this industry is low.

Bargaining power of suppliers

The providers are supplied with services and customers by the enterprise development agencies. They review loan applicants and their plans, provide training, coaching and other services. Thanks to these organizations entrepreneurs are linked to the banks and other financing organizations. There are several of these business development support organizations scattered over the country, these can be both NGOs and private companies. There are many NGOs stimulating entrepreneurship in specific localities (for instance Stabij in The Hague, Ondernemershuis in Amsterdam) as well as specific target groups (for instance IntEnt, focusing on returning migrants). Many more can be named in almost all regions and cities of the Netherlands. Also some private companies are active in this field, such as IMK and the B&A group, who often work for government or EU-funded projects in advising entrepreneurs. The actual costs of the BDS services rendered are not yet borne by the banks but often by government and project funding through subsidies.

There is some competition amongst those suppliers (both the commercial ones and the NGOs) enabling providers like the government to engage in price bargaining. However, in some regions suppliers are not present and there are fewer options for bargaining. Providers do need the suppliers to assist them in providing microfinance because of their knowledge and their access to the customers. Since they can use their unique position in the bargaining process regarding access to customers, the bargaining power of the suppliers can be said to be medium.

Bargaining power of customers

At the moment there are three groups of customers:

- Potential start-ups can come from different backgrounds, and do not necessarily adhere to a specific description regarding the sectors they want to start their enterprise in. These potential start-ups are planning to start a business and have a business idea. They are looking for finance to be able to start their company.
- Start-ups that are in the early stages of forming their enterprise; they mostly have less than one year in business. Some have just started, with little preparation in advance and realize they need finance; others have prepared a business plan and have undertaken careful consideration. The last group is well aware of their needs regarding finance for the start-up period.
- Existing microenterprises that run into a cash-flow problem, need working capital or need an investment for the growth of their business.

The bargaining power of customers is extremely low. The final decision about granting a loan always remains with the bank. Potential customers cannot influence the price, for example the interest that must be paid, and have to fulfil all kinds of other (reporting) requirements. In particular customers from vulnerable groups have difficulty in finding the right access points when asking for a loan from a provider. FACET BV (2006) mentions that there is a cultural difference between banks and micro-entrepreneurs. In principle, the customers have the option to shop for a loan at all providers. Also, there are many projects around that are looking for customers, but in reality both options are limited. Since most projects take place locally, potential customers from other regions have no access to the services and do not have any influence over these location decisions. Customers can decide just to stop their business when they do not get a loan and go and work for a boss instead, or more likely fall back on social benefits.

Threat of new entrants

With the gap left by the competing providers, there might be a possibility that new entrants will come to serve the potential clients who are excluded. Slowly new NGOs are starting to appear, some of them using money from private investors to provide microloans. One example is the Hands On Foundation in Amsterdam.[20] Online peer-to-peer loan providers might also be possible new entrants, although the only Dutch peer-to-peer loan provider, Boober.nl, is so far focusing on consumer credits. However, the entry barriers for anyone wanting to start delivering financial services are high, for example Boober.nl has had a lot of trouble obtaining a licence to enable them to provide credit.[21] Regulations and rules for lending operations are extremely strict and complicated, and are even more so for saving schemes. The new entrants might therefore possibly come from new retail and savings banks like the DSB bank, who wants to tap into this market. At the moment the threat of these new entrants to the position of the main providers is low.

Threat of substitute products

Micro-entrepreneurs will look for different ways of finding finance when access to microfinance is limited. This can be through using personal money, loans from friends, supplier credit or other (potentially illegal) ways. Research (FACET BV, 2006) has shown that 36.3 per cent of start-up companies are financed completely by the owner. This personal investment may well come from an extra mortgage on the house or a personal loan. Also 14 per cent of start-up companies borrowed money from family and friends, while only 20.7 per cent obtained credit from a bank.

Conclusion of the industry analysis

This analysis reveals that we are dealing with an imperfect industry in which providers have all the power and can decide whether or not to deliver the product, no matter how high the demand. Although this industry analysis encompasses many aspects of the microfinance sector in the Netherlands, it does not yet tell us much about the enablers and stimulators of microfinance in the Netherlands.

The enabling environment

Several organizations have a role in the enabling environment. The government has increased its efforts to promote entrepreneurship. Through the Ministry of Economic Affairs and the Ministry of Social Affairs, programmes are developed to directly target micro and small entrepreneurs. The state guarantee schemes (explained in more detail below) support banks in rendering financial services for the intended target groups. The Ministry of Education is focusing on ensuring that entrepreneurship receives more attention in the curricula of the formal education system. The Chambers of Commerce play an important role, both on the regulatory side and on the promotion side.

The Council for Microfinance in the Netherlands is promoting access to financial and non-financial services for micro-entrepreneurs. This high-level council includes HRH Princess Máxima and lobbies at a high level with the government, banks and other (potential) providers of microcredit and related services. It also provides advice to government as to the steps forward.

Enterprise development agencies try to increase the numbers of entrepreneurs in the Netherlands by providing them with guidance and assistance where needed. They also promote entrepreneurship amongst vulnerable groups as a means to gain economic independence.

Universities (of applied science) and intermediate vocational education institutions stimulate their students to become more enterprising. Alongside this, research is carried out in the field of microfinance by several students of the main Dutch universities, although university research mainly focuses on microfinance in developing countries. One university of applied science (INHolland) has started focusing specifically on microfinance in the Netherlands itself through the establishment of a professorship in 2007.

Both the microfinance sector and the enabling environment are not yet mature. Many steps must and will be taken by both government and the private sector to improve the situation.

Model of microcredit granting in The Netherlands

There is no official model for microfinance and provision of microcredit in the Netherlands. Based on an analysis of the initiatives that have taken place so far, the following model is the one most commonly used in the Netherlands. In this model three organizations play dominant roles:

1. *Regular banks* carry out the actual lending and administration of the loan to the microenterprise.
2. They base this on advice from *an intermediary*, such as enterprise development agencies, NGOs or schools. The intermediary provides

business development services like coaching and training in the preparation of business plans. The costs of these are paid by external parties and sponsors, or volunteers are used.

3. *Others* (like the government, European funds, projects) support banks with a guarantee.

They all three operate along the following lines:

1. Micro-entrepreneur seeks loan.
2. Goes to intermediary with a loan application.
3. Intermediary coaches the micro-entrepreneur with the loan proposal (often business plan).
4. Loan application request is sent by the micro-entrepreneur to the bank.
5. Bank asks for advice from the same or other intermediary.
6. Bank requires collateral (or checks availability of it) or a guarantee after receiving positive advice.
7. Bank provides the loan (or not).
8. Micro-entrepreneur receives a loan.
9. Micro-entrepreneur gets ongoing business development services from intermediary.

This leads to the following model shown in Figure 18.3.

It is logical that the banks do not want to pay the costs incurred in selection and coaching. Clients are not in position to pay for it, but so far no schemes exists for (co)funding of those. The way this is handled will determine how the microfinance industry develops in the Netherlands.

This model does not take into account the opinion of the entrepreneurs. Do entrepreneurs want to receive all this coaching or do they just want to obtain financing from the bank? A culture of dependency might be created by this model, ignoring the fact that an entrepreneur wants to be seen as an independent person.[22]

FACET BV (2006) recommends that experiments with more models are needed at local and regional level. Some, like the Hands On Foundation, are already running. They operate as a one-stop-shop, offering all steps within the organization. Some banks have small projects under their corporate social responsibility programmes. They might offer unsecured lending (Rabobank with school-leavers and Stason[23]) and sometimes even pay for the intermediary work (Fortis).

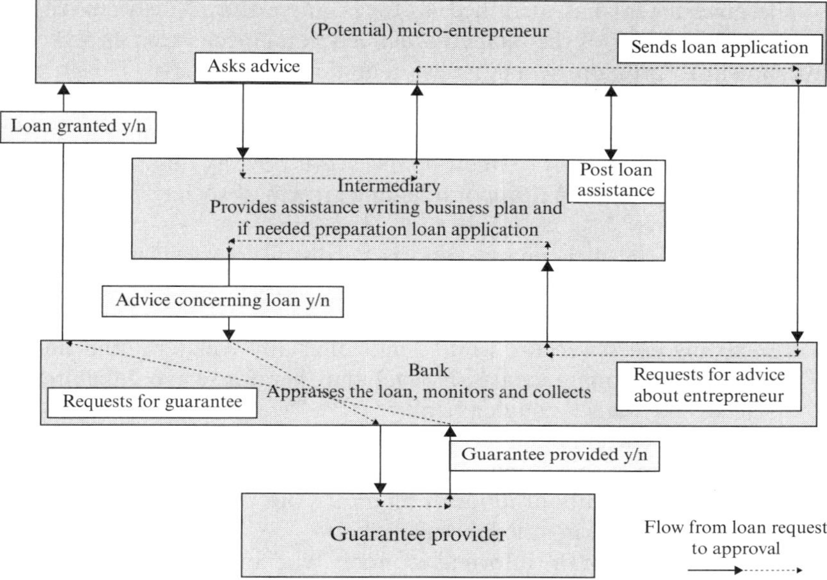

Source: Author, August 2007.

Figure 18.3 Most often used microfinance model in the Netherlands

Target groups in the Netherlands

FACET BV (2006) reported that at present there is no explicit reporting about the use and effects of microcredit, nor is it clear how and which target groups are reached by the banking sector. FACET argues that it could be opportune to divide the target groups and programmes into those that serve customers with additional income-generating activities with loans below €5000 and those that serve microbusinesses that need loans between €5000 and €25 000.

The current projects and programmes have a large social component and focus on women, specific districts, specific ethnic groups or young people. Exceptions are some of the bank programmes that focus on start-ups from all backgrounds.

In most programmes the focus has been on start-up companies and not on existing micro-entrepreneurs. This last group has been left behind while for the start-up companies it remains a challenge for the finance sector to adjust their system to really include them. A more scientific approach is needed to determine which groups actually can benefit most from microfinance activities.

The government has identified 40 focus or 'problem' districts (covering the major cities of the Netherlands). Microfinance is seen as a proper instrument to promote social inclusion and combat poverty. This in turn might result in getting people out of the welfare system.

The FACET report states that overall policies are still unclear in the Netherlands with respect to microfinance: 'is it poverty alleviation, social inclusion, escape from welfare or dynamic growth of society?' that society wishes to achieve?[24]

The Council on Microfinance reports a growing consensus on the target groups[25] to be reached:

- existing entrepreneurs who cannot offer any collateral and do not have an adequate education level and therefore have difficulties in accessing loans through a bank;
- start-up entrepreneurs coming from a (hidden) unemployment background; this often concerns people with low incomes, from backward neighbourhoods or migrants, but also school-leavers and women re-entering the labour market;
- people active in the informal economy who are not now encouraged to start entering the formal economy;
- people holding paid jobs who would like to be entrepreneurs if the right conditions existed. Half of these are people from backward neighbourhoods, migrants or low educated people.

Financial terms and conditions

For the different microfinance projects in the Netherlands there are no standard financial terms and conditions. Each project follows its own set of rules concerning repayment period, flexibility in repayment schedules and interest rates within the legal boundaries. For several of the current microfinance projects the interest rates and other conditions are given in Table 18.1.

The regular banks providing overdraft facilities to small enterprises charge commercial rates for this facility. The rates of these fluctuate and are different for each bank and are negotiable for regular customers. Also the other conditions differ, with most banks demanding a positive bank balance in a certain period each year. Since it is not a regular loan for which a repayment period is agreed, this leads to flexibility for the entrepreneur on the one hand but uncertainty on the other as the overdraft facility can easily be withdrawn by the bank when they feel the entrepreneur is misusing the facility.

The business services provided are mostly assistance in formulating a business plan and other pre- and post-loan coaching for the entrepreneur.

Table 18.1 Financial conditions on 25 July 2007, these are subject to fluctuations and change

Organization	Interest rate	Repayment period	Other conditions for the borrower
Fortis Bank – microfinance programme	Fortis basis interest (currently at 4.75%) plus 4%[a]		Onetime costs €250 Free coaching trajectory
Hands On Foundation[b]	6%	12 or 18 months	One-off €250 for costs Monthly €25 for business development services (obligatory)
BBZ, social services	6%[c]	Depending on size loan	Payment by local government for pre-loan and post loan advisory services
Women@Work in Action Microcredit[d]	5%	36 months (women start repayment 3 months after receiving the loan)	Free mentoring programme Peer review
Startersfonds Amsterdam Zuid Oost[e]	5%	3 years	
Kunstenaars&co with Triodos Bank[f]	2.25% or 4.5% (depending on status of artist)	< €1000 1 year < €2000 2 years < €3000 3 years Loans above €10 000 have a fluctuating interest and repayment period	

Notes:
a. Information based on interview with F. Groeneveld of Fortis Bank.
b. www.handsonmicrokrediet.nl and confirmation by telephone with Hands On Foundation.
c. Ministry of Social Affairs and Employment, W&B/URP/07/14065, 6 June 2007.
d. Huijstee (2007).
e. www.ondernemershuiszuidoost.nl.
f. www.kunstenaarsenco-cultuurlening.nl.

Source: Author, August 2007.

This is normally not done by the organizations providing the loans but by intermediary organizations. Using these services is often a pre-condition for granting a credit. Only the Women@Work in Action initiative uses a mandatory peer-group approach.

Other microfinance products

So far the focus of this chapter has been on microcredit and not on other microfinance products. Some other microfinance products can be found in the Netherlands. FACET BV (2006) advises that there is room for more microfinance products and programmes to be developed alongside those already in existence.

Since the arrival of migrants in the Netherlands, first from Indonesia and Surinam and then from other countries, there have been savings and loan groups based on traditions of migrants' home countries. The traditional Indonesian *arisan* and Surinam *kasmoni* groups still flourish today but are mainly used for consumer credit or for social events like weddings and funerals. There is no evidence so far that they have been used to finance starting enterprises.[26] New immigrant groups have their own versions of savings and loan groups, often in the form of Rotating Savings and Credit Associations (ROSCAs). These savings and loan groups are local initiatives with a clear bottom-up approach, differing from most microfinance approaches in the Netherlands that are organized top-down.

Fortis Bank have started with a pilot in June 2007 in which they provide microinsurance in addition to credit. They are the only formal provider offering microinsurance at the moment.

The basic bank account covenant that was developed between the banks and the Salvation Army can also be seen as a financial product for inclusion.

Government support

The government uses several financial support systems to stimulate entrepreneurship.

Welfare support for self-employed

Bijstandverlening aan zelfstandigen (BBZ) or 'welfare support for the self-employed' is aimed at assisting recipients of welfare benefit to start a small business and at helping self-employed people with temporary financial problems. This consists of a loan scheme, supplementary income facility and business development services. When the income of the entrepreneur is below welfare level, supplementary income is provided for a maximum of 36 months. A subordinated loan (with interest) can be granted up to a maximum of €31 502. Also, one can get access to business development services.[27] This programme operates at municipality level. According to FACET BV (2006), several studies mention the success of this programme and the reasonable life-span of the companies created. Between 1500 and 2000 people a year start from a welfare situation[28] and probably use the BBZ regulation. According to Velden et al. (2004) local civil servants tend to take a conservative approach to entrepreneurship being a way to reach financial independence. The attitude of civil servants towards entrepreneurship determines whether they will discuss this as an employment option with their clients or not. For those with a work disability benefit a similar scheme is available. This scheme still excludes those who receive unemployment benefits based on their last earned wages rather than at welfare level. This large group is receiving the benefits from the national unemployment agency which does not participate in the BBZ scheme.

Guarantee facility

In order to improve the above-named BBZ system and to make it more inclusive, in July 2007 the Ministry of Social Affairs and Employment[29] launched a one-year pilot with a guarantee scheme for start-up credit for people with either unemployment, welfare or work disability benefits. In Rotterdam, Leeuwarden and Lelystad, eligible potential entrepreneurs will be able to get a loan from a bank more easily to start their business. If they submit a good business plan (which will be evaluated by enterprise development agencies), the government will provide the bank with a guarantee of 80 per cent of the loan amount. A maximum of 300 entrepreneurs should gain access to loans ranging between €10 000 and €15 000, with a maximum loan amount of €31 500.[30] Depending on the results of this pilot a decision will be taken to roll out the programme on a nationwide scale.[31]

The national guarantee scheme for SMEs has a long history. The first SME scheme was introduced in 1915, and in 1965 the first all-embracing Loan Guarantee scheme for SMEs was introduced, replacing the many old specially tailor-made schemes.[32] Nowadays any entrepreneur in the Netherlands can apply for a loan guarantee at their own bank and such services are now provided by some twenty banks. The government provides a partial guarantee for a loan given by a bank. This loan is only granted when the SME complies with regular financial parameters (like liquidity and solvability). For starters, the maximum loan amount is €100 000 while for 'normal and innovative' entrepreneurs it can go up to €1 000 000.

EQUAL programme: ESF projects

Many projects have started in the Netherlands through the ESF programmes of the EU. Some of these projects are aimed at start-up entrepreneurs and focus on vulnerable groups of people with fewer opportunities in the labour market.[33]

Regulation and fiscal treatment

Microenterprises as such do not receive special treatment in the Netherlands. All companies need to be registered with the Chamber of Commerce. Until a couple of years ago a trade licence was necessary in order to start a business. This licence is no longer required, but for many businesses a variety of different licences and permits are needed. These can for instance be in the field of hygiene for caterers, and environment for personal service providers and retailers. Depending on the type of company, licences can take considerable time and effort to acquire.

All businesses selling services or products are obliged to register with the tax office. One needs to follow certain administrative rules about keeping accounts and payment of VAT to the tax office. The only exception for microenterprises is that when the total VAT to be paid to the tax office is below €1345 per annum one can be exempt from paying it (as a compensation for the time spent in account-keeping).[34]

A start-up company can get some tax benefits and deductions. One needs to prove that one is engaged for at least 1225 hours a year in the company to be able to be eligible for such deductions. This excludes a large group of entrepreneurs, especially women who work on a part-time basis. If the entrepreneur starts his or her enterprise midway through the year it is difficult to reach this number of hours in the first year. The new government has promised to look into the tax deductions for part-time entrepreneurs as well as into relieving the administrative burden. There used to be a government facility for income support for women entrepreneurs who become pregnant but this has been stopped. Complicated insurance has replaced this facility. Because of heavy protests the government has decided to re-introduce the income support for pregnant entrepreneurs from mid-2008.[35]

The 'Aunt Agaath' regulation makes it attractive for family members to lend money to (starting) entrepreneurs. According to FACET BV (2006) this regulation is underutilized and even unknown amongst migrant entrepreneurs. The regulation allows for an exemption from capital tax, and any losses (meaning the relative not paying back) can be deducted from income tax.[36]

Financial and operational sustainability

Figures about sustainability are not available at the moment. Since most programmes are financed through funds or subsidies or with guarantees it can be assumed that operational sustainability is not achieved. One can also assume that the overdraft facilities that banks provide reach financial and operational sustainability, otherwise banks would no longer provide the product.

The level of interest rates of microloans has always been a point of discussion in the Netherlands. Following the awarding of the Nobel Peace Prize in 2006 to Prof. M. Yunus and the Grameen Bank, this discussion was rekindled, and the general public got involved through the press.[37] Although experts would explain the logic of these high interest rates from a commercial and sustainability point of view, the common people felt that microcredit equals low interest (even lower then normal).[38] Experience shows that in order for microfinance products to be sustainable, cover losses, risk and operational costs, a higher interest rate needs to be used. In developing countries this can be between 20 per cent and 40 per cent. This might prove a hindrance in setting up sustainable microfinance products in the Netherlands as high interest rates are socially and legally unacceptable. The interest cap for consumer credit[39] is set by the government at the Statutory Interest Rate[40] set by the Dutch National Bank (DNB) plus 12 per cent; this amounts to 18 per cent at 1 July 2007.

The neo-liberal approach in which the customer pays in full for these financial and non-financial services is hardly acceptable in the Netherlands, and additional co-financing will thus remain necessary.

The future of the sector in the Netherlands

The future looks bright for microfinance in the Netherlands. With the new Council for Microfinance in the Netherlands, a professor specifically focusing on microfinance in the Netherlands at INHolland University of Applied Science, and government, banks and NGOs starting their own microfinance programmes, a new momentum seems to be created.

It remains important that the objective for microfinance in the Netherlands is clearly defined and that it is also acknowledged that microfinance is an instrument and not a sole solution for poverty alleviation, social cohesion and dynamic growth in society. It would be beneficial if all actors could agree on the definition of microfinance and microcredit for the Netherlands so that a common language is used and common understanding is achieved. Although the sector analysis shows that we are dealing with an imperfect microfinance market, activities are already being developed to improve on that situation. Lessons can and should be learned from both developing countries and other European countries on how such imperfect markets can best be stimulated.

Several national meetings and symposia have taken place in the last year bringing old and new actors together to share experiences and build better networks. In the future, those new established relationships can be built upon further to create a dynamic microfinance sector.

With all current activities and the upcoming advice of the Council for Microfinance for a new (or improved) model for microfinance in the Netherlands, an exciting future lies ahead for microfinance in the Netherlands.

Notes

* Collaborator: Klaas Molenaar.

1. The EMN Charter on microfinance is used as a basis for this description of the situation in the Netherlands which includes that microloans have a maximum amount of €25 000, loans are used to finance start-ups or the development of existing business, and limited collateral is available.
2. NVB (2001).
3. CBS (2007).
4. Ministry of Foreign Affairs (2007).
5. CBS (2000: 93–9).
6. Kuiper (2007).
7. NIBE-SVV (2002: 75–9).
8. FACET BV (2006).
9. FACET BV (2006).
10. 'The European Social Fund, created in 1957, is the European Union's main financial instrument for investing in people. It supports employment and helps people enhance their education and skills. This improves their job prospects.' (http://ec.europa.eu/employment_social/esf/index_en.htm).
11. Bureau Bartels (2004).
12. 'The mission of the EQUAL Initiative is to promote a more inclusive work life through fighting discrimination and exclusion based on sex, racial or ethnic origin, religion or belief, disability, age or sexual orientation. EQUAL is implemented in and between Member States of the EU and is funded through the European Social Fund.' (http://ec.europa.eu/employment_social/equal/index_en.cfm).
13. INHolland University, June 2007.
14. *Staatscourant*, February 2007, page 11.
15. http://www.regering.nl/regeringsbeleid/balkenende4/beleidsprogramma/index.jsp.
16. Council for Microfinance in the Netherlands, interim advice June 2007 to Secretary of State of Economic Affairs.
17. Porter (2000: p. 6, figure 1-2).
18. Fortis (2007).
19. FACET (2006: 27).
20. Zorg en welzijn (2007).
21. Boober.nl press release, 28 August 2007.
22. Amels (2007: 33 and 50).
23. www.stason.nl.
24. FACET (2006: 10).
25. Based on a personal interview with members of the council.
26. Bijnaar (2002).
27. Ministry of Social Affairs and Employment, www.szw.nl.
28. Velden et al. (2004: 43).
29. Ministry of Social Affairs and Employment, 07/047, 5 June 2007.
30. Although this amount is higher than the €25 000 used in Europe for microcredit, in the Netherlands this is still considered to have the characteristics of a microloan.
31. Ministry of Social Affairs and Employment, W&B/URP/07/19997, 5 June 2007.
32. Input provided by Roland Starmans of Senter Novem.

33. FACET (2006: 33).
34. www.belastingdienst.nl, www.kvk.nl.
35. Ministry of Social Affairs, press release, 3 September 2007.
36. MKB Nederland (2004).
37. Chakrabarty (2006).
38. NRC (2006).
39. Law on consumer credit, 1991.
40. www.dnb.nl, interest rates.

References

Amels, W.P. (2007), 'Microfinance and entrepreneurship as engine for social integration and social capital, integration and poverty alleviation in the Netherlands', first draft (unpublished), University of Amsterdam.

Bijnaar, A. (2002), *Kasmoni, een spaartraditie in Suriname en Nederland* (a savings tradition in Surinam and the Netherlands), Amsterdam: Bert Bakker.

Bureau Bartels (2004), 'Kleine kredieten aan kleine onderneming' (small credits for small enterprises), commissioned by the Ministry of Economic Affairs, Amersfoort.

CBS (2000), 'De Nederlandse economie 2000' (The Dutch economy 2000).

CBS (2007), 'Sociaaleconomische trends, 1e kwartaal 2007' (Social-economic trends, 1st quarter 2007).

Chakrabarty, Arnob (2006), 'Microkrediet helpt armen niet' (Microcredit does not help the poor), Opinion, *NRC Handelsblad*, 24 October.

Council for Microfinancing in the Netherlands (2007), Interim advice June 2007 to Secretary of State of Economic Affairs, the Netherlands.

FACET BV (2006), 'Microkredieten in Nederland, Een nog onontgonnen gebied, Kansen en Uitdagingen' (Microcredits in the Netherlands, a still unexplored territory, chances and challenges), commissioned by the Ministry of Economic Affairs, April.

Fortis (2007), press release, 25 June 2007.

Huijstee, N. van (2007), PowerPoint presentation by Women@Work in Action Microcredit, expert meeting, 23 May, INHolland University.

INHolland University (2007), Kort verslag themabijeenkomst 'Microfinanciering in de Nederlandse Praktijk' (short report meeting 'Microfinance in the Dutch Situation'), School of Economics, The Hague, June.

Kuiper, K. (2007), 'Microkrediet is ouder dan Yunus' (Microcredit is older than Yunus), *Vice Versa*, no. 2.

Ministry of Foreign Affairs (2007), 'Kerncijfers Nederland 2007' (The Netherlands in Figures), May.

Ministry of Social Affairs and Employment (2007), press release, 'Proef met starterskrediet voor uitkeringsgerechtingenden van start' (Start of pilot with start-up credit for benefit receivers), 07/047, 5 June.

Ministry of Social Affairs and Employment (2007), Letter to the lower-house by state secretary, 5 June 2007, W&B/URP/07/19997.

Ministry of Social Affairs and Employment (2007), 'Wijziging rentepercentage' (Changing interest rate), besluit bijstandverlening zelfstandigen (welfare support decision for self-employed people), W&B/URP/07/14065, 6 June.

MKB Nederland (2004), 'Financiering, prijs en toegang, vreemd vermogen in het MKB' (Finance, price and access, financing for SMEs), January.

NIBE-SVV(2002), 'Inleiding bankbedrijf over geld en financiele instellingen' (introduction to banking).

NRC (2006), 'Microcredit fraud or solution?', 11 December, Opinie (Opinions), available at http://weblogs.nrc.nl/weblog/discussie/2005/12/11/microkrediet-oplichting-of-oplossing/.

NVB (2001), convenant inzake een pakket primaire betaaldiensten (covenant concerning a package of primary payment services).

Porter, M. (2000), 'Concurrentievoordeel, de beste bedrijfsresultaten behalen en behouden' (Competitive Strategy 1985), Uitgeverij Business Contact, Amsterdam-Antwerp.
Staatscourant (2007), 'Instellingsbesluit Raad voor Microfinanciering in Nederland', no. 26, February 2007 p. 11.
Velden, J. van, C. Jansen, I. Vossen and E. van der Boom (2004), 'Ondernemend de uitkering uit, onderzoek naar het starten van een bedrijf uit een uitkeringssituatie' (Starting a business from unemployment), ECORYS for the Ministry of Social Affairs and Employment.
Zorg en welzijn (2007), 'Met 5000 euro je eigen telefooncentrale' (Your own telephone service centre for 5000 euros), May 2007.

Conclusion

Karl Dayson

Microfinance in Europe displays the characteristics of a continent divided for much of the twentieth century, with the MFIs in Eastern Europe linked to the economic renewal following the collapse of the Berlin Wall, while those in the West desired to include all within wealthy societies. It was noticeable that the chapters in microfinance in Eastern Europe took the early 1990s as the historical starting point. This was in sharp contrast with Western Europe where considerable stress was placed in antecedents from previous centuries.

More specifically, both Italy and Portugal mentioned church-based charities in the fifteenth century, while Germany, Sweden, Belgium, the Netherlands and the UK chapters discussed the early cooperative societies during the Industrial Revolution. It would be unlikely that the cooperative movement was completely absent from Eastern Europe, though it is undoubtedly the case that the Industrial Revolution proceeded earlier in the West. What this historical discontinuity indicates is partially the authors' own perspective, but also the cultural disconnection that occurred in Eastern Europe during the twentieth century. Thus, when capitalism was reintroduced, a new discourse on microfinance had to be established, much of which was imported from the USA. By contrast, the Western European nations were able to draw upon historical precedent for contemporary microfinance activity. This was undertaken because microfinance was associated with NGOs, particularly NGOs from the USA, which sought to promote economic growth in the developing world. To suggest a 'reverse colonialization' of policy carried political risks. Instead, supporters of MFIs sought to draw inspiration from developing world exemplars, while couching their arguments within an indigenous historical framework, knowing it would be easier to persuade cautious civil servants of the benefits of microfinance if it was possible to show that it had occurred previously. In reality, any direct connections between microfinance today and its alleged antecedents is often illusionary (building societies in eighteenth century Britain) or in some cases a product of state intervention, such as the role of savings banks in Spain.

If financial organizational evolution only offers limited evidence of the source of European microfinance, a stronger case can be made for neoliberal macroeconomic policy. For example, the Austrian national context section talks of the need to improve flexibility and geographic mobility within the state. Examining the chapters, there seem to be *two* trends operating that are encouraging the development of microfinance.

1. Economic liberalization demands that economies are 'opened up' to competition through greater workforce flexibility and a stress on entrepreneurship. Such reform has driven nations to policies that facilitate, or to be precise, appear to facilitate, a more entrepreneurial society. Microfinance is but one of a number of policy initiatives that fit within the rubric.
2. An impact of these changes has been an alleged, and in some cases, namely in Britain, an actual weakening of existing welfare systems. Naturally, politicians have sought to ameliorate this development through a reconfiguration of the welfare system towards greater self-reliance. Thus, microfinance offers an affordable mechanism within a new type of welfare support. Evidence in support of this argument is indicated in the number of chapters where microfinance policy and support was targeted at specific groups. In Belgium it was women, in Bulgaria the long-term unemployed, and migrants in Sweden and Spain. By this confluence of purpose, microfinance has been able to appeal to various political strands and interest groups across Europe. The only exemption was Sweden where Swain and Jonsson argued that the connection between microfinance and self-employment has yet to occur. Perhaps this is not surprising given the strength of Sweden's socio-economic system.

Certainly neo-liberalism is not unique to Europe, and the role of microfinance globally is linked to the economic policy of the World Bank and a variety of United States-based NGOs and foundations. While it could not be argued that all of these are agents of neo-liberalism, it would be fair to ask whether it is a coincidence that international support for and promotion of microfinance arose as neo-liberalism was being pushed on developing nations, particularly through IMF and debt repayment policies. Microfinance's narrative of individual self-reliance and pursuit of MFI sustainability comfortably sat within the broader neo-liberal philosophy. Sometimes in contradiction to this, MFIs were also local NGOs that contributed to the expanding global social economy network of NGOs, with their emphasis on independence from the state and a commitment to campaigning for higher levels of social protection in financial services.

In Europe the chapters have indicated that both these impulses are present and a number of contradictory arguments in favour of microfinance have been advanced. Therefore, while Eastern European MFIs have been supported by US aid agencies and foundations as part of the post-Soviet control adjustment, in Western Europe there was much greater stress placed on the successful NGOs in the developing world. Only in the UK did these coincide to produce a synthesized outcome. Here, the MFIs were inspired by the Community Development Finance Institutions (CDFIs) in the USA and MFIs in Eastern Europe and the developing world. This led to a series of institutions that were established independently of the state and then sought to incorporate microfinance within the emerging enterprise agenda of the prospective New Labour government in the mid-1990s. Beyond the UK, it is difficult to find evidence of a European microfinance policy community, although there were nodes of activity which did communicate with each other, alongside, but often subsidiary to their connections with non-European MFIs and foundations. Only when EMN was established in 2003 did the process of creating a European approach begin to be formulated. This is still under construction and it may be that a single European perspective is impossible until the economies within the EU are better aligned. Whatever the outcome, the chapters have shown the importance of global networks of funders and NGOs in the development of Europe's microfinance community. It is likely that activities and policies outside the EU will continue to have a profound effect on MFIs within it.

Though economic policies, narratives and networks were all crucial in the development of MFIs in Europe, the role of charismatic individuals should not be omitted. In some chapters, such as France and the UK, a specific person was named, elsewhere it was the leadership provided by a particular institution, either funder or MFI founder. There seems to be no causality between the key entity and what organization they worked within. For example, in Poland, it emerged from an MFI (Fundusz Mikro) and Romania from a funder (Soros Foundation). Moreover, there was inclusive evidence that subsequent success of a nation's MFI sector was related to the type of organization the key actor worked for. All that can be assumed is that an activist is required to engage with policy makers and persuade funders to further experiment.

While there is always considerable focus on social actors, the state invariably has an important contribution in Europe. Beyond helping to frame the policy environment, the state is also responsible for the legal and regulatory requirements and often supporting the sector in its incipient phase. Unanimously, the country chapters stated that there was no dedicated MFI legislation in any nation. Instead their legislative framework was taken from a mixture of credit, banking, cooperative, and sometimes usury laws. In terms of legislation, Germany, followed by Italy, appeared to be the most MFI-unfriendly. German MFIs require a credit licence and need to work with banks as it is almost impossible for them to attain the appropriate qualification. Though the rules were slightly less onerous in Italy there were still extensive restrictions on credit issuance.

By contrast, MFIs in most of the other countries operated under credit rules that were distinct from deposit-taking regulation. It also seems that the European Commission would like a more liberal regime for MFIs as it stated in its Communiqué on 20 December 2007 that member states should be proportionate to the costs and risks and not 'put a brake on the supply of micro-credit and the growth of specialist MFIs' (EC 2007:8). Across Europe, most MFIs were not deposit-taking institutions, but this places a reliance on capital growth through profit accumulation and share issuance. This contrasts with credit unions that are exempt from EU prudential regulation. Although a few MFIs are credit unions, the majority are not and so therefore to build stability of the sector a limited deposit-taking role may need to be considered in the years ahead. Any legislation of this kind should be connected with consolidation and harmonization of MFI regulation across Europe.

With regard to funding pilots, there was a clear demarcation between East and West Europe. In all Western European nations, the state had a significant role in the initial funding and support for the sector; for example the UK established a dedicated fund for MFIs, the Phoenix Fund. However, the state often worked in partnership with the private sector, such as with Aide in France, or foundations – savings banks in Spain. These partners may provide some financial assistance though they are usually engaged for technical expertise, guidance and the possibility of providing microfinance services through their extensive branch networks. By contrast, the private financial sector was much less developed in Eastern Europe, while the states had little money for policy programmes in the 1990s. Instead they relied upon strategic investment from international foundations, such as USAID, CRS and the EU in Bulgaria, and Opportunity International in Romania.

Although it was not possible to ascertain from the origin of funding whether this difference in initial funding fundamentally altered the relationship between the state and the MFI, it could partially explain how sustainability is viewed across Europe. The first and most important observation is that accounting methods used by MFIs differ within some nations (CDFA 2008) as well as across the continent. Almost every country chapter (again with the exception of Sweden) states that they are pursuing sustainability, but finding reliable methods to compare sustainability has not been possible. Problems arise because sustainability is defined differently (should it include non-earned income funding?) depending on the MFI and also because the tasks MFIs perform are fundamentally different.

Although the UK MFIs tend to be free-standing entities with little, if any, relationship with the banking sector, this is not the case in France where Aide has a complex symbiotic relationship with the private banking sector. In the latter case loan delivery costs can be transferred to the banks, while Aide can concentrate on reducing the loan approval and support costs. In the UK, the MFIs often find themselves encumbered with the business support costs as well as all the loan approval, support and delivery costs. It is perhaps no surprise that the UK MFIs have the highest interest rates in Europe. This is not to say that one system is correct, rather that any pan-European comparison should be treated with caution. In reality, the most sustainable MFIs are in Eastern Europe, in particular Bulgaria (where some have become joint-stock companies), Poland and Romania. Even in these countries, the MFIs are currently unsustainable. It is also possible that paucity of the banking sector in the 1990s provided Eastern Europe MFIs with a unique opportunity and that many of the clients they serve would have been able to access mainstream services in the West. This goes to the core of debates about MFIs in Europe: are they adjutants of the formal banking service providing a social policy imperative, or are they free-standing financial institutions that happen to serve the most excluded? At present they are both of these things, which explains why sustainability remains a vexatious topic.

Evidence from the previous chapters and differing views of sustainability have demonstrated the variation in the types of microfinance institutions and practices that operate in Europe. A danger with this superficial heterogeneity is that it obscures communalities and similarities, and instead becomes fixated with local cultural relativity and economic context. Essentially there are three categories of MFIs in Europe: public agencies, NGOs and the private sector, with sustainability being the main determinant of what category the institution falls into. Thus, all the private sector or quasi-private sectors are found in Eastern Europe and the national and regional public programmes found in countries like Belgium.

Additionally, a nation could have two or more categories operating simultaneously, such as the state-funded intermediaries and private savings banks in Spain. The most problematic category is the NGOs, mainly because they are either reliant on state funding for survival or they are integrated within a process of delivering economic inclusion. France is the best example of both these arrangements. The rise of complex interrelations between MFIs, the private and public sectors is a feature of Western European MFIs. The exceptions are Italy, where the sector is in its infancy and a product of local government support, as well as the UK, where the state is unwilling to impose any engagement obligations on the private sector. It is possible to see the Aide type approach as a Complex

Interrelationship MFI (CIMFI), which is expected to ensure that the state's social inclusion policy is delivered in areas of entrepreneurship and financial services, but also expects the private and public advice sectors to contribute. In this model, the CIMFI would take clients prepared by the business advice sector and issue loans through the mainstream banking sector. The loan itself is partially underwritten by the state, and the banks benefit through having access to a proven set of potential clients. Variations on this model have emerged, or are emerging, in Spain, Belgium, Holland and possibly Sweden. Moreover, the emerging policy from the European Commission accords with the CIMFI model.

Until recently, the European Union had a relatively minor role in MFI policy, mainly because it sat astride three different policy areas: social, enterprise/economic and employment. As Unterberg (2008) argued, this made it difficult for microfinance to be placed within an EU institutional framework, though this also offered an opportunity because it enabled the sector's proponents, the European Microfinance Network and its president until September 2008, Maria Nowak, to shape the agenda. In the early part of the decade much of the MFI activity, linked to EU funding, was limited to local partnerships under European Regional Development Fund (ERDF) and European Social Fund (ESF) support. By 2007, the European Commission began to publish outlines of a more strategic European approach to microfinance. The outlines of this approach were sketched out in the communiqué of 20 December 2007 in which four elements were highlighted:

1. improving the legal and institutional environment in Member States;
2. further changing the climate in favour of entrepreneurship;
3. promoting the spread of best practices;
4. providing additional financial capital for new and non-bank MFIs.

In terms of policy implementation, the first stage will concentrate on a pilot project on technical assistance entitled JASMINE (Joint Action to Support Microfinance in Europe). Support is likely to include mentoring and peer learning, and private sector financial sector firms will have a role in financing the initiative. In the longer term it is hoped that MFIs will attain certain standards that will make them attractive investment vehicles for the private sector. Thus a model of EC microfinance policy is likely to develop that assumes an 'upskilling' role for the EU, a client interaction role for MFIs and a financial investment role for the banks, though a delivery partner role is not ruled out. This would seem to be very close to the development of the CIMFI outlined above.

At its core, microfinance is a remarkably simple concept: the provision of credit to those who cannot access it from other affordable sources. 'Affordable' is the contentious word and is open to many interpretations. Should affordability be viewed morally and thus set at a minimum threshold? The problem here lies in defining what is a minimum acceptable rate and what is classified as usurious. Some European states, such as Germany, sought to resolve this dilemma by setting rates nationally. This institutionalization of morality absolves MFIs from pursuing aggressive sustainability strategies and pushes them towards reliance on the state and cooperation with other financial providers. Such an approach can be described as corporatist, involving the state, private financial sector and NGO MFIs in a coordinated assault on credit exclusion. At the other extreme, the state refuses to define affordability and allows MFIs to operate unencumbered by extensive legislative and economic–cultural control. These can be seen as market-based solutions. Between these dichotomies reside a range of mixed market approaches; some arise because the state has changed its policy direction and the remnants of previous regime remain, while others are part of strategic attempts to address slightly different social problems.

The former, a type of residualization approach, often operates in tandem with the pragmatic perspective of the latter. But as the chapters have shown, the situation is rarely static and the social actors involved seek to reframe the policy to their benefit. Thus, the financial sector may seek to overturn corporatist strategies in the name of national competitiveness or globalization, while some MFIs may want to minimize their reliance on the state and hopefully gain full independence. This may be sought because the MFI has an ideological commitment to freedom and believes its mission can only be achieved through sustainability. This can be described as a market-NGO approach. Still others seek reassurance from the state, especially as attempts at sustainability prove elusive, and pursue corporatist NGO approaches. As such, MFI policy in Europe is dynamic and often precarious, reliant on continued support from the state and to a lesser extent the private sector (see figure below).

This review chapter has shown there is also emerging evidence of a

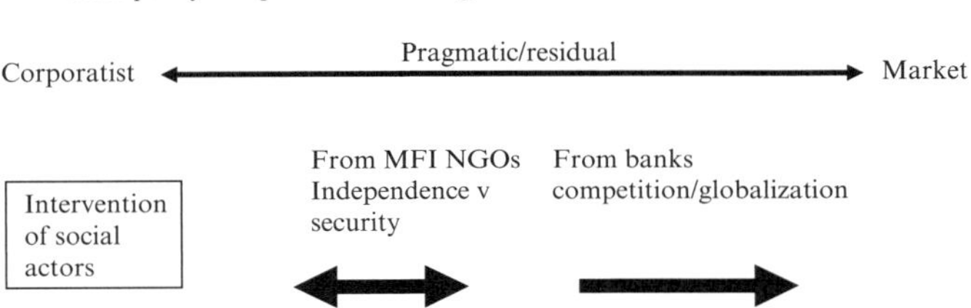

new model for the delivery of microfinance in Europe, particularly in Western Europe, which was described above as Complex Interrelationship Microfinance Finance Initiatives (CIMFI). Currently, only the contours of this are apparent but it is a model that can be utilized throughout the continent and does offer a way to serve those most excluded. It assumes that most Europeans will have access to financial services and the focus should be on including the remainder, either through direct connection to the mainstream or through intermediary organizations, such as MFIs. Because it accepts that the market for MFIs in Europe will be more limited than in the developing world, while the costs of delivery will be higher, it is necessary to spread costs across a delivery partnership. Therefore, public enterprise advice agencies will be expected to ensure service users are properly prepared before referral to an MFI, MFIs will focus on client guidance and support through the loan application process, while loans will be issued through the banks. In nations where the MFIs are already sustainable it is likely that they will conduct the last two tasks. Such models offer the most realistic opportunity for MFIs to become sustainable and consequently become attractive investment vehicles for mainstream financial institutions. Without a CIMFI approach, states will have to accept that MFIs will require the freedom to charge interest rates sufficient to cover their costs – the alternative is an MFI sector that is perpetually reliant on public support.

Consequently, any nation that wishes to maintain a cap on interest rates and have a sustainable MFI sector is likely to gravitate towards a CIMFI model. This is not to say that mistakes will not be made, but ultimately in a highly sophisticated financial services environment MFIs in Europe will require a different and more integrated model than is utilized at present in the developing world or indeed in Europe. This review has shown that the MFI sector in Europe is diverse and multi-layered, driven by sometimes complementary and sometimes competing forces. However, in certain places, it has been staggeringly successful and incredibly innovative, demonstrating the continued potential for microfinance in Europe.

References

CDFA (2008), *Inside Out: The State of Community Development Finance*, London: CDFA.

European Commission (2008), 'A European initiative for the development of micro-credit in support of growth and employments', communication from the commission to the council, the European Parliament, the European Economic and Social Committee and the Committee of the Regions, Brussels, 20.12.07 COM(2007) 708 final/2 EN.

Unterberg, M. (2008), 'Microfinance as a European policy issue: policy images and venues', European Microfinance Conference, Nice, 8–10 September, available at http://www.microfinancegateway.org/files/54395_file_25.pdf.

Index